INSTITUTIONAL SYSTEM ANALYSIS IN POLITICAL ECONOMY

T0326185

To My Beloved Daughter

Institutional System Analysis in Political Economy

Neoliberalism, Social Democracy and Islam

TANER AKAN
King's College London, UK

Routledge
Taylor & Francis Group

LONDON AND NEW YORK

First published 2015 by Ashgate Publishing

2 Park Square, Milton Park, Abingdon, Oxfordshire OX14 4RN
711 Third Avenue, New York, NY 10017

Routledge is an imprint of the Taylor & Francis Group, an informa business

First issued in paperback 2017

British Library Cataloguing in Publication Data
A catalogue record for this book is available from the British Library

The Library of Congress has cataloged the printed edition as follows:
Akan, Taner.
Institutional system analysis in political economy : neoliberalism, social democracy and Islam / by Taner Akan.
    pages cm
Includes bibliographical references and index.
ISBN 978-1-4724-6402-6 (hardback)
1. Turkey--Economic policy. 2. Institutional economics. 3. Neoliberalism--Turkey. 4. Islam and state--Turkey. 5. Socialism--Turkey. I. Title.
HC492.A535 2015
330.9561--dc23

2015014526

ISBN 978-1-4724-6402-6 (hbk)
ISBN 978-1-138-55982-0 (pbk)

Contents

List of Figures and Tables

Figures

Tables

Acknowledgements

This book is based on a research funded by Turkish Scientific and Technologic Research Institution, TUBITAK, and was conducted at the Max Planck Institute for the Study of Societies, the MPIfG, Cologne. I should thank the TUBITAK's anonymous panellists for their interest in and confirmation of this project as well as the BİDEB's staff for dealing with some complex bureaucratic issues that emerged during the conduct of this research.

My special thanks go to the supervisor of this research, Prof. Wolfgang Streeck of the MPIfG. Without his unprecedented guidance and help, this book could not have been publishable. He always inspired me to think and defend what I had to say throughout the one-and-a-half years' duration. Of course, all shortcomings in the book are mine.

I should also express my gratitude to Prof. Richard Hyman of the London School of Economics for his enduring support of me. My research under his supervision in Spring 2008 comparing the political economy of European social democracy and Turkish Islam was the beginning of my journey that continues with this book.

The friendly interest and help of the MPIfG's distinguished staff of various units made me feel like I was studying in my own home, for which I am grateful. On this occasion, I should cite the following names: Claudia, Ruth, Gabi, Thomas, Susanne and Jürgen Lautwein.

I am also very glad to have the chance to thank Murat Yenigün, Volkan Özvatan and Markus Burtscheidt, who gave a remarkable amount of their valuable time to deal with my recurring demands, particularly in having access to various academic resources.

Finally, I wish to thank Ashgate's distinguished editorial staff for dealing with the processes of review and publication very kindly and tolerantly. And the anonymous reviewer of the book enabled me, *inter alia*, to clarify my argument, for which I request her/him to accept my thanks.

London, 15 May 2015

Acknowledgements

Introduction

A dichotomy has become embedded between social structures and social theories in capitalist times: the more complex the former becomes, the more mono-disciplinary methodologies the latter adapts. The outcome of this dichotomy for the science of political economics is this question raised by the Queen of England at the LSE, London School of Economics and Political Science, with regard to the ongoing global recession: 'If these things were so large, how come everyone missed them?' (*Daily Telegraph*, 2009).

This failure is nothing new for mainstream economists. For example, Irvin Fisher, a prominent neoclassical economist, had lost all his private wealth while playing a *financial game* at Wall Street in the autumn of 1929, just before the Great Depression erupted, having predicted that 'Stock prices have reached what looks like a permanently high plateau' (see Galbraith, 1954: 95). In this respect, the Queen's question revealed, albeit unintentionally, that nothing changed for the neoclassicals in undervaluing social complexity.

Since the dawn of this tradition in the early 1870s, its adherents have adapted methodological functionalism, a theoretical pre-acceptance that the growing complexity of science-making, inevitably, ends up with specialisation in positive, social and also intra-social sciences with the mentality that 'equip yourself to fulfill usefully a specific *function*' (Durkheim, 1994 [1893]: 2; Jevons, 2005 [1888]: 26). As a consequence, for neoclassical schools, the discipline of political economy becomes the statistical study of utility and self-interest rather than the study of systemic intersections between polity, economy and society (Jevons, 2005 [1888]: 33).

A recent example of such a monolithic methodology is Acemoğlu and Robinson's study of 'Why Nations Fail' (2012). In this book, the writers do not see any need for systemically bringing the question of *why the American economy fails* or more essentially *why the American social system produces overseas crises* into analysis. Instead, they aim to provide the *other* nations with the recipes of economic success: to secure private rights, create a level playing field exclusively for the holders of this right and then stimulate new investment in technology and human capital. According to them, the role of polity in this equation consists mainly of preparing the ground for this right to be played more freely and the culture cannot have any pivotal role in the structuration of such an *inclusive* set of institutional stock.

If it is so simple, uncomplicated and unidirectional in methodological terms for every nation to reach economic success by adapting these recipes, why did Acemoğlu himself (2009) seen *a need* to write a paper entitled 'The crisis of 2008: Lessons for and from economists', including, *inter alia*, the following paragraph?

Whether or not the second half of 2008 will be featured in history books, however, it is a critical opportunity for many in the economics profession – unfortunately, myself included – to be disabused of *certain notions that we should not have accepted in the first place*. It is an opportunity for us to step back and consider which, among the conclusions to our theoretical and empirical investigations led us, remain untarnished by recent events – and to figure out what intellectual errors we have made, and what lessons these errors offer ... As of March 2009, the crisis is still evolving, and *there remains much uncertainty about what happened in the financial markets and inside many corporations*. We will know more in the years to come. From what we know today, many of the roots of our current problems are apparent; but most of us did not recognize them before the crisis (Acemoğlu, 2009: 186–7).

In this book, it is suggested that the most critical notion that the neoclassicals have yet to accept is the very reality that social structures are complex evolving wholes and that their constituent parts, at least their major political and cultural constituencies, cannot be subsumed into the *complementary details* of the economic myths generated by the neoclassical themselves. With this insight, this book proposes an analytic frame, 'institutional system analysis in political economy', that aims to explore social complexities by unravelling their *evolutionary entanglements* between polity, economy and society. To better explain its purpose, let me first elaborate on why we should develop a systemic analysis of evolving institutional structures rather than perform a functional, ergodic or punctuated analysis on the basis of one-fits-all recipes. In this introductory section, I will then present a concise guide on how to use this book, explaining the contents of its parts with their role in conveying the general message of this book.

Why A Systemic Analysis of Institutional Interactions is Needed?

Social systems and their national, regional and international products, as depicted at Figures I.1 and I.2, co-evolve in a highly complex, multi-dimensional and multi-actor context. The lines between the national, regional and international actors in political economy depicted in Figures I.1 and I.2 denote the institutional axes that interconnect actors and orchestrate their interplay.

Politico-economic institutions range from national laws that structure the policy-making boundaries of political parties to transnational regulations, such as the dispute settlement system of the World Trade Organization (WTO), which imposes both regulatory sanctions and liberatory rights on member countries. At the regional level, for example, the European Union's Maastricht Criteria could be defined as an institution that conditions fiscal and financial structures and the magnitude of social expenditures in member and acceding countries. In the international sphere, the conventions of the International Labour Organization (ILO) establish the standards for regulation and the conduct of individual and organised labour relations. Thus, they obligate governments to draft and enforce the necessary regulations to ensure that individuals and organised labour have the opportunity to exercise the rights recognised by the conventions.

Specifically, Figure I.1 depicts the dynamics of the Turkish (national) social system and its constituent components. And Figure I.2 integrates this complex national relationship into regional and international contexts and depicts their evolutionary cycles. The lines in these figures are symbolic and much more complex axes can be contemplated in each context. The vertical and horizontal axes between sub-units or sub-institutions in the figures denote the mutual interactions among the various units and the complex web of institutional interconnections. It should at this point be noted that social systems and their institutional structures do not come into being or evolve over time through their hierarchical organisations, but through interconnections between their constituents. In this sense, Figure I.1 depicts the national system in terms of its macro-institutional intersections for the ease of illustration rather than to emphasise a layered organisation of institutional interactions. Otherwise, both figures would purport to be a *biological alignment* of major organs, as Durkheim assumed.

Institutions are interactive constituents that condition and constrain one another's structures and evolution on a multivariate basis. The channels or axes of interaction among economic, social and political democracy, as the principal institutions of national governance for example, unfold, as depicted in Figure I.1, among the government, political parties, non-governmental organisations, organised labour, business associations and so on. Political democracy intersects with economic democracy by entitling organised labour to participate in the neo-corporatist councils that have the authority to take binding decisions regarding socio-economic issues. Based on the inclusion of organised labour in these councils, social democracy is rooted in the functionalisation of economic democracy, on the one hand, and the formation of an organic linkage between the working class and politics, on the other. The very nature of the economic system impinges on the liaison between political institutions and organised labour or business associations, thereby establishing the institutional boundaries of economic and industrial democracy.

The national intersections among this trilogy of democracy might also be affected by regional or international actors. For example, in Turkey, as depicted in Figure I.1, an acceding country to the European Union (EU), this process encounters the constraining and enabling impacts of, *inter alia*, the Maastricht criteria, such as restrictive austerity measures that prohibit governments from leveraging the budget to pursue discretionary policy choices and the Social Charter, which stipulates that organised labour has the right to organise and strike. Over the decades between 1998 and 2008, the International Monetary Fund, an international organisation, wrought havoc on the country's economic policy-making processes, ranging from development plans to the decisions of the Economic and Social Council, the major neo-corporatist institution in Turkey. (In the second and succeeding parts, I will elaborate on the cross-interactions depicted in both figures.)

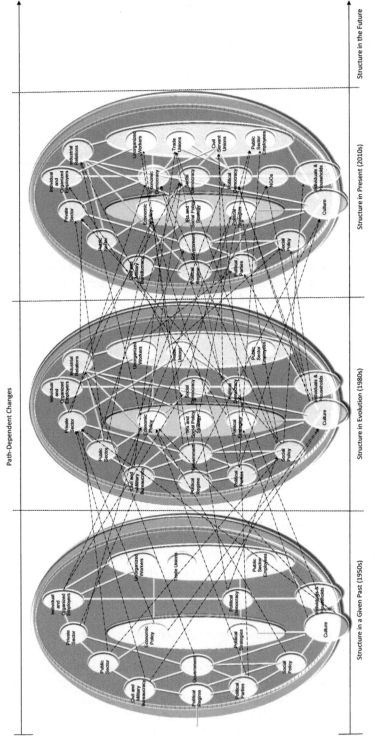

Figure I.1 Structural evolution of Turkish political economy between 1950s and 2010s

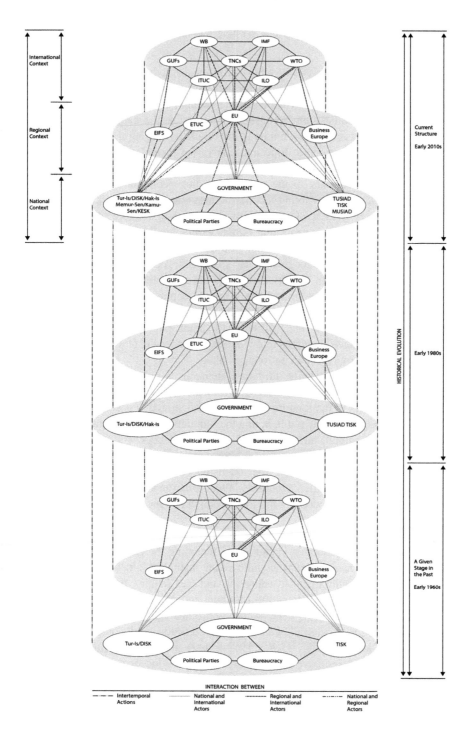

Figure I.2   Evolution of transnational institutional environment of Turkish political economy between the early 1960s and 2010s

Such a structural analysis of inter-institutional interactions, albeit adapted to describe a multi-context and multi-actor perspective, falls short of identifying the process-based *evolutionary* dynamics of the national or international intersections in a politico-economic system because it only describes the static structure of these interactions. However, dynamic interaction requires bringing the change or path-dependence of institutions in time into analysis with their inter-complementary and inter-repulsive implications.

For example, contrary to the putative verdict, economic development as a fundamental element of evolving social structures is a *process* of multi-dimensional transformation consisting of a diminishing role of agriculture, changing trade patterns, the increased application of human capital and knowledge in production and, finally, undertaking fundamental institutional change. Including politics in this process essentially recognises that sustainable economic development, as in the case of East Asian countries, requires the adaptation of a dynamic (rather than a linear) strategy that shifts from simple to sophisticated exports with high value added. This is an endeavour that entails constant guidance and assistance from the public sector to the private sector being phased out under optimally designed performance standards that would also hinder the rent-seeking activities of unproductive firms through patronage linkages.

Altering an export profile ultimately demands a public-private partnership enforcing a high-road strategy that would create self-reinforcing or efficiency-enhancing impacts in the long run. The high-road strategy consists in, as Keynes (1964 [1936]) systemically put it, laying the foundation for and sustaining optimal endowments of capital, technology and human resources while simultaneously maintaining social equality, individual liberty and economic efficiency. Of these parameters, technology creation, the touchstone of economic development and its application to production processes, alters a nation's production possibilities frontier and creates the potential for greater output and income (Cypher and Dietz, 2004, Easterlin, 2006: 58–9).

The generation of new technologies is a strenuous process that is subject to a society's social and economic institutions – including the existing class structure, land tenure relationships, financial and banking institutions, ideology, religion and superstitions, its commitment to education and free inquiry, the openness of the state to scientific and educational infrastructure and so on. In this regard, although technologic change, *prima facie*, seems a mechanically structured process, in systemic terms it is 'a culturally-contingent phenomenon and it comprises the stock of aggregated skill of a society' (Ayres, 1962: 111–2). In brief, economic development is the sequential quantitative and qualitative reorientation of a society's cultural, political and economic institutions from basic changes in the level of education to governance structures involving government, business and labour organisations.

Importantly, evolution (of economic development) is not a two-stage, linear process moving from foundation to evolution. It is a four-stage, non-linear process: the foundation, evolution, current and future stages are conditioned by path-dependent changes in space-time, as shown in Figures I.1 and I.2 (the straight lines depicted between these stages represent major interactions. However, their evolution is neither unidirectional nor synchronous). Including the transnational outgrowths of these processual interactions further confounds the picture presented in Figures I.1 and I.2. The nature of the international political economy at a certain period in time, as the structure imposing rules on national social systems, the individual impacts of the former's actors on the latter and the ebb and flow of these interactions on the basis of processual, non-linear and non-synchronous evolution, provides us with an extremely complex structure to disentangle.

The key analytical question is at this point how we can conceptualise the abovementioned complex relationships. This book suggests that social complexity, as depicted in Figures I.1 and I.2, can be explained only through adapting a systemic approach between economy, society and polity. In principle, a systemic approach is used to explicate structures comprising a relatively large number of variables. This stems from the ever-increasing density and variety of cross-institutional interactions, as the number of actors, variables, interactions, concepts and instances, along with the asymmetric structuration and destructuration of this institutional complexity, increases at the national or transnational levels with each cycle. In this context, as partly noted above, the aim of this study is to propose an analytic framework, *the institutional system analysis in political economy*, to crystallise the above-noted complex, complementary and repulsive interactions of political, economic and social institutions from a process-based, evolutionary perspective. The book makes this a complex and systemic political economy analysis with reference to the cross-institutional intersections between (neo)liberalism, social democracy and Islam in the Ottoman-Turkish case. The following sub-section explains in which sequence this aim is carried out in the book at the level of theory and praxis.

How to Use this Book?

In Part I, Chapter 1 examines the institutional system analysis in political economy with its four constituent variables: (i) the *institutional environment* under which institutional interactions unfold; (ii) the *actors* that mediate these interactions; (iii) the *power relationship* among the actors as the process of institutional interactions; and finally, (iv) the *path-dependent institutional changes* that arise upon the inter-actor power relations evolving over and under the rule-imposing institutional environment.

Chapter 2 offers a systemic and cross-paradigmatic analysis of the liberal and neoliberal, social democratic and Third Way and Islamic political economies. I will examine these three major paradigms by proposing a systemic taxonomy of their macro-economic, political, social policy and industrial relations institutions. This particular chapter aims to furnish the reader with an intensely and systemically constructed theoretical insight into the practical intersections and evolutions of Islam, liberalism/neoliberalism and social democracy/Third Way in the Ottoman-Turkish territory.

In the next parts of the book, in light of the explanatory framework of the institutional system analysis, the Turkish political economy will be examined in terms of: (i) the formation of its Islamic, secular and capitalist path-dependencies; (ii) its evolutionary change under the constraints of these path-dependencies between Islam, (neo)liberalism and social democracy; and finally (iii) its future prospects again among these three paradigms.

In Part II, in this context, I begin by examining the Ottoman Islamic institutionalism in Chapter 3 as the source of the *primordial* path-dependencies that evolved into the contemporary structure of the Turkish political economy. This analysis is necessary for understanding the patterns of path-dependent changes and the essential dynamics of inter-actor power relations from the early nineteenth century to today's Republican Turkey, as well as the current structure and the future prospects of the Islamic polity and economy in the country. Then, in Chapter 4, I probe the changing dynamics of these path-dependencies among Islam, secularism and capitalism in terms of the power relations among the Empire's major actors in the period 1808–1918. Next, in Chapter 5, I will examine the main dynamics of the first great divide in Anatolia in the period 1923–50 when Orthodox Kemalism became embedded as one of the major path-dependencies in the contemporary Turkish political economy. In this period, with the accumulated dynamics of change accruing from the previous period, Turkey's secular political, economic and judicial regimes as well as the strategic convergences in the inter-actor power relations among civil-military bureaucracy, businessmen, workers and political forces became embedded among Kemalism, etatist liberalism and civil Islam.

In Part III, I will first examine the institutional environment and the main national, regional and international actors of the Turkish political economy in the period 1960–2013 when Islam, social democracy and neoliberalism have become intertwined. The investigation in Chapter 6 aims to explain the institutional framework and the actors under and with which the actors of Islamic, social democratic and neoliberal institutionalism in the Turkish context have become engaged in a power relationship throughout this period. Then, Chapter 7 deals with the evolutionary dynamics of Turkish social democracy during the period 1960–2013. To do so, it examines the formation, evolution and current stages of Turkish social democracy in a comparative perspective, with the theory of social democratic and Third Way political economies that were examined in Chapter 2 of the book. In Chapter 7, the reader can pursue the application of path-dependent change patterns, proposed in Chapter 1, to the evolution of Turkish social democratic parties under the constraint and opportunities imposed by the institutional environment of the Turkish political economy and the inter-actor power relationships that these parties took part in during the period 1960–2013.

Afterwards, in Chapter 8, Turkish Islam is brought into discussion first in terms of the waxing and waning of the Just Order. As the politico-economic project of the National Outlook Movement, the Just Order was introduced in the last quarter of the twentieth century to re-accumulate the discontinuing path-dependencies of Ottoman Islam under the constraints of continuing path-dependencies of the

Kemalist establishment and (neo)liberal national and international environment. In terms of the current structure of the Turkish political economy, this particular chapter is of significance for explaining the path-dependent genesis of the incumbent Conservative Democrats, as examined in Chapter 9, out of this political tradition, the multivariate composition of their policy strategies and the delicate power relationship they developed with the pro-cyclical or countercyclical actors of the period 2002–13. In this context, I will bring Turkish Conservative Democracy into analysis as the paradigmatic manifestation of the second great divide in Anatolia at the crossroads of continuing changes and changing discontinuities among the path-dependencies of the Ottoman Empire, the Just Order, the neoliberal national and international environment and the Kemalist political establishment.

In Part IV, I will deal with the *next* stage of Turkish Islam, neoliberalism and social democracy from a political economy perspective. This part will examine their future prospects with reference to the accumulated dynamics of their encircling environment.

In this sense, Chapter 10 gives a full-fledged analysis of the future prospects of Turkish social democracy in light of the two sets of variables. The first is composed of: (i) the policy programmes and the practical performances of the Turkish political parties that adapted social democrat, Kemalist and Third Way strategies; (ii) the endogenous dynamics of path-dependent changes of these parties' policy strategies; and (iii) their systemic power interactions with national, regional and international actors. The second is the evolving national, regional and international environmental circumstances, the actors' strategies at each level, the potential power relationships in which these parties could or should engage and the path-dependent changes that these parties would experience.

Chapter 11 provides a full-fledged analysis of Turkish Islam's future prospects in light of its evolutionary dynamics. In doing so, the political and economic pillars of the Islamic theory of political economy, the Ottoman Islam, the Just Order and the Conservative Democracy have been examined in a comparative perspective to explain the institutional changes and path-dependencies that both have brought the Conservative Democracy into existence and would shape Turkish Islam's future prospects. This comparative analysis has been contextualised into the constraints and opportunities that the national and international institutional environment offered in the past and would offer in the future, and the power relations in which the proponents of the Just Order politics and the Conservative Democracy engaged in in the past and would engage in the future with pro-cyclical or countercyclical national, regional and international actors.

The book concludes with a systemic inquiry into 'what is next' for the Turkish social system within Islam, neoliberalism and social democracy. In doing so, the conclusion aims to pour the long and detailed investigations in the book into brief but expedient responses to this inquiry in systemic terms.

Before concluding this introductory section, I wish to bring two points to the readers' attention. Firstly, in Part I, as noted above, the institutional system analysis in political economy is suggested as an analytic framework to explain the complex evolutions of politico-economic structures. The case study section in Parts II–IV aims to demonstrate how the analytic tools of institutional system analysis can be used to explain the evolutionary dynamics of the Ottoman-Turkish case within Islam, neoliberalism and social democracy. The reader can pursue this complementary link between the theoretical and case study sections in Chapters 3 to 11.

In other words, Chapters 3–9 aim to present qualitative and quantitative data on the political, economic and cultural dynamics of the Ottoman-Turkish social system in reasonable detail using the analytic tools of the institutional system analysis in political economy. In addition, Chapters 10–11 integrate these data to make a full-fledged analysis of the evolutionary dynamics and the future prospects of the Turkish political economy within Islam, neoliberalism and social democracy. This detail is important in pointing out the fact that the comprehension of all details in Chapters 3–9 is necessary to comprehend the systemic analysis in Chapters 10–11.

In methodological terms, this means that the comprehension of all major details about the political, economic and cultural institutions of a social structure with their evolutionary dynamics is the *cost* of having a *systemic insight* into its current structure and future prospects. To be in the position of sharing this 'risky' point with the reader is a strange feeling for an author who, like all his colleagues, wishes to be read by a respectable number of readers! But at the end of the day, I could not find an alternative to taking this risk at all costs by adapting such a methodology in this book and therefore request the reader to tolerate me for doing so.

Secondly, this book is an initial but not an end-product of my research on the institutional system analysis in political economy. Thus, it will always be in need of improvement in line with its readers' comments in time.

PART I
Institutions, Social System and Political Economy

Chapter 1

Institutional Interactions in an Evolutionary System Perspective

When used in conjunction with the *social*, the term *systemic*, in view of its mechanic and stern overtones in the *normative subconscious*, stands on the knife's edge. For this reason, to conduct an institutional analysis from a *systemic* perspective, a dynamic trade-off should be established between formal and informal institutions with respect to their inter-repulsive and inter-complementary inclinations and among micro-constituencies of a social system, such as individuals, groups and organisations, and macro-constituencies, such as governments, the bureaucracy, and so on. This is because the static and sharp-edged analytic apparatuses of mainstream social systems theory have prompted system analysis to lock in the monolithic, univocal and unidirectional premises of structural functionalism.

Societies are complex systems comprising mutually contingent interrelationships of individuals, organisations and social groups of various types. These relationships generate certain structural principles that bind the *overall clustering of institutions* across time and space. As the holistic manifestation of this clustering, a social system is the interwoven and interacting stock of formal and informal institutions evolving in a specific timespace. What distinguishes a social system from other systems, such as biologic, ecologic, physical and so on, is that its constituent parts are human-established or artefact institutions based on non-routine and unpredictable behaviours in complex interaction. The latter comprises the mechanic amalgamation of commensurable units such as atoms, cells, microorganisms and so on.

As the basis of social systems, the institutionalisation of social interaction, in an accumulating fashion, paves the way for structuration across time and space. In this sense, institutions, in evolutionary terms, are structure-forming properties of social systems. And a social structure takes on a systemic form because it mediates the patterned or ordered intersections between institutions, thereby obtaining an integrative scope (Giddens, 1984: 16–24). Structures, however, are discontinuous systems, as their principles or institutional underpinnings are subject to constant change. Dynamic structures may contain the changing and evolving character of social systems, but they also fail to capture inter-temporal changes. Thus, including a structure, with its cyclical changes, in an analysis demands a process-based approach. This is because the 'process is a structure in time' (Dopfer, 2005: 17).

In terms of the conceptual basis of a systemic analysis of social structures, there are two points that should be clarified. The first is to identify the contradistinctions among structures, regimes and social systems in institutional terms, as these three terms are used interchangeably in an ambiguous manner. According to Andersen (1990: 2), for example, a *social policy regime* refers to 'the relations between state and economy, a complex of legal and organisational features are systematically interwoven'. The fundamental prerequisite for a regime is hence an embedded institutional structure that relies on a coherent and inter-complementary, but not necessarily an effective, relationship among its constituents. In this regard, a regime can be defined as a *structured ordinariness* of institutional interactions.

In political economy terms, the term system, unlike regime, does not require a coherent interconnection, but rather lasting and relational interaction among its constituents. The inter-constituent liaison in *social* systems, contrary to functionalist structuralism, can generate stable or unstable, but not static or functionally dissipated, structures. Stability and equilibrium are not preconditions for a system to exist or evolve. Rather, social systems arise based on the institutionalisation of norms and values at the formal or informal levels, and the inter-repulsive and inter-complementary tensions between these institutions are mediated by organisational, economic or political actors. (The term *inter-repulsive* denotes that two or more constituents interact in a way that suppresses or restrains each other's abilities to enforce certain aims, respectively.) Thus, I will use the term *system*, in a social sense, to denote structures that have individual or organisational constituents interacting through value-rationally or purposive-rationally in shifting proportions and evolving inter-complementarily or inter-repulsively over time and space.

In brief, structures are static elements of a social system, while regimes signify the patterned alignment of these structures. Social systems are patterned or unpatterned structures in evolution, intersecting with the relational interactions between its formal and informal constituents. Social systems might exhibit regime characteristics, but a lack of these characteristics would not eliminate their systemic nature.

The second conceptual problem is related with a seemingly minor but analytically major distinction. The asymmetric structuration of subdivisions, their relational interaction in a social system and the cross-interactions among various social systems in multiple periods pose a formidable challenge in developing a systemic conceptualisation. This quandary purportedly circumvents a non-functional analysis of social systems. An underlying reason is an analytic misapprehension of the contradistinction of *systemic* and *systematic*. Systematisation relies on the functional hypothesis that the (rational) behaviours of A and B have kindred characteristics consisting of linear, measurable and predictable variables; their overall causes and effects and institutional manifestations would be gauged quantitatively by standard benchmarks, and the normative implications of these tenets are not an independent variable in the conduct of social action (Buckley, 1967: 76).

For example, the game-theoretical explanation of institutional interactions is rooted in the fact that institutions jointly regularise social behaviour, and this regularised conduct of behaviours enables each actor to assume that 'his opponents are rational, that they mode the game exactly as he does, and that they assign the same correct priors' (Greif, 2006: 129). In other words, in a game-theoretical analysis, it is pre-accepted that players have a common knowledge of rationality, the mainstay for an *equilibrium* game to be played by rational actors (Greif, 2006: 124). The institutional environment consists of a restricted web of regularised rules that provide the actors with common (standard) knowledge for making the rational choices. As a result, 'games need to be kept very simple: few actors, few options' (Pierson, 2004: 61). This denotes that in analytic terms, the cognitive complexity of identifying Nash equilibria falls short of making a holistic analysis in case the number of independent players and the variety of their strategic options increase beyond a very few. Furthermore, the sequence or evolution of inter-actor games cannot be interrupted because 'sequence, in these models, refers to an ordered alternation of "moves" by "composite actors" with preferences and payoffs fixed in advance' (Scharpf, 1997: 105).

For these reasons, the game-theoretical methodology is far from enabling us to develop such a systemic perspective. (It is true that as noted above, institutions are the products of societal norms and values. But this fact cannot be used as the main basis for a determinist, functionalist explanation of inter-actor relationships under an *ex ante* restricted and standardised setting.) Because a systemic analysis of institutional interactions should include: (i) the potential and irregular extension or contraction of the boundaries of an institutional environment; (ii) all major actors that exert impact on the conduct of a system, their changing pro-cyclical and countercyclical positions under changing composition of coalitional constellations, and the irregularity of their reactions to each other at each institutional system cycle; (iii) changing composition, density and trajectory of power relationship between the actors; and (iv) the *ex ante* undeterminable and unsystematic sequence of path-dependent change dynamics in timespace. (Each of these analytic points will be elaborated in due course.)

Of particular importance for a systemic analysis of social action, in addition to the above listed ones, is the incorporation of informal institutions (norms and values) into analysis as an independent variable rather than a means to regularise or communise the purposive-rational action. For example, Weber (1947: 168) proposes the commonly employed measures of rational economic action as follows: the *systematic* acquisition, production and distribution of utilities. If one presupposes that the core of *systemic* analysis relies on the *systematic* delineation of the normative implications of social interactions, then developing a non-functional system analysis of an institutional whole becomes inconceivable. Systemic analysis, nonetheless, does not or must not rely on the systematised or imbricated (regularly overlapped) resources of social knowledge. Its essence is to include the combined impact of the normative or rational implications of inter-institutional interaction in the analysis.

Systematicness cannot be systemic in this sense, as it omits both the purely normative and normatively contingent or value-rational implications of social conduct. When adopting a systemic perspective, a social analyst should presuppose that there are *cryptic constellations*, ineffable niches of social phenomena, in these interactions that would not be standardised by numeric measures. Instead of generating abstract knowledge at the expense of theoretical concretism, she/he aims to conceptualise institutional interactions in terms of their intersectional implications at the level of the social system and its subdivisions. This would, in effect, help the researcher to understand and identify the framework of the overall stock of institutions and manage the co-evolution of formal and informal institutions to determine the best available combination of mutual-enforcement. (The latter does not refer to top-down design but rather the orchestration of the institutional structure.)

Ultimately, a systemic analysis of institutions should neither be overvalued nor undervalued because it is implausible to expound entire institutional interactions (through a *panacean* systemic analysis), especially given their informal implications. It would nonetheless be tenable: (i) to perform a reciprocally dependent and inter-repulsively or inter-complementarily contingent inquiry into institutional interactions within a social whole; and (ii) to ascertain the interlaced and process-based evolution of these interactions over time and space. In this book, the institutional system analysis is proposed to be a framework for performing these two interconnected objectives in an evolutionary perspective. As can be seen in Figure 1.1, the main constituents of this analysis are composed of institutions, actors and their strategies, power relations between the actors and path-dependent changes arising out of these relations. What makes this institutional analysis *systemic* is that it first offers a holistic perspective that interconnects these four constituents and then explains their interactional dynamics in a *co-evolutionary* perspective.

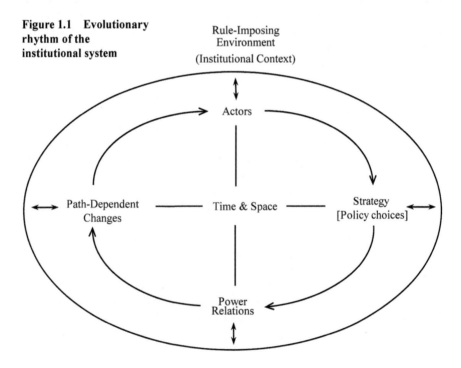

Figure 1.1   Evolutionary rhythm of the institutional system

Therefore, while proposing such an analysis, on the one hand, in addition to constructing its general framework, I will also try to explore a combined way of thinking over institutional environment, actors, power relations, and offer new patterns of path-dependent changes. Besides, I will naturally utilise the available concepts, definitions or investigations proposed in the relevant area of research. While citing these concepts or definitions or exploring the others, my ultimate purpose is to bring the four constituents of institutional system analysis together in tandem with its general explanatory framework.

Institutions as Interaction Channels

In a systemic analysis, institutions are the core constituents of the integrated structures of societies because they are the *interaction channels* that give life to the embodiment of a social system. Ascertaining and clarifying the definition of an institution is therefore a significant primordial step for institutional theory, as the former specifies the trajectory along which the latter's analytic path develops. In a systemic perspective, institutions can be defined as the *building-blocks of social order; they represent mutually related rights and obligations enforced by specific categories of actors to regulate, liberate or expand individual and collective action* (Streeck and Thelen, 2005: 9; Commons, 1959). An underlying feature of this definition is that, as *interaction channels*, institutions structure mutual relationships among individuals and organised actors. In this sense, they are constitutive of social and economic intercourse (Bromley, 2009: 45).

Institutions are constraining and enabling, namely liberating and expanding the right to act in certain forms. Here, constraint is used in the sense of *structural constraints*. It refers to the structuration of social systems as spaces of asymmetric power, denoting that constraints allow or disallow some actors from instrumentalising the structure's resources to enforce their goal and aims (Giddens, 1984: 170–176). In Streeck's words (1997: 197), (beneficial) constraints exist because 'a society requires a capacity to refrain advantage-maximising rational individuals from doing things that they would prefer to do, or to force them to do things that they would prefer not to do'. The object of constraint-contingent structuration is to sustain the trilogy of the social optimum (economic efficiency, social equity and individual liberty) by proactively regulating destructive interactions of unfettered utility-maximisers.

This is a structural crossroads where institutional interaction encounters the trilogy of conflict, dependence and order (Commons, 1959: 118). In the economic realm, for example, every economic transaction is bound to set off a conflict of interests because each actor or economic unit intends to obtain as much, and give as little as possible. On the one hand, such a mutually destabilising interaction creates dissensus among its participants. On the other, for social systems to maintain their existence there should be a trade-off point, an order, upon which *workable mutualities* can be predicated on the basis of mutual dependencies. As orders, especially the capitalist *order*, are barely sustained by voluntary action, there should thus be collectively binding arrangements to compel each party in the interaction to comply with the prerequisites of the social order by exhibiting performance, avoidance or forbearance.

A social analyst who disregards the inter-complementary quality of the conflict, dependence and order is likely to make a bounded definition of institutions. For example, to North (1990: 3), institutions are 'the rules of the game in a society or, more formally, are the humanly devised constraints that shape human interaction'. And the economic institutions 'define property rights, that is the bundle of rights over the use and the income to be derived from property and the ability to alienate an asset or resource. The function of rules is to facilitate exchange ... Political institutions ... reduce uncertainty by creating a stable structure of exchange ...' (North, 1990: 47–50). The boundedness of North's definition stems from his failure to even tangentially address the issue of *power* and its role in the process of economic change and performance, as he concentrates on smooth economic processes rather than their rough political manifestations at the level of social economics and social politics.

In political economy terms, does it matter that a rule in a country's constitution stipulates that the state should take the action necessary to ensure and sustain equality of opportunity if there is not a level playing field for the underprivileged to obtain this opportunity? Within this context, Streeck and Thelen (2005: 11) draw attention to the authority, obligation and enforcement-creating nature of institutions. For a rule to impose a workable constraint upon an action, it should hence have systemic, complementary linkages to other constraining tools within a structure to enforce its aim. This is the precondition for an institution to be an *effective* institution, the *de jure* presence of which then becomes a *de facto* constraint on actors. In this case, the actors will become aware that it is highly likely that they will be sanctioned for a potential noncompliance. The reverse is true for ineffective institutions.

Formal and Informal Institutions in Interactional Perspective

Institutions, formal or informal, are not mutually exclusive but inter-complementary or inter-repulsive (Dopfer, 2005: 26). Formal institutions such as state-enforced rules (legal frameworks, constitutions and so on) or organisational procedures regulate social action. This need not come in the form of a purely rational initiative, but may also be a normatively contingent rational initiative. As an integral part of culture, informal institutions such as norms, values, habits, standard practices, customs, traditions and conventions are the products of communicative action among individuals (Mantzavinos, 2001: 101–52). They are, in this regard, socially shared rules, namely forged, communicated and enforced through social interaction.

Informal institutions are, in a broad sense, composed of values and norms. Values are conceptions of the preferred or desirable combined with the construction of standards through which existing structures or behaviours can be compared and assessed. A value system is, in other words, a rule that an individual uses to select which of the mutually exclusive actions he/she will undertake (Arrow, 1967: 3–4). Norms, including ethical and moral codes, specify how things should be done. They define legitimate means to *valued* ends (Scott and Meyer, 1994: 58). As they appear in socially shared expectations, norms are benchmarks for a given pattern of behaviour (Elster, 1989: 97).

Values are shared beliefs regarding what is good/bad or true/wrong, and therefore underlie the structure of a society and the variety of its culture. Internalised values also determine the action orientations of individuals, groups and so on. In conjunction with values, norms are created to monitor and enforce cultural values, shared rules of conduct, that orient individuals regarding how they should act in specific situations (Horne, 2001: 4). The *normative* defines the domain of these shared rule-conditioned or value-rational actions (Elster, 1989: 150–151).

When it comes to a systemic perspective, the interactional explanation of formal and informal institutions becomes paramount as it is an analytical priority to shed light on the structuration, restructuration or destructuration of social institutions in terms of their inter-complementary and inter-repulsive inclinations. Habermas' conceptualisation of *communicative action* can be suggested to be the best available means for making such an interactional explanation of institutions.

The communicative action literature stems from Mead's symbolic interactionism, Wittengstein's concept of language games, Austin's theory of speech acts and Gadamer's hermeneutics. As the contemporary proponent of this tradition, Habermas (1984, 1987) contextualises communicative action within three societal constituencies – personality, culture and society – into the lifeworld and social system, two areas of interaction that unfold in an inter-repulsive process. Personality denotes the competences that make a subject capable of speaking and acting. Culture is the stock of knowledge that supplies its participants, persons, with interpretations during communication as they attach meanings to something in the lifeworld. Finally, societies are the systemically stabilised complexes of action of socially integrated groups, and thus they are the legitimate orders through which participants regulate their memberships in social groups and secure solidarity. The dimensions along which communicative action extends comprise the semantic field of symbolic contexts, social space and historical time.

The identity formation of a person, to Habermas, which he drew from Mead, centres on the social world to which the person belongs and a subjective world that is delineated from the social world. The latter is an external world of facts and norms facing the person. The confluence of these two relevance structures at the level of personality materialises in the interrelationship of the 'I' and the 'me'. The 'I' is the expressively manifested subjectivity of a desiring and feeling nature, and thus symbolises acting autonomously beyond the *institutionalised individual*. As a result, it is the particularising and impermeable element of the lifeworld and constitutes the essential reason that social structures are unpredictable. On the contrary, the 'me' stands for the other component of personality that is shaped through social interaction or socialisation.

Throughout the process of communicative action, the validity claims of participants in dialogical communication evolve from gesture to, in turn, symbol, grammatical speech and discourse that mediate the participants in their attempt to achieve an understanding within a cultural setting that supplies persons with interpretations to attach meanings to social phenomena. A gesture is a validity claim of alter and ego in discourse that morphs into shared understandings. By their utterances, the alter and ego share their subjective understandings and thus evince their inner thoughts self-reflectively. It is a shared language that makes this self-reflective interaction possible. By construing a situation and arriving at some agreement in communicative action, participants pursue their plans cooperatively on the basis of a shared definition of the situation. In other words, the validity claims of the alter and ego by means of linguistically mediated discourse pass into the values and norms that form the basis of rule-consciousness or shared meanings framed in institutional settings. The shared meanings do not arise from a sequence of cause-and-effect but rather from *self-reflexive* interaction between two or more individuals. This is why Habermas criticises Mead's delineation of social action as the totality of common meanings that individuals attach to the same symbols, as social action cannot be conceived of as the totality of individual actions.

In institutional terms, the production and reproduction of both informal and formal intersubjectivities originate in the formation of a common language between alter and ego, from gesture to symbol-mediated interaction to normatively guided interaction. As this process flows among millions of egos and alters in varying and dynamic combinations, but not in a linear sequence of cause-and-effect, communicative action gains an imponderable and undeterminable complexity over time and space. As the naked manifestations of communicative actions by interacting persons around shared but not identical meanings, institutions in evolution gain a variety of compositions at each social cycle, as the ego does not give the same signal to the alter's behaviour recurrently, and thus social action becomes unpredictable *ex ante* due to the this non-routine human action.

Habermas argues that, in historical time and space and within the sequence of tribal, traditional and modern forms, societies are differentiated both as systems and lifeworld. Lifeworld is the 'culturally transmitted and linguistically organized stock of interpretive patterns' that encompasses three elements of communicative action, culture, society and personality. In this regard, lifeworld stands for normatively regulated action, whereas the social system comprises rationally constructed structures. Social interaction is differentiated between system and lifeworld because the complexity of the former and rationality of the latter gather pace over time. This is not a linear but a dialectic process that, in contemporary capitalist societies, narrows the lifeworld into a subsystem of the social system in the sense that the rationally structured media of the latter, formalised structures, in due course, chips away at the social realm of the normatively structured constituencies of the former. An example of this so-called process is the formation of *norm-free* structures in modern societies in which members are prone to engage in formally organised action systems that are marshalled via economic exchange and political power. The result is that norm-confirmative and identity-forming social memberships are made peripheral (colonised) and gradually wither away.

Thus, normatively guided interactions among persons morph into strategic attitudes adopted in a consequentalist or intentionalist mindset. Media such as money and power spread social action through empirically motivated bonds on the basis of rationally motivated value commitments. In institutional terms, money is an exchange mechanism that mediates the interlinkages among the state, business and households in the context of the institutionalisation of wage labour, as a dependent constituency of the capitalist enterprise and tax-based regulation of this intercourse by the state. Teleological action, the driving force of monetarily steered social systems, works to bring about a desired state by choosing strategically calculable options that are expected to yield the most lucrative outcomes in utilitarian terms. (This model of action underlies game-theoretic approaches in economics, sociology and social psychology [Habermas, 1984: 85].) It is the particularising effect of the 'I', the rationally motivated aspect of personality, which comes to the fore as a result of the receding scope of norm-confirmative or value-rational behaviour in the operation of a social system.

At this point, it should however be noted, in terms of the institutional system analysis, that a social system embraces both formal and informal institutions, and the lifeworld is an integral component of it. As a result, unlike Habermas' perspective, culture cannot be reduced to the lifeworld. This is because his orientation is to address the social system as the norm-free institutionalised form of the lifeworld. Nevertheless, as Figure I.1 illustrates (p. 4), culture, as the cement of social action, as Habermas himself put it, shapes the intersecting meaning structures of formal and informal institutions. If we regard the system as the whole of its constitutive components, juxtaposing the lifeworld against the social system is analytically dissipative. This is because the *systemness of society* is not *systematicness of society* and vice versa. Systemness comprises both normative and rational constituencies, but systematicness only includes the rational, knowledgeable or intelligible (Turner, 2010: Chapter 6). Instead, I prefer to analyse the social system as a whole consisting of formal and informal institutions.

The underlying logic is that while Habermas' communicative action authoritatively demonstrates the institutionalisation of formal and informal institutions, it fails, to a certain extent, to theorise on their dialectic evolution in timespace. Informal institutions, norms and values, are constitutive elements of formal institutions and structure the normative conduct of social systems. In other words, normativeness is not limited to informal institutions. In many contexts, informal institutions, ranging from bureaucratic and legislative norms to clientelism and patrimonialism, shape political behaviour and outcomes (Helmke and Levitsky, 2004: 725). In Luhmann's words, they are the *connective value* of the overall stock of institutions. In another respect, the structuration of formal institutions with a purposive-rational mentality is not detached from informal institutions, as this rationally constituted structure of formal institutions in due course is also suffused with informal values. The dissolution of cultural stock, as reflected in extreme individualisation, consequentialist personalisation or purposive-rationalisation, illustrates that, in this regard, there is an incessant and evolutionary reciprocality between the two types of institutions rather than a unidirectional and irretrievable bifurcation.

Habermas' reaction to Parsons' or Durkheim's functionally articulated systems approach does not validate the unsophisticatedness of this sharp-edged balkanisation. However, Parson's 'social systems' theory represents a much more obfuscatory example of an examination of culture from an unsystemic perspective. He includes the culture and social system in the analysis as two separate units. The segregation of culture from the social *system* in Parsons' work (1951: 15) inevitably leads to a quandary, as his analysis fails to address where culture is forged, shared, transmitted and learned. This is the social system itself. In Parsons' terms, what is its *status*? He uses the social system and society interchangeably: 'A social system, which meets all the essential functional prerequisites of long term persistence from within its own resources, will be called a society' (1951: 19). Thus culture is a separate unit of what? In this sense, addressing culture as an adjunct unit of the social system is a structural analytic *deficit* in this sense, which is evinced in Parsons' conceptualisation of *adaptive change*. Without interlinking the subjectivities among actors, who interact along the institutional axes, in terms of the evolution of cultural rhythms of formal and informal institutions, we cannot explicate the evolutionary dynamism in the system. Thus, we have to say that: the structure is as such and the actors must abide by the given rules. Who changes these rules and for what reason? Our discussion, in the following, proceeds to delve into determining an answer to this question through the four constitutive elements of the institutional system analysis.

Institutional Structure: the Environment for the Inter-Actor Relationship

In a systemic analysis, after defining institutions as the channels through which actors interact, the next task is to inquire into the overall institutional structure, the institutional environment, within which this interaction unfolds. The increasing velocity of individual and societal rationalisation of politico-economic structures provides an impetus to address the encompassing social environment as something composed of subsystems functioning under the cement of unifying differentiation. As discussed below, for example, Luhmann's social system analysis relies on such a theoretically functional analysis (albeit wielding some unsystemically assembled normative utterances such as black boxes). However, it is the institutional interactions unfolding in a social environment that are the driving force of the formation and evolution of social systems. And this interaction is not unilaterally determined by rational action but also affected by a normative one as well.

In this respect, the social environment structures the context within which in-system or inter-system interactions unfold, and thereby gains its meaning through the intersectional manifestations of informal and formal institutions.

Essentially, it is implausible to ascribe a definite boundary for the limits of the social environment due to the complex structuration of institutions at the national, regional and international levels. An analysis of institutions should nonetheless be placed in a certain context to make it possible to illustrate which institutions and interactions will be examined from a systemic approach. The solution of this dialectic challenge is that an environmental analysis of institutions should be based on the intersectional scopes of inter-actor relationships, not on the formal boundaries encircling this interaction. This means that, analytically, the domain of the environment would expand or contract according to the boundary of institutional intersections mediated by actors, and therefore the analysis would not be strangled by the *ex ante* domain of the environment. *The environment, in this regard, is the institutional structure that encompasses, regulates and constrains the inter-actor relationships.*

Regarding the sub-section of social theory that approaches social interaction using a systemic approach, two analyses come to the fore concerning the environment of the institutional structure. The first is Luhmann's auotopiesis-theoretic exegesis of social systems, and the second is Wallerstein's world system analysis of the capitalist world economy. In the following, these two analyses are discussed and compared, and then the key principles of an institutional environmental analysis will be proposed in terms of the interaction-theoretic perspective of institutional system analysis.

Society, to Luhmann, is the all-encompassing social system that includes everything social (1995: 408). There is one society, world society, which has no boundaries in time or space and is constituted by its elemental units (communications). As everything is embodied, evolves or changes within it, it is a stable, self-substitutive order. At each circulation, a system stabilises and re-stabilises its instabilities (p. 218). In Luhmann's theory, self-substitution manifests itself in *self-referentiality*, the action of a system to address its structured environment. A self-referential system comprises the least particular element of a general social system, establishes relations within itself and differentiates these relations from its environment, that is, its negative correlate or its everything else (p. 181). In other words, its existence resides in the fact that it differentiates and maintains its boundaries with its environment, an action that provides it with an idiosyncratic identity or meaning. What enables a system to be self-referential is its functional elements that make its self-constitution possible, independent of all surrounding others or its environment. Luhmann terms such a system *autopoietic*, in an effort to capture a system's self-producing and self-sustaining competence in continuing encounters with other systems. It is the self-organisation of an autopoietic system rather than environmental functions that determine its internal and external boundaries and its functional role.

Luhmann argues that the boundary of a system does not denote a cut-off point. It is a systemic element arising from the system's differentiation from the others that makes it possible for the system to interact (establish interboundary relationships) with other systems. In other words, the boundary distinguishes the elements of various social systems from one another but not necessarily their relations. It allows causal effects to pass through (p. 29). This is the *communicative differentiation* in a structural sense. To Luhmann, the function of a structure is to make autopoietic reproduction possible by unifying functionally differentiated subsystems evolving in an unpredictable complexity. The functional differentiation of systems does not refer to a secession or detachment from their environments. Instead, a system, to maintain its autopoietic existence, must adapt its structure to its environment.

Scientifically, according Luhmann's perspective, on the one hand, the functional explication of social systems, in essence, aims to place each function in the proper place in its environment and describe the causal interlinkages between different functions. Therefore, functional analysis can clarify latent relationships. However, he also emphasises systemic complexity, which stems from differentiating the identities and meanings, of systems. Luhmann argues that meaning is what distinguishes a system from the others, and thus a system only gains meaning when it refers to other meanings. Complexity is the meaning of inter-systemic *interaction*, a phenomenon that cannot be traced through the differentiating identities of its constituent systems, as there is no counterpart from which it can be differentiated. He states: 'Every element (event, action, etc.) is then determinate and indeterminate at the same time: determinate in its momentary actuality and indeterminate in its *connectivity*' (p. 49).

Complexity, in this sense, signifies indeterminacy or a lack of information, and hence is not accessible to scientific analysis or simulation (p. 14). He terms these indeterminate spaces in social systems *black boxes*. The open horizons originating from the potentiality of an ever-expanding number of relationships between systems delimit social complexity (p. 17). A further insight from Luhmann relevant to conceptualising complexity is that, in addition to arguing that complexity is a self-reflective process, as noted above, complexity also reduces complexity itself by allowing systems to develop new elements to differentiate themselves from others to maintain their existence in the face of increasing environmental change resulting from ever-expanding complexity or indeterminacy, and this differentiation in turn causes their differentiating identities, meanings, to become clear (p. 26).

Underlying social complexity is the dialogical communication of ego and alter under a double contingency. Luhmann contends that communication is the processing of selection or a selective occurrence in time. It cannot be reduced, as Habermas did, to an action-theoretic element, nor can the process of communication be regarded as a chain of action. The selection of ego, alter, alter ego, alter ego's alter ego and so on unfolds under double contingency, as each of them makes their selection in tandem with their diverse identities and within a complex environment. In addition, the double contingency of alter and ego's communicative selections expand in a spiral fashion over time and space because, in the presence of continuous circularity and asymmetric information, their communication unfolds within black boxes or undeterminable areas of interaction. Therefore, communication cannot be observed but only inferred.

According to Luhmann, the evolution of a social system is the concomitant evolution of a system and its environment, and a social system reshapes its unifying difference as a result of this cyclical dependence to its environment. Cyclical dependence manifests itself in the interpenetration of systems by introducing their own already constituted complexity into one another. In another respect, the complexity increases with each institutional system cycle, as the interaction of a system with its environment in mutual adjustments, amendments or supplementations does not unfold synchronically or linearly. A critical point in Luhmann's analysis is that this causal interaction between a system and its environment is incidental to the autopoietic reproduction of the system itself, as he conceives of the latter as its reason for *being a system*.

Wallerstein provides an alternative interpretation of institutional environment in his study of world system analysis. He conducts an interaction-theoretic explication of inter-actor relationships in terms of the environmental boundaries of social action. As a system theoretician, he contextualises his inductive analysis within the 'world system'. Social reality, to him, hinges on the inter-complementary linkages, the division of labour, in this world system rather than multiple nation states. The system's institutional elements consist of states and the interstate system, productive firms, markets, households, classes and identity groups of all sorts. The interlinkages among these elements constitute a matrix that makes the system operate a conflict-ridden (rather than stable) path dating back to the sixteenth century.

The mainstay of Wallerstein's analysis, *historical social science*, is the diachronic evolution of this matrix at multi-temporal and multi-spatial horizons with a focus on the existence of a division of labour along core periphery axes among states encircled by the webs of private property. The social division of labour occurs in the world economy, a large geographic zone in which the substantial exchange of basic goods and the flows of capital and labour circulate cross-nationally (2011a: 351). This world economy and its capitalist mode of production are interconnected through a complementary, but not cause-and-effect relationship, and constitute the Capitalist World Economy (CWE) (Wallerstein, 1980: 6).

Geographical conceptualisation is another methodological theme through which world system analysis attempts to explain cross-national linkages among the system's elements. Wallerstein argues that, provided that we accept that the world-system is the essential social system, the hallmark of this system is the emergence, consolidation and political roles of classes and status groups. The cross-national confluence of these elements, not exclusively class-consciousness or occupational status, should be addressed when their roles are the subject of debate (2011b: 348–9). While having a conflated structure of economic ties around combined division of labour, in this respect, the CWE comprises a wide variety of cultures, political regimes, civic movements and numerous religions, languages, traditions and so on. While the elements of the CWE develop certain common cultural practices, termed geoculture (2011b: 277), this does not mean that a homogenous socio-political structure is a reasonable probability. This is because the elements of the CWE do not shift their structures equidirectionally or simultaneously, as 'the social system is built on having a multiplicity of value systems within it, reflecting the specific functions groups and areas play in the world division of labour' (2011a: 356).

Without falling into the trap of 'social physics', Wallerstein first delineates the respective evolution of politico-economic interactions at the world system level by concentrating on the structuration of centre and peripheral areas of economic action in terms of *relational* interactions among the elements of this system. His core concern is to contextualise economic action with respect to the spatial context in which it unfolds rather than to explain it through organically structured conceptual apparatuses. In other words, the CWE is based on a systemically ordered explication of economic relationships in terms of their *socially embedded idiosyncrasies*. What makes his analysis normatively contingent is that he does not subsume national varieties within the systemic nature of the CWE. At issue is that the environment of the CWE consists of the elements for which their roles, impacts and relational intersections vary across time and space. Wallerstein begins his four-volume work with this brief paragraph: 'Change is eternal. Nothing ever changes. Both clichés are "true". Structures are those coral reefs of human relations which have a stable existence over relatively long periods of time. But structures too are born, develop, and die' (2011a: 3).

Unlike Wallerstein, Luhmann's theoretic core resides in general systems theory. When compared with the rudiments of GST, it becomes evident that Luhmann reduced sociology into living systems theory in terms of a system's environment, autopoiesis, equilibrium, autonomy and so on. This can be detected in his emphasis (1994: 15) that 'we therefore will exclude the (highly controversial) direct analogy between social systems and organisms or machines, but not, however, an orientation toward a general systems theory that seeks to address more encompassing demands'. This premise is how he establishes the pillars of his systems theory. For example, like Habermas, he also contextualises interlinkages between social systems in terms of self-reflexive and communicative interaction between alter and ego. Nonetheless, as Luhmann singles out *rational* but not *normative* implications when developing the central pillars of his analysis, he fails to explain the colligated embodiment, re-embodiment or disembodiment of formal and informal institutions at the national or transnational levels. Instead, he focuses on how human experience is ordered, differentiated and hierarchised.

A sort of *totalitarian particularism* asserts itself in Luhmann's distinction between general and subsystems in terms of their environment. However, a system cannot be considered independent of its environment. Its communicative action with other systems, inter-system interaction, in the environment constitutes the environment itself. Luhmann loses sight of the fact that the macro-environment of a social system is not the totality but the aggregate meaning of the shared environment of subdivisional systems. In other words, a differentiation-based identification of systems and their environment cannot allow us to conceptualise the interaction-based liaisons between them in terms of the encompassing institutional structure.

Closed systems are static and have a bounded scope of interaction within their environment. In addition to being dynamic and ever-expanding environments, open systems have the potential to interact with other systems and develop a more complex structure. In Weber's approach, for instance, *open* and *closed* refer to whether something is closed to interaction (1978: 43). In Luhmann's analysis, however, the closedness or openness of a system is at best fuzzy, as he overvalued the self-renewing and introverted nature of social systems and undervalued inter-systemic interaction.

As a result of the above discussion, let me assert three basic principles of an environmental analysis that I will follow throughout this study:

1. It is essential not to lock in the imbricated or numerically *concatenated* structure of the environment; instead one must determine the range of intersections at which institutional axes unfold. In other words, there is no *minus-plus* hierarchy for inter-system spaces, but rather interaction-contingent spatial horizons in complex evolution.

2. There are no statically segregated and *ex ante* defined environments consisting of functionally disjointed parts and their *symbiotic* evolution in terms of their status, location and interactions; instead, the scope, size, impact, status and intersections of both the environment and its constituent elements change under the trilogy of conflict, dependence and order. Thus, the cyclical and unintermittent adaptation or adaptive differentiation between the former and the latter are analytically insubstantial.

3. In political economy terms and under contemporary modes of production and power relations, no system, sub or upper, can survive independently without engaging with the others within a given institutional structure. In other words, a systemic identity is obtained not through isolation but interaction. *Isolationist interaction*, symbiotic relationship of isolation and interaction, is a chimera in both theory and practice if there is, as Luhmann claimed, a single world society or more than one society in this one world. This is because *interaction* could not unfold without *reciprocal* action.

Actors and Institutional Structure between Rule-Making and Rule-Taking

Defining institutions as the binding elements of the inter-actor relationship denotes that they determine the idiosyncrasies of the structure, the institutional environment, in which actors interact. Therefore, the independent variable in political economy is institutions rather than actors. In terms of the systemic rhythms of the institutional structure depicted in Figure 1.1 (p. 16) the actors are the constituents of social systems that act to operationalise their aims through long-term strategy or short-run policies. Strategies are future-oriented actions to create the most effective match of potential strengths and weaknesses with available opportunities and threats within the existing institutional structure. By doing so, a strategising actor's aim is to contextualise its action within the least risky pathway throughout which enforcing tactics would be phased out most effectively (David, 1993). A competent strategy should manage imminent opportunities and challenges in timespace without systemically diverging from the initial targets. Naturally, such a competency is contingent on the evolution of the encompassing institutional structure and rival actors' strategies and tactics (Besanko et al., 2000: 497–9; Keane, 2005). Each actor might not (or might lack the ability to) devise a long-term or *evolutionary strategy* and enforce it with tactical policies, but instead make non-strategic (short-run) policy choices. (For the term evolutionary strategy, see Whittington, 1993: 17–21.)

In systemic terms, *strategic* does not necessarily refer to rational-purposive actions, nor are non-strategic policy choices due entirely to the actors' inability to craft effective strategies. The complexity of the social structure and unpredictability of future action are the primary ways in which the institutional structure could disable actors, even purely rationalist ones, namely firms, from determining long-term strategies and structuring them to address conjunctural drifts, especially during periods of crisis (Boisot, 2003). Within this context, institution building is not a mere exercise of technocracy, as public or private bureaucrats cannot *ex ante* control the evolution of micro- or macro-supranational and national social structures, including economic sectors, in tandem with the specifications of their plans (Chang, 2007: 13).

In addition, the actors' aim need not be interest maximisation, a metaphysical claim that action has become stripped of its informal qualities or wholly rationalised. In line with the intriguing structure of the social system, human and organisational behaviour is too complex to be defined by an unsophisticated assumption that overlooks non-wealth-maximising values (North, 1990: 15). The individuals or organisations' incentive to act varies with context, size and composition (Olson, 2002 [1965]: Chapter I; Jackson, 2010: 71), and hence cannot be determined *ex ante*. In social space and time, in other words, the action-frame of actors cannot be decoupled into two separate divisions, as Weber did, value-rational and purposive-rational. Even if we accept that the 'I', a non-institutionalised or non-codified individual, entirely stands for a denormativised individual, even then, this claim would not be vindicated. This is because the 'I' cannot be removed from the 'me', an institutionalised individual, in that both of them are intersecting 'actors' but not functionally dissipated units. To put it in Weber's own words (1978: 4–5): 'We shall speak of "action" insofar as the acting individual attaches a subjective meaning to his behaviour – be it overt or covert, omission or acquiescence. Action is "social" insofar as its subjective meaning takes account of the behaviour of others and is thereby oriented in its course'.

In other words, the interlaced evolution of individual and organisational action with time-lags and in various sequences comprises various gravities of purposive- and value-rationality, and a barometer to disentangle their binary coexistence has yet to be developed. This intriguing phenomenon asserts itself in Weber's statement that 'understandable and non-understandable components of a process are often intermingled and bound up together' (1978: 23). In addition, the different contextual worlds of the interpreter and the interpreted in communicative action occurring at various levels highlight the abstruseness of social phenomena (Jackson, 2009: 147). Further obfuscating social action is the pragmatic oscillations of human behaviours between theory and praxis. This denotes that the actors' discursive or declarative manifestations might be at odds with real and enforcing actions. As a result, to identify all sub-social processes and to count them is a futile task as far as the change-laden cycle of the social system is concerned.

This futility is evinced in *bounded rationality*, implying that, at least in finite time, agents fall short of exhibiting substantively rational behaviour as they: i) do not have full knowledge of all possible contingencies; ii) are unable to exhaustively explore the entire decision tree; and iii) correctly evaluate and understand the utility values of all mappings of actions, events and outcomes (Dosi et al., 2005: 261). Kaplan's (1965: 58) contextualisation of national action is of explanatory value in this regard. According to him, under the constraints of their values and essential rules, national actors differ in their appraisals of situations and the extent to which they will allocate resources among national and transnational objectives in situations of equal urgency. Therefore, to refer to all of the actions of national actors as self-interested obscures practically and theoretically substantial aspects of behaviour. As a consequence, under bounded-rationality conditions, institutional interactions should be analysed context-dependently and in terms of the actors' discourses and practices and pursue their ebb and flow in the process of power relations.

In terms of institutional context, actors develop, sustain or reorganise the institutions that affect their operational ambit. In principle, they are rule-takers, as the institutional structure imposes the power distribution channels and rules under which they act, as depicted in Figure 1.1 (p. 16). In other words, institutions are 'actor-binding' and 'coordinating elements'. As Beckert (1999) noted, actors, however, are not only 'constrained entities' but acting subjects that instrumentalise the existing opportunities in the institutional infrastructure to layer, convert or displace dominant institutions through an incremental power struggle. However, it is utterly reductionist to claim, as actor-centred functionalists have, that institutions exist to serve the interests of those that created them (Pierson, 2004: 95). The exchange-theoretic delineation of social networks in the new institutionalist perspective, for example, is predisposed to develop an *actor-conditioned* perspective on social interaction, albeit incorporating the pure existence of informal institutions in the operations of this network (Richter, 2008: 173–5).

At this point, the lingering question is: what is the independent variable of social action, institutions or actors? No actor *per se* can impose, rework or restructuralise institutions, nor does the existing stock of institutions always conserve the same quantity of power to constrain actors' actions at the same density. Instead of locking in a determinist presupposition, we can formulate this ancient puzzle in this way: the trajectory of the social system is determined by the confluence of the strategies and policies of pro-cyclical or countercyclical actors, *both under and over* the evolving institutional cycle. The underlying principle is that institutional structures, their actors and their intersectional combinations vary over time.

A powerful constellation of change agents could prevail over the institutional structure. The outermost range of what they can do, in most cases, is nonetheless to restructure the pre-existing structure rather than annihilate it and erect an entirely new architecture. Insurrectionary or subversive actors might displace or convert an institution or a constellation of institutions such as a social security system, the economic structure and so on. In addition, in terms of the overall or subsystemic institutional structure, they could not enforce their aims at a critical juncture but have to pass through a processual transition, at best. This point is the distinguishing *architecture* of social systems that relies on the integrated evolution of formal and informal institutions over time and space, as we discussed with reference to Habermasian communicative action. The quintessence of communicative action is that *actors are the products of instrumentalisation* or *institutionalised structures.* In other words, they are not *spontaneous organisations*, as Hayek claimed (1998a: 27). Ultimately, the power of institutions is a structurally objective phenomenon that cyclically desubjectivises temporarily subjectivised power by the actors. To put it simply, it is the institutional establishment that retains the 'roots' of power resources. This is what Habermas (1974: 22) describes as 'the self-reflection and the objectification of the whole'.

Furthermore, the new competition between the actors will, ultimately, recurrently concern the current form of the pre-existing structure, and the actors or a peculiar constellation of institutions will ultimately change. However, what would not change is that social systems should have an institutional structure, restructured or destructured, situated in time that begets either the embodiment of new actors or the recasting of inter-actor relationships. Reducing the institutional structure to outcomes or the rules of the game followed by the actors is in this respect untenable. Institutions are not unidirectionally or equidirectionally manipulable tools for actors' strategic choices, but the underpinnings that pro-cyclical or countercyclical actors should consider an independent variable of their interplay.

In terms of inter-actor relationship under an institutional environment, *action per se* does not mean exerting a *coercive* impact on others and we cannot speak of a power relationship if there is no *interaction.* Interaction is action but not dominance of one over another. Being an actor hence does not necessitate being a dominant over others but taking place in the institutional environment, even with a tenuous impact. In other words, being an actor necessitates performing the act of acting irrespective of its status in terms of power relations. An act might serve the master. This impact is also introduced into the system through which the master cultivates the power of enforcing its dominance (Wrong, 1979: 57). In Foucauldian terms, actors are both wielders of power and subjected to power and there is a contingency of reversibility in most cases (Foucault, 2003: 27). This implies that power is not an isolated constituent but an instrumental component of social systems and does evolve with the institutional, formal or informal, environment in which it is generated, disseminated or transferred. In this respect, if we disregard passive actors in unfolding of power relations, we cannot extrapolate power substitution between the subject and the object. As a result, actors can be defined as those *constituents that convert policy strategies into impacts* in social systems.

Friedland and Alford (1991: 240–242) argue that an authoritative exegesis of society should comprise a trilogy of actors involved in social action, 'individuals, organisations and institutions' competing and negotiating, in conflict and coordination, and in contradiction and interdependence. By contrast, methodological individualism argues that the latter two could not have aims or develop teleological action (Rutherford, 1994: 32). In conjunction with this liberal mindset, Easton (1965), as a system theoretician, suggests that variables regulating the inflow of the demands and impacts of their members within the social system are termed *intermediary* organisations.

Easton's definition is flawed because it fails to acknowledge that intermediary organisations are not agents but genuine actors that collectivise the demands of their members. Namely, it is not the mere sum of those demands but their collectivised manifestation at the level of organisations that is introduced into the system as a separate niche of impacts on the institutional structure. In this sense, an organisational actor not only mediates its members' demands but also transforms them into organised impacts on the social system (Easton's perspective originates in his development of a power-free analysis of political systems). The quintessence of this fact for a systemic analysis is that having a system-regulating, structuring, destructuring, restructuring or changing impact requires an organised action to realise certain *common aims*. The organised action does not have to unfold under the unifying shelter of a single organisation. Instead, the cooperation between various actors to achieve their common ends can also be considered as an organised or a coalitional action. Scharpf (1997: 55) defines coalition as the common action of actors that have *separate purposes*. It should be added that what makes a coalition or a coalitional organisation possible is the *common ends* of their constitutive actors and this does not rule it out for them to pursue their separate purposes in or outside this coalition.

I will label actors as pro-cyclical or countercyclical with respect to their coalitional constellations given the existing stock of institutions. Pro-cyclical or countercyclical actors produce path-sustaining or path-changing strategy and policy choices, respectively, to realise their aims or consolidate their positions. The institutional environment is the path-imposing structure of the inter-actor relationship, as depicted in Figure 1.1. This binary definition, however, does not imply that the two types of actors have unidirectionally pro-system or anti-system aims; instead, their strategies, in terms of their core constituencies, are congruent or incongruent with the existing institutional structure to varying degrees. Hayek (1998a: 39) points out that 'purposive ... mean[s] merely that the elements have acquired regularities of conduct conducive to the maintenance of the order – presumably because those who did act in certain ways had within the resulting order a better change of survival than those who did not'. What should be added is that not only the purposive but also the value-rational actions of actors have the same *purpose*, to maintain an order that supports their aims.

A veto-theoretic definition of actors and their power resource, veto-points, presupposes that the institutional system is, in an analytic perspective, subsidiary to the spatiotemporal flow of the actors' ratificatory actions in a cause-effect sequence (Tsebelis, 2002). The deductive delineation of actors' intersectional points around veto-points prevents the analyst from inductively locating them in the broader alignment of social interaction. Instead, the analytically significant component in the definitions of pro-cyclical or countercyclical is that the concepts are rooted in the power relations among actors in the institutional system, where their actions take their roles in the development of the existing structure. In political economy terms, for example, this means that an intra-party group's vetoing of a new vision or identity for their party should be examined not only in terms of the party's political career but also the conduct of political system, the economic policies of the incumbent government and the future of the relationship among political parties, business associations and non-governmental organisations, including trade and civil service unions. This does not preclude delineating the particular veto points of this group, but proposes that such an effort be placed within the 'social system of politics and economics'.

Finally, as an adjunct to pro-cyclical and countercyclical, actors can also be categorised as national, regional, international, supranational, transnational and so on. Kaplan (1965: 54–84) primarily categorises actors as national or supranational. The latter comprise bloc actors such as the USA and the USSR during the Cold War and universal actors such as the United Nations. Actors can also be defined as state or non-state actors (transnational corporations and non-governmental organisations) (Bieler et al., 2004); internal or external; active or passive and so on. In this sense, it would be expedient to distinguish actors by using their boundary and spatial limits to attach a particular identity to their frame of action. In institutional systems analysis, however, pro-cyclicality and countercylicality are the principal terms for defining the statuses and positions of actors in terms of power relations and the unfolding of subsequent, path-dependent changes that take root in the inter-repulsive and inter-complementary dynamics of inter-actor relationships.

Power Relations as the Process of Institutional Interactions

In a systemic account of the politico-economic environment, power inheres in the tension between inter-actor relationships and the encompassing institutional structure. In other words, power is a dynamic that shapes the tensions in inter-actor rivalry that flows through the evolution of institutional cycles. To put it in Foucauldian terms (2003: 29), 'power passes through networks', and therefore it is the background motive of everything.

As a background motive, power is in fact an amorphous element (Weber, 1978: 53). However, its effectual manifestation can be observed at actors' impacts over institutional structure and their rivals' actions. With reference to its instrumental nature, power can thus be defined as *the actors' ability to formulate, implement and revise strategies or policy choices that aim to organise a micro or macro-institutional structure according to their objectives vis-à-vis their rivals' countervailing actions* (each of these three forms of ability is inter-complementary and interdependent. For example, having the potential to formulate a powerful strategy is the precondition for implementing it).

To organise a social structure, the actors should have a systemic power. *Systemic* nature of power rests upon the fact that a constellation of actors have the amalgamation of available power resources as far as to enable them to determine and manage the cyclical course of a given section or the whole of a social system in a certain period of time. Put it differently, it is not a prerequisite for pro-cyclical or countercyclical actors to grasp all resources of power at equal or highest gravities. In this sense, systemic power is not a monadic or static whole but a dynamic combination of core and complementary types and sources of power, depicted in Figure 1.2, at various levels and contexts and among various actors (Kelly, 2008: 35–7). Nor is its core unit to control inter-actor relations in a static timespace but to manage the dialectic encounters with countercyclical actors that could change the structure of in-system power distribution in time (Brucan, 1975). An example of an inter-context manifestation of power is the intermeshing linkages of various segments of systemic power, power at the national, regional and global levels in economic, political, technological, cultural realms and so on, and essentially the relational or intersectional dynamics that their encounters unleash at varying intensity and complexities (Bowles and Gintis, 2005; Bowles, 2005: 265; Borch, 2005: 158, 164).

Historically, for example, at international level, three nations had the ability to enforce systemic power: the United Provinces (the contemporary Netherlands) in the mid-seventeenth, The United Kingdom in the mid-nineteenth and the United States in the mid-twentieth centuries. The criteria that must be satisfied to enjoy such a status are: establish the major rules of the international order, dominate economic intercourse (in production, commerce, and finance) and formulate the popular means of culture (Wallerstein, 2004: 57–8). That these countries exerted a controlling power over the other nations in these three major areas does not invalidate the fact that the other nations continued to create notable impacts into the international system and generated strategies to determine the future of their own societies. Instead, the former kept control of the centre of gravity of power relations as far as to organise the international division of labour in parallel with their own objectives. The latter determined those strategies under the constraints of the international environment dominated by the former.

The segmentation of power at various social structures or levels is rooted in the fact that each actor or a group of actors, expectedly, aims to enforce its basic objectives. This purposive or/and value-rational action might require having only certain kinds of power out of Figure 1.2. For example, a university can have systemic power in the area of higher education through holding the sources of power of knowledge such as innovative power in some specific high-tech areas over its national or international competitors. Naturally, a university cannot be expected to have a systemic power in an entire social system. Instead, by the agency of an established school of, for example, economics theorised by its members, a university can provide theoretical power with those actors holding systemic power at their hands to discourse, justify and consolidate their objectives and strategies (Dugger, 1980: 899–902). The very phenomenon of 'Chicago Boys' is a case in point. This title refers to those economists who have been designing the Chilean political economy by standard neoliberal recipes after getting trained at the University of Chicago under Milton Friedman's leadership and then being assigned to the top posts in the Chilean governments and bureaucracy, particularly during the reign of General Pinochet in the mid-1970s. They had then the opportunity to restructure the country's economic stock under Pinochet's systemic power over the entire population. Furthermore, beyond Chilean borders, this locational restructuration came to be a niche of structural knowledge and justificatory power for global neoliberalism to consolidate its reign across the continents.

Given the segmented nature of power resources, the varieties of power should be contextualised into a complementary set of systemic power. Figure 1.2 aims to propose a model of power to achieve this purpose. As can be seen, in terms of a given institutional structure, five types of power lie at the core of systemic power: institutional, theoretical, structural, discursive and the cyclical manifestation of all four of these patterns, evolutionary power. These power patterns acquire their meanings through their complementary or coalitional partners, as depicted in Figure 1.2, such as justificatory, strategic, knowledge or consolidative power. Let me engage with the main patterns and then their complements.

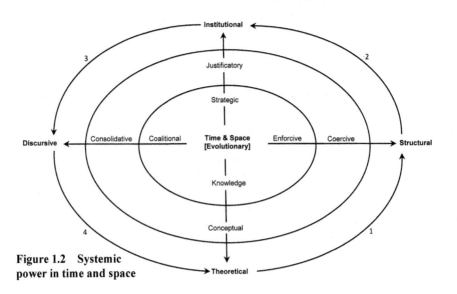

Figure 1.2   Systemic power in time and space

Major Patterns

- **Institutional power**: Foucault notes that 'I don't believe this question of "who exercises power?" can be resolved unless that other question of "how does it happen?" is resolved at the same time' (Kritzman, 2003: 103). In this sense, the power of institutions originates in the fact that, as noted above, they hold the origins and foundations of power over and under which actors compete. In other words, institutions, formal or informal, serve as a power resource for the actors, whose aims, strategies and policy choices are fed back by them. Informal institutions such as shared values and norms can be expected to bestow a relatively longer-term power on their adherents. Because their institutionalisation evolves in a process through which respective norms and values are gradually infused into the social subconscious through their scaring and accumulated effects, the dissolution of this type of power would also require a longer period of time. This can be traced through Islam's lingering impact on the Turkish people's civil life and particularly its rising ascendance with a modern face at the very centre of Turkish political life nearly one century later, a process to be examined in the next parts of the book. Formal institutions such as governments would provide their holders a relatively shorter term of power, as their resources, such as political support and popularity, might well be expected to be much more fluid in nature.
- **Structural power**: a particular deployment of politico-economic institutions at a certain period in time, the structure, determines the potential impacts of actors at the national or transnational levels. The neoliberal structuration of European political economies, for example, enabled the Third Way ideas to have structural power over classical social democrat ones particularly during the mid-1990s in that the latter failed to propose a genuine alternative to the systemic power of neoliberal policy-making. The proponents of the Third Way politics and economics such as the British Labour Party and the German SPD did so by proposing a new mix of efficiency and equity under the confines of *positive welfare*, a strategy to be implemented through workfare schemes.
- **Evolutionary power**: the continuity of both the core and complementary types of power depends on their evolutionary continuum. Evolutionary power, in this respect, is the ability to sustain and accumulate both types of power in time. Their holders cannot sustain these different types of power at equal levels during each institutional system cycle, as their co-evolution unfolds in various combinations of power resources. This is because the impact of each constituent varies both conjuncturally and cumulatively (see Kennedy, 1998: xv). Within this context, inter-temporal changes in the impacts of relative weights of power elements on the conduct of aggregate systemic power, if pro-cyclical, would spur the inculcation of dominant structures. Otherwise, if countercyclical, they would pave the way for or contribute to the regression of the dominant structure.

In broad strokes, for example, the neoliberal ideas started accumulating in the early or the mid-1970s and became embedded during the 1990s. After more than three decades, with the outburst of the ongoing great recession during which fiscal stimulus and monetary expansion have become widespread practices across the world, Keynesians come to have the potential of re-defending their thesis, as can be observed at Skidelsky's (2009) impressive work, *the Return of the Master* (Keynes). Nowadays, a hypothesis of *the time for visible hand* has become a popular image, a concrete indicator that neoliberal ideals have already started to de-accumulate (Stiglitz, 2010; Williams, 2010). Yet the adherents of neoliberal status quo, the neoclassicals, still continue to dominate the global production of economic knowledge (as to be discussed below, for example, Acemoğlu and Robinson [2012] still continue to vehemently defend Friedman's ideas). Apparently, this is possible due to the accumulated embeddedness of the systemic power resources of neoliberal institutionalism in time. These resources of power range from the institutional and structural such as *Central Bank independence* and the *power to invest* (at businessmen's hands), respectively, to discursive and conceptual such as an attractive emphasis on *technical progress* and the justification of unequal distribution of power with the motto of *equality of opportunity*, respectively.

- **Theoretical power**: theory provides actors with the power to establish knowledge resources, by the agency of concepts, in a consistent framework that feed back into the formation, implementation or justification of their aims and strategies. In political economy terms, the formulation, expansion and systematisation of a theory would become a structural leitmotiv for the enforcement of certain praxis, as seen in the 'political power of Keynesian economic ideas' (Hall, 1989). Keynes' General Theory, in this sense, as the theoretical constituent of the post-war *settlement*, became a countervailing (theoretical) force that, in a crisis environment in which the praxis of laissez-faire came into disrepute, fed back the destructuration of the neoclassical basis of theoretical economic knowledge and its discursive and structural manifestations in practice by theoretically inducing a countercyclical (systemic) change, state intervention in the economic structure.
- **Discursive power**: discourse, in political economy terms, is the recontextualised theoretico-practical voice that actors use to popularise or/and consolidate their aims (Leeuwen, 2008: 17). Given the pragmatist conduct of contemporary capitalism, discourse can be suggested to be a connective voice that conciliates the coexistential conflict between theory and praxis. This resides in the popularity-contingent nature of politico-economic processes such as gaining social trust or entrenching clientelist linkages in *public markets*. The inculcation of neoliberal institutions through a justificatory theorisation of their praxis is the contemporary representative of the *image-maker-ness* of discursive power. The consequence is that, throughout neoliberal era, one witnesses the emergence of a prominent group of *global standard institutions*: political democracy, an independent

judiciary, a professional bureaucracy, a small public-enterprise sector, a developed stock market facilitating hostile mergers and acquisitions, a regime of financial deregulation allowing for the unfettered flow of speculative capital, an independent Central Bank, shareholder-oriented corporate governance and flexibility-contingent labour market institutions (Chang, 2007: 20). Wallerstein (2004: ix) explains the systemic impact of the neoliberals' discursive power in this way: 'We are told that there is not alternative to globalization, to whose exigencies all governments must submit. And we are told that there is not alternative, if we wish to survive ...'

Minor Patterns

- The power of knowledge enables actors to predicate their actions on rational pillars, thereby specifying their raison d'être as featured by their goals and objectives. The variety of knowledge ranges from practical, theoretical to scientific or technical (Adler and Bernestion, 2005: 295). Drawn upon these rational knowledge resources, the concepts are patterned utterances or lexical frameworks used by the actors to express interconnected meanings that they attach to social facts. In time, these patterned utterances coalesce into theoretical power, the combined manifestation of inter-complementary concepts and ideas by which the actors contextualise their actions into an overarching or coordinative framework that offers them a consistent, if not viable, policy proposal.
- Strategic power enables actors to generate feasible objectives particularly in the middle and long term. With the effective implementation of these objectives and thus having further access to institutional power resources, the actors gain the power of justification that capacitates them to embed their policy choices in the interactional linkages of prevailing institutional environment. Strategic power capacitates the actors to justify their actions through setting a workable mutuality between their objectives and the constraints that an institutional environment imposes (Beetham, 1991: 60–61). In time, with the incremental legitimation, increasing scope and consolidated rigour of the actors' impact, they gain institutional power to reorganise political or/and economic order in line with their objectives.
- Enforcive power stands for the actors' ability to ensure that their policy choices come into effect. Its mainstay is not the direct implementation, but the realisation of the actors' policy choices, as argued by Lukes (2005: 74). In other words, having potential or latent power for realising an objective is the same as enforcement in case B unwittingly does what A wants because B feels A's potential power (Wrong, 1979: 7). This does not have to be in the form of coercion. For example, as Clegg (1989: 77) put it 'powerful may not attend to, may not listen to, or may not "hear" demands articulated

by the less powerful'. In this case, the objectives of the less powerful do not come into being.

Enforcive power gains a coercive nature in case it comes into effect in the way that A *directly requires* B to do what A wishes, although B does not wish to. Enforcive power practically enables the sequel of coercive power: because A cannot be expected to coerce B to take A's policy priorities if A is unable to enforce its own policy choices (Russell, 1997 [1938]: 23). In time, those actors having both enforcive and coercive powers can grasp the potential of setting a new trade-off in inter-actor relations, the structural power, in line with their policy choices.

- Coalitional power originates from a group of actors who collaborate to enforce their common objectives. This common initiative provides them with the opportunity to consolidate their aims and objectives. Such a consolidative power rests upon not only the effectuation of each actor's individual impact, but of the organised impact of all actors in the coalition, as discussed above. In time, their consolidated position provides the actors in coalition with a discursive power that enables them both to theoretically embed and practically extend their policy choices across the institutional structure by pragmatically manipulating the gap between their theoretical utterances and practical (*de facto*) performances. Furnishing actors with the power of discourse are the complexities or implicit niches of social interaction that make it possible to conceal the reality between theory and fact.

Complementary Adjustment and Strategic Convergence of Power Patterns

Note that the above classification is not an end in itself but a means to explain the basic forms of power interactions in time. In this sense, beyond their above-noted segregated classifications, the major and minor patterns of power enable the actors to exert their impact particularly when their various major and minor patterns come together in an inter-reinforcing manner. For example, the coexistence of institutional, structural and theoretical power enables pro-cyclical actors not only to reorganise the entire institutional stock to realise their conjunctural objectives, but also to make profound changes even in the regime characteristics of this stock in line with their theoretical or ideologic claims. To do so, at stage one (see Figure 1.2), theory provides the actors with a holistic frame of knowledge for the systemic formulation of these changes. At stage two, structural power enables the actors to embed their power resources in the pre-existing institutional setting. The structuration of these power resources is a presage for redesigning a given part or the whole of an institutional stock in a stable and sustainable manner, thereby gaining institutional power at stage three to execute policy objectives in a relatively long-run perspective. At stage four, the discourse enters the scene both to consolidate the reorganised version of the relevant institutional stock and justify its imperfections by manipulative recontextualisations between its theoretical pillars and practical manifestations, as noted above. The evolutionary power starts to accumulate when this institutional power becomes embedded across the social system. It should be noted that this examination of major power patterns in numeric sequence aims merely to exemplify the evolutionary complementarity of these major power patterns. The sequence of this complementarity can well be expected to change under the changing circumstances of each institutional environment and inter-actor power relationship.

I will further pursue the aggregational varieties of these major and minor (complementary) patterns of power in an evolutionary perspective with reference to the Turkish case in the following parts, particularly in the fourth part, of the book.

Yet, it should be noted here that combinational manifestation of the types of power can be observed in the form of 'strategic convergence' in social systems. The concept of *strategic convergence* defines the centre of gravity towards which any social system or its sub-units incline in a certain time and space. It indicates that the formation, evolution and change of institutions are determined by the centre of gravity in the power relations among the actors involved, which interact within institutional structures. Its analytic functionality lies, *inter alia*, in the diminution or pragmatisation of the monolithic ideological conceptualisations of contemporary political economies. (Strategic convergence is not akin to a win-set: because there are no tangible game-theoretically specifiable or step-by-step negotiable cases, alternative sets of *patterned* choices, ceteris paribus agreement points with mathematically representable zero-sum or positive-sum opportunities and so on [Putnam, 1988]).

Figure 1.3 depicts the strategic convergences and divergences of *pure* Islam, neoliberalism and social democracy, and their context-specific and situation-dependent repercussions in Turkish political economy: the Just Order, Turkish conservative democracy, social democratic Kemalism or Kemalist social democracy. Embodying the strategic convergence between *pure* and *applied* forms of these paradigms is the reformulation of their proponents' strategies or policy choices to conciliate or reconciliate their structural statuses through the exigencies of dominant institutions, thereby sustaining their organisational entities and gaining access to institutional power resources. The Just Order represents a middle ground between pure Islam and the institutional structure of Turkish political economy between the 1970s and 1990s; Turkish conservative democracy represents a combination

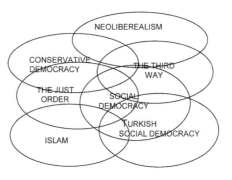

Figure 1.3   Evolutionary convergence across paradigms in the Turkish context

of the Just Order, the Turkish political context at the turn of the millennium and neoliberalism; social democratic Kemalism is a hybrid of Kemalism, the official ideology of Turkish Republic, and *pure* social democracy in the 1970s, the late 1990s and the first half of the 2010s.

These evolutionary reformulations and incremental adjustments allow for cross-paradigmatic intersections at the level of theory and praxis between ideology and pragmatism. For example, as I will elaborate in the third part, conservative democrats of the Adalet ve Kalkınma Partisi – AKP (Justice and Development Party) – which has been in power in Turkey since late 2002, adopted an industrial relations strategy combining various extents and combinations of Islamic, neoliberal and social democratic motives at the level of theory and praxis. The aim of this initiative is to co-manage the politico-economic resources of power by establishing a balance among dependency, conflict and order. The politicians' motivation is that, as they are confronted with a secular political regime, they have to symbiotically offset their countercylically Islamic position through more generous social welfare provisions and a social democratically voiced discourse on the rights of workers without damaging neoliberally structured, austere economic policies. This 'government's dilemma' compels them to generate a set of strategies and tactics counterbalancing the suppression of and support for organised labour.

Political Economy of Path-Dependent Institutional Changes in Time and Space

Institutional cycles, in systemic terms, evolve through the inter-actor power relationship over and under the environmental entity of institutional structure. And as discussed in the previous sections, this interrelationship is the main catalyst of path-dependence or change dynamics of social structures. Thus, in this section, the varying manifestations of institutional change and path-dependency will be discussed within this context. In the meantime it should be borne in mind that institutional structures do have other dynamics, in addition to and in cyclical connection with inter-actor relationships, that exert impact on institutional changes or path-dependencies. These dynamics do to a great extent bear on informal institutions ranging from receding norm-contingent or ideology-dependent attitudes to rising market or money-consciousness of individuals in both private and public spheres. The examination of this impact of informal institutions is, due to their normative contents, hard to initiate in this book: because this study deals essentially with political economy of institutional structures (in terms of its practical implication). For this reason, I concentrate on formal manifestations of colligated evolution of formal and informal institutions and refer to informal institutions as a background motive.

Institutional systems analysis, in its analytic essence, relies on the holistic and knitted explication of formal and informal institutions to crystallise the complexities of an evolving social whole in terms of their inter-complementary and inter-repulsive proclivities. In mainstream tradition, path-dependency and change dynamics, two major concepts describing the evolutionary pathways of social institutions, have however been conceptualised as mutually exclusive phenomena from a reflexively reactive perspective rather than in terms of their inter-complementary or inter-repulsive inclinations between accumulation and de-accumulation over time and space (see Figure 1.4). Such a sharp-edged delineation between these critical concepts strangles social analysis from delving into the varying manifestations of path-dependence and change dynamics and causes such analysis to ignore how these change and path-dependencies ebb and flow between continuity and discontinuity.

In hindsight, the long *duree* of history has demonstrated that change is eternal but not discontinuous and, equally important, that path-dependency is a persistent but not eternal phenomenon (Roberts and Westad, 2003; Kennedy, 1998; Woodruff, 2002). In Ayres' words (1962: vi), 'two forces are eternal in all human behavior of all ages; a progressive, dynamic, productive of cumulative change; the other counter-progressive, static, inhibitory of change'. To disentangle the complexities of social reality, it is thus necessary to follow its evolutionary ebb and flow from a systemic perspective between path-dependence and change in time and space, rather than lock in its sharp ripples at the so-called critical junctures which are supposed to give rise to the path-dependencies. The latter succeeds only in dissociating past from present and vice versa, a methodological fault which results in the unquestioned acceptance of timelessly reified justifications.

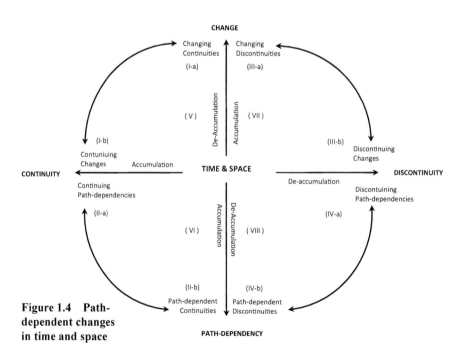

Figure 1.4   Path-dependent changes in time and space

Change, Path-Dependence and Path-Dependent Changes between Continuity and Discontinuity

Accumulation and de-accumulation are the gradual waxing and waning, respectively, of social institutions in a dialectic process. Their regressive or progressive cumulation means that the waxing or waning of institutional structures occurs gradually, simultaneously and haltingly, but not abruptly, linearly or equidirectionally. In this context, changes over time can be conceived as a process of accumulation or de-accumulation in terms of the yardstick used to define them. Two intersubjective yardsticks can be suggested for this purpose, continuity and discontinuity, which are, respectively, processes of uninterrupted and interrupted dynamics in social institutions across time and space. Defined by continuity and discontinuity, change signifies, respectively, a process of the de-accumulation of continuities (sections I-a and I-b in Figure 1.4) and the accumulation of discontinuities (sections III-a and III-b).

The underlying implication is that, once a change sets in, continuities and discontinuities pass through a gradual waning or waxing, respectively, in overlapping and varying but not linear cumulations. Thus, on the one hand, change denotes the accumulation of discontinuities or new elements in the sense of setting off the process of the interrupted flow of the pre-existing structures. On the other, it reflects the de-accumulation of continuities in the sense of the gradual waning of pre-existing structures versus the gradual waxing of the change initiated by the new elements. Thus, in terms of the initiation and progress of change, the de-accumulation of continuities and accumulation of discontinuities are interwoven and accommodative processes across time and space.

Pure continuity *per se* features the uninterrupted *flow* but not the gradual *embedding* of social institutions. In other words, continuities can be associated with the *static or unaccumulated flow* of social institutions. Path-dependency is, however, a process of the accumulation of continuity or the incremental embedding of the social institutions. It originates in the uninterrupted flow of self-reinforcing continuities generated by the pre-existing structures. The distinction between pure and accumulated continuities manifests itself in their interaction with a change. As with pure continuities, path-dependencies also begin or continue to de-accumulate once change sets in. Yet the scale of inter-repulsion between the latter and change is more intense, as the latter has become entrenched, but not locked, in the structure concerned and de-accumulates over a relatively longer period of time. This implies two facts. The first is that change and path-dependency cannot be boiled down into the linear accumulation or de-accumulation of continuities. Therefore, the second is that a clear differentiation between pre-existing and nascent structures is inconceivable for social systems during their transitional periods. Put differently, it is the turning points and relational transitions, but not critical junctures or cut-off points, between past and present that symbolise the changing path-dependencies of embedded institutions.

As a joint process of path-dependency and change, *path-dependent change* fundamentally means that social institutions undergo change within the confines of the accumulated continuities of pre-existing structures. Underlying is the ebb and flow between path-dependency and change upon the range of inter-repulsive accumulations and de-accumulations structured between continuity and discontinuity in time and space. This can be traced through the vertical line with arrowheads at both ends in Figure 1.4. Path-dependent change can be defined bilaterally in terms of continuity and discontinuity. By continuity, a path-dependent change means the de-accumulation or gradual waning of social institutions within the confines of accumulated continuities. In this definition, as seen to the left of the horizontal and vertical lines, change and path-dependency are coupled with the de-accumulation of continuities (section V in Figure 1.4) and the accumulation of continuities (section VI), respectively. By discontinuity, path-dependent change refers to the accumulation of discontinuities within the confines of pre-existing institutional structures. This can be traced through the right side of the horizontal and vertical lines. In this definition, change and path-dependency are aligned, respectively, with accumulation of discontinuities (VII) and de-accumulation of discontinuities (VIII).

Varieties of Change and Path-Dependence

Defining change and path-dependency in terms of the accumulation and de-accumulation of continuities and discontinuities facilitates the provision of insights into the various forms of change or path-dependency as depicted in Figure 1.4: (i) changing continuities (I-a) or continuing changes (I-b), changing discontinuities (III-a) or discontinuing changes (III-b); (ii) continuing path-dependencies (II-a) or path-dependent continuities (II-b), and discontinuing path-dependencies (IV-a) or path-dependent discontinuities.

i.   Changing continuities refer to continuities that continue to de-accumulate at an incremental pace under the transformative impact of gradual changes, thereby featuring a process of *becoming transformed* (I-a). Social democracy is a continuing social institution in change, even if as a background motive, under the transforming impact of capitalism. Manifesting its continuing change is the new social democracy or the Third Way that can be designated as identificational searches of its proponents to contextualise social democracy within a workable pathway under the rule-imposing and disidentifying structure of the dominant neoliberal institutions.

ii. Continuing changes denote that changes continue to transform the continuities in an accumulative manner (section I-b). The argument is therefore on the process of an uninterruptedly transforming impact of changes or the uninterrupted transformation of the continuities. Instantiating this argument is the lingering transformation of contemporary societies from industrial to post-industrial or network societies under rapidly changing technologic endowments.

iii. Changing discontinuities demonstrate that changes start or continue to affect discontinuities (III-a). First, discontinuity is not the evanescence or extinction but the deactivation or passivisation of certain institutions, generally because the actors buttressing or utilising these institutions as their sources of power have fallen into a subordinate position through the process of power relations. When they are subject to changes such as displacement (Streeck and Thelen, 2005), previously dormant or latent institutions are contingently reactivated or become dominant in a transformed fashion as a result of internalising the constraints that the pre-existing institutions impose on them or transform their intrinsic structures as a counter-manoeuvre to gain new or regain their previous power resources.

The transformation of contemporary Turkish politics into Islamic terms well epitomises changing discontinuities. The unifying power of the Islamically structured political regime of the Ottoman Empire *de facto* ceased to exist at the end of the first quarter of the twentieth century as a result of a long process of de-accumulation. At the end of the 1960s, its socio-political dynamics began to re-accumulate again in a transformed fashion. And two decades later, as of the early and, particularly, mid-1990s, a political party as the main actor of this transformation, *Refah Partisi* – RP, the Welfare Party, which advocates the re-establishment of an Islamically organised political system, the Just Political Order (JPO) – came into office as the major partner in a coalition government. The JPO is rooted in the reformulation of the building blocks of Islamic politics in line with the rule-imposing framework of secular democracy in Turkey. In the aftermath of the subsequent closure of the RP and its successor after a post-modern military intervention, AKP was founded by some of the early forerunners of the Just Order politics. This party developed the notion of *Conservative Democracy* as a Third Way strategy combining Islamic conservatism and secularist democracy in politics and market progressivism and Islamic solidarism in economics. In brief, as a *de facto* discontinuing image, systemically structured Islamic politics goes on to incur continuing changes under the constraining impacts of the secular (state) capitalism in Turkey.

One can legitimately challenge the dissimilarity between the patterns of changing continuities and changing discontinuities. Across Western Europe, social democracy is not a discontinuous image, as it has not systematically ceased to exist and has had immediate potentiality to re-accumulate as in the mid-1990s. Yet the political establishment of Ottoman-Turkish Islam began to *de facto* decline, especially with respect to its socio-economic pillars, at the beginning of twentieth century and *de jure* withered away at the end of first quarter of the century.

iv. Discontinuing changes symbolise the process of interrupted transformations across time and space (III-b). This does not imply that changes abruptly cease to exist but that they de-accumulate or become dormant or latent. In Turkish politics, as a response to the ascendancy of Conservative Democracy, Kemalist social democracy, the official ideology of the main opposition Republican People's Party (the founding party of the Turkish Republic), has been *de facto* reconverted into the social democratic Kemalism by the party's subversive reformists, who currently hold power within the party. This process was carried out with a particular emphasis on the reformation of the social security system from an egalitarian perspective (social democratic Kemalism was also formerly the prime strategy of the RPP during the mid-1970s). Yet this change, to an enormous extent, lost momentum because intra-party skirmishes thwart the reformist actors, who advocate for the emphasis of social democratic strategies over the radical protection of the secular regime, encountered the restrictive force of Kemalist social democrats, who advocate the reverse. Currently, the change that the party experienced before the elections of 2011 has wound down, but it is not extinct. Instead this change remains on the party agenda and is expected to be rekindled.

v. Continuing path-dependencies (II-a) refer to the uninterrupted embedding or intensification of accumulated continuities, while path-dependent continuities (II-b) mean that continuities continue to accumulate in an overlapping manner. The market-based society that originates in the unbridled human greed in capitalist economies is an enduring example of continuing path-dependencies (this will be discussed below). From the great transformation on, a turning point with antecedents dating back to the sixteenth century, there has been a continuing image whose constituents obtained path-dependent pecularities at certain turning points. For example, Polanyi (1989 [1944]: 24–6) drew attention to the inculcation of money-consciousness in peoples' minds in the 1930s. Crucially, continuing path-dependent institutions are not linear processes and are consistently subject to change. It is a well-established fact that during the post-war period, market economies, particularly in Western Europe, underwent a transformative change due to their confluence with social or beneficial constraints (Streeck, 1997). However, the image of the market economy then came to re-accumulate under a layered type of change, sophisticated securitisation and over-financialisation. The ascendancy of shareholder capitalism with a destructive speed of diffusion can, in this sense, be suggested to be a path-dependent continuity under the auspices of network technologies. A feature of this process is that, in a path-dependent process, the global capitalist economy continued to be centred around finance-capital, but with an increasing intensity through the insertion of new elements, an ever-increasing variety of high-risk financial derivatives.

In terms of path-dependent changes and the inter-repulsive inclinations of path-dependency and change dynamics, the first (II-a) comes to the fore as it reflects the outermost range upon which path-dependencies repulse changes exponentially. Vice versa, the continuing changes (I-b) also reflect the outermost range upon which changes come to exponentially repulse path-dependencies.

vi. Discontinuing path-dependencies (IV-a) refers to the process of the de-accumulation of path-dependencies over time. The embedding of the outsider model against the insider model in Germany, the disorganisation of an organised model, denotes the de-accumulation or disembedding of the path-dependent flow of organised capitalism (Streeck and Thelen, 2005: 3–4).

vii. Finally, the path-dependent discontinuities symbolise the de-accumulation or de-embedding of continuities in either an overlapping or accumulative manner. The commodification of informal values in network societies, particularly from the onset of neoliberal institutionalism with a substantial power to disidentify, may be suggested to epitomise the path-dependent disembedding of the discontinuing presence of the society of values.

Path-Dependent Institutional Changes in a Political Economy Perspective

Methodologically, the nonlinear inter-repulsion between path-dependence and change asserts itself in the interwoven analysis of normatively and rationally instituted constituents of social systems. For contemporary capitalist societies, the sharp distinction between formal and informal institutions with respect to their normative and rational implications is a *chimera*. Rather, as previously discussed, it would be more optimal to suggest that formal institutions, such as relationships of exchange in the private or political markets mediated by price and patronage, respectively, are constructed on the basis of the norms and values (informal institutions) of a particular society, the rule-imposing environment, but then come to disqualify their normative conditionalities with a rationally structured power of repulsion.

This, nevertheless, does not imply that formal institutions are entirely stripped of normative values; rather, the rational values retain the driving force behind social evolution in contemporary societies. Put within the context of this study, the repulsive intersubjectivity of formal and informal institutions between rationalisation and normativisation forges the main area of interaction around which path-dependency and change dynamics revolve. Despite this, neoclassical or path-dependent theoretic arguments reduce this rationally structured intercourse to critical junctures, points of unaccumulated change or into constant path-dependencies such as unchanging general equilibrium to explain institutional evolution, as they perceive the exchange value of economic instruments as the unique determinant of the conduct of politico-economic circulation (in what follows, I will first discuss the impasse of norm-free articulation of the political economy as it appeared in the ongoing global crisis; then, I will engage with the critical juncture and path-dependence literature in the context of the path-dependent changes).

Schumpeter (2008 [1934]: 56), for example, argues that there is not a whole of social values but a social system of individual values. In exchange relations, these individual values interbreed with each other within the individual's economy. In systemic terms, interconnecting the individual's values, to Schumpeter, is the price system. In Smithian parlance, it is the labour of businessmen to produce and reproduce that engenders the unique resource of value enabling the political economy to circulate (Smith, 1976 [1776]: 343–5). Thus noneconomic values are incidental to rationally instituted exchange relationships in the market. Contemporaneously, with a continuing path-dependent perspective, rational choice institutionalism eviscerates politico-economic analysis from its social implications, focusing on the mechanic sequences, in Veblen's words (1912: 284), thereby locking in the *institutional statics* (Streeck, 2009: 6). A case in point is Acemoğlu and Robinson's recent study of the institutional pillars of 'Why Nations Fail'.

As one of the forerunners of game-theoretic or value-free science-making, Acemoğlu (2009), even if with some hesitation, in his examination of the lessons of global economic crisis for the economics profession, professed that scientific causation in game-theoretic terms was unable to predict or authoritatively account for the crisis (see p. 1 in Introduction). Yet in his recent study co-authored with Robinson (2012), he did not hesitate to fervently re-emphasise the exigency of systemic disorganisation and the deregulation of economic structures to acquire and sustain wealth and prosperity and the determinativeness of critical junctures, but not culture, for the formation and evolution of the political economy.

Evolutionarily speaking, they do not go beyond rehashing the systemic preconditions for cultivating liberal, but not social, welfare, namely capital welfare, formerly repeated by Friedman (1980: 56–64). In their repetitive analysis, unsurprisingly, no response can be found for the question of how extractive or inclusive institutions, Acemoğlu and Robinson's analytical concepts, have come into being. As a result, it becomes a chimera to explain *the continuing path-dependence of the unfettered and unbridled greed of risk-ridden individuals* 'who [are] too ignorant or too weak to attain even their own ends' (Keynes, 1964 [1936]: 372). It is this greed for irrational risk-taking that makes up the very formative cause of the ongoing global socio-political and economic crisis, but not the high-risk financial derivatives created in the sub-prime market. Because it is the former, the very informal value of neoliberal establishment, that demanded, designed, structured and ventured into the latter for speculative purposes and unleashed an interdestructive complementarity.

The aporia in Acemoğlu and Robinson's analysis is the question of 'what is the strategy of neoliberalism for de-accumulating the so-called continuing path-dependency of homo-economicus in unleashing overseas crisis?' In hindsight, it is in most cases Keynesianism, as in the post-war period, a policy strategy that systemically deranges the liberal economic establishment by bringing the interventionist state back in. Thus, neoliberalism is not a self-corrective or self-perpetuating system of political economy. If it is not so, where are its positive feedbacks to recover from, in Keynes' words, the second *end of laissez-faire capitalism*? It is quite ironic that Acemoglu and Robinson have not addressed the unfictitious reality that the most catastrophic crisis of the twentieth and twenty-first centuries, the great depression and the housing bubble, have essentially originated in the disorganised capitalism of the United States, a social system that they argue in a fictitious obsession has the most lucrative resources of power and prosperity. A social economist who underscored the crucial role that social values play in the steady development of an economic system, Keynes (1964 [1936]:

142), a voice from eight decades ago, reminds us of both of the origins of enduring path-dependency in casino capitalism in the crisis in general and the very specific reason why the ongoing crisis erupted:

> Speculators may do no harm as bubbles on a steady stream of enterprise. But the position is serious when enterprise becomes the bubble on a whirlpool of speculation. When the capital development of a country becomes a by-product of the activities of a *casino*, the job is likely to be ill-done. The measure of success attained by Wall Street, regarded as an institution of which the proper social purpose is to direct new investment into the most profitable channels in terms of future yield, cannot be claimed as one of the outstanding triumphs of *laissez-faire* capitalism – which is not surprising, if I am right in thinking that the best brains of Wall Street have been in fact directed towards a different object.

In economic parlance, from a reflexively reactive point of view, Arthur (1994) enunciated the *increasing returns* in the face of a diminishing returns hypothesis of conventional economics. He argues that increasing returns economics has strong parallels with modern nonlinear physics, and it is this nonlinearity in supply and demand flows in the economy, market imperfections in neoclassical terms, that makes increasing returns possible. Instead of the negative feedbacks that lead to predictable equilibrium prices and market shares, small fortuitous events – unexpected orders, chance meetings with buyers, managerial whims – would set the stage for the direction of economic change. If a product, due to these small fortuitous events, reaches a competitive position by chance, it tends to sustain and undergird this position in the market. In addition, once a potential inefficiency or unpredictable event is substituted for the invisible perfections of the market mechanism, a single equilibrium could no longer be guaranteed; even individuals are assumed to be rational actors (the nonlinearities that generate increasing returns, self-reinforcing effects, consist of high start-up costs, learning effects, coordination effects and adaptive expectations).

As a result, the economy may become, due to small historical events, locked in to a technological path that would be inefficient, inflexible and *ex ante* unpredictable. To Arthur, three paths of technological adaptation would be plausible. The first is that, *ex ante*, we cannot prognosticate which technological endowment will dominate. Second, the dominant technology is not necessarily the best or most efficient. Finally, once the dominant technology generates self-reinforcing feedbacks, it is difficult to change it.

In the political literature, Pierson (2004) has transposed Arthur's theory into political science in terms of critical junctures. He argues that critical junctures are the early sequences when a particular event that eventuates in disproportionately large effects on later events occurs with a threshold impact. Subsequently, in the second stage, the repercussions of the event, institutions become more impervious to change. Ultimately, in the third stage, the path locks in or change becomes bounded as a result of the continuing positive feedbacks. Pierson's adaptation of Arthur's ideas into politics is methodologically unsound. As Steinmo and Thelen (1992) note, political science, particularly in its evolutionary version, could not be structuralised by analytic parameters transplanted from economics. The reason is that the evolutionary pathways, continuities and discontinuities in political and economic institutions exhibit different spatio-temporal predispositions, as their peculiar institutional frameworks enfold normative and rational implications to varying extents. This is a factor that straightforwardly impinges upon the actions of their constituencies such as political parties, entrepreneurs and so on, and their interactions.

For example, as Pierson himself (2004: 34) noted, the mediating institution of political processes, patronage, the price of politics, is intricately structured by the informal values of the society, as politics is based on authority rather than exchange, and political authority hinges on and develops through patronage linkages. Conversely, economic analysis also cannot be structuralised by political arguments, in that it has a relatively more rationalised institutional environment structured by price-mediated exchange relationships, where informal values fall into a subordinate position in market societies. In this sense, extreme normativity based upon the mechanical idea of unchanging path-dependency of social institutions in the very determinativeness of informal institutions is also untenable.

It is true that path-dependency is more persistent for the norm-contingent constituencies of the social system, whereas change is expected to be more fluid for relatively norm-free structures such as financial systems (Hechter and Opp, 2001: 406–8). Nonetheless, it is now a well-established fact that, throughout the operation of the cycle in which *values engender conduct* (institutional structure) *and conduct engenders values*, as mentioned above, rationally structured institutions (formal institutions), though not in all cases, have come to engender their respective values, such as the greed of outrageous risk-taking, even at the cost of global society, and dictate them to the human lifeworld.

The distinctive evolution of political and economic phenomena in their idiosyncratic trajectories, however, does not require that they be nonintersecting constituents. Instead, under the unifying fabric of the social system, political and economic actions constrain each other, as the major social institutions that regulate political and economic actions coincidentally hold, in most cases, and sway over the behaviours of their actors. Our discussion on the process of economic development in the introduction demonstrates this point in reasonable detail. The result is that path-dependency and change dynamics should be dealt with from a holistic political economy perspective that considers the inter-repulsive inclinations of the normative and rational implications of formal and informal institutions in a particular social system.

Such an intermeshed perspective requires an extension of the analysis to encompass the cross-path-dependency, cross-changes and cross-path-dependent-changes that sprout out of the co-evolution of accumulated and de-accumulated continuities of formal and informal institutions across time and space. Cross-path-dependent changes, methodologically, concern the predicament of the indeterminability of *social complexity* that originates in the connective value of social institutions and pervades the intertwined waning and waxing of accumulated continuities in various sub-social systems. This is what makes complexity an imponderable subject of analysis.

Within this context, the paradigm of path-dependent change is a process-based explication of path-dependency and change dynamics in terms of accumulation and de-accumulation of continuity and discontinuities. And it rests on the very reason that the social system is an evolving whole across time and space with both formal and informal institutions and, hence, should be analysed in terms of the intertwined existence of its normative and rational implications. A linear or nonlinear articulation of social phenomena in terms of critical junctures, path-dependency or increasing returns, nonetheless, reifies, fragmentises and *de-accumulates* social evolution. The reification is due to the fact that these articulations disconnect the politico-economic analysis from its social intricacies and thus subjugate it to a flattened flow of equidirectional continuities, unchanging path-dependencies or unaccumulated changes (the critical junctures). This results in the congealing or constriction of accumulations or de-accumulations in undialectical or static processes and thereby in the fragmentation of analysis into pure economic and political segments dismissive of their mutually constraining implications.

Path-dependent change, methodologically, does not feed on the perception that there is an uninterrupted flow of equidirectional accumulations downward or upward, but on inter-repulsions between continuity and discontinuities over time and space as depicted at Figure 1.4. This is because of the following: (i) the social complexity of this evolution renders us unable to make clear-cut conceptualisations, such as unchanging path-dependencies; (ii) neither positive nor negative feedback in terms of Veblenian cumulative causation is permanent; instead, (iii) the density of positiveness or negativeness in the *social* feedback shifts in each institutional system cycle; and (iv) due to the non-routine nature of human activity, the sequence and timing of the change or path-dependence vary according to the stickiness, solidity or social embeddedness of the institutional structure concerned.

A case in point for cross-path-dependent change is Ayres' reasoning on the frontier temperament of cultural contact and cultural diffusion between Europe, the Middle East and Asia in the process of accumulating scientific knowledge. Contrary to Acemoğlu and Robinson's (2012: 103) rationalist claim that the industrial revolution 'was a break from the past made possible by scientific inquiry and the talent of a number of unique individuals', he proposes, after a meticulous investigation of the sequential advancement of technological knowledge, that the foundations of Europe's industrial revolution are based on the transfer of inventions, such as paper from China, the Hindu-Arabic numerals including the symbol for zero, wind and water mills introduced into Europe during the Crusades and so on:

> It is not the occurrence of inventions that distinguishes modern civilization but the organization of society to bring this about. The primary instrument for such organization is literacy. If anything so subtle can be dated at all, it should be dated with reference not to the steam engine but to printing (Ayres, 1962: 152).

His analysis features first the inter-temporality and multi-spatiality of the accumulated continuity, or path-dependency, and second the accumulated discontinuity of knowledge generation at certain points in time, such as the invention of the steam engine. The first implication means that advances in science are primarily based on printing, namely, that this is a path-dependent process of accumulation. Without accumulated knowledge by means of experience and experiment, the modern sciences could not have come into existence. In another respect, the second implication means that the modern sciences revolutionised the accumulated stock of knowledge, thereby de-accumulating their continuities. This is the inter-repulsion of pre-existing and incipient knowledge over time across the continents. It is the change that always changes pre-existing knowledge but, equally important, the path-dependency of change predates the change and makes it a change, de-accumulated continuity or accumulated discontinuity. A compelling note from history where, as a Swiss historian pointed out, 'history is the one subject where you cannot begin at the beginning' (Roberts and Westad, 2003:1), might be more revealing regarding this delicate balance of path-dependent change:

> The appearance of a new civilization in the eastern Mediterranean owed much to older Near Eastern and Aegean traditions. From the start we confront an amalgam of Greek speech, a Semiotic alphabet, ideas whose roots lie in Egypt and Mesopotamia, and reminiscences of Mycenae. Even when this civilization matured it still showed the diversity of its origins. It was never to be a simple, monolithic whole and in the end was very complex indeed. For all that integrated it and gave it unity, it was always hard to delimit, a cluster of similar cultures around the Mediterranean and Aegean, their frontier zones blurring far outwards into Asia, Africa, barbarian Europe and southern Russia. Even when its boundaries with them were clear, other traditions always played upon Mediterranean civilization and received much from it (Roberts and Westad, 2003: 172).

Taking Stock of the Institutional System Analysis in Political Economy

Institutional system analysis is aimed at crystallising the repulsive and complementary interactions of social institutions from a process-based evolutionary standpoint. The systemic nature of this institutional analysis is rooted in the multi-level, multi-actor and multi-dimensional complexity of social action stemming from the ever-increasing density and variety of cross-institutional interactions.

In the context of institutional system analysis, societies have been defined as complex systems consisting of mutually contingent intersubjectivities of individuals, organisations and social groups of various types. The structural principles that these relationships generate constitute the basis for the overall clustering of institutions across time and space. The holistic manifestation of this clustering, the social system, is the interwoven and interacting stock of formal and informal institutions evolving in a specific timespace. This definition rests upon the fact that, in institutional terms, (i) the structuration and re-structuration of both informal and formal intersubjectivities originate in the formation of a common language between alter and ego from gesture to symbol-mediated interaction and then to normatively guided interaction, and therefore (ii) culturally conditioned institutionalisation underlies the structuration of politico-economic entities, as Habermas argued.

Social systems rely on continuing and relational interaction among the actors in a social structure, and this interaction would unfold on a stable or instable, but not a static or functionally segregated, pathway. In this book, therefore, the term *system* has been used in a social context for those structures in which individual or organisational constituents interact with value-rationality or purposive-rationality to varying extents and evolve inter-complementarily and inter-repulsively over time and space. And it has been suggested that evolutionary dynamics of social systems unfold through the path-dependent changes that arise from the inter-actor power relationships over and under an institutional environment, as depicted at Figure 1.1 (p. 16).

As the building blocks of a social system, institutions are the *interaction channels* that represent mutually related rights and obligations enforced by specific categories of actors to regulate, liberate or expand individual and collective action. In institutional system analysis, it is the interlaced symbiosis of the *connective values* of institutions that requires adopting a systemic analysis to explicate the intricacies of politico-economic action. Formal and informal institutions are not mutually exclusive but interbreeding and interconstitutive. The former, such as state-enforced rules (legal frameworks, constitutions and so on) or organisational procedures, regulate social action, not only through a purely rational but also a normatively contingent, rational initiative. As the origin of the former, the latter are the cement of social organisation, which take various forms such as norms, values, habits, standard practices, customs, traditions and conventions.

The dialectic evolution between formal-informal institutions varies according to the institutional environment in which in-system or inter-system intersections unfold. The *institutional environment*, from a systemic perspective, can be defined as the institutional structure that encompasses, regulates and constrains inter-actor relationships. In this book, three constituents have been proposed for an institutional environment analysis: (i) it is essential to determine the range of intersections in which institutional axes unfold rather than to lock the analysis in *ex ante* restricted boundaries; (ii) there is the changing scope, magnitude, impact, status and intersections of both the environment and its constituent elements under the trilogy of conflict, dependence and order; and (iii) institutional environment gains a systemic identity not through isolation but interaction.

The necessary dynamism, power, that makes institutional structures evolve, is created by the inter-actor relationship. In other words, actors generate the dynamism that underlies social change. Actors are the constituents of social systems that act to operationalise their aims and objectives through long-term strategy or short-run policies. Strategies are the future-oriented actions to contrive the most effective match of potential strengths and weaknesses with available opportunities and threats within the existing institutional structure. In contrast to neoclassical perspectives, human and organisational behaviour cannot be confined to interest-maximising behaviour but should be addressed through the intermeshed evolution of purposive-rational and value-rational behaviours.

In this inter-repulsive mode of action, the actors develop, sustain or reorganise the institutions that feedback into their operational ambit. In principle, they are both rule-takers and rule-makers in their interaction with the institutional environment. The former originates in the fact that the institutional environment imposes power distributional channels and rules under which the actors interact. The latter occurs when actors have the necessary power resources, particularly systemic power, to streamline the institutional stock in line with their strategic choices. As two major actor patterns, pro-cyclical and countercyclical actors produce path-sustaining or path-changing strategy and policy choices, respectively, to realise their aims or consolidate their positions. At this point, power relations emerge.

Power is the ability to formulate, implement and revise strategies or policy choices vis-à-vis one's rivals' countervailing actions. In institutional system analysis, power is a dynamic that shapes the tension of inter-actor rivalry flowing through the evolution of institutional cycles. Regarding social-system-wide power relations, power gains a systemic niche, *systemic power*, that consists of five major (institutional, structural, theoretical, discursive and evolutionary) and eight complementary types (strategic and justificatory, knowledge and conceptual, coalitional and consolidative and enforcive and coercive), which constitute one another evolutionarily. For a group of actors to have systemic power, they need not retain all of these major-minor power resources, but rather a combination of these resources that enables them to determine and manage the cyclical course of a given section or the whole of a social system within a certain period of time. The combinational manifestation of major-minor patterns of power emerges in *strategic convergence* in social systems that define the centre of gravity towards which any social system or its sub-units lean at a certain point in time and space.

The outcome of inter-actor power relations under the constraints of the institutional environment is the path-dependent institutional changes that unfold over the accumulation and de-accumulation of social institutions in a dialectic process. Accumulation and de-accumulation gain their meanings through continuity and discontinuity, respectively, which are the processes of uninterrupted and interrupted dynamics in social institutions across time and space. Path-dependence is a process of the accumulation of continuity or the incremental embedding of social institutions, whereas change indicates a process of the de-accumulation of continuities or accumulation of discontinuities. Thus, path-dependent change signifies the de-accumulation or gradual waning of social institutions within the confines of accumulated continuities.

In social systemic terms, it is the repulsive intersubjectivity of formal and informal institutions between rationalisation and normativisation that forges the main area of interaction around which path-dependence and change dynamics revolve. In the context of institutional system analysis, I have concentrated on the *systemic* variations of path-dependent changes and proposed eight major patterns: changing continuities, continuing changes, continuing path-dependencies, path-dependent continuities, changing discontinuities, discontinuing changes, path-dependent discontinuities and discontinuing path-dependencies.

Overall, the evolutionary rhythm of the institutional systems can be seen in Figure 1.1 (p. 16). However, it should be noted that their evolution does not occur in a linear manner as depicted in this figure: because social systems evolve gradually, simultaneously and haltingly, but not abruptly, linearly or equidirectionally. This means that we cannot pursue the traces of social evolution like watching the progression of clock time. Instead, we should focus on the idiosyncratic evolution of a social system in terms of the inter-actor power relations with its path-dependencies, changes or path-dependent changes in time. And it can be suggested that this evolution will help us find out the right analytic timing to catch up with the evolutionary cycles of this social system.

Chapter 2

A Systemic and Cross-Paradigmatic Analysis of Islamic, Neoliberal and Social Democratic Political Economies

In the succeeding parts of the book (second, third and fourth), I will try to explore the evolutionary dynamics of the Ottoman-Turkish political economy by using the analytic tools of institutional system analysis. Before doing so, this particular chapter examines neoliberal, social democratic and Islamic institutionalism.

A cross-paradigmatic analysis of these three paradigms can furnish international readers with an insight into the specific alignment of two or three of these paradigms in their countries. This analysis has specifically been added into this book as the basic axioms of these paradigms and the cross-intersections of these axioms have constituted the basis for the evolutionary dynamics of the Ottoman-Turkish political economy, particularly from the 1960s onwards. Underlying this is that these paradigms have been adopted by various political and economic actors or they define the patterned alignment of the Turkish political economy at certain periods of time. Thus, the analysis of the institutional stock of these three paradigms will make it possible to explain the specific characteristics of the Turkish political economy or its major actors' policy formulation and performances.

The institutional rudiments of the three paradigms are illustrated in Table 2.1. As there is a vast literature comprising distinct analyses of various institutions adopting these paradigms, in this chapter I will scrutinise their inter-institutional implications rather than separately analysing each institution in depth. As illustrated in Table 2.1, the main criteria for this analysis are methodology, institutional basics, macro-politics, macro-economics, social policy and industrial relations. While examining the institutional stock of these paradigms, a systemic perspective has been adopted in terms of (i) the path-dependence of and changes in these major paradigms between theory and praxis; (ii) their formational and evolutionary dynamics within the context of the interactions between their formal and informal institutions; and (ii) the inter-actor power relationship over and under their institutional stocks.

The methodological basis of a political economy paradigm is the strategy that its adherents employ to generate, change or keep its knowledge sources path-dependent over time. In systemic terms, the source and production of knowledge is the most path-dependent in Islam, as Muslims must engage in reformations under the eternal validity of a pre-structured divine theory of Islamic institutions as set down by Allâh and implemented by the Prophet Muhammad. This instrumental rationality of Muslims in executing an *ex post*, mundane praxis should unintermittently consider the consistency between theory and praxis as long as the world revolves around the sun. It is therefore *a priori* true that Muslims must not transform Islam into a pragmatist theory or a practical ideology (Tibi, 2001: 159–66). The underlying reason is that Islam is not a theoretical ideology or an ideologic theory, as its theory rests with Allâh, a superhuman entity exempt from human faculties, including thinking and developing ideas. The margin available to social democrats and liberals to employ pragmatist or utilitarian discretion is therefore not available for Muslims. Rather, Islam stipulates a continuing stability in terms of Muslims' political economy practice.

Table 2.1 A systemic taxonomy of Islamic, neoliberal, social democratic and Third Way institutions from a political economy perspective

Paradigms / Policy Parameters	Islam	Neoliberalism	Social Democracy	Third Way
Methodologic Basics				
Basic source of knowledge	Pre-structured divine theory and its *ex post*, mundane praxis	Mythic rationalisations based on non-virtual models	Consistent theorisation on the practice of institutional interactions	De-ideologising theoretical postulates to attune them to practical conduct
Knowledge generation strategy	Instrumental rationality conditioned by divine principles	Methodologic reductionism	Holistic conciliation of theoretical postulates with the institutional environment	Reconciliatory conceptualisations between theoretical postulates and the institutional environment
Theory & practice	Theoretico-practical adaptation	Theoretical pragmatism to justify practical conduct	Theory-practice moderation	Theoretical pragmatism to justify adaptive changes
Institutional Basics				
Order	Tawhid-conditioned equilibrium	Spontaneous equilibrium	Solidaristic compromise	Flexible compromise
Regulation	Organising regulation	Deregulative regulation	Positive-sum regulation	Deregulative regulation
Constraint	Equilibrating constraints	Constitutional rules that constrain public discretion	Decommodifying constraints	Unsystemic de-constraining

Paradigms / Policy Parameters	Islam	Neoliberalism	Social Democracy	Third Way
Evolution	Practical changes constrained by theoretical path-dependencies	Static equilibrium	Changing theory path-dependently in tandem with the institutional environment	Drift in compliance with the dominant institutional environment
Macro-politics				
Aim of existence	Steering social harmony and economic stability	To feed back into the operational ambit of market exchange	Orchestrate the social optimum	Market-friendly regulator
Political democracy	Elections – Principle of *ijma* [consensus] – Majority rule as the second best	By elections and majority rule	By elections, interest-mediation, and organic relationships with class constellations	By elections and majority rule
Economic democracy	*Shur'a* [governance] under equal decision-making power	By exchange	Trade and civil service unions participating in economic and social councils	'Organised exchanges'
Social democracy	Organised right-seeking by trade and civil service unions	Norm-free equality of opportunity on the basis of 'individual democracy'	By including a voice for individual rights of social citizenship at the level of macro-political economy	Norm-free competitive solidarity
Public-private choice	Provision of infrastructural public goods to stimulate productivity and the full employment of economic resources without crowding-out private investment	Public discretion should be confined to securing private property, public education and public works	Public investment for redistributional and full employment purposes	– Restricted redistribution by the state – The privatisation of publically owned enterprises
Taxation	Progressive [Indirect taxes disqualified] – Based on the ability to pay and the benefit-cost principle	Regressive – equality of inequality in taxation	Progressive	Marginalised progressive taxation with competition-friendly corporate taxes

Paradigms / Policy Parameters	Islam	Neoliberalism	Social Democracy	Third Way
Debt and deficit	Balanced or surplus budgets, in principle – Deficit financing for development purposes or providing a minimum standard of living [Asset-based debt or interest-free borrowing] –No deficit financing by money creation	Imposing upper-limits on governmental discretion in fiscal leveraging and monetary expansion	The possibility of but not a preference for deficit-borrowing to finance social expenditures	Balanced budgets or constrained debt and deficit-financing only for subsidising investment
Monetary policy	Maintain price stability – Arrange credit flow for productive investment, principally by *mudaraba*	Maintain price stability and remain aloof from real variables such as output and employment	Expansionary policy to reduce interest rates in the presence of underemployment	Price-stability
Macro-economics				
Market	A means for the realisation of human needs and welfare	The temple of human interaction	A means of obtaining decent work	The moderator of the human lifeworld
Development	Public-private coordination under a planned, demand-constrained strategy and a combination of material and spiritual components	Pursuit of self-interest (capital accumulation) [a micro-economic issue]	Positive-sum synergy between the factors of production under the frame of International Keynesianism	…
Growth	Productive investment structuralised by *mudaraba* [venture capital] and joint risk-sharing	Capital-led technological innovation and productive investment by free-riding entrepreneurs [a micro-economic issue]	Productivist solidarity	Capital-led technological innovation and the enhancement of human resources

Paradigms \ Policy Parameters	Islam	Neoliberalism	Social Democracy	Third Way
International trade and finance	Regulated foreign direct investment and interest-free foreign portfolio investment – speculative financial flows disqualified	Comparative advantage under floating exchange rates	Controlled exchange of international commercial and financial flows under a fixed-exchange rate regime	Free flow of international commerce and finance *loosely* constrained to attenuate their deleterious impacts
Inflation	A market imperfection caused by arbitrage-seeking capital	A function of monetary expansion above real output	The cost of employment creation (Phillips Curve)	Monetary phenomenon
Interest	Main drag on full employment, an equal distribution of income and the efficient allocation of productive resources	Main source of savings and investment	The cost of borrowing funds	…
Unemployment	Caused by deficient demand and diminishing marginal propensity to invest	– Voluntary [a micro-economic issue] – The result of temporary deviations from the natural rate of employment	Deficient demand [Involuntary]	A micro-economic issue arising out of market rigidities
Business cycles	Arising out of speculative initiatives or demand shocks	Structural imperfections caused by governmental intervention and institutional rigidities such as labour law and minimum wage regulations	Deviations from full employment caused by fluctuations in productive investment due to decreased or increased rate of the marginal efficiency of capital	Structural imperfections
Social Policy				
Principles	The principle of self-enforcement, prioritises equality of opportunity through the structural provision of the equality of outcomes	Individual responsibility on the basis of equality of opportunity	Social citizenship with a guaranteed minimum income – Universal welfare regime	No rights without responsibilities

Paradigms / Policy Parameters	Islam	Neoliberalism	Social Democracy	Third Way
Strategy	Redistribution by wealth and inheritance taxes – Equality of opportunity by *mudaraba* and public education – Citizenship-based equal and universal rights to social security	Commodification of social rights – Social exclusion – Means-tested [selective] benefits	De-commodification of social risks through full employment, positive-sum redistributive and regulative measures, direct and progressive taxation	Positive welfare
Inequality	Meritocracy-based prosperity balanced and constrained by redistributive measures	An equal inequality of income	The equality of outcomes [in principle]	Equality of opportunity
Poverty	A structural challenge to be erased using funds from the wealth tax [*Zakat*] and by solidarist social self-help	Privately bestowed temporary assistance through voluntary organisations	Eliminable by adopting universal social citizenship	Poverty alleviation or social assistance programmes by third sector agencies
Active/Passive labour market strategy	ALMPs for lifelong learning	An issue of individual marginal productivity	PLMPs are dominant	Activating lifelong training programmes or welfare-to-work schemes
Industrial Relations				
Structure	Positive-sum compromise through the reconciliation of interests	Contract-based, voluntary and uncollective compromise	Positive-sum compromise through bargaining	Opt-out compromise by concession bargaining
Employment pattern	Performance and meritocracy-based permanent contracts	Performance-based flexible contracts	Permanent with generous social allowances	Flexicurity
Wages	Based on ensuring decent living conditions – Minimum wages – Equal pay for equal work	Marginal productivity of labour	Minimum wages, and wage-restraint	Wage restraint

Table 2.1 *Concluded*

Paradigms \ Policy Parameters	Islam	Neoliberalism	Social Democracy	Third Way
Trade and civil service unions	Solidarist and conciliative organisations	Rent-seeking institutions	Political mediators of power moderation and price-setting institutions	Negotiators as representatives of workers as social 'partners'
Collective bargaining	Necessary for creating equal bargaining	A means of labour monopoly	A means of balancing power between workers and their employers	Passive governance mechanism
Strikes	Justifiable for acquiring earned and contract-based rights	A means of labour tyranny	A legitimate and systemically adopted right	Defunctionalised

Selected Sources: for Islam (Mannan, 1983; Asad, 1961; Ahmad, 1991; Al-Faruqi and Al-Banna, 1984); for neoliberalism (Friedman, 2002 [1962], 1980; Buchanan, 1999 [1962], 2000 [1977]; Hayek, 1998a, 1998b, 1998c); Rawls, 1996, 1999 [1971]); for social democracy (Keynes, 1964 [1936]; Przeworski, 1993; Notermans, 2007; Meyer and Hinchman, 2007; White, 2004); for the Third Way (Giddens, 1998; Whyman, 2006; White, 2004; Howell, 2004).

Islam only allows for flexible practices to maintain the continuity of its institutional system on a stable path. In this sense, Islam tolerates *changing continuities* provided that they are path-dependent. Continuing path-dependency is hence necessary for the systemic functionalisation of an Islamic social entity. In other words, with respect to institutional renewals, Islam rejects discontinuing path-dependencies but not changing continuities, as the former, in systemic terms, result in the de-accumulation of Islam's accumulated continuities or the flexibilisation of its inflexible stabilities (Reader, 2003: 48–52).

For example, the discontinuation of the principle of social-equity-first structuralisation of politico-economic institutions cannot be accepted in an Islamic perspective, as such a step is deemed to destructure its systemic coherence. Reorganising the practical conduct of Islamic institutions would change the methods and strategies used to provide social equity, but systemic destructuration is simply repudiated. In general terms, systemic destructuration signifies the dissolution of *tawhid*-conditioned equilibrium or the equilibrating constraints of Islam by pragmatist *Muslims*. One of the most frequently emphasised directives in the Qur'an is the necessity for theory-praxis consistency: 'Those who fulfil the Covenant of Allah and fail not in their plighted word' (Qur'an, 20: 20).

This is not tantamount to the Marxian rejection of engagement with capitalism. The presuppositions of the Marxist ideology might be considered revisable in response to changing earthly circumstances because Marx was a human and might have left some institutional points unaddressed or in need of revision or change to ensure a more workable socialist or communist system. Islam's fundamentals are, on the contrary, eternally unchangeable, and Muslims do not consider Allâh capable of any mistake, theoretical or practical. In a sense, this might be suggested to pose a challenge to Muslims' ability to develop a change-theoretic rationality, as they must, on the one hand, maintain Islam's eternal facts while rationally adapting the institutional stocks of their societies to contemporary capitalist structures, on the other. This is an arduous task for Muslims as Islam, a normatively contingent social system, entails pursuing its norms and values at the level of *group feeling* and developing dynamic civilisational discretion to modernise these norms and values without disrupting the interbreeding co-evolution of formal and informal institutions (Muslehuddin, 1999: 94–130). Muslims' vacillations between the systemic coherence of Islam's divine principles and the incoherence of their worldly implementation of these principles seem to illustrate this arduousness.

At its outset and during its golden age, social democracy was a politico-economic regime structured on the basis of conciliative theorisation of the socialist ideology combined with capitalist practices. Theory-practice moderation, in this respect, resulted in a theoretical pragmatism, and the pragmatist theory of social democracy thus emerged on the basis of both continuing and discontinuing path-dependencies in the sense of maintaining the egalitarian postulates but not the anti-systemic core of socialist ideology. The symbiotic existence of *decommodifying constraints* and their *utilisation* to realise positive-sum regulation or productivist solidarity are the systemic repercussions of the continuity and discontinuity of socialist ideology at the level of social democratic theory and praxis, respectively (Przeworski, 1993). The fact that the path-dependent continuities of social democracy were dependent on those of capitalism, as the dominant institutional environment, allowed for its path-dependent discontinuity, as observed in the emergence of the Third Way with the extinction of the *conjunctural* dynamics of the social democratic establishment (see Giddens 1998).

Therefore, in essence, the Third Way symbolises the continuing change or path-dependent discontinuity of socialist and social democratic premises in the face of the path-dependent continuities of liberal capitalism. The former and latter are due to the fact that the Third Way is the double commodification or de-accumulation of socialist premises or the commodification of social democratic de-commodifications due to reconciling or resubjecting both with or to capitalist practices. This process of de-accumulation from socialism to the Third Way is characterised by the systemic dissolution of socialist and then social democratic premises as a result of continuing ideologic pragmatism, which has created institutional *double-shuffles* rather than inter-complementarities in both the theory and praxis of the Third Way. The *hard* evidence of this is that there is not, in systemic terms, a precise definition of what the Third Way is and whether social democracy continues or discontinues. The result is a stalemate that prevents the proponents of these ideologic currents from identifying new sustainable pathways under the pressure of timespace compressions.

From its outset, liberalism has evolved over a path of theoretical pragmatism to justify a flexible or unfair praxis of capitalism through mythic rationalisations rooted in non-virtual conceptualisations such as spontaneous or static equilibrium. Thus, in this respect, path-dependent pragmatism with a purposive rationality constitutes the core unit of liberal paradigm, making change an accommodating auxiliary to capitalism. The change here refers to continuing flexibility or path-dependent instabilities between theory of liberalism and its praxis, capitalism, rather than exclusively to the continuing changes in the theory of liberal ideology. The latter comes into existence when ideologic premises or consistencies begin discontinuing, whereas the former materialises when ideologic postulates go through an uninterrupted drift between the consistencies of a theory and the inconsistencies of its praxis.

Inconsistencies between the theory and praxis of Islam and social democracy and the emasculation of the inter-complementary meanings of their theoretico-practical postulates originate in their dialectical intersections with this uninterrupted drift of liberal capitalism, the dominant institutional framework encircling this intersection. It is not, initially, an encounter of theories but praxes. As Islamic and social democratic practices have failed to countervail capitalist praxis, their proponents come to intersperse liberal premises into their theories. The result is 'liberal Islam', 'Islamic liberalism', 'social democratic liberalism' or 'liberal social democracy', the Third Way and so on. As a result, it becomes unlikely to expound the long-run oscillations or conduct of a politico-economic system using the analytic concepts of a single theory such as Islam, liberalism or social democracy. For this reason, I will discuss the Turkish political economy in terms of the intersectional manifestations of Islam, neoliberalism and social democracy in this idiosyncratic context.

At the foundational stage of an Islamic state or civilisation, the politico-economic policy choices of its members, as Ibn-i Khaldun (1967 [1375]) argued, are institutionalised under the theoretical postulates of Islamic theory, as he exemplified with reference to the evolution of taxation in earlier Islamic societies. (This verdict applies to early Islamic civilisations and might not be valid for their contemporaries.) At this *movemental* stage, group feeling among its members gives way to strategic convergence among these choices, ensuring the path-dependent continuity of Islamic social systems. In Habermasian terms, the communicative action of Muslim personalities under the unifying power of Islamic culture underlies their group feeling and the continuity of their social organisation. Power and money are subjected, at this stage, to systemic complementarities or strategic convergences among the norm-contingent rationalities of Muslims of various classes. Yet, with the *formal* organisation or professionalisation of the movemental spirit, this norm-contingent group feeling, in due course, becomes a power- and money-conditioned competition among Muslims. At issue is the similarity between Ibn-i Khaldun (1332–

1406) and Habermas' analyses of societal dissolution, despite that they analysed culturally different societies, Islamic and Western, respectively. Thus, what is the distinguishing feature of Islamic societies as religion-conditioned organisations?

If not affected or dominated by an external force, the fate of a human or a society naturally rests with its own actions. The Qur'an (20: 11) explicitly and emphatically declares: 'Verily never will Allâh change the condition of a people until they change it themselves'. As a result, if Muslims dissociate their actions from Islamic values, these actions come to be identical to those of liberals with respect to developing pro-cyclical pragmatist attitudes (Allâh does not compel them to conform their actions to Islamic principles). Thanks to the disidentifying power of group feeling among its subjects, Muslims or non-Muslims, liberal capitalism or worldly interests thus pose a potential threat to Muslim communities by substituting norm-conditioned action for a power, prestige and money-conditioned one. The greatest challenge for contemporary Muslims is, as highlighted above from a different approach, that the systemic power of neoliberal institutionalisation over *social* structures is to dissociate the 'I' from the 'me'. And the reversal of this process depends on both contemporary Muslims establishing the necessary power channels to reduce the barriers capitalism erects to normatively contingent development and the re-establishment of institutional infrastructures for the resurgence of the 'me' in the face of the 'I'. Throughout these encounters, as noted above, one would expect converging divergences between Islamism and neoliberalism to appear such as liberal Islam, Islamic neoliberalism, and so on.

The same preconditions hold for a social democratic revival, as social democrats should encourage group feeling in society, at least among their electorate, and embed it within political, economic and legal organisations in a structural sense. Moreover, as seen in the post-war period, conjuncturally, this process does not rest with the autonomous discretion of social democrats but, substantially, with the cyclical evolution of capitalism. The feature distinguishing social democracy from Islam is that the former is a middle-ground theoretico-practical paradigm between capitalism and socialism, while the latter is a pure theory that requires unconditional implementation. Yet, in praxis, as in the emergence of 'Conservative Democracy' in the Turkish context, when secular capitalism dictates its institutional adaptations, Muslims would also have to develop a middle-ground theoretico-practical paradigm. Therefore, they must also counter the double-edged challenges facing contemporary social democrats. What would be the ultimate result? Would they demonstrate a more consistent attitude than social democrats or pursue the same *conservative* pragmatism? I will grapple with this question in the following parts.

When it comes to liberal institutionalism, its value- or norm-free nature enmeshed with a deep-seated theoretico-practical pragmatism makes it feasible to infuse itself into and persist in every type of social structure. *This is what provides neoliberalism with its systemic power*, which makes it possible for liberal capitalism to preclude the de-accumulation of the 'I' in the face of the 'me' throughout its dialectic encounters with its rival paradigms such as Islam and social democracy. Naturally, there emerges a structural question: 'flexible markets, stable society'? (Streek, 2008) The response, in theory, is obvious: 'no'. In praxis, the issue is that contemporary societies are unable to rid themselves of the dull stability of the flexibility of neoliberal theoretico-practical premises to redeem a group feeling that would enable themselves to voice the so-called 'no'. The macro-political economy of Islam and social democracy takes shape under the tense pressure of responding to this question: 'in fact no, but yes'.

The systemic functionalisation of an Islamic political economy requires the imposition of necessary constraints on individual or business actions. However, these constraints, in praxis, are worldly regulations that may be de-functionalised by those (the political authorities, and so on) expected to enforce these constraints. In this regard, the practical implementation of Islam demands the establishment and *maintenance* of the delicate balance in which Muslims should act in conformity with Islamic principles without being conditioned by worldly constraints that are, as human-devised apparatuses, instrumental arrangements to provide for the worldly establishment of the eternal or divine facts of Islam (Chapra, 2000: 59–61). Muslims are required to abide by these constraints as an exigency of their responsibility to Allâh, the imposer of Islam. Thus, institutionalisation and the stability of politico-economic organisation around individual and social Islamic action is not an option, but a necessity.

As noted above, the social democrats have to functionalise similar humanitarian dialectics between formal and informal institutions. However, they do not have eternal divine support, at least in theory. This means that they must confront capitalist praxis through a path-dependent egalitarianism deriving from their humanly constrained *decencies*. In contrast to widespread perception, liberalism also relies upon the institutionalisation of a cultural background that interest-seeking personalities *socialise*. As this decollectivising socialisation resides in the elimination of binding constraints, the mainstay of group-level consistency, liberalism stipulates the extermination of the decommodificatory role of politico-economic organisations.

Under the confines of this decollectivising power of liberal establishment, Islam and social democracy assume the structuralisation of the social optimum through political and economic democracy, the major constraints on governmental and business actions. That *shura*, the Islamic governance, is not rooted in secular structures does not matter in terms of the role democracy plays in the establishment of the social optimum, as the latter's essence is giving voice to bottom-up demands in macro-politics and economics to forge a reciprocal *power control* among the actors but not the cultural references of this voicing. Beyond power control, in Islam, the key principle in adapting or maintaining an institution is consensus, while majority rule is considered second best. This is because a thoroughly Islamic politics would only be enforced by integrating all citizens equally, requiring participatory democracy in major processes. In Islam, *shura*, in this respect, would be the essential means of inspiring individuals to behave Islamically; namely, it is the practical means for achieving theoretical consistency (Asad, 1961). Yet the consensus-theoretic alignment of social institutions by way of *shura* has not, in praxis, been implemented on a large scale, even among Muslims and Muslim countries, as a result of the emasculation of Islamic group feeling at the family, organisation, region, state or international levels.

The aim of Islamic politics, in a systemic sense, is to ensure social harmony and economic stability. An Islamic state's role is thus to stimulate productive and full employment by providing infrastructural public goods while avoiding crowding-out private actors. In Islam, a free-market economy constitutes the general environment for economic action. Yet, the market is a means for realising human welfare. And the state should enforce decommodifying constraints on private action such as progressive taxation as the means of state intermediation of reciprocal control in favour of the have-nots in the process of distributing income or inhibiting national or international arbitrage-seeking, speculative financial flows to prevent the exploitation of a country's productive resources. In the same vein, despite the priority placed on balanced budgets in Islamic economics, a government is entitled to engage in deficit-financing for redistributional and development purposes through asset-based or interest-free borrowing, but not by money creation, which is assumed to empower speculative financiers. To ensure a stable economic system, (Islamic) governments or Central Banks are expected to maintain price stability and regulate credit flows to ensure productive investment. The aim of this policy is to promote full employment of the factors of production and create equal opportunities among the citizens of various classes (Mannan, 1983).

Despite this smooth delineation of inter-institutional interaction, the systemic implementation of an Islamic political economy *requires* reciprocal power control that flows through inter-organisational interaction, in which the relevant actors are the state and the government; individual or collective business organisations; the civil service or trade unions as the workers' representatives; the state officials; the retired; women's and environmental organisations and so on. The reason for this is that mono-directional control by the state might be highly vulnerable to the pragmatist and the patronage-based exploitative tendencies of Muslim rulers or employers. Moreover, being a Muslim does not absolve anyone from malpractices such as imposing unequal taxes or reducing real wages to obtain patronage or financial power, respectively. For example, without the involvement of trade and civil service unions in the economic decision-making process, how can a social optimum obtained through positive-sum compromise be expected to materialise in the long run? This is crucial for the stabilisation of conjunctural pragmatisms and the establishment of public-private partnerships and coordination under a planned and a demand-constrained strategy.

In Islamic social policy, equality of opportunity based on self-enforcement can thus only be provided by establishing the structural means for creating an equality of outcomes: full-employment-oriented fiscal and monetary policy, progressive taxation including Zakat and inheritance taxes and so on. In brief, the establishment and management of a genuine Islamic system depends on the effective operation of economic and political councils in which the actors share equal power to reach consensus or majority decisions, not only for an equal but also a solidaristically devised, productivist development, which is the only means of sustainable economic growth (Choudry, 1999: 259–61). Without the establishment of such an institutionalised power balance, the system is likely to be unable to manage inflation and interest cycles by eliminating arbitrage-seeking or speculative opportunism without causing a decline in aggregate demand or demand shocks, which entail unemployment, recessions and so on. This is because the patronage and power relationships would not be harnessed to coerce governmental authorities and business organisations to comply with the structural pillars of an Islamic economic regime.

Despite emerging on the basis of theoretical pragmatism, the achievements of social democracy, especially in Scandinavia, namely the ability to sustain a comparatively equal distribution of income and power, should be taken into account. The issue is that, in social market economies, the collective welfare of the masses is realised through the practical functionalisation of democratic processes through organic or inorganic collaborations between social democratic parties and organised labour. It thus becomes possible to democratise political democracy and make productivist solidarity implementable. The primary target of a social democratic government is to offer a decent life on the basis of the rights of citizenship and by way of full employment and a generous welfare state, including the strategies of welfare without work, progressive taxation and so on (Meyer and Hinchman, 2007).

The sustainability of a social democratic regime centres, in the structural sense, on state intervention in harnessing market imperfections in addition to the effectiveness of trade unions in industrial or macro-level decision-making processes in sustaining positive-sum dialectics. However, in the event that such governments avoid institutionalising binding constraints on private action and adopting expansionary monetary and fiscal policy during dull years to decommodify market imperfections and optimise effective demand, the regime of social democracy would become unfeasible. The reason is that trends in output and employment are deemed to have a destabilising effect on business cycles due to speculative financialisation and ensuing deviations from full employment. First, at this juncture, social democratic parties would and in fact did adopt a pro-cyclical strategy that shifted the balance of power away from the have-nots to enable an investment-first, pro-austerity strategy and the pursuit of catch-all politics. Second, this process does not have to unfold in a linear progression; for example social democrats could make tactical use of neoliberal prescriptions to cultivate funds for a social democratic resurgence. These two trends demonstrate the converging divergence and *re*diverging convergence between social democracy and neoliberalism (Hou, 2009: 311).

The determinant parameter in these regressive or progressive trends in social democratic institutions is, as discussed above, the establishment, development and maintenance of an organised and solidarist group feeling. As a result of the relative perpetuation of this feeling in advanced capitalist countries, social democratic regimes, albeit frequently interrupted by various other political currents and impoverished by the emergence of Third Way politics, managed to maintain comparatively equal income distributions with a high degree of international competitiveness (see OECD, 2014; WEF, 2013). It is true that some European nations that represented social democratic values in the past obtained a certain portion of the capital needed to establish this comparatively equal welfare distribution through colonialist or neocolonialist incursions. Equally true, however, is that they managed to transform these *funds* into sources of internally organised, positive-sum interactions. Admittedly, as a social system can only unfold through the perpetuation of the consistencies of formal-informal dialectics, the former does not necessarily overshadow the latter, in systemic terms.

Liberal political economy, in contrast to the organised interaction in Islam and social democracy, is rooted in the encouragement of interest-seeking individual action and the elimination of market-constraining regulation. On the basis of a norm-free equality of opportunity and individual responsibility, this catallactic disorder is assumed to create an equal inequality of income (Hayek, 1998b: 107–9). As market exchange is considered the unique regulator of the inter-individual distribution of power and income, regulative or redistributive initiatives by the government or bureaucracy are claimed to allow rent-seeking behaviour by organised actors such as trade unions. Instead, a liberal government is expected to develop a regressive taxation strategy by expanding its tax base.

Monetary aggregates in liberal theory should be determined by supply-and-demand cycles (rather than the state's expansionary discretion) in tandem with the growth in output and employment (Friedman, 1968). Rather than decommodificatory purposes, the sole objective of state intervention or regulation is to secure private property through constitutional rules as a catalyst for both political and economic development (Buchanan, 2000). This is because development is an economic rather than a social issue, which can only be realised under capital-led technological innovation at the firm level. Constitutional rules should also constrain and, in fact, reduce the state's discretion in borrowing to support the public budget and coerce it to adopt a strict austerity strategy by prioritising price stability and the investment climate. Because unemployment is simply a voluntary issue, and a temporary deviation from its natural rate precipitated by governmental intervention creates labour market rigidities such as the enactment of labour laws or minimum wages. Instead, the state should enact flexible working arrangements that allow employers to determine their employees' wages on the basis of the marginal productivity of labour. If the state were to enact organised rigidities, these and the ensuing power balance between employers and employees would result in the suppression of business interests, through worker tyranny and the productive organisation of free enterprises.

These major interactions among liberal institutions, when intermeshed with their capitalist practices, create a power- and patronage-dominated social structure in which these sympathetically serviced (theoretical) institutions are bound to become extractive institutions. It is true that liberal capitalism created material progress for humanity to a structural extent. However, at what cost? As discussed earlier, without the use of Keynesian approaches, neoliberal postulates lack any dynamic to stimulate market exchange. This signifies that liberalism, or neoliberalism, is not a self-sustaining system of political economy and is the most concrete exemplar of the inconsistency of its theory and praxis.

The institutional alignments of Islam and social democracy, as previously discussed, converge in the structuralisation of the macro-political economy at the social optimum. Islam diverges from classical social democracy in terms of the source of knowledge and its production, the principality of consensus, the state's role in organising market exchanges while not making direct investments for redistributional purposes, a more conservative deficit-financing strategy and not using money creation to finance public deficits, the principal adaptation of a flexible exchange rate regime, a strict prohibition against financing the private or public sectors by borrowing at interest, realising equality of opportunity by ensuring the equality of outcomes, institutionalising social self-help as a poverty alleviation mechanism and prioritising ALMPs over PLMPs (active and passive labour market policies, respectively). Despite these methodological divergences, I believe that they share the common goal of structuring institutional interactions on the basis of the social optimum. The decisive factor is which of them would inspire their actors to establish, sustain or develop the necessary group feeling for Islamically or social-democratically designed institutions in the face of the destructuring impact of liberal capitalism and the structuration of an organised relationship on the basis of equal power sharing among the actors in a politico-economic system.

A possible intersection between Islam and liberalism in the sense of the former's praxis being modified by that of the latter would be expected, first and foremost, to marginalise, if any, the power balance among the actors in a political economy. This is because liberalism, systemically, requires the subjugation of countercyclical actors to pro-cyclical ones in a capitalist environment, and the unique way of so is to eliminate the former's power resources. Specifically, the dissolution of common decision-making processes based on achieving the social optimum is the prime target of such a dissolution, resulting in the uprooting of the original consistencies of an Islamic social system. In this case, the system comes to depend on the conjunctural policy adaptations of political authorities and market forces and the patronage and power linkages between them. This would be expected to generate dichotomous practices that vacillate between Islam and neoliberalism. The political authority would be inclined to pursue deficit-financing to functionalise its strategy of catch-all politics or develop an ALMP-oriented full employment strategy while allowing the continuance of interest-bearing financial circulation for developmental purposes, the liberation of international financial flows irrespective of their speculative disposition, increasing indirect taxes vis-à-vis direct taxes from a supply-side perspective and so on, in varying degrees or combinations.

The same trends hold for the encounter between social democracy and neoliberalism, in the form of the institutional pillars of the Third Way. The most 'concrete' dissolution of social democracy by Third Way politics is the shattering of the solidarity-contingent constraining rigour of the social democratic system as reflected in the declining power of organised labour to engage in binding collective bargaining and participate in politico-economic decision-making processes. This predisposes the political authorities to steer institutional interactions using their conjunctural inclinations. Further de-ideologising the social democratic establishment, the Third Way, in this respect, develops a *flexible compromise*, the orientation of which is driven by the practical dictates of the neoliberal environment. Crouch's definition (2001: 94), 'the Third Way is what the New Labour does', well describes the inconsistent nature of this orientation. Major policy tools of this inconsistency are privatisation, marginal progressive taxation, including competition-friendly corporate taxes, the prioritisation of austerity and disinflation vis-à-vis full employment and governmental discretion, confining economic development to the free flow of micro-economic market forces, the liberalisation of exchange rates and international financial flows and so on. As in the case of Islamic parties, formerly social democratic parties would adapt a varying mix of these social democratic and neoliberal institutional strategies.

Finally, it should be noted that the cross-institutional interactions among neoliberalism, Islam and social democracy are, naturally, expected to vary according to the context-specific circumstances of the dominant institutional environment and the power competition between pro-cyclical or countercyclical actors. In the following parts, I will delve into these varying adaptations of Islamic, neoliberal and social democratic policy strategies by Turkish conservative democrats and social democratic Kemalists vis-à-vis the dominant liberal or neoliberal institutional environment. In the light of the cross-paradigmatic discussion in this chapter, the analytical apparatuses of institutional system analysis will enable us to unravel the intriguing manifestations of these entanglements from an historical perspective, to which I now turn.

PART II
Formation and Re-formation of Path-Dependencies among Islam, Secularism and Etatist Liberalism

The first part of this book proposed an institutional system analysis to explicate evolutionary dynamics of a social system from a path-dependent change perspective. In this second, third and the following fourth part, the path-dependent institutional changes in the Ottoman-Turkish political economy will be analysed through the theoretico-practical lens of institutional system analysis. An outline of this and the next chapters is illustrated in Figure II.1.

The major watersheds and cross-intersectional dynamics of the institutionalisation, deinstitutionalisation and reinstitutionalisation of Islam, social democracy and liberalism in the context of the continuing changes in Turkish political economy can be summarised as follows:

→The idiosyncratic institutionalisation of Ottoman Islam as the source of the path-dependencies on the basis of which the contemporary Turkish political economy developed in the twentieth and the twenty-first centuries and its changing continuity due to imperial pressure from rising European capitalism in the nineteenth century.

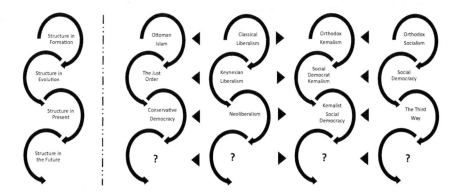

Figure II.1   Theoretico-practical interaction of the Ottoman-Turkish political economy with the European and global capitalism

→(i) The reformative institutionalisation of orthodox Kemalism as the theoretico-practical ideology of the Turkish Republic; (ii) its path-dependently changing continuity under the banner of 'social democratic Kemalism' in the late 1950s and the 1960s, and the paradigmatic embedding of the latter in the 1970s; (iii) the resurrection of social democratic Kemalism within the pattern of continuing path-dependence by the mid-2010s following the reformational experiences of third way Kemalism and Kemalist social democracy between the mid-1980s and 1990s and between 1995 and 2010, respectively; and (iv) the discontinuing change in social democratic Kemalism after the July 2011 general elections.

→(i) The changing discontinuity of Ottoman Islam under the title of 'the Just Order' in the late 1960s and the path-dependent discontinuity of the Just Order following the creation of Turkish conservative democracy conceptualised based on the perspective of theoretical pragmatism at the beginning of the twenty-first century when Turkish state neoliberalism came to a halt under the ideologically embedded practices of orthodox Kemalism; (ii) the changing continuity of the Just Order re-envisioned in a more egalitarian and solidaristic form by the HASPAR movement in 2010 under the leadership of a professor of social policy; and (iii) the merger of HASPAR into the AKP in 2012.

The long-term examination of these systemic cycles within the regional and global institutional environment requires an attention to both permanent niches and the various changes to these niches at structural turning points. From this methodological perspective, the above-noted evolutionary dialectics of Islam, social democracy and neoliberalism during the Ottoman and the Republican periods gave rise to a *cryptic* structure. The ebb and flow of this structure's institutional stock between norm-contingent rationality and rationality-conditioned normativity in timespace make uncoupling it an arduous task. Analytically, its ebb and flow prevents us from adapting a unilinear methodology of rationalisation, as proposed by Habermas and Khaldun, from a normatively ordered lifeworld to a mechanically ordered social system. Rather, the attempts at resurrection pursued by both Islamic and social democratic institutionalism, with their adaptive compositions, in response to the neoliberal establishment, require basing our arguments on the process of *normative rerationalisation* (in due course, these processes will be explained in detail).

Infusing the intricacies of the normative niches into the actional subconscious of individual and organisational actors in the Turkish political economy is, from the beginning, a *constrained* task. An attempt to disentangle the cryptic constellations in the Turkish context by conducting theoretico-practical investigations would thus ultimately produce, on the one hand, limited inferences, despite that adoption of an institutional system perspective. Despite its boundedness, employing an institutional system analysis is, on the other, inevitable in the Turkish case, as the systemically woven structure of theoretico-practical investigations into the knowable manifestations of the Turkish case would redound to the explanatory power of our arguments.

The enduring impact of politics, as the central representative of normative demands in the Turkish context, on economic and social development is another structural justification for employing a holistically organised, inter-temporal perspective to analyse the institutional bridges among political, economic and cultural constituencies (although Turkish state capitalism seems to reflect discontinuing path-dependence). An additional parameter is the ever-increasing impact of regional and international actors on the Ottoman-Turkish context from the nineteenth century onwards, as these external impacts augment the complexity of relational interaction between internal and external actors influencing the Ottoman-Turkish political economy.

Overall, an integrated examination of the reciprocally dependent and inter-repulsively contingent relationship between the internal and external or pro-cyclical and countercyclical actors urges us to employ an institutional system analysis. In doing so, I will use the interactions-cum-interconnections among the theoretical components of institutional system analysis, namely the institutional environment, the actors and their strategy or policy choices, the power relations and path-dependent institutional changes. This methodology entails concentrating on the inter-actor power relations in the constraining atmosphere of the contemporary institutional stock in lieu of advancing purely idealistic, econometric or sharp-edged conceptualisations. A disjointed set of quantitative or qualitative data cannot, in other words, be utilised as systemically explanatory niches for a political economy analysis. This is because tracing the long-term pendulum of path-dependencies and changes requires a focus on the relational manifestations of these two types of data at the level of formal and informal institutions. In this sense, I will present pure data on major macro-economic, political and social indicators and a systemic interpretation of their evolutionary, conjunctural and relational implications.

It should be noted that, in the second and third parts, the institutional system analysis will be employed for explaining the formational and evolutionary dynamics of the Ottoman-Turkish political economy, particularly with reference to the path-dependent changes of these dynamics in terms of their political, economic and cultural implications. But, it is the fourth part and the conclusion that will bring the analytic tools, particularly the systemic power of the institutional system analysis, together to explain the current structure and future prospects of Turkish Islam and social democracy under the constraints of the neoliberal national and international environment. In this sense, although the explanatory value of the institutional system analysis can well be pursued throughout the second and third parts, this value can essentially be recognised in the final part and in the conclusion. This is because I have to discuss first the analytic material in moderate detail throughout the second and third parts that should be brought into together to make a fully fledged systemic discussion in the fourth part.

Chapter 3
Primordial Path-Dependencies: The Ottoman Islamic Institutionalism

The Ottoman state was a transcontinental empire with a political and commercial existence stretching from the Balkans and the Black Sea region through Anatolia, Syria, Mesopotamia and the Gulf to Egypt and most of the North African coast throughout the six centuries before World War I (Pamuk, 2014: 1–2). This extensive spatio-temporal coverage predisposed the Empire's major actors to structure its institutional stock in a manner that ebbed and flowed among the theoretical consistency of Islam, the practical exigencies of its geostrategic and geocultural interlinkages and conjunctural pragmatic choices. Irrespective of this, and in parallel with the factional balkanisations in Republican Turkey, there has been a sharply bifurcated, instead of a systemically organised, approach to Ottoman institutionalism: either appraising it with regard to its Islamic institutional stock and civilisational achievements, in humanitarianism, multi-cultural cosmopolitanism, military triumphs and so on, or to denounce it for its religious pillars that are alleged to have constrained the embodiment of an innovative industrial and democratic mindset compared to its European contemporaries.

The upholders of the former are far from responding to the question of why the Empire failed to counteract European capitalism and lagged behind in catching up with industrial progress. The latter group fails to account for how the Ottomans were able to found a substantive world power, especially during the fifteenth century, while the Turkish Republic, despite its formally secularised institutional stock, continues to await a mythic hero, for example, to produce a local brand of automobile and has yet to enact a civic constitution, the prospects for which appear gloomy at the ninetieth anniversary of its foundation. Thus, to read the history of the Ottoman Empire and Turkish Republic from a 'yes or no' position triggers a crude precision at the expense of losing sight of the dialectic nature of the Empire's institutional stock in terms of its change-blocking, path-sustaining or path-dependently changing dynamics.

The issue for this research is in this sense to identify the institutional pillars, the major constituents of which are illustrated in Table 3.1, which formed the basis of and sustained the Empire's existence over more than six centuries, their changes over time and ultimately their path-dependencies that have informed the Turkish political economy. To fulfil these three objectives, our analysis centres on 'Ottoman Islam' as the main framework of the Empire's social system. Ottoman Islam refers to the idiosyncratic formation of the Empire's institutions from the pattern and regulation of production to state-society and state-business interlinkages by nurturing a complementary thread between its spatial and cultural practices and the *unifying cloak* of Islamic theory.

This formational dialectic between Islamic theory and practical idiosyncrasy unsurprisingly produced, at certain times, flexible, pragmatic or diplomatic adaptations to domestic and external politico-economic reconstructions. The result was the genesis of an institutional stock based on a *delicate balance* that compelled the Empire's administrative units to craft practically feasible policy choices that, at times, forced the limits of Islamic theory. In fact, it was again this delicate balance between the inter-repulsive dynamics of the Empire's institutional stock that precipitated its ultimate demise. Methodologically, this institutional delicateness over a voluminous spatio-temporality requires that researchers not indulge in constant generalisations while studying Ottoman institutionalism.

Table 3.1   The major institutional constituents of the Ottoman political economy

Institutional system	Ottoman Islam	Public-private choice	State regulation of private production through precisely defined rules and selectively enforced price controls
Institution-building strategy	Theory-praxis conciliation with an exemptional orientation towards practical pragmatism	Market	A means of pecuniary exchange under the priority of provisionism and traditionalism
Political democracy	–Shûra-based state administration –The absence of intermediary linkages for civic public to participate in macro-political decisions –Strong commitment to the rule of law in judicial matters	Growth and development	–A demand-constrained, stable and planned production system conditioned by a solidaristic division of labour –Territorial expansion and pragmatic engagement with transnational commercial opportunities
Economic and social democracy	A solidarity-based form of market governance between the guilds and state-led economic governance between the local and central administration and the guilds on the basis of order, dependence and rare conflict	International trade and finance	–Provisionism-focused import enhancement and export-restriction –Engaging with international and private financial institutions to fund state expenditures and manage revenues

Taxation	Institutionalised according to Islamic law and to the priority of the state's survival	Interest	Principally prohibited, rarely implemented
Fiscal policy	Austerity	Social policy strategy	Executed by the *waqfs* on the basis of religiously motivated and organised voluntarism
Monetary policy	–Sustain price stability in tandem with fiscal balances –Debasements for financing budget deficits	Labour relations	Day-long working hours, decent wages, conflictual compromise with state authorities, prohibition of trade unionism

The politico-economic regime of the Empire, contrary to widespread presuppositions, was not under the unilateral control of the state, but structured based on state-led reciprocal power balances among the major actors. As in the case of consigning security, tax collection and military training to *tımarlı sipahi, timariot*, for instance, the central government generated structural conciliations with the local notables, occupational groups, the guilds and religious leaders. On issues ranging from price arrangements to security and tax issues, the local notables were consulted by *Kadı*, the local governor of a city or a municipality (Ortaylı, 2004: 24–5). Another implication is that the Ottoman state crafted a flexible rigidity in its rule over conquered areas, not by disintegrating the ingrained institutions of their inhabitants, but by developing a socio-economic diplomacy of engagement with them. As will be elaborated below, these balances were also well embedded in intra-state governance between political and ecclesiastical authorities, economic governance between political and market forces and judicial mediation between political power and the rights of citizens.

Another offset was that the economic system functioned on the basis of establishing a dynamic stability between organising market relations to provide the optimal amount of goods and services from well-organised suppliers acting under predetermined rules of competition and prioritising the maintenance of state power as the guarantor of this balanced society-market nexus. Voluntary social organisation and production of basic public goods and services, from education to social aid for the needy, served to complement this state-society-market interaction. These balances persisted until traditional path-dependencies began to change in the early eighteenth and then gathered pace in the nineteenth century. Let us begin to examine these balances through main axes in the Empire between politics, society and the market in terms of the interactions between their major actors.

The Interface among Ottoman Political, Social and Market Actors

The Ottoman Empire was, in systemic terms, an Islamic state with respect to: (i) the sorting and taxation of its citizens according to their religious affiliations; (ii) the composition of the judicial apparatus and legislative sources, from inheritance to commercial law; (iii) the main courses, materials and knowledge sources in the educational system; (iv) the underpinnings of craft and agricultural production; (v) the constitutive element of the family and social life and so on. (A counter argument to this thesis is the widespread practice of common law in the Empire. This claim loses sight of the fact that common law is also a secondary source of Islamic law.) As noted above, this principal foundation was not divorced from pragmatism, such as allowing lending at interest, albeit exceptionally, on the basis of perpetuating the socio-economic interests of the society. To designate the Ottoman state as 'Islamic', in this respect, we do not have to identify an overall strategic convergence between Islamic theory and its Ottoman praxis. Rather, we should consider what constituted the *centre of gravity* in the Empire's politico-economic strategies and their *de facto* practice. In terms of the abovementioned pillars of the Empire, considering it an Islamic state is not, in this sense, an issue of controversy. Examining these pillars will help us to clarify this argument.

During the classical period, the administrative system of Ottoman politics was divided into two main axes: the centre and the provinces. The main actors of the central administration were the Sultan and the Palace; *Divân-ı Hümayun* (The Ottoman Imperial Council) and its affiliated bureaus, Vezir-i azam (the Grand Vizier) and *Bâb-ı âli* (The Sublime Porte); *Bâb-ı fetva* and the organisation of *ilmiyye* that issued *fatwa* (Islamic adjudication) and education; the revenue board and financial organisation; *Kapıkulu ocakları* (the troops under the Sultan's direct command); and the navy. The Sultan was initially dubbed *bey* to indicate that he was the leading actor of a political *movement* rather than an *organisation*. The characteristic distinguishing a *bey* from a *sultan* is that the former particularly governed through mores, customs and in conciliation with prominent social groups and the members of dynasties. During the reign of Mehmet II, (who reigned as Sultan during the periods 1444–46 and 1451–81), the heads of the Ottoman state adopted the title of sultan, *padişah*, as the leader of a sedentary organisation under the principle of the authority to rule, passing as an inheritance from father to son (Ortaylı, 2008: 139–260). Beginning in the seventeenth century, this practice gradually transformed into the succession of the oldest member of the House of Osman (Faroqhi, 2009: 97). In later periods, the title of Caliph, the leader of the Islamic *ummah*, came into use under Selim III (1789–1807).

As the highest institutional actor in the Empire, *Divân-ı Hümayun* was a conciliatory council responsible for the administrative, judicial, financial or customary affairs of the Empire with the aim of assisting the Sultan in making his ultimate decisions (beginning in the eighteenth century, when the bureaucratic organisation of the Empire was divided into specialist organs, the *Divân-ı Hümayun* took on a ceremonial role). Its major permanent members were the *grand vizier*, *defterdar* and *kazasker*. The *grand vizier* was the second man of the Empire, responsible for all administrational issues, apart from judicial and financial ones, which were dealt with by *kazasker* (a military and high-ranking judge subordinate to the *şeyhülislam* [shaykh al-Islam] and *defterdar* [financial director]). The *şeyhülislam* was responsible for the structuration and settlement of the Empire's judicial system according to sharia law.

The *kazasker* was a respected figure as the *şeyhülislam*'s representative in the *Divân-i Hümayun*, and he was the member of *Heyet-i Vükela* as the minister of Shar'iyya, founded during the reign of Mahmut II (1808–39). As the salaried officials of Ottoman state, the *şeyhulislam* and the religious staff were affiliated with the sultan's rule in terms of their assignment, dismissal and relegation. Yet the class of *ilmiyye* was relatively independent and respected, because it represented the theoretical, discursive and particularly the enforcive powers of Islamic law over the rest of society. And these power resources allowed them to play critical and determining roles during political cycles, including, at times, overthrowing sultans and initiating major wars in addition to the organisation of social customs and mores, from permitting the drinking of coffee to the foundation of printing houses (Dursun, 1989: 240–242). For example, İnalcık (1964: 44) notes: 'In the eighteenth century it became established practice to seek the *şeyhülislam*'s opinion on every governmental matter of importance'.

The main administrational strategy of the Empire under the rule of this central organisation, as summarised by Mustafa Naima, the seventeenth century Ottoman chronicler, in his formulation of the *cycle of equity*, was: '1- There could be no *mülk* (rule) or *devlet* (state) without the military; 2- Maintaining the military requires wealth 3- Wealth was garnered from the subjects; 4- The subjects could prosper only through justice; 5- Without *mülk* and *devlet* there could be no justice' (cited in Shaw, 2002 [1976]: 112). As a transcontinental organisation, the Empire's systemic power relied on its military institutions, and thus it erected an Islamically contingent political organisation based on this source of institutional power. The Ottoman state imposed taxes on its subjects according to Islamic law and assigned the role of collecting these taxes to military personnel as their primary means of making their living. The state expected military officials not to oppress the peasants using their enforcive power to collect taxes (this balance, at least until the late sixteenth century, was generally maintained).

The inter-class transitions between social actors at various layers were, in terms of socio-political justice, relatively consonant with Naima's conceptualisation. Ottoman society was, by and large, divided into two main parts, the *askeri* and the *reâya*. The *askeri*, the military, comprised the Sultan himself and the officers of the court and the army, civil servants and the *ulemâ*, who had executive or religious powers. The *reâya* were the Muslim or non-Muslim subjects (İnalcık, 1964: 44). Despite the traditional path-dependency of peasants to perpetuate their status, it was possible for them to become *ulemâ* by pursuing education in a *medrese*. The son of a peasant family would become an *âskeri* if he was assigned to state service through *devşirme*, the Christians conscripted to be raised to become *janissaries.* Moreover, through indirect means, a *timar* could be acquired by the peasants themselves (Faroqhi, 2006: 122). Ortaylı (2004: 15–8) reminds us that the transition to the *İlmiyye* class was, however, quite limited due to inheritance-conditioned and strict in-class boundaries.

Another structural issue in parallel with Naima's conceptualisation was the invalidity of the general *crude* perception that *padişah* had an absolute coercive power over his subjects, including the *askeri*, and executed his own discretion at all costs. A scholar from Israel's Hebrew University, Gerber (2005: 246) argues that on the contrary, the *padişah* was not a despot but a strict adherent of Islamic law, and he exemplifies this thesis with the fact that the 2,500 decisions contained in the Vianna Complaint Register of 1675 prove that the *padişah* directed all complaints to the *Kadı* to make a decision according to the law. He (1994: 181–2) emphasises that:

> Most of the complaints were filed by low-class individuals, mostly villagers, often against very high officials. All the complaints include exact names and addresses, which evidences a lack of fear that is to my mind remarkable. Another aspect of the complaints that seems to me impressive was the serious and fair treatment accorded to each by the central government. Every complaint was sent to the nearest *kadi* with a strongly worded order to look into it diligently. In no case do we find any effort, direct or veiled, on the part of the sultan to whitewash a case to save a high-placed official. Furthermore, the fact that thousands of villagers sent complaints to the faraway sultan seems to imply that complaining was meaningful in achieving results … As far as central government policy was concerned, the line of authority in judicial matters was clear and undisputable — *kadi* decisions had to be heeded by governors and police officials because this was the wish of the sultanate; the policy was clearly anchored in Islamic ethics. The overwhelming weight of the evidence indicates that this was also the social reality.

In addition to this justice-centred political governance, which cannot be divorced from occasional unlawful practices throughout the Empire's lifespan, between the organised political and unorganised Ottoman civic society, there was a truly economic governance mechanism within the extent of the organised Ottoman guild system and the local and central organs of political administration. A concise elaboration of the functioning of this mechanism, I believe, would enable us to capture the politics of artisanal production as a systemic nexus of the power relationships in the Empire. Yet it should be kept in mind that only 10 per cent of the population lived in the cities and was occupied with the crafts affiliated with the guilds and other non-agricultural work (Pamuk, 2003: 56–7). The vast majority of economic output consisted of agricultural production, which constituted the backbone of the Empire's budgetary income and military organisation. Agricultural production was performed by peasants who lacked coalitional power to confront state officials or civic authorities responsible for collecting ordinary or unordinary taxes. Thus, this proportional division should be taken into account when interpreting the systemic nature of the political economy of production relations in the Empire. In addition, the guild system, despite its existence until the end of the Empire, began to de-accumulate with the retrogression of central authority's systemic power over the periphery in the seventeenth century, and the sale of guild-affiliated workshops to capital-owning military officials, state rulers, *ulemâ* and merchants was facilitated.

Functioning on the basic principle of *futuwwa* (brotherhood), *Âhi* (friendship) organisations (until the mid-fifteenth century) and the Ottoman guilds, in a more professionalised manner (from the beginning of the sixteenth century to the end of the Empire), institutionalised the solidarist, altruistic and tolerant civic consciousness of the Empire's people in their internal and external relationships with political authority (Arnakis, 1953: 237; Lewis, 1937: 29). Despite primarily recruiting their members among craftsmen, the *Akhis* were more diverse than the guilds in both a compositional and functional sense. Their functions embraced the ecclesiastical and socio-economic realms in addition to the political one. As they existed before the consolidation of the Empire's bureaucratic tradition, they were more independent and influential in their principally conciliative relationship with the state. However, in the event of conflict, they did not hesitate to take countercyclical action. Arnakis (1953: 235–6) writes, 'Akhis acted as a check on the absolutist trends of local emirs and of the first two Osmanlı sultans. [...In this context, as] the authority of Murad I was [...] distasteful to the Akhis, popular discontent increased, and in the reign of his successor, Bayazid the Thunderbolt, it broke into open rebellion'.

From the early sixteenth century to the end of the Empire, Ottoman guilds also comprised a diverse membership, ranging from the *ulema* to peasants. Their membership base also included Rum, Armenian, Serbian, Bulgarian and Christian artisans and craftsmen. A *Şeyh* served as the religious leader of the guild and was responsible for external administrative affairs. The intra-organisational composition of guild-affiliated workplaces consisted of a three-tiered structure: *usta* (masters), *kalfa* (senior apprentices) and *çırak* (regular apprentices). Their functions included tax collection, control over the quality of products and weights and measures, *narh* (fixing of prices) and wages, determining the composition and size of the workforce and recruiting their members as civilian auxiliaries for the army in times of war. Of these, the most salient was their intermediary role between the government and their members by performing the general supervision of their members and issuing a guarantee for their compliance with governmental orders and announcements (Baer, 1970: 28–50).

The government intervened in the guilds to provide physical infrastructure and sufficient raw materials for their production, market supervision and price fixing, and the collection of regular and irregular taxes. Despite this, government intervention never became an unchallenged authority. For instance, the government did not interfere with intra- or inter-guild matters that the guilds themselves could manage, and they also had input into fixing official prices. In their internal affairs, the guilds acted under the principles of cooperation, mutual control and reciprocal privilege. They sought to restrain the intra-guild competition and external incursions into the sectors in which they operated. Their tolerance of one another was nonetheless limited to establishing internal agreements. When a conflict among them emerged, it was generally resolved by the state, a means for the latter's balanced intervention in production and exchange relationships (Faroqhi, 2005: 177–93).

The Ottoman guilds maintained their functions under the rule of the *Kadı*, the head of a province in the Empire. Minor conflicts with low-ranking officials were settled under his authority. In cases of substantive and recurring conflicts, the guilds filed a petition to the *Divân-ı Hümayun*, which functioned, *inter alia*, as the supreme court in Istanbul. Petitions were substantial means through which the guilds communicated with the state. Any petitions filed by one or more guilds, the most salient of which concerned taxes, were handled by the political authorities in a relatively fair manner. In addition, they also brought their internal problems to the *Divân*, as they believed that the state would judge the matters fairly. With this state-centred perception of justice, '[they] looked to the Ottoman state for help against anyone who might undermine their economic position' (Faroqhi, 1991: 43; 2005b; 95–6). The state took their demands seriously, aware that in the event of conflict, the guilds could spontaneously incite rebellion or become part of an anti-government countercyclical action. Another factor was their intermediary role in the collection of taxes, the provision of services to the army commissariat and enforcement of official rules in the marketplace (Faroqhi, 1991: 42). Yet, as Yi emphasised (2004: 212): 'Ultimately, it was the government, however receptive it was, that had the right to formally approve or disapprove guild affairs, and guilds could not always ensure that the government made the decisions they wanted'.

A Provisionist and Traditionalist Austerity between Islam and Pragmatism

The first period of the Ottoman economic system, from the foundation to the last quarter of the fifteenth century, witnessed a structural power competition between the local notables and central officials who were selected through recruitment. From the last quarter of the fifteenth to the end of the sixteenth century, the *classical system* of production relationships based on the tax-based administration of the land, cities, guilds and trade by the state reached its zenith in terms of operational optimality. During the second half of the sixteenth century, however, the Ottoman economy suffered the adverse effects of a number of developments such as inflation, foreign trade and changes in military technology. These effects damaged the delicate cosmopolitan balances in the organisation of the Empire and hence resulted in the emasculation of the state's systemic power over the periphery.

However, the peripheral forces, especially local notables, could not grasp the structural power resources necessary to overrule economic surplus, but they instead were able to share it with the forces of the central government to ensure the survival of both camps (Faroqhi, 2009: 19–20). Despite its de-accumulations over time, the classical economic system of the Empire, which was institutionalised between the fourteenth and sixteenth centuries, did not undergo a structural shift until the first part of the nineteenth century. The period from the early nineteenth century until World War I symbolises the opening up of the Ottoman Empire to the world economy, during which the central tendencies did not fade away but maintained their existence by adopting a mode of state capitalism. Beyond the conjunctural variations, in this respect, three main principles can be suggested to define the basic pillars of the Empire's economic conduct (Genç, 2000: 47–69):

i.   *Provisionism*: The object of economic action under state direction was to provide necessary goods and services to provide a decent life for consumers but not a suitable investment environment for maximum profit and surplus. The supply of ample, qualified and inexpensive goods and services was hence the quintessence of economic transactions. State intervention was primarily intended to preserve and consolidate this principle throughout the economy, from the first producer to the final consumer. For example, in agriculture, the state did not grant individuals with complete property rights to agricultural lands. In this regime of property ownership, entitled *miri*, the right to cultivate the soil was rented and transferred from father to son, but the right to sell and purchase was confined to the state, and its dedication to others was prohibited. The farmers were not allowed to keep the soil fallow, so as not to prompt a decline in agricultural production or immigration to cities or other regions by leaving the soil. The essence of this system was that the state did not permit changes in the sizes of family businesses, which were allocated land of between 60 and 150 acres according to the productivity of the soil, by being divided into parts. The vast majority of arable land was harvested by small or middle-sized peasant families, which forestalled the genesis of alternative political currents *vis-à-vis* the central state (Pamuk, 2003: 38–43). Unless they satisfied the needs of a town-scale region comprising a population of between 3,000 and 20,000, agricultural products could not be marketed to other regions. In addition to this locational constraint, the purchasing, processing and selling of foodstuffs and raw materials of agricultural production was the monopoly of the towns.

There were separately organised guilds for each good and service consisting of workplaces run by the craftsmen and their apprentices and regulated to not exceed predetermined average sizes, as was the case in agricultural workplaces. As noted above, instead of competition and conflict, cooperation and conciliation were prioritised by the guilds with the aim of reducing competition over prices, wages and productions to the bare minimum. As a result, income differentials between the richest and the poorest crafts were, for example, at most between four to seven times in nineteenth century and three to six times in seventeenth and eighteenth centuries. Although these ranges became relatively larger in the commercial sectors, there were significant constraints on the opportunities for private capital accumulation, such as strictly enforced profit margins, in addition to the limited possibility for cross-sector capital investment.

The primary aim was to maintain the balance between production and consumption. After domestic demand, including the other regions of the Empire, was met, it was permissible to export the remaining production, which required a special permit and the payment of a high customs duty. In contrast, importing was free of all constraints, as it was, in parallel with the principle of provisionism, an action confined to the products that were not produced in the Empire or were to a limited extent. In later periods, the capitulations were to be a ramification of this inward-looking strategy (this does not mean that the Ottomans were unaware of the functions of import duties).

The Empire's practice of ensuring decent wages could be suggested to be another pillar of provisionist or demand-sided nature of the Ottoman economy. From the mid-fifteenth century to 1914, researchers have found that, for instance, the wages of Ottoman construction workers in Istanbul increased in real terms. These wages were higher than the amount required for the subsistence of a human being. For example, in the sixteenth century, an unqualified construction worker could buy 8 kg of bread, 2.5 kg of rice or 2 kg of mutton with his daily wage. Qualified construction workers earned one-and-a-half to two times more than their unqualified colleagues. These rates were close to those in Antwerp, Amsterdam, Paris and London. A similar trend can be observed in the real wages of construction workers, which increased by more than 300 times between 1489 and 1914 (Pamuk, 2000: Chapter IV and VI).

ii. *Traditionalism*: The principle of provisionism created its own consolidating associate, traditionalism, which averted the de-accumulation of accumulated structures. In agriculture and commerce, the key concern in this respect was to eliminate the possibility of scarcity due to a small decrease in production or a small increase in consumption. The *men-i isrâf*, sumptuary laws, hence aimed to preserve this balance by inhibiting luxury consumption. The supply side was also subject to controls, except for a surplus amount that would finance the purchase of compulsory import goods. The reason was that the interchange of capital or labour in various sectors would destabilise the established balances.

Another ramification of traditionalism was that the basic source of knowledge in economic regulation was shariah. The central principle of dispute resolution in economic transactions was *not to do business in opposition to established traditions*. Yet, the areas not explicitly or implicitly regulated by shariah were regulated by other means such as *Kanunnâme*, codes of law, issued by the *padişah* as the head of the Empire, or customs and mores. These secondary sources were binding, as they were also codified as a complementary institution to the general principles of shariah.

iii. *Fiscalism*: This principle entails increasing state income and preventing its decline as strictly as possible, requiring budgetary austerity. In the Empire, the state's opportunities to cultivate additional income from the economy were bounded, as productivity and the level of production in the economic structure were low and limited, transportation was gruelling and costly and production for markets was constrained. The volume of monetary transactions was also restricted, as it entailed the potential to create financially powerful new strata to challenge political control over the socio-economic system and thereby destroy institutional balances between fiscalism and provisionism. A complementary institution to this strategy, the system of *narh*, price control, was implemented as a *de facto* constraint on the rate of profits that artisans and merchants could obtain: that they were not to exceed the rate of 15 per cent. It was not necessarily levied on a regular basis during periods of economic stability; the aim of the narh was to curtail exorbitant prices on commodities through frequent inspections and lasted until the mid-nineteenth century. Pamuk (2003: 90–91) concludes that narh lists were only prepared during periods of scarcity, monetary fluctuations and extraordinary instabilities from the sixteenth century onwards. It resumed, nevertheless, with the increasing number of wars and deteriorating financial balances, continuing until the second quarter or even the middle of the nineteenth century.

These three principles illustrate that the Ottoman state extensively regulated private production through precisely defined rules and selectively enforced price controls. The Empire also intervened directly. It owned more than half of the agricultural land and always represented the largest share of physical capital investment, including nearly all mines and metallurgical plants. In addition, the Ottoman state directly built or controlled certain areas of investment, such as bedestans, bazaars, dyehouses and so on that required vast amounts of capital, or maintained them as public property through the *waqfs*. Furthermore, the state regulated the labour market by adjusting the mobility of the *reâya* and the number of craftsmen, *kalfa* and apprentices among the city artisans (*esnaf*).

Despite such substantial direct involvement by the Ottoman state in economic matters, the essence of its interventionism was, in a systemic sense, its tax strategy. The Ottoman state divided all assets and real estate, including workshops, market places, mills, docks, custom gates and so on, into three parts according to the their incomes: *has*, *zeâmet* and *timar*, representing, respectively, the most to the least income-yielding parts. The incomes of the first two were assigned to the sultan or high-ranked state officials as their salaries. The last was left to the *timariot*. In the Ottoman system, there were two types of taxes. According to the first, *Şer'i*, Muslim and non-Muslim subjects were subject to the *öşür* (tithe) and *harac* taxes, respectively, that equalled one-tenth and from one-tenth to one-half of the harvest according to the size of the land. Non-Muslims were also subject to the *cizye*, in proportion to their financial power, due to their exemption from military service. In addition, there were, *inter alia*, traditional taxes such as the *çift resmi* (land tax) for Muslims and *ispence* for non-Muslims and the *avâriz* that were collected during extraordinary periods such as wars and so on. The *timar* system constituted the mainstay of the Empire's economic strategy of adapting the main principles of Islamic taxation to its geocultural realities. The right to collect taxes from state lands, entitled *miri*, was granted to the *timariot* with the aim of sustaining their participation in a *sipahi*-heavy military force and its self-control to improve participation during wartime. It can be suggested that the organisation, harvesting and taxing of agricultural production and the formation of a regular army were the basic tenets of societal reproduction and fiscal and economic structure in the Empire (İnalcık, 1994).

The *iltizam*, another pattern of taxation, involved granting the enforcive right to collect taxes to the *multezim*, the tax-farmer, who paid a substantial sum to acquire this right for one to three years. Arising from the ranks of capital-owners, high-ranking officials from the military class, the *ulema*, moneychangers and, to a certain extent, the merchants, *multezims* collected taxes and exchanged a certain amount of in-kind taxes from a given tax, the *mukataa*, into cash and delivered it to the state in a predetermined amount. Over time, part of the timar system was converted into the latter for meeting the state's need for cash, primarily for financing budget deficits, as the *iltizams* began to be sold to capitalists including the non-Muslim *sarrâfs*. Gathering pace in the second half of the seventeenth century, this strategy aimed to reduce budgetary expenditures by granting the right of *iltizam* to a group of *ulufeli*, the salaried class, who came from the ranks of the central army and bureaucracy (Darling, 2006). In parallel with the state's inspection of the timariot, the mukataas of those multezims who decided to impose an amount in excess of that stipulated by the central government were immediately cancelled and their *muaccele*, advance payments, were not refunded.

The state enjoyed a strong financial position until the second half of the sixteenth century, due to the additional incomes yielded by conquests. Yet, in the second half of the century, the state resorted to short-term financing from Jewish bankers, authorising them to participate in the largest *iltizam* auctions with effective privilege; these bankers thereby secured the right to do business in the most attractive mukataas. Towards the end of the second half of the century, due to increasing financial challenges, the state commenced to borrow without interest from high-ranked officials including the sultan, viziers and so on. The most significant impact of the financial depression was the dissolution of the timar system. With the pressure of rising inflation and devaluations, the timar system became marginalised for both peasants and the timariot, as their incomes began to lose value and extraordinary taxes such as *avaris* were imposed with increasing frequency. (Therefore, the *iltizam* system came to prevail over a wider segment of society.) Akdağ (1963: 65–6) notes that:

> Even at the beginning of the 16th century, like the ordinary public, the government also suffered from the scarcity of money. The fact that the sons of Beyazıd II, then provincial governors, were in bad straits appears to be solid evidence of this.

The retreating level of income resulted in the fact that many of the Kapıkulu soldiers entered into commercial activities, used their salaries (*ulufe*), at times by pooling, as capital for interim usury and exploited the public by sharing the land of peasants, whom they lent to, at a lower cost ... Deriving de facto power from the treasury and the *waqfs*, an evil group (*ehl-i şer*) from the *Kadı*, müderris and müfti, in addition to *multezims*, embarked upon farming and animal feeding by obtaining vineyards and orchards and arable fields and plains in the villages.

The dissolution of the timar system coerced the peasants to migrate to the city centres to work in the crafts or merchant businesses, and the regression of the central state's coercive power over the periphery sparked off the *Celâli* rebellions, a structural indicator of the marginalisation of social balances. The *umerâ*, governors and high-ranking officials in the provinces organised their own armed forces and employed mercenaries in these armies. Unemployed ex-peasants were among those who participated in these armies, entitled *sekban*, which rioted against and defeated the military forces of the central administration in certain areas. In 1698, *sekban* troops marched towards Istanbul, and the state had to come to terms with these troops. As an alternative to these troops, the state attempted to collaborate with a group of local notables and representatives of the ordinary public, *the ayans*, who came from the ranks of the military classes, merchants or capital owners, the *ulemâ*, provincial governors or *kadı*. In the seventeenth century, the ayans began to gain the status of *mütesellim*, entitling them to collect taxes from *reâya*, commerce, guilds in the cities and the other sources at the *sancaks*. As an intermediary agent of surplus transmission, they established patronage links with high-ranked officials and took control of the *mukataas* in the eighteenth century, and their structural power culminated in the *Sened-i İttifak* (1808) agreement recognising the power of the *âyan* and declaring the *âyan*'s commitment to the Sultan.

In addition to the dissolution of the timar system as a result of social confusion, military stagnation, reducing tax incomes from conquered lands and the rising number of salaried *Kapıkulu* cavalry overburdened the Empire's finances. To assuage this burden, the Empire, *inter alia*, resorted to a devalutionary monetary strategy. The Empire had a bi-metal system and regulated the relative exchange value of gold and silver coins. At the end of the sixteenth century, the Ottoman state began to devalue silver coins, and then in the eighteenth century, gold coins also came to be a means to issue more money in the market and thus provide additional income (seigniorage) to the treasury (Pamuk, 2003: 113–5). The 1585 *tağşiş* (debasement) to finance budget deficits was, in this sense, a turning point for the Empire's monetary policy. As a result, rising prices and diminishing purchasing power prompted *Yeniçeri*, Janissaries, to revolt in a number of instances. In 1589, for example, the Janissaries demanded and obtained the execution of the chief treasurer and other state officials they considered responsible for paying their *ulufes* (salaries) in debased coins. In due course, to compensate for their decreasing level of income, as noted above, they engaged in craft and commerce (Faroqhi, 1994: 434).

The artisan and merchant guilds also encountered operational challenges as a result of continuing static *narh* and *ihtisab* rules despite rising inflation and an increased cost of raw materials. As they could not compete with the European merchants in various foods and raw materials such as leather, cotton and so on, they had to apply to the state for export protection. In compliance with its provisionist strategy, the state did not implement effective measures to constrain imports. Furthermore, in commercial diplomacy, the Ottomans did not abstain from granting unilateral privileges and exemptions to the rivals of their rivals, such as Venetians, the French or the British, to secure their dominance of Mediterranean commerce. With the exploration of the India road through the circumnavigation of South Africa and thus the emergence of the risk of the dislocation of the commercial roads passing through the Middle East to the oceans, the Ottomans began to recognise privileges, entitled capitulations, to attract European merchants to the Mediterranean. These privileges consisted of engaging in commerce and making a journey, transporting their goods from one location to another in the Empire, using the ships carrying the flag of their own nations and so on. With the extension of their operational scope, these merchants were granted the right to settle their commercial disputes in these courts.

In addition, customs duties were kept at a minimum, even lower than those faced by national merchants in most cases. With the decline of the Ottoman's political power in the seventeenth and eighteenth centuries due to the rise of the European nations, the European merchants rushed to extend the ambit of these capitulations. The Armenian, Rum and Jewish merchants in the Empire also began to affiliate themselves with these merchants to appropriate these privileges that placed them in a more advantageous position than their Ottoman counterparts (Eldem, 2006). Moreover, the minority merchants financed the multezims, *âyans* and the farm-owners and collected agricultural goods for export. Over time, the Europeans collaborated with the minority merchants to utilise their interior networks to organise commercial linkages between the Empire and the outside world.

The regression of the Empire's central enforcive power to regulate and sustain financial balances not only resulted in the diminution of its operational scope in international commerce but also in the gradual loss of its internal financial autonomy to various groups of capitalists. From the mid-eighteenth century onwards, in this context, the moneychangers began to provide short-run credit to the Ottoman state. Moreover, they managed the individual wealth of the Ottoman Sultans and bureaucrats and gained control of the market for commercial paper, thereby becoming financial capitalists specialising in money and credit affairs. Founding their first bank in the 1840s, they were called 'Galata bankers'. The Armenian members of the moneychanger guild were assigned to the managerial positions of the *Darphane-i Amire*, the Ottoman mint. In the 1840s, the affiliated members of the Galata bankers increased in number to encompass the Jewish and the Levantines coming from Europe. However, they had to compete with the European banks and bankers that provided long-term credit to the Ottomans, gaining substantive power with the foundation of the Ottoman Bank (Pamuk, 2010: 64–74).

Thus, the Empire's economic policies ebbed and flowed between a commitment to Islamic theory as the structural background of its social system and adaptation to practical exigencies to ensure the state's *bekâ* (permanence). The Empire's policy of international commerce, as discussed above, is a case in point. The foremost proof of the Ottomans' economic pragmatism lies, however, in their surreptitious approbation of interest-bearing credit transactions and the utilisation of state-provided tax incomes by a minority of high-ranking state officials to invest in trade and land to acquire profits. In principle, there was a relatively developed non-interest credit financing system. However, exceptionally, interest-bearing transactions were also conditionally approved for social purposes. The principality of non-interest and exceptionality of interest-bearing credit funding, I believe, well illustrates the pragmatic boundaries of the match between the Empire's theory and praxis in the form of delicate balances. What makes this pragmatism more extensive in the Ottoman social system is the functionalisation of interest-bearing transactions under the title of one of the pivotal institutions of the Empire, the *waqfs*. A closer examination of these relatively cosmopolitan interlinkages would furnish us with a more nuanced perspective.

During the middle ages, in Islamic societies, alternative financing methodologies were developed such as various business partnerships and credit arrangements, debt transfers and letters of credit and so on, to the extent that throughout the twelfth and the thirteenth centuries, in the Eastern Mediterranean, credit and finance institutions were more advanced than in Western and Southern Europe. Ottoman credit and finance institutions remained within this tradition without being affected by the developments in Europe until the end of the seventeenth century. In particular, it is obvious that there was pronounced economic activity in the Empire funded by credit-financing. Business partnerships were implemented in the manner of *mudaraba, muvafada, inan* or *vucuh* within the basic principles established in Islamic economics, not necessarily for funding productive activities but also for long-distance commerce. In addition, a partnership with a common responsibility for capital, profit and loss, the *mufavada*, was another partnership methodology, albeit with a limited scope. In settling disputes among partners or labourers, the Ottoman jurists used classical Islamic principles as main reference point from the fifteenth to nineteenth centuries (Çizakça, 1996: 64–85).

These types of business partnerships are, as in Islamic theory, geared towards the provision of a solidaristic growth model. In the Empire, another institution was established to provide voluntarist support for solidarism-based social sustenance and dynamism, the *waqfs*. Organised by an Islamically motivated voluntary initiative, the *waqfs* came into being with the allocation of income from a private asset for the public interest and beneficence (Pamuk, 2003: 83–4). (It is a reasonable argument that the Ottomans were, in establishing the waqf institution, influenced by Byzantine, Mesopotamian, Jewish, Buddhist and especially Sasanid traditions: see Çizakça, 2000: 1–26.)

The purpose and the areas in which the wafqs' capital and resources could be used were stated in a deed of endowment, submitted to the public authorities, such that, under ordinary circumstances, even the Sultan could not intervene in their operations. The revenue of a waqf, as stipulated by its founder and managed by a trustee, was earmarked either for a pious purpose or for a group of beneficiaries. The economic magnitude of the *waqfs* represented up to one-third of arable lands in the Empire in the early eighteenth century. This is significant in the sense of redistributing the national income among the haves and the have-nots through a voluntarily organised social transfer mechanism, in addition to their contribution to employment. (At the turn of the twentieth century, the Ottoman *waqfs* employed 8.2 per cent of the total workforce.)

Ottoman *waqfs* would, by all means, be considered as a pivotal component, like the timar system, of the Empire's social system, rather than a mere philanthropic institution because most public goods were provided by the *waqfs*, from education to social aid. These include the foundation of all primary, secondary or higher education institutions (until Tanzimat); the provision of social services, social security and social assistance; offering a great number of services under the responsibility of municipalities, the services of the guilds and the military fraternal services and so on. Although they established commercial centres such as bazaars, *han* (inns) and so on, the public goods the Ottoman *waqfs* provided were in essence aimed at meeting the needs of the underprivileged and the poor rather than those of the general public. The rationale behind this is to *institutionalise* social self-help in compliance with their key principle of operation, *continuity* (Kazıcı, 2003: 128–31). Their possessions comprised a wide range of entities, ranging from shops and residences to production facilities, mosques and so on. In its Ottoman practice, it is assumed that the consecrated tenets of the *waqfs* were in 'Allâh's possession', and the *de facto* ownership of these tenets passed on their users while the absolute ownership rested with Allâh. This means that the waqf endowments could in no way be sold to private persons (Akgündüz, 1988: 110).

In addition to their immense societal functions, the *waqfs* also provided financing. It was within this context that the Cash *Waqfs* in the Ottoman-Empire were established by well-to-do individuals allocating a given amount of their money for *pious* purposes. This amount was lent to borrowers who were required to return an extra amount in addition to the principal, to be transferred to various social purposes. Dated to as early as the beginning of the fifteenth century, this type of *waqfs* became extremely popular by the end of the sixteenth century throughout Anatolia and the Empire's European provinces (Çizakça, 1996: 131).

Çizakça's study indicated that only four of these *waqfs* employed a *mudaraba* style of financing and the rest lent money to borrowers, including moneychangers, with a rate of return of between 9 and 12 per cent. Furthermore, the moneychangers lent the money borrowed from the cash *waqfs* to ordinary customers after adding an extra amount. Another unexpected and astounding reality is that they were 'the trustees who were borrowing from the very endowments that they themselves were managing'. The amounts these trustees borrowed were lent at a higher rate of return to the money dealers, *sarrâfs*, in Istanbul. Therefore, 'a secondary capital market had emerged in the Ottoman economy with the cash *waqfs* providing the cheaper money and the *sarrâfs* re-lending it a higher rate of interest to the merchants and tax-farmers' (Çizakça, 1996: 131–4).

In the Empire, there were two groups who held the greatest amounts of capital, *sarrâfs* and high-ranking state officials. As noted above, *sarrâfs*, the moneychangers, lent to the peasants, guild members and merchants and were involved in commerce and non-agricultural production. The largest moneychangers lived in Istanbul and lent to high-ranking state officials and the state itself. The sarrâfs who undertook transactions concerning government finance departments acquired the greatest fortunes (İnalcık, 1978, Chapter XI1: 137–8). Yet, the high-ranking staff, the *askeri* or the governing elites, holding tax incomes from the high-income-yielding *dirlik* and *zeâmet* was so wealthy that even the largest merchants could not rival even a mid-level member such as a junior governor, *sancakbeyi*, and remained under the control of these political classes (Faroqhi, 1994: 546). The influential groups in the Empire's political cadre were committed to the principle that trade and agriculture should be reserved for private individuals, the taxpaying subjects. An active minority among them, nonetheless, invested their tax incomes in various economic activities including lending and commerce, thereby acquiring substantial profits. Faroqhi (1994: 548, 552) notes: 'Quite a few viziers of the sixteenth century engaged in trade on their own behalf'.

Chapter 4

Burgeoning Secular Capitalism Between Changing Continuities Versus Continuing Path-Dependencies

During the nineteenth century, the Ottoman state encountered an accumulated stock of restructuring dynamics arising out of the economic imbalances, military decadence, social dissolution, political skirmishes and a retreating vision of the Empire in the international division of power. On the one hand, to enforce these restructurings was quite a challenging task, as the Ottoman social system, as discussed above, relied upon delicate balances that started to become unfastened during the second half of the sixteenth century. In this sense, the processes of conjunctural recoveries and then deteriorations stretching forward to the nineteenth century resulted in the accumulation of substantial discontinuities. On the other hand, such a restructuring was an out-and-out requirement for the perpetuation of the Empire's traditional balances, the mainstay of the Ottoman social system. Thus, in the nineteenth century, the panorama of the Ottoman political economy was that its leisurely continuities should be changed in a manner that would not disrupt the building blocks of its continuing path-dependencies. This arduous nexus ineluctably brought capitalism into the very core of the *Empire's civilisational equations* with its inseparable attachment, secularism.

In understanding the intertwined accumulation of Islam, neoliberalism and social democracy throughout Turkey's Republican period, the legacy of the late Ottoman Empire, at this point, acquires a retrospective significance in terms of three parameters: Islam, secularism and capitalism. Amongst them, capitalism was what initiated the secularisation of an Islamically structured, although ethnically mosaical, alignment of the socio-economic foundations of the Ottoman Empire, essentially from the early eighteenth century. Gathering an infusive pace into the interiors of the Empire in the nineteenth century, capitalism, primarily European in origin, resulted in the dissolution of its institutional system on the basis of the weakening of the harmony among civic dynamics and the political management of economic processes, the economic crisis of the Empire in the face of rising European dominance, the de-accumulation of its embedded structures and the beginning of a reinstitutionalisation initiative by the *Bâb-ı* Ali, the *Sublime Porte* and, overall, a widening disjunction among the state, economy and society. The evolutionary dynamics of the Ottoman political economy in the period 1808–1918 can be seen at Table 4.1. This sub-section examines these dynamics, as can be seen in the table, in the light of the analytic apparatuses of the institutional system analysis.

The impact of capitalism was not only entwined with the volume of economic exchange but also with the dynamics of civilisational and institutional formations, reformations and changes in the face of structural chaos, crisis and exhaustion. One of these substantial dynamics, secularism, the major source of the tension between capitalism and Islam, came to be the main anchor of countercyclical forces, primarily the ITF (The Party of Union and Progress), which defended, as detailed below, the subjugation of religion to rationality in the organisation of Ottoman society, from political authority to inter-human relationships. With this mindset, they vehemently denounced the Empire's institutional stock for impeding the genesis of an *Ottoman Renaissance*. The consequence was that, from the early eighteenth century onwards, the reciprocal stress among Islam, capitalism and secularism left its mark on the change, path-dependency and path-dependent changes of Ottoman-Turkish institutions. Moreover, the paradigmatic repercussion of this tension over time manifested itself in the dialectic evolution of Islam, liberalism and social democracy.

The ebb and flow of Islamic and secular reformism in the Empire took root in the early eighteenth century, specifically from the Tulip Era onwards, the period following the Treaty of Passrovits (1718), when the Ottoman ruling elite recognised European ascendancy and set the stage for the discovery of European capitalism by delegating a staffer in 1720, *Çelebi Mehmet*, to make observations and file a report on the socio-political and -economic structure of France, the gateway to the Empire's modernisation (Europeanisation) adventure. While having a symbolic connotation at first glance, this case was to lay the ground for the methodology of cultivating the philosophy or substance of institution-building (including the social democratic ones erected in the second half of the twentieth century) in the Ottoman-Turkish political economy. This methodology was pursued through the feedback contributed by the agency of those Ottoman or Turkish figures delegated, particularly for educational purposes, to pivotal Western countries, the foreign experts or academics employed at indigenous educational institutions such as military or medical schools that were founded in the second half of the eighteenth century. These schools, such the *Hendeshane*, the school of military engineering, became the gateway for the introduction of modern sciences to the Empire through the translation of books on geometry, physics, medicine and so on into the Ottoman language (military and medical schools, in the second half of the nineteenth century, were to become shelters of countercyclical movements). *Translation* was therefore to become the core formal *institution* interconnecting the Empire with Europe.

The impacts of the eighteenth century represented a threshold for the embodiment and infusion of the pattern of a dependent modernisation strategy on the part of the Empire on the road to *Tanzimat* (1839), the Reorganisation. Out of this reorganisation emerged a more programmed, integrated process of modernisation following the transitional period of the reign of Selim III (1789–1807), the first real countercyclical actor in the Empire's modernisation history. He undertook a vigorous reform package entitled *Nizam-ı Cedid*, the New Order,

Table 4.1 Evolution of the Empire's institutional system, 1808–1918

The period	Institutional environment	Major actors and strategies	Power relations	Path-dependent changes
1808–76	–Systemic de-accumulation of Ottoman Islam under the pressure of politico-economic restructuration –Accumulating engagement between the social structure and market capitalism and the commercialisation of agricultural production –A slow de-accumulation of guild-based production dynamics –Rise, fall and resurgence of state-led industrialisation	–Mahmud II and the consecutive Tanzimat bureaucracy: to restructure the main institutional stock under an equivocal blend of normative and rational conditionalities –Rising countercyclical intellectual crusade by the Young Ottomans against Tanzimat reformers with a demand on normative-conditioning of institutional changes	–Reestablishment of the structural power of the state over the periphery by centralising the tax collection system and suppressing the economic power of local notables –The declaration of the Constitutional Monarchy of 1876	Changing continuities in the face of continuing path-dependencies: Dualisation of the institutional stock through modernising secular and state-led market reforms under the constraints and accumulated dynamics of the embedded Islamic and conventional establishment
1876–1908	–Rising tensions among Islam, secularism and capitalism –Increasing financial dependence, budgetary constraints and economic downturns –Peripheralisation in the international division of production	–Abdulhamit II and his pro-cyclical bureaucratic allies: blending rationalist modernisations with convalescent Islamic normativity through adapting a balancing posture between diplomatic and authoritarian political action –ITF: militarily-organised, elitist crusade against the Abdulhamid administration –European capitalists and Galata bankers: to capitalise raw material and internal market demand under quite low import taxes free from domestic customs and engaging in loan-based financial extraction and control over state revenues	–Abdulhamit's success in perpetuating its power and decelerating civilisational downturn –Initial failure but accumulating enforcive power of the ITF cadres in the declaration of the Second Constitutional Monarchy of 1908	Continuing path-dependencies in the face of changing continuities: re-consolidation of the Empire's normative political dynamics with overseas impact (Pan-Islamism) challenged and ultimately subdued by the rationalising impact of continuing institutional reforms and the ITF-led coup d'état of 1908
1908–18	–Initiation of the process of systemic secularisation of the Empire's institutional stock –Accumulating dynamics of military-dominated, nationalist politico-economic infrastructure	ITF: to execute a top-down and overall institutional design, to accelerate industrialising attempts with a nationalistic niche	ITF's infusion into the educated social classes, composing a dedicated bureaucracy to its own ideals, banning organised action and purging intra-party liberal and Islamic lines by wielding conspiratorial tactics	Continuing changes with path-dependent discontinuities: De-accumulation of Islamic spirit of bureaucratic establishment, Waqf-centred paternalist egalitarianism and solidaristically organised economic governance

conditioning the restructuring of state finances and administration in addition to the establishment of new military and naval schools, a second state-of-the-army independent of the Janissaries and provincial troops (Shaw, 1979: 1–54). As it would dislodge the then basic structural axes of the Empire's political economy, the pro-cyclical actors triggered a mutiny and toppled Selim III, claiming that he had come under the control of *Frenks* and the *Nizam-ı Cedid* was intended to destroy the institutional harmony settled by religious pillars (the strongholds of these actors were the ulema, the Janissaries [the royal army], the *Âyan* [local notables] and even some of Selim's own ministers, who vetoed the change through a bottom-up social uprising). This was the first, but not the last, structural power skirmish between the pro- and countercyclical actors during the first genuine reformation/ modernisation of Ottoman institutions: because a continuing structural power resource was available to the subversive ruling class, the countercyclical actors. The Empire was in the midst of a drift process due to losing ground in territorial integrity, economic stability and political grandeur, and there was no alternative exit from the embedded structure. Mahmut II (1808–39) transformed this resource into a path-making opportunity, who, despite his tactical manoeuvre at the outset of his rule to ally with the Janissaries and local notables and sign a letter of agreement (*Sened-i İttifak*, 1808), advocated for Selim III's layering reforms. He did so by annihilating the Janissary corps in a despotic manner, consolidated state power over society, essentially through recentralisation and the foundation of a new officialdom. In the context of this recentralisation he organised the central government into ministries and established new military, naval, engineering and medical schools to train new elites and curb the clout of many of the provincial power holders, essentially the âyans (Neumann, 2006: 60).

In complete opposition to their pre-existing counterparts, the new military and central bureaucracy, the majority of whom came from the secularly educated strata, were the key coalitional forces for the Sultan as the then prime countercyclical, subversive actor (Ali, Fuat and Reşit Pashas). The leader cadre of Tanzimat Era (1839–76) were all graduates of *Tercüme Odası*, the Translation Bureau. In parallel with the transitory structure of the Tanzimat epoch, these individuals and their leaders, the Pashas, held diverse viewpoints ranging from liberal and European sympathisers to conservative and anti-European ones (Ortaylı, 2006: 96). It was these absolutist and central new bureaucratic officials, although functioning within a dualistic structure along with the traditional bureaucratic system, who launched a new array of reforms under the banner of Tanzimat. In its quintessence, Tanzimat had become a transition period between Islamism and secularism that witnessed the introduction of equal citizenship, a common citizenship, Ottomanism, for Muslims and the other ethnic and religious groups, the security of private property, life and honour with a ubiquitous emphasis on the fact that the Empire's decline primarily stemmed from disobedience to *Şeriat*, Islamic law.

Tanzimat bureaucrats enforced far-flung codifications ranging from trade and punishment to the law of real property, thereby paving the way for the dualisation of political and religious establishments by isolating the latter from the former. Their methodology was first to delve into the legal codes of various European countries and then to conflate them with an *alaturca* spirit, as in the Constitution of 1876 (Ortaylı, 2006: 123). Tanzimat statesmen carried out these reforms discretionally, sparingly and pragmatically to arrive at a middle ground between tradition and modernisation. Yet their pragmatic reformism evolved into, one generation later, a political ideology, group and individual skirmishes and triggered a programmed opposition in the second half of the century, especially following the *Islahat Fermanı*, The Edict of 1856, which further consolidated the equality of citizenship among Ottoman subjects irrespective of their religious affiliation, granting the non-Muslims the right to become civil servants, pay the same amount of tax as Muslims, establish their own councils to govern their internal affairs and so on.

The mounting resentment among the Muslim subjects in the face of absolutist enforcement of the Tanzimat reforms, the retrogression of Islamic law in the central administration and the increasingly privileged position of the Christian minorities of the Empire under the aegis of the European powers not only found expression in conspiracies, popular uprisings and anti-Christian riots such as those in Syria in 1860, but also engendered a second generation of reformists, veto players over the Tanzimat reformists (Zürcher, 2010: 74). The Young Ottomans, *Jeunes Turcs* to use the title they were known by in Europe, unleashed an intellectual crusade against Tanzimat reformism and unanimously advocated supplanting the absolutist regime with a parliamentary monarchy, although they held divergent views on how to bring it off. They thought that, by this way, the ruler and the government would be brought under the control of the representatives of the people, the organs of which were envisaged by their prominent figure, Namık Kemal, as *Şura-yı Devlet* (the council of state), a *Şura-yı Ümmet* (national assembly) and *Meclis-i Âyan* (a senate).

Their critique focused on three points: the economic plight of the masses, the political marginality and dependence on the European powers and the financial follies of the ruling strata. Their enduring anti-Western posture notwithstanding, methodologically, they supported modernisation, but not the unconditional imitation, of industrial, economic, educational institutions under the indigenous discretion of the Ottoman state rather than the pressure of European forces. Namık Kemal, who was to play a pivotal role in the making of the Constitution of 1876, denounced the Tanzimat reforms in this regard, on the grounds that they undermined the historical existence of the Muslim community and the Islamic foundations of the state. Islam was, to him, the unique social system associating moral virtue with justice and superior to the philosophical reasoning of the European mindset (Berkes, 1964: 204–18).

In December 1876, the *Kânun-i Esâsi* (The Basic Law), which legalised the First Constitutional Monarchy, was promulgated by Abdülhamid II to quiet the abovementioned internal social unrest and outmanoeuvre the European, primarily Russian, offensive against the Balkan provinces, which was to be negotiated at the international Istanbul Conference, discussing how to further the European hold on the Ottoman economy and government. This occurred following a series of meetings imbued with political skirmishes among their attendants (the socio-political elites, namely the religious, administrative and military dignitaries and two pre-eminent figures of the Young Ottomans, Kemal and Ziya. Stipulating a two-house assembly, one to be chosen by public and the other by Padisah himself, the Constitution granted the Padisah the right to dismiss the National Assembly and prorogue the Constitution (Tanör, 1992: 104–18). In the case of a disagreement between the assembly and the government, the Padisah had the right to dismiss one or both of them.

After two years, in February 1878, Abdülhamit prorogued the Constitution and parliament until 1908, when the new group of secularly minded reformists, the Young Turks, reproclaimed it and inaugurated the era of Second Constitutional Monarchy in 1908. Despite his absolutist vision, Abdülhamid II maintained the Tanzimat's regulatory and rationalising, but not secularising, reforms as a firm believer in the necessity of modernisation, promoted the functional effectiveness of higher education institutions, pushed for the establishment of telegraph and railroad networks throughout the state, updated the agricultural system, constructed industrial establishments and so on. In addition, it was during his reign that private enterprise gained momentum and the first modern Muslim bourgeoisie emerged, initially in the agrarian and then in the commercial sector. In view of Abdülhamit's reformist initiatives, Karpat (2001: 204) notes that, in essence, without this relative ease in the socio-cultural agenda, the Young Turks era and the foundation of the Republic would have been unimaginable.

Abdülhamid, thanks to his diplomatic skills in shifting between authoritarianism and reformism, was able to calm the social tension at the top of the political pyramid but could not hinder the formation of an elitist and arcane political organisation in the underground, the Young Turk movement. Inspiring the genesis of this countercyclical movement was the reconsolidation of the religious establishment under the reign of Abdulhamit II, the weakening of the Ottoman state in the face of external forces and the encroachments of foreigners and local Christians (Zürcher, 2010: 72). In retrospect, the first revolutionary ideas among the Movement's members were taking root in higher education institutions, primarily in the medical schools and, to a lesser extent, the schools of engineering, veterinary medicine, law, civil service and commerce that were Westernised, cosmopolitan and comfortable with a foreign language and culture, mostly French (Berkes, 1964: 275).

Offering a relatively strong coalitional feedback was the expansion of secular education and the secularising impact of the press with its widening scope and impact by opening the people's mind to the material world. The Movement aimed at re-establishing the constitutional and parliamentary regime with the aim of *saving the state*. While they were crushed in 1896, after a 10-year interval, they regrouped as *İttihâk ve Terâkki Fırkası* – ITF, The Committee of Union and Progress. Following their defeat, the reformists were primarily active as exiles in Cairo, Geneva and particularly in Paris during the interval when the movement crystallised into two distinct factions: the nationalist and centralist one around

Ahmet Rıza, *İttihad ve Terakki Cemiyeti* – the Community of Union and Progress – and the liberal and decentralist one around Prince Sabahattin *Teşebbüs-ü Şahsi ve Adem-i Merkeziyet Cemiyeti* – the League for Private Initiative and Decentralisation (Hanioğlu, 2008).

From 1906 onwards, the Young Turks' progress gathered pace, especially among the Ottoman armies in European Turkey, and then the military influence in the Movement grew rapidly (Zürcher, 2010: 74–5). This progress unfolded where the Christian bourgeoisie was at the forefront of societal life in the Balkans, the Agean and İstanbul, both providing them with a model of modernity and agitating their reactionary sentiments, as they lived at the margin of the increasing wealth and power of the non-Muslims. The vast majority of the ITF's leading force, the members of which included Enver, Cemal and Mustafa Kemal Pashas, who played critical roles throughout the period, were the graduates of higher education institutions providing secular education and a career in the state. Expectedly, their secular education imbued them with a science-focused, materialist worldview. Moreover, some of them were also influenced by European thinkers. The prominent among them were Ziya Gökalp by Emile Durkheim, Prince Sabahattin by Camile Demolins and Ahmet Rıza by Auguste Comte. Under the impact of their theoretical and practical observations, their international vision came to be a part of the Europe-centred regional and world system, not as peripheral forces but as partners such as Japan (Mardin, 2000: 166–8).

The ITF-led coup d'état of 1908 ultimately forced Abdülhamid to restore the Constitution of 1876, symbolising the Second Constitutional Monarchy of 1908. This coup d'état was not a large-scale popular uprising or a liberal reform movement, but a well-planned military insurrection outlined and executed in European Turkey by a conspiratorial organisation, the ITF (Hanioğlu, 2001: 210–278). The first five years of constitutional government, founded by the members of the Islamic, liberal and the secular nationalist factions of the ITF, were marked by a constant struggle for political power in which the last group, the core cadre of the organisation, ultimately emerged victorious. Capturing power in 1913, following a military coup d'état, the *Raid on the Sublime Porte*, by eliminating the liberal and Islamist segments, under the rule of secular nationalists, the ITF governed the Empire until the end of the World War I. As a ruling group, the ITF sought to maintain itself in power, first by gaining the support of the military and attempting to manipulate it. After achieving a certain compromise with the army, which had become preoccupied with the War, the Unionists sought organisational support from the lower- and mid-level intellectuals, lower ranking bureaucrats, some army officers and a variety of aspiring economic groups in the countryside, such as small merchants and petty landowners (Karpat, 2001: 208).

The consequence was that the ITF never became a mass party to mobilise the masses to restructure the country. Although they did not overtly outlaw political parties and parliament to capitalise on its legitimising force, they were convinced that a strong parliament would undermine the regime and aggravate ethno-religious conflict. With such an authoritarian viewpoint, since 1908, the Unionists had come to believe that the complete transformation of the entire fabric of their society was necessary to save and rejuvenate the decaying structure. Maintaining the *status quo*, as the Ottoman liberals proposed, would prove suicidal, and a social revolution that would take Turkey into the modern world was vital for its survival (Ahmad, 2003: 40).

Economic Nationalism, Paternalist Egalitarianism and Authoritarian Interventionism

In the nineteenth century, the economic recession in the Empire, combined with continuing losses in war and budgetary constraints, resulted in a number of changes. The economic power of local notables was suppressed, and the tax system was centralised. Continuing debasements, rising inflation and diminishing tax revenues brought about a large stock of domestic and foreign debt borrowed from the Galata Bankers and European capitalists. The accumulating financial dependency of the Empire on European capital from the 1854 onwards in conjunction with increasing borrowing rates and higher interest payments, a process that accelerated in the mid-nineteenth century, resulted in the moratorium of 1875–76. *Düyun-u Umumiye*, the Ottoman Public Debt Organisation, was founded in 1881 to authorise European finance capital to collect a part of tax revenue to service the Empire's debts (Issawi, 1980: 383–4). In addition to its strong hold on the public sector, Western European capital also obtained substantial competitive power in the Ottoman private market. The *Baltalimanı* Free Trade Treaty, which remained in force until the end of the World War I, abolished the Empire's monopoly power (in imposing export/import bans or quantity limitations or extraordinary trade taxes) over foreign trade. It first drove export duties up to 12 per cent and then down to 1 per cent between 1860 and 1861 and initially levied import duties of 5 per cent and then increased them to 8 per cent in 1861, in addition to exempting foreign merchants from paying domestic customs.

In the face of the economic downturn, beginning in the 1830s, the Ottoman state embarked on establishing factories using steam engines with the aim of meeting the needs of the army. At the end of this decade, the productive capacity of these factories exceeded the military's needs and their products began to be sold on free markets. The process of the Empire's industrialisation gathered pace in the 1840s with new investments in sectors such as leather, weaving, foods, glass, porcelain, paper and so on and paved the way for the establishment of factories producing investment goods. In the 1850s, state investment to establish new plants came to an end, and the state introduced subsidies and investment facilities for private enterprise. This was because most of the previously established factories had to be closed due to their incapacity to resist import competition, which also caused traditional crafts to lose ground and demand that the state impose protective measures. Although the state did not take these demands seriously at the time, it complied with this demand during the 1860s, as noted above, by sacrificing the principle of fiscalism and raising import duties. In the 1880s, domestic industries began to be protected through differentiated import customs duties.

The second wave of industrialisation in the 1880s with an open-economy structure, in comparison to the first, was relatively resistant to foreign competition in the sectors where the cost of labour and raw material was relatively advantageous for competition in import goods. The artisans in the cities, despite their attempts to adapt themselves to the new circumstances and their resistance in certain sectors in which transportation costs were expensive, could not compete with the European goods, especially in sectors such as textiles where transportation costs were not high. Yet, by becoming specialised in labour-intensive branches, they maintained their existence until the end of the Empire (Quataert [1999] challenges the thesis of a unilinear and plummeting decline in Ottoman manufacturing). In the late nineteenth century, the Ottoman state began to directly engage in international competition for commerce by establishing infrastructural investments (primarily railroads, mining, water, gas and electric) using foreign debt. These investments, especially the railroads, aimed to operationalise the Empire's new role in the international division of labour, exporting raw materials and importing manufactured goods from Europe (Pamuk, 1994: 16–36).

The ITF's economic strategies shifted the route of the Ottoman economy towards a secular and etatist liberalism. During the first years following the 1908 coup d'état, in fact, the ITF first attempted to establish a liberal regime, claiming to provide a stable investment environment for entrepreneurs, increasing the tax-paying power of the masses and so on. Cavit Bey, the Minister of Finance in the ITF governments, was an ardent liberal, claiming that 'there would not be equality between the various income levels, as there is not equality between human beings'. Yet the liberalisation caused small-sized artisans to lose ground under difficult competitive conditions while consolidating that of non-Muslims and foreigners, who monopolised Ottoman commercial life. In addition, the Ottoman state was unable to import even 3 per cent of the goods that it had imported before the war. In reaction to this dichotomous result, the ITF, after consolidating its power in 1913, adopted a *national economy* perspective under the aegis of the German historical school.

Ziya Gökalp, a Durkhemian social analyst and the most influential social theorist in the ITF, contended that liberal economics is the economics of advanced capitalist countries, such as Britain, to exploit the national wealth of the less developed nations. Instead, by adopting an organic solidarity, the Empire would acquire self-sustaining economic power through its own internal dynamics on the basis of the fact that *national demand creates national supply*. The state's role was to provide all of the opportunities to the ethnically Muslim-Turk entrepreneurs by subsidising their participation in industrial, commercial and financial activities to increase economic welfare. Ethnic unity was a prerequisite, as a multi-cultural society could not yield the *organic division of labour* necessary to forge this productive motivation.

In this context, adapting Freidrich List's 'political economy' approach, the ITF planned to construct *national unity* through organic integration among the country's political, economic and cultural *facts*. The consequence was the interventionist and organiser economic policy of the Empire (Toprak, 1982). With the outbreak of World War I, the capitulations were cancelled unilaterally in 1914 (to be reimposed with the Treaty of Sevres of 1920), specific customs duties were imposed gradually at a rate of 15 and then 30 per cent, exchange transactions were controlled by *Kambiyo Muamelatı Merkez Komisyonu*, the Exchange Transactions Central Committee, with the aim of protecting the young industries in the country, and a national bank, *Osmanlı İtibâr-ı Milli Bankası*, was founded in 1917 in the form of a publicly owned investment bank to finance the development projects of all types. As a complementary step, the Anatolian branches of the ITF organised the operationally strong Muslim merchants by founding credit and sales cooperatives.

With the declaration of the Second Constitutional Monarchy, the number of corporations notably increased, especially national corporations between 1914 and 1918. Foreign capital was, until the World War I, considered indispensable for economic development and allowed investments to be made, between 1908 and 1913, on the basis of foreign-domestic capital partnerships. (Between 1849 and 1907, 86 corporations were founded, and this figure increased to 236 during the period 1908–18.) Despite this judicial allowance, as a part of the nationalist strategy for economic development during World War I, the ITF did not hesitate to confiscate certain strategic corporations such as ports, railways and so on owned by foreign capital. For the ITF, the unique way of forging a modern Empire was the genesis of a *Turkish bourgeoisie*.

Its major attempt to achieve this purpose was to issue a subsidy law to enhance the national entrepreneurship, *Teşvik-i Sanayi Kanunu*, The Law Encouraging Industry of 1913. The abolition of the right to strike in 1909, in the immediate aftermath of the mounting waves of strikes after the endorsement of this right in 1908, was rooted in this ideal of creating a national bourgeoisie. Direct involvement by the ITF's members was another way of executing this strategy. Kara Kemal, one of its leading members, for example, founded a corporation named *Heyet-i Mahsusa-i Ticariyye* to meet the demands of Istanbul's inhabitants for basic goods during the war years. Another example, *Anadolu Milli Mahsulat Osmanlı Anonim Şirketi*, was founded by the same individual to buy and sell goods such as cereals, wool, leather and so on.

In a partial divergence from the change in the path-dependence of the Ottomans' classical provisionist, traditionalist and fiscalist strategy by the ITF towards more nationalist, secular, interventionist and capitalist lines, the ITF chose to perpetuate the then existing social welfare and labour relations regimes to a great extent. This can be understood based on the fact that the ITF was initially a militarist organisation that would be assumed, at best, to cultivate a paternalist egalitarianism in social policy and an unconflictual compromise with the working classes. These two strategies did not require making essential changes, but the perpetuation of the status quo. As the ITF's main strategy was to establish an independent national economy under an authoritarian political regime throughout the rather volatile decade between 1908 and 1918, this consequence was not unanticipated, apart from the institutionalisation of an inchoate social security regime.

The mainstay of the change in the Ottomans' voluntaristically organised centripetal welfare system was the centralisation of the waqfs' financial accounts under state budget and gradual formalisation of their administrative structures through emerging bureaucratic apparatuses. Thus, state primarily took on the role of protecting the poor by making monthly and yearly payments to *muhtacin*, the needy. Following the decentralisation of the state administration, the mayoralties began to protect, feed and meet the health needs of the poor, orphans, widows and so on. A partially modern advance in this period was the institutionalisation of retirement and health services in the wake of the establishment of civil officialdom as a permanent pattern of employment in the public sector. In the second half of the century, the retirement system, institutionalised under *Tekâud Sandıkları*, the Retirement Funds, was extended to include non-civil service employees in addition to the foundation of the *Teâvun Sandıkları*, Solidarity Funds, for providing cash and in-kind aid to the employees and their families in the event of illness, disability or death. In 1910, an act was passed to determine the eligibility criteria for retirement and levels of salaries for the workers, orphans and widows. The primary action taken by the ITF in the area of social policy was to found a new institution, *Müessasat-ı Hayriye-i Sıhhiye*, to unify the health and social welfare institutions in Istanbul (Özbek, 2006: 26–84). Another conspicuous development in this area was the extension of the voluntary social aid initiatives undertaken by civic associations.

In the area of industrial relations, the bureaucratic elites introduced a number of regulations ebbing and flowing between being emancipatory and authoritarian. These were issued, primarily, to tackle the burgeoning labour organisations and unorganised workers' strikes, beginning in the second quarter of the nineteenth century. The first in this kind was the *Polis Nizamnamesi* of 1845, The Police Regulation of 1945, transposed from the French Penal Code, which banned the establishment of worker organisations and actions at a period when there was not any worker movement in the Empire. For its part, the Second Constitutional Monarchy legalised the right to organise and establish associations, thereby paving the way for the establishment of trade unions. With *Tâtil-i Eşgal* (The Ottoman Strike Law), this right was banned for public sector employees in the face of the waves of strikes in 1908. Transposed from two French legal conventions, the French Labor Law of 1892 and the Act of 1894, the Law aimed to circumvent the politically agitative actions of the workers under the motivational enhancement of then vivid European trade unions (Gülmez, 1982: 330). This declaration made by *Ali Bey*, then representative of the Ministry of Commerce and Public Works, is worth quoting here as a path-making note;

> I do not recognize either the laborer or the capitalist. I just take care of the interest of my country. I am paying effort to make both employer and laborer equal persons for the sake of my country's salvation ... If we grant the laborer the right to organize in a period when we most urgently need foreign capital, the capitalists will be under the threat of the laborer ... It is expected that trade

unions would define some representatives among the laborer, and they will
settle the matters in the mind of the capitalist and laborer. Who would do this is
nobody else but the state itself ... the government is granting the laborer their
freedom by banning trade unionism (Takvim-I Vâkayi, 1909a, p. 13, quoted in
Gülmez, 1982: 330).

Between 1876 and 1923, a few labour organisations, such as *Amele Perver Cemiyeti*
(the Pro-Laborer Association) and *Osmanlı Amele Cemiyeti* (The Ottoman Laborer
Association), were founded mainly for self-help purposes but then shut down on
the ground that they would disrupt the public order. Throughout the period of
1872–1908, in total, 23 strikes were initiated essentially by unorganised workers
and overwhelmingly for claiming their earned rights rather than for new interest
purposes (Mentzel, 1994: 95–141). Their style of action was first to approach the
state with a petition for helping them reclaiming their rights, and then to go on
strike if their demands were not met with a satisfactory response (Karakışla, 1995:
19–20).

I have hitherto examined the institutional system of the Empire and its path-
dependent change in the nineteenth century as illustrated in Table 4.1. At this
juncture, the analysis of the Empire's institutional stock using Islamic theory
would be plausible. I prefer, however, to analyse the systemic consistency or
inconsistency, evolution and path-dependent change of Ottoman Islam, the NOM's
'Just Order' and the incumbent AKP's Conservative Democracy simultaneously
in the fourth part in terms of the theory of Islamic political economy and the
contingent consequences, as discussed earlier, that its systemic intersection with
the liberal establishment would generate. This is because our ultimate target is
not to specifically identify the systemic nature of Ottoman Islam's institutional
stock and its comparison with pure Islamic theory, but the path-dependent change
of its institutional stock evolving into the embodiment of the Just Order and then
Turkish conservative democracy in timespace. Such a cross-temporal exploration
in light of an enduring theoretical base will enable us to make a more definitive
investigation into the future of the Turkish political economy.

Chapter 5

The Embedding of Orthodox Kemalism and Etatist Liberalism in Analotia Between Continuing Changes and Path-Dependent Discontinuities

Therefore, a great ideal should be born out of the intensification of only that group which, in addition to being the richest and most powerfully organized, is in a position to bring together and assimilate all other groups in its own organization (Gökalp, 1959: 80).

The period of 1923–50 in the Republican Turkey's history makes sense essentially with the incessant single-party authority of the Republican People's Party. As there did not appear any countercyclical actor that could embark on an insurrectionary initiative, it becomes untenable to make an analysis of power-centred interaction for this period. In this respect, this chapter aims to examine the period 1923–50 in terms of (i) the formation of one of the two major path-dependencies in the CHP's party identity, the Orthodox Kemalism, and (ii) the evolutionary trends, particularly the embedding of secular capitalism in this period with reference to the accruing path-dependence and change dynamics from the earlier periods.

In this period, following the defeat of the Empire in World War I and the flight of the Unionist leaders, Mustafa Kemal and his proponents led the development of a single-party, secular and elitist political regime. The pioneers of this regime by and large came from the Unionist cadres, including Mustafa Kemal himself and his successors as prime minister, Fethi Okyar and İsmet İnönü, Mustafa Kemal's old friends from the ITF. The new regime was thus constructed by an 'intelligentsia composed of military and civilian groups who formed the hard core of the Kemalist movement' (Ahmad, 2003: 76). Mustafa Kemal founded *Halk Fırkâsı*, the People's Party, in September 1923 (in 1935, the name of the party became *Cumhuriyet Halk Partisi* – CHP, the Republican People's Party) and political activity revolved around this party until the first genuine general elections in May 1950.

The CHP was the successor to the *Anadolu ve Rumeli Müdafaai Hukuk Cemiyeti*, the Association for Defence of the National Rights of Anatolia and Rumelia, founded region by region to ensure the independence of Turkish territory. In other words, it can be suggested that the CHP was superimposed upon a grassroots movement of popular resistance and defence. The leading cadres of these associations were the upper and middle classes in Anatolia and Thrace, comprising the landlords, local merchants and craftsmen, ulemâ, schoolteachers and lower ranking government officials. It was the ITF's members who merged these associations under the roof of Defence of Rights Association (Karpat, 2004: 211–3). After its abolition in April 1923, the Association was transformed into the *Halk Fırkası*, many prominent figures of which were members of the ITF (Kili, 1975: 21–3, 45).

For a political organisation to maintain its existence for nine decades from 1923 onwards, there should be a common ground between its organisational pillars and the aspirations of, at least, a certain segment of a society. This liaison for the CHP was its embodiment of the bottom-up motivational spirit of the Defence of Rights Association, furnishing the party with the necessary operational margin to initiate far-reaching countercyclical socio-political reforms vis-à-vis the then cement of Turkish society.

The reforms aimed to further accumulate the path-dependent discontinuities of the Ottoman legacy and therefore intensify the accumulation of continuing changes. For this purpose, the religious schools were closed; the Caliphate was abolished; the Republican Directorate of Religious Affairs was founded in 1924; *Medreses* were closed and the Ministry of National Education was founded in 1924; Religious courts were abolished; in November 1925, all male Turks were compelled to abandon the *fez* and in its place wear a hat with a brim; the Gregorian calendar was adopted as the single time-measure of the Republic in 1926; the Swiss Civil Code, the Italian Penal Code and a Commercial Code transposing various sections of the German and Italian codes were enacted in 1926; the new Turkish alphabet was formed on the basis of Latin letters in 1928; Sunday was made the weekly holiday; and women received the right to vote and stand for office in 1930 and 1934, respectively.

Expectedly, this process evolved under arduous debate between Kemalists and religiously sensitive groups, especially regarding the maintenance of the Caliphate. When they initiated their political struggle in 1923, the Kemalists were in the minority in the National Assembly following the elections held in June 1923, but they then purged the religiously sensitive and liberal Westerners in the National Assembly and established their rule over the central political establishment.

The discontinuing path-dependencies, namely the de-accumulation of the systemically organised and normatively contingent unity of the Ottoman politico-economic institutions particularly in the eighteenth and nineteenth centuries, had paved the way for the opportunist subversives, primarily the ITF, to enforce their prescription of a top-down rationalist, nationalist and secular institutional design between 1908 and 1918 (Kazancıgil, 1995: 199–200). The ITF's socio-economic reforms, in this sense represented, for the first time in Ottoman-Turkish history, the de-accumulation of the path-dependent continuities of Ottoman Islam, albeit partially, by a political party in power. The CHP's role was to extend this discretion to a systemic extent via sharply executed and secularly embedded rational changes, breaking through the normative path-dependencies in the minds of the ordinary public. As a complementary initiative, the process of the above-listed *institutional break-offs* was planned to be expeditious, so as not to leave room for the re-accumulation of religiously embedded path-dependencies that would discontinue the *systemic* accumulation of continuing secular and rationalist changes, particularly from 1908 onwards.

Gökalp's proposal in the epilogue was thus materialised in a formal respect. His conceptualisation of the 'ummah', 'state' and 'nation', in this sense, also sheds light on the conceptual matrix of the then great divide in Anatolia between Islam and Kemalism. He proposes that:

> A collectivity (*hey'et*) united by religious mores and subject to a religious authority is called an *ümmet*, the ummah. A collectivity united by political mores and subject to a political authority is called a *state*. The collectivity which is the product and the union of cultural *mores* under a cultural authority is called a *nation* ... The fact that in organic society only a part of the institutional life rests on religious *mores* while in primitive society all institutions rest on religious *mores* should not lead us to think that religion is serving a more useful task in primitive societies. Religious *mores* invest the institutions to which they are related with a supernatural or, in clearer terms, a charismatic power and value. This power may be useful in its relation to institutions which are relatively spiritual and represent the collective conscious of society, but it becomes harmful when it is extended to worldy or secular and especially to material, institutions because it prevents these institutions from adapting themselves to the expediences of life. Therefore, the predominance of religious *mores* over all institutions is not something to be desired for organic societies. In organic societies religious *mores* still exist, but they cover only those ideals and sentiments which have to remain spiritual and sacred ... One of the great tasks of religion in organic society is to leave other institutions free within their own spheres (Gökalp, 1959: 183–5).

Despite this unconflictual justification in theory, the sharp institutional break-offs, as the methodology of practising these theoretical premises, required the systemic control of society. The easiest way of enforcing this aim was to erect a single-party administration and justify it by manipulating political pluralism. It is within this context that the first opposition party in Turkey, *Terakkiperver Cumhuriyet Fırkası* (TCF), the Progressive Republican Party, was closed in June 1925. In August 1930, with the urging of Mustafa Kemal, *Serbest Cumhuriyet Fırkası* (SCF), the Free Republican Party, was established to save face for the regime and sooth political tension rather than establish multi-party democracy, as was popularly claimed. Albeit tactical, the SCF was enthusiastically welcomed by the people in large crowds, and all opposition to the regime coalesced around it, a process resulting in the closure of this party, too, in November 1930 (Kalaycıoğlu, 2005: 45–66). A month later, a rebellion broke out, the *Şeyh Said rebellion* of 1925, initiated by a group of Sunni Muslims led by a cleric in Menemen, a town in western Turkey, with the demand of restoring Islamic law and the caliphate.

Table 5.1   Main strategies of the ITF and the CHP in comparative context

Period	Economy	Polity	Social Policy	Industrial Relations
ITF, 1908–18	–Formation of a national economy –Forming an etatist economic regime and creating a class of Turkish/Muslim bourgeoisie by issuing the Law Encouraging Industry –Dismantling the Ottoman Public Debt Administration and abolishing the capitulations	–Re-establishing Constitutional Monarchy and fortifying Europeanisation with cultural reforms –Replacing the political value of religion with nationalism, and confining the former's scope to private faith and ritual by executing secularising socio-economic reforms	–Unifying the health and social aid institutions –Central regulation of scattered social security funds –Sidelining the peasants by not enforcing the land reform	–Passivising workers' movements and actions for preventing the outbreak of social disorder and improving the investment climate
CHP, 1923–50	–Path dependence in the formation of a state-led national economic strategy but change in the application of a broader and more generous set of incentives for entrepreneurs –Strategic change in participating in the IMF and the World Bank and in accepting foreign aid from the USA	–De-accumulating (secularising) path-dependencies through sharp-edged and systemic institutional break-offs –Embedding the continuing changes using authoritarian measures	–Paternalist provision of social aid and services –No rights but responsibilities	–Paternalist authoritarianism –Positive discrimination in favour of civil servants against private sector workers

After the suppression of this rebellion, the CHP devised a new ideology entitled 'Kemalism' or 'Atatürkism' to theoretically justify the continuing changes vis-à-vis the discontinuing path-dependencies of Ottoman Islam, the clarification of an ongoing search for identity since the party's foundation. With the onset of the Great Depression and the failure of the liberalisation strategies between 1923 and 1929, liberal democracy had been discredited on the part of the CHP. The single-party regimes, especially fascist Italy, offered an attractive alternative. The Party sympathised with the Bolsheviks, with whom the new Turkey had established cordial relations during the national struggle, but a socialist administration was at odds with the main strategy of the Party, particularly due to the prospective risks of a classless (socialist) society (Jacoby, 2004: 93–7). Then, the pro-CHP press argued that fascism did not permit opposition parties but rather intra-party criticism. However, a fascist party could in no way allow a critique of its fundamental principles. This vision was the mainstream mindset of the ruling elite when the regime headed for a mono-party system. In addition to the inclusion of 'Republic' to the Party's title in 1935, following the example of the Nazis in Germany, the CHP passed a resolution uniting the party and the state and therefore the secretary general and the chairmen of the provincial organisations of the Party became the minister of interior affairs and the governors of the provinces, respectively.

The ideology of Kemalism was introduced into the Turkish Constitution in 1937 as its supreme constitutive element consisting of *six interwoven and unchanging arrows*: Republicanism, Nationalism, Populism, Etatism, Laicism and Revolutionism: (i) Populism was adopted as a discursive tool to justify the top-down realignment under the aegis of a theoretical definition – national solidarity structured on a classless (homogeneous) society; (ii) Laicism was perceived in the sense that Islam could no longer be manipulated by religiously sensitive individuals for political purposes. Instead it should be confined to the individual or civic-cultural sphere under the state's disorganising power; (iii) Statism refers to the process of political and economic *modernisation* by the central bureaucracy and military; (iv) Republicanism is suggested to refer to the sovereignty of the nation to govern its *common* interests in the face of international challenges in tandem with the principle of national independence or nationalism; (v) Gökalp (1959: 80) put it, nationalism is the cement of the Turkish Republic as the upper identity emanating from having the same ethnic unity, the same language, the same faith and *homogenous* ideas; and finally (vi) Revolutionism is the title of the Kemalist discretion to de-accumulate the religiously inspired path-dependencies of Ottoman-Turkish society (Köker, 2005). This principle would, *prima facie*, be claimed to evoke a change-making connotation. In the aftermath of uprooting the formal antecedents of Islamic institutionalism from the formal pillars of state organisation, for the CHP's strategies, Revolutionism became a path-sustaining power of resistance to safeguard the Kemalist establishment.

Following the death of Mustafa Kemal in 1938, the founder and eternal leader of the CHP, İnönü became the Party's *permanent chairman*. He was the prime minister of the Party between March 1925 and September 1937, when Mustafa Kemal sacked him. İnönü also acquired the title of 'national chief' and the regime adopted a truly fascist form, aptly described by the Party's slogan 'one party, one nation, one leader'. With this new vision, in the wake of the outbreak of World War II in Europe, the CHP launched a second tide of authoritarian interventionism involving nearly every aspect of Turkish life. The National Defence Law of 1940 outfitted the government with extensive emergency powers to control prices and the supply of goods in the market, coercing the peasants to engage in *angarya* (forced) work, confiscating agricultural products at low prices, provisionally confiscating private businesses, extending working times and so on. In 1943, the tithe, abolished in 1925, was reinstated in the form of a 'payment-in-kind tax' on agricultural products (Kazgan, 2004: 73–6).

Under rampant inflation, substantial declines in real wages, negative growth and so on, the war years imposed a hard burden on Turkish society. In January 1942, the government was forced to ration even bread, the staple of the Turkish diet. While the common man suffered great deprivation and hardship, in November 1942, İnönü bitterly complained about the hoarding, black-marketing and profiteering. Ten days later, parliament unanimously passed the dichotomous 'Capital Tax Law' designed to impose extraordinary taxes on the businessmen accumulating wealth during the War, particularly non-Muslims and the owners of large farms (Ahmad, 2003: 70). In essence, the Law was enacted (i) to suppress the commercial supremacy of the minorities and empower Turkish businessmen and (ii) to appease the masses by creating an anti-capitalist image.

Another act was the Land Reform Bill of 1945 that aimed to allocate a certain part of the holdings of large landowners to the peasants who had no land or a tract inadequate for optimal harvesting. The result of these successive regulations was the profound destruction of the bonds among the government, the Muslim or non-Muslim bourgeoisie and large farmers and the military-civilian bureaucracy established during the War of Liberation. Four members of the CHP, on the grounds of the emerging authoritarian management of politico-economic cycles, broke off from the party and founded the Democrat Party in 1946; the businessman-banker Celâl Bayar, the bureaucrat Refik Koraltan, the historian Professor Fuad Köprülü and the cotton-growing landlord Adnan Menderes (Vanderlippe, 2005: 114–25).

The failure of the path-dependent continuity of the CHP's single-party political strategy after a long period of attrition also left its imprint on economic policy. In view of its rule between 1923 and 1950, the Party's economic strategy was, by and large, etatism along with the creation of a national bourgeoisie by public incentives, namely the path-dependent continuity of the ITF's national economy strategy. Yet it vacillated between liberal etatism and etatist liberalism during its 27-year incumbency. Its initial strategy was liberal etatism between 1923–29, as negotiated at the Izmir Economic Congress, the first economic governance platform in the Republican period. In reaction to the onset of the Great Depression, in addition to internal structural reasons, the Party came to hold an etatist liberal mindset beginning in the 1930s. Between 1946 and 1949, at the end of its single-party authority (1923–50), the party relaunched liberal etatist strategies in response to the Democrat Party's ascending vision under the sponsorship of liberal premises in addition to the burgeoning new international order.

Etatist Liberalism, 1923–29

This strategy of economic development was first discussed at the Izmir Economic Congress of 1923, held to symbolically negotiate the economic policy strategies of the Turkish state and overwhelmed by industrialists and merchants. The Congress was truly a state-business *contract* for constructing the division of labour with the confirmatory participation of labour. Endorsed at the end of the Congress, the principle of gaining *economic independence* brought in the strategy of *national economy*, the main principles of which were to be developmentalism, the subsidisation of domestic capital and peasants by the state, encouragement of foreign investment and primarily accumulating productive and capital power in the hands of domestic entrepreneurs.

Between 1923 and 1932, two basic acts were enacted for these major purposes. The first was the Law for the Encouragement Industry of 1927 that provided enterprises with extensive exemptions, privileges and subsidies, ranging from the selling of the goods and services produced in the public sector at a discount and an exemption from income and customs taxes to requiring public sector institutions to purchase the products and goods of the companies subsidised by this Law if their price was not more than 10 per cent more expensive than imported goods (Kepenek, 2007: 47). The second was the foundation of *Sanayi ve Maadin Bankası*, The Turkish Industry Bank, to remain in operation until 1932, to grant credits to the private sector, establish joint stock companies with private firms, operate state-owned enterprises, henceforth SOEs, temporarily, and then ultimately hand them over to the private sector. The Bank, before 1932, did not transfer the SOEs to private sector but retained its shares in 16 private enterprises. However, as the private enterprises could not abide by their capital commitments, the Bank also failed to achieve its targets.

Throughout this period between 1923 and 1929, the Treaty of Losan banned differentiated prices for imported and domestic goods, except those of the latter that were produced in the public sector. To exploit this gap, the state developed monopolies in a variety of sectors to provide additional income for the state budget. In praxis, these monopolies became the primary means of *training* national capitalists from the privileged private strata and companies with shareholders who were high-ranking civil or military bureaucrats and politicians. This mode of *business making* therefore came to be a highly lucrative rent extracting methodology for the *state-business coalition*. Founded primarily by the donations of Indian Muslims to the Turkish state during the War of Liberation, *Türkiye İş Bankası*, the Isbank, was the official arbitrator and sponsor of this rational *interplay*, the prime and unique function of which was to be the financial bridge between private and public capitalists. To enhance the *productivity* of this model, the state executed extensive confiscations, such as railroad and tobacco enterprises, and banned cabotage by foreigners who then invested in the Turkish market by buying shares in the joint-stock companies (Boratav, 2007: 39–43).

As Table 5.2 shows, during the first period between 1923 and 1929, a high growth rate was generated with a moderately low level of inflation, predominantly stemming from resilient agricultural production after World War I and the War of Liberation. Due to the unprotectedness of domestic producers under the constraints of the Losan Treaty, the balance of payments, on average, showed a deficit of 1.8 per cent of GDP. With the imposition of customs duties after the termination the Treaty's relevant items and the lifting of the capitulations, the balance of payments recovered during a period when the volume of international trade declined due to the underemployment conditions of the Great Depression. Throughout the period, despite high unemployment rates compared to the succeeding periods in the single-party era, the CHP government did not intervene through expansionary measures (Keyder, 2009: 98–101).

Rather, the Party clung to budgetary austerity (the financing of agricultural products by a state bank, Ziraat Bank, also remained limited during this period), and public employment constituted a trivial share of total employment, 2.7 per cent. The increasing proportion of indirect taxes in this period indicates that the tax burden was imposed on the peasantry and working class. Real wages in the public sector increased slightly until rising, between 1930 and 1932, to one of the highest periodic averages in real terms throughout the Republican period, 19 per cent. The period 1930–32 witnessed the continuity, even a slight loosening, of strict budget austerity despite the depressive signals in the economy with zero growth, a rather large, negative rate of inflation and a moderately high unemployment level (Akalın, 2008: 155–86). The slight rise in final consumption expenditures was far from sufficient to stimulate output and employment. Furthermore, public employment diminished by more than its average increase during the previous period.

Practical, Authoritarian and Theoretical Variants of Liberal Etatism (1933–39/1940–46/1947–49)

The CHP's 1935 programme highlights that 'The role of the state is to prioritise, regulate and control the private entrepreneurs *as well as to make direct investments*' (CHP, 1935: 10). Under the auspices of a conjuncture when the theoretico-practical premises of liberal capitalism were discredited (during the Great Depression) and the planned economy policy of the Soviet Union had achieved relative success, Turkey embarked on an inward-looking import-substitutionist strategy of industrialisation, primarily for producing mass consumption goods. The development plans, beginning in 1934, came to be the path-guides of the Turkish economy, and the state emerged as the principal entrepreneur, establishing SOEs in a number of key industries. During this period, in parallel with the previous one (1923–32), conducting business with the public sector was the essential *job* of industrialists, whereas the commercial bourgeoisie lost its advantageous position due to the protectionist policies.

Between 1933 and 1939, a high growth rate was achieved along with a low level of inflation, and unemployment receded to moderate levels in spite of negative growth in public sector employment (see Table 5.2). Real wages in government continued to increase at a relatively high level in addition to the moderate increases in the agriculture and manufacturing sectors. The CHP did not change its balanced budget strategy, whereas final consumption expenditure increased slightly. The low-level inflation was a direct outcome of this persistent austerity combined with increases in the direct and indirect tax burden. During World War II, however,

Table 5.2 Main indicators of Turkish economy, 1923–50

Notes: *Annual Growth Rates.
Source: 1- TUIK (2012);
2,3,4-Bulutay (1995: 203, 256-8, 305).

	GDP	Annual Sectoral Growth			Budget Balance /GDP	Balance of foreign trade /GDP	Taxes/GDP	
		Agriculture	Industry	Services			Direct	Indirect
1923-1929	10,8	15,9	8,0	8,1	0,2	-1,8	0,4	4,8
1930-1932	0,0	-6,1	14,9	7,7	-0,3	0,3	0,9	5,4
1933-1939	8,5	11,2	10,3	7,9	0,2	0,5	1,7	5,9
1940-1946	-1,1	1,3	-2,0	-2,3	0,7	0,7	2,2	4,6
1947-1949	1,1	3,6	2,8	7,2	0,2	-0,8	2,4	5,0

	Final Consump Expend. /GDP*	Wholesale Price Index[1]	Unemployment[2]	Public Employment	Real Wages in Government	Real Wages and Salaries in Agriculture[3]	Real Wages and Salaries in Manufacturing[4]
1923-1929	4,8	2,9	5,3	2,7	2,8	16,0	0,7
1930-1932	5,7	-17,4	3,6	-3,6	19,0	-9,6	14,4
1933-1939	6,8	1,8	3,2	-2,2	8,6	5,1	4,4
1940-1946	7,1	28,9	2,8	3,9	-9,7	1,8	-9,2
1947-1949	6,3	5,6	2,5	4,7	9,5	0,4	10,4

monetary growth soared, despite a negative average growth rate, and increased real inflation in the wake of the Central Bank of Turkey's decision to discount the treasury-guaranteed securities of the public sector institutions or to open credits in return for these securities, namely to finance public deficits. As a result, in 1946, for the first time, the Turkish Lira was devalued by 113 per cent, a competitive devaluation to increase exports and decrease import rates, thereby reducing the domestic debt stock proportionally.

Between 1940 and 1945, Turkish economy incurred all of the negative externalities of World War II, even though the country did not participate in the War. In addition to a contraction in real output and consequent rampant inflation, real wages and salaries in the public and manufacturing sectors declined remarkably despite the steady increase in agricultural wages. The National Defence Law of 1940, the Capital Tax Law of 1942 and the Land Reform of 1945, under these circumstances, aimed to ward off social upheaval by taking advantage of the state's enforcive power in cultivating the funds necessary to provide food, heating and wear to the large cities (Boratav, 2007: 82–9). General price levels skyrocketed to 94 and 73 in 1942 and 1943, respectively, paving the way for exorbitant gains. The Capital Tax Law, elaborated above, was a result of this process.

Overall, the period 1940–46 was perceived as a concrete indicator of the fact that the Turkish economy was unable to make strides with a state-led private sector due to the accumulation of speculative commercial but not productive industrial capital under an economic structure that was not based upon technological know-how, a systemic macro-micro organisation for efficient production, professional entrepreneurial power and expansive marketing strategy (Kazgan, 2004: 80). In other words, between 1923 and 1946, the oscillations between etatism and liberalism accumulated the internal dynamics of a new turning point. Conjuncturally, for the genesis of this point, there also emerged an external stimulus. In the context of the Truman doctrine and Marshall Plan, Turkey had been expected to morph into a market economy from an etatist one.

In the Economic Congress of 1948, it was suggested that Turkey should attract foreign capital to cultivate foreign exchange resources to finance import goods and overcome the scarcity of development capital, thereby engaging in a liberal trade regime. Beforehand, in parallel with these internal/external conjunctural dynamics, at the 1947 CHP convention, a private-sector-led etatist strategy was articulated with the prospect that state would not make direct investments, especially in industrial sector, but that such funds should feed back into the operational capacity of the private enterprises and attract foreign capital by making infrastructural investments (Önder, 2005: 110). This outward-oriented development strategy resulted in the influx of import goods with changing consumption patterns and therefore in the current account deficits between 1947 and 1949 that were to continue throughout the rest of the Republic, except its infrequently balanced or positive rates during exceptional periods. One per cent growth with moderately low inflation and unemployment was achieved between 1947 and 1949. In addition, public sector final consumption expenditures slowed, but public employment experienced the largest average increase between 1923 and 1949 and the real wages in both the public sector and manufacturing registered substantial increases, of approximately 10 per cent.

Accumulated Dynamics of a Prospective Social Democratic Restructuration?

The single-party era fell into, as noted above, a vicious circle in the mid-1940s with wartime food shortages, heavy taxation and inhuman exploitation of labour. This inevitably caused the CHP to re-examine its policy choices of an authoritarian political system, a closed economy and an introverted foreign policy. In this regard, it was the deep economic crisis, the possibility of social upheaval and, most important, the foreign pressures on Turkish politics for democratisation that coerced the party to conduct this examination (Turkey had become a member of the League of Nations and the ILO in 1932, and later the United Nations in 1945).

The UN's pressure on Turkey to fulfil its membership requirement and Turkey's engagement with the Western Block were the major external factors for democratisation. Its membership in the IMF and the World Bank, begun in 1946 and 1947, respectively, was strategically the most significant step taken by the party in terms of Turkey's engagement in global capitalism. Under these intertwined pressures, the CHP administration shifted its policy choices to a multi-party system, an open economy, private sector enhancement, the enactment of the Trade Union Act of 1947 and a strategic attempt to attract foreign capital (Karpat, 1959: 140–143). In addition, the universities were granted administrative autonomy, and the press law was liberalised.

The most structural shift in the CHP's policy choices was the introduction of a course of religion in primary and middle schools, on the basis of preference, and the foundation of a faculty of theology at Ankara University in 1949. Kili (1975: 108) argues that, as another structural indicator of the discontinuing path-dependency of the CHP's denormativist perseverance, during this period, the Party came to sideline the Village Institutes, founded in 1938 to train schoolteachers as agents to develop a nation holding a Kemalist ideology. The religious *concessions* were in fact tactical steps to isolate the Democrat Party (1946) and the Nation Party (1948) founded by the conservative dissidents among the Democrats.

The change in the CHP's route emanated from the tension that the Party's failure to engender a progressive nation through the accumulated order, an appeal that was desired by the Party's hardliners who denounced this structural change. Those who enforced this change were the moderates in the Party who aimed to politically position the party as liberal etatist, more conservative and less sharp-edged reformist (evolutionary but not revolutionary), socially inclusive and so on. These countertendencies then revealed the structural skirmish between the ideologically stable and pragmatically flexible segments of the Party. The former persisted in executing their ideologic priorities at all costs, irrespective of the institutional environment, while the latter, pragmatically, intended to reconcile their ideologic priorities with environmental ones. The key debate, at the seventh congress of the party in 1947, in broad strokes, concerned whether and how to attune the party to the changing national and international circumstances or maintain the six arrows without any modification (VanderLippe, 2005: 171–4): manifesting its engagement in market capitalism and centralist positioning in electoral politics, the debate has consistently remained a quintessential challenge to the CHP throughout the Republican period.

In examining the politico-economic reforms and practical performance of the CHP between 1923 and 1949, for the purposes of this research, it is sensible to identify, in general, the *formational pillars* of its strategy and policy choices and, specifically, whether we can ascertain the accumulated dynamics of the social democratic restructuring the Party pursued during the 1960s and 1970s. In systemic terms, it seems more convenient to designate this particular period as the vicious circle of the Party between crafting a supreme *theoretical ideology* and adopting *practical pragmatism* with the aim of enforcing the premises of this ideology through authoritarian measures. As the Party constructed and embedded a countercyclical paradigm, Kemalism, in the face of the civic Islamic legacy, it had to use institutional break-offs to engineer social restructuring (Akural, 1984).

The theoretical ideal of Westernisation but practical implementation of a design-centred institutionalisation destabilised each other in the fullest sense of the word. In economic policy, a similar oscillation of the Party's strategies between liberal-authoritarian etatism and etatist liberalism well illustrates the Party's incompetence or unwillingness to fine-tune a theoretico-practical consistency by mobilising the democratic and spontaneous evolution of Turkish society. Instead, the boom-bust cycles of the political economy circumvented the embodiment of a democratic dialectics between state and society, an extremely significant niche underlying the sharp-edged balkanisation of contemporary Turkey's major social actors. In other words, *the continuing changes, from the ITF-period onwards, on the basis of authoritatively engineering or embedding the path-dependent discontinuities on the socio-political front can hence be suggested not to yield the institution of a secular social optimality of individual liberty, economic efficiency and social equity.*

These formational pillars, in terms of the Party's politico-economic strategies, should not be considered to feed back into a social democratic construction to be practised on the basis of productive solidarities among the state, society and market. In structural terms, the introduction of multi-party democracy by the Party was not rooted in its own spontaneous initiative, but in the intertwined pressure from internal and external (f)actors. This argument becomes more convincing because that the Party has always perpetuated, albeit de-accumulatedly, its political coalition with the civic-military bureaucracy, even at the turn of the twenty-first century, to re-establish its institutional and structural powers. The embedded etatism could be argued to form the basis for an interventionist regulatory tradition towards a social democratic pathway.

Yet this interventionism, too, was not aimed at striking a balance among the market, state and social dynamics of economic development, but to engender a bourgeoisie capitalism, an effort that ultimately stimulated trade and encouraged industrial capitalists to exploit the subsidies and crisis-ridden circumstances of the country, especially during the conditions of war. In the industrial sector, the Party could not transform an optimal endowment of production factors to obtain robust productivist development. Instead, at its first stage, industrialisation was primarily executed by small and middle-sized enterprises and focused on the processing of agricultural products, mining, weaving and so on, whereas imports essentially consisted of investments and basic consumption goods.

The positive fiscal balances were not the result of output and employment productivity, but the suppression of organised rights, and gradually and periodically increasing the tax burden. The growth in public sector employment remained limited throughout the Party's incumbency, whereas direct taxes increased slightly but steadily. The fact that the increase in indirect taxes was limited compared to that of direct taxes resides in the large real increases in the latter during World War II. Yet the former, apparently, was quite high in proportion, and it is not conceivable to claim that the CHP pursued a progressive tax strategy. In this sense, the real increases in public sector wages, rising to record levels in some periods, can be proposed to be a paternalist inclination and a result of positive discrimination in favour of civil servants vis-à-vis agricultural and industrial workers.

In addition to the tax strategy, the distributional policy choice of the CHP was not predicated on social citizenship but voluntary procurement of social aid and services. Its *etatism*, in this respect, was not a social democratic but a paternalist one that did not accept poverty alleviation or redistribution as *systemic* tasks for the state but a patrimonial requirement of national order and unity. Underlying this was the motto conceptualised by Gökalp, 'no rights, but responsibilities', and the Party's open declaration: '*The Party* does not discriminate between men and women while *giving responsibility* to its citizens' (CHP, 1935: 5). Featuring this is an approach that perceives public aid or services to citizens as endowments bestowed by the unique values of the Turkish social system, the state or CHP itself.

An example of this patrimonialism was the CHP's substantial intervention in applying price controls to ensure that the citizens had access to basic goods, the ability to purchase agricultural products at low prices or to distribute these goods and products unreciprocally. The main issue of social policy until the end of World War II was to broaden the geographic coverage of protective health policies to safeguard the already diminished population and care for war orphans. In this era, the primary strategy of the CHP administration was to reinforce the foundation and operations of the civil and para-official institutions such as *Hilâl-i Ahmer Cemiyeti, Türkiye Kızılay Cemiyeti* (1935) and so on, offering services in the fields of public health, social aid to the poor, orphans, migrants, combating natural disasters and so on (Özbek, 2002: 274–320). Yet, after World War II, a series of social security institutions were successively established. After the foundation of the Ministry of Labour, workmen's compensation and maternity insurance (1945), the Social Security Institution (1945), illness insurance for workers and the retired including their dependants (1950) and life insurance (1950) were established.

The CHP's unsystemic management of social policy issues in political economy terms, albeit promising institutionalisation of social security regime, comes into view more prominently in the Party's industrial relations strategy throughout the single-party era (1923–46). The Party determined a truly authoritarian strategy of labour relations management by legal arrangements. The first of its kind, *Takrir-i Sükun*, The Law for the Maintenance of Order of 1925, banned the right to organise for worker movements. Astonishingly, a year later, Turkish Civil Code of 1926, transposed directly from the Swiss Civil Code, *de facto* legalised the right to establish worker organisations. Another initiative, in this vein, was the word-for-word transposition of the Swiss Code of Obligations from the French text to form the Turkish Code of Obligations (Gözaydın, 2004: 291), entitling the workers to sign collective contracts during a period when there was no labour movement.

The Labor Act of 1936 was the first separate act regulating employee-employer relationships, issued to create a space of action for etatist liberal strategies. Along with banning the right to strike, the Act regulated compulsory arbitration of labour relations conflicts. Taken together with the ban on the right to organise by the Act of Associations of 1938, therefore, the authoritarian nature of the then etatist regime became entrenched in structural terms. Under this restrictive and volatile environment, only two labour organisations were founded. The first was disbanded due to the operational challenges, whereas the second was closed down in 1928 with the passage of *Takrir-i Sükun*. The CHP supplanted these organisations with *İş Bürosu*, the Labour Bureau, and *İşçi ve Esnaf Cemiyetleri*, Worker and Artisan Associations, to control and ideologically predispose the workers towards an unconflictual compromise strategy. Expectedly, apart from a few inconclusive strikes initiated for wage concerns at enterprise level, there did not emerge a wave of labour conflict to challenge the operational unity of the Party's strategies.

Right after the inception of the multi-party democracy, CHP's industrial relations strategy was intriguingly transformed overnight with the enactment of the Trade Union Act of 1947 under pressure from the UN and the ILO. The dichotomy was that the Act recognised the right to organise but not the right to strike and prohibited the engagement of trade unions in politics. This face-saving nature of the Act was best described by the following declaration of the then Ministry of Labour:

> As a matter of fact, there is no doubt in the fact that this Act is one of the steps, such as introducing the multi-party system, taken as a requirement of taking part in the realm of big democratic states. The Act was also issued largely under the compulsion of the external political and military actors after the World War II (Tuna, 1969: 256).

Parla and Davison (2004) suggest that Kemalism formed a 'solidaristic corporatism'. Dividing corporatism into two segments, fascist and solidarist, they argue that defunctionalising the individual, class and tradition as the cement of a social entity, 'corporatist formulations derive models of society and forms of political and economic organization from "occupational groups", professional organizations, or corporations' (p. 12). They draw attention to three interrelated features of corporatism: (i) its ideologic niche between economy and society, namely its functionally segregated organic and inter-complementary alignment on the basis of occupational groups; (ii) its economic and class instruments for interest representation; and (iii) its peculiar political institutionalisation with an authoritatively integrated decision-making process.

The CHP's corporatism, if any, was totalitarian in its organisation of inter-group relations on the basis of their unifying differentiation, as Durkheim theorised. Moreover, it also tended to be authoritarian by forbidding the organisation of workers or employers, let alone their organised interaction. Instead, the Party, even in its programme, highlights its strategic choice to command the actions of individual workers and employers under its party organisation along with the compulsory arbitration of employee-employer conflicts. Thus, to term the CHP's political economy strategy *corporatist* seems untenable. The practical blend of totalitarian and authoritarian inclinations under the unifying bond of Kemalist ideology does not feed back into the embodiment of a corporatist *regime* whatsoever *in the absence of worker or employer organisations* for interest representation.

Instead, it can be suggested that the CHP of 1923–49 developed an *ideologic theory*, Kemalism, and began to manage the ebb and flow of the practical volatility and dichotomous outcomes of its politico-economic strategies and policy choices by authoritarianly constructed shallow interventions in market and industrial relations. The explicit evidence of this fact is the Party's adaptation of liberal etatist, etatist liberal and then liberal etatist policies. On what basis did the Party choose this course of volatile action? Analysing the Party's programme leads one to the conclusion that it aimed to symbiotically both single out the private sector and to equip the state with the power to enforce price controls. The state's controlling and regulatory task, as imposed by the same programme, resulted neither in an effective coordination of private-public economic action nor in a progressive bourgeoisie organisation, which was the Party's initial target, but an *institutional volatility* that had drifted under the *driving force* of reactionary strategies.

The Party's clinging to austerity with respect to the consolidated budget or balance of payments could not create a dynamic match between human and capital factors of production. Instead, the Party opted to outfit indigenous entrepreneurs with manipulative opportunities rather than systemically crafted and monitored subsidies. The workers' lack of the right to organise, apparently, facilitated the rent-extractive action of the leisure class of entrepreneurs. The adoption of an optimal tax base, which would not overburden society, as declared in the Party's programme, did not materialise, given the extensive gap between direct and indirect taxes: 1.5 and 5.1 per cent of GDP on an average between 1923 and 1949. The most salient discrepancy between the Party's programme and its praxis is that solidarist development through *rational work*, a term used in the

Party's programme, was substantially damaged. Systemically speaking, this was in substance not conceivable by exclusively relying on authoritarianly crafted pragmatist interventions.

The democratic interaction between social forces can be suggested to enhance *institutional dynamism*, the core of creating productive solidarity on the basis of equal power sharing. Throughout this period, the CHP tended to eliminate all prospective dynamics of power competition using either the market or civic forces. Naturally, as noted at the beginning of the chapter, in the absence of notable countercyclical actors, we cannot conduct a dialectic analysis of the power relationship in this particular period, 1923–49. Instead, it seems more reasonable to state that, under the subconscious reference that Ottoman Islam could not engender a self-reconstructive and rationally designed reformist dynamism in the face of European capitalism, the CHP manipulated the knowledge, discursive and justificatory power of its theoretically secular political vision to inculcate the non-normative means of nation-building (Webster, 1939). No less important than this civilisational reference was the CHP's structural power stemming from its being the founder of the Turkish Republic through, at least ostensibly, a grassroots movement. This structural power authorised the Party to fundamentally perpetuate and embed the ongoing changes in the institutional environment. In the absence of effective countercyclical actors, the Party did not have any difficulty in enforcing its policy choices through coercive regulations.

Chapter 6

The Institutional Environment and the Major Actors in the Turkish Political Economy During the Period 1960–2013

The Turkish political economy between 1960 and 2013 lay partway between volatile stability and chaotic flexibility. This is an idiosyncrasy that requires the examination of this country's institutional environment with reference to its structural adjustments in certain sub-periods. It would, only in this way, be possible to apprehend the long-run evolutionary dynamics of Islam, social democracy and liberalism in terms of the interactions between the actors supporting these paradigms and acting over and under this institutional environment. Underlying is the analytic necessity to comprehend the sub-periodic ebbs and flows within the structural dynamics accruing from previous periods, especially in instances of political or economic volatilities. And such a long-term perspective that presents the evolution of the Turkish political economy in terms of the main turning points of its institutional environment can provide the readers with an overall approach to contextualise *short-run fluctuations* in this period within *systemically explanatory long-run trends*.

In this sub-section, in this context, the structural idiosyncrasies of the period 1960–2013 are examined as the institutional environment conditioning and being conditioned by the actors of Islamic, social democratic and liberal/neoliberal institutionalisms. (The period 1950–59 has also been added to this section as it is relevant for its impact on changing the path-dependencies of the orthodox Kemalist institutional environment and creating liberal conservative feedback into the present.) At the end of this chapter, I will offer a condensed outline of the national, regional and international actors that affected the Turkish political economy between 1960 and 2013: these actors consist of two groups (see Figure I.2 p. 5). The first consists of the proponents of the above-noted three paradigms, and the second is the regional and international governmental or financial institutions, and business, interest or non-governmental organisations, primarily the trade unions. In the next chapters, I will elaborate on the former in detail. The definition of the latter with a brief explanation of their strategic policy choices aims to provide the reader with the necessary background to understand with whom the former interact (elaborating on the latter in this book is both impossible, due to space limitations, and unnecessary since our primary aim is to explain the evolutionary dynamics of the three paradigms in terms of the power relationship between their proponents).

In broad strokes, the period 1950–2013 can in this sense be divided into three main phases. In economic policy terms, these phases are the outward liberal etatism of 1950–59, import-substitutionism of 1960–79 and etatist neoliberalism of 1980–2013. In political terms, these phases are: (i) the conservative secularism of *Demokrat Parti* – DP, The Democrat Party of Turkey in the period 1950–59; (ii) the inter-repulsive dialectics among the ideologic theories of the CHP, *Milli Nizam and Milli Selamet* (National Order and National Salvation Parties), *Milliyetçi Hareket Partisi* – MÇP (Nationalist Action Party) and *Adalet Partisi* – AP (the Justice Party of Turkey) in the period 1960–79; and (iii) the volatile interflow of changing continuities and continuing path-dependencies of the political dynamics of the previous era under crisis-ridden etatist neoliberalism and with adaptive adjustments to the prevailing international order in the period 1980–2013. Let me start with a brief overview of the evolutionary dynamics of basic macro-economic aggregates in the Turkish economy in the period 1950–2013 and then pursue their periodic developments with their political implications in the above-noted three phases.

A Brief Look at the Reactionary Structurations in the Turkish Economy

As Figure 6.1 shows, the period 1950–59 features relatively high growth (6.9 per cent), a balanced budget (-0.08) and a noticeable current account deficit (-0.9) with a limited volume of foreign trade (6) and moderately high inflation (8.77), as an average: in the next period, 1960–79, despite the relative persistence of the high-growth trend (5.1), inflation (15) and unemployment (5.8) nearly doubled, in addition to a more than a one-quarter increase in the current account deficit (1.2) with nearly the same foreign trade volume as in the previous period (6). The distinguishing feature of this period is that it exhibits the highest rate of public fixed capital formation (6.8). The third period, 1980–2002, is the longest in terms of scope and crisis-ridden cycles of structural transformations. What comes to the fore in this period is a low level of growth (3.8) with hyperinflation (62) and high unemployment (8.3).

Despite institutional dissolutions to downsize the public sector, PSBR (public sector borrowing requirement) soared to 5.9 per cent, public fixed capital formation receded only slightly (5.8) and the capital account deficit was at its lowest between 1950 and 2002, whereas the foreign trade volume increased to 22 per cent of GDP. In the last period, under the rule of AKP governments, the average growth rate observed in the second period, 1960–79, resumed with a relatively higher rate of PSBR (1.9), a moderately lower level of inflation (10.1), but nearly double higher unemployment (10.8) precipitated by a receding public sector fixed capital formation (3.4), half as much as that in 1960–79. The striking trend in this period is the phenomenal increase in the current account deficit (5.2).

Overall, the most prominent trend across the four sub-periods is that the structural transformation between 1980 and 2002, in spite of neoclassical theory, initiated an *uncreative destruction* in systemic terms. The receding growth with

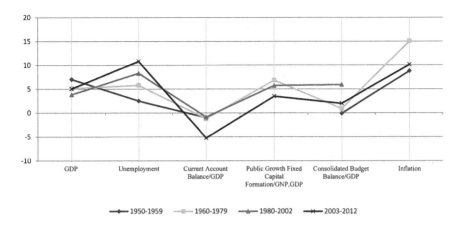

Figure 6.1   Major internal variables of the Turkish economy 1950–2012
Source: TKB (2013a).

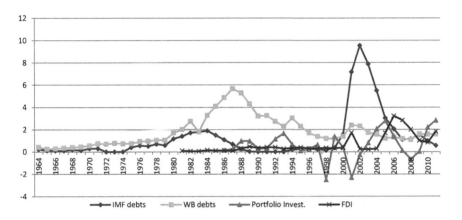

Figure 6.2   Major external variables of the Turkish economy, 1964–2011
Source: TUIK (2012, Chapter 15).

both high inflation and unemployment despite the rather high PSBR demonstrates the destructive impact of *volatile, untimely and reactionary restructurations*, rather than the stabilising impact of neoliberal policy recommendations. The persistence of unemployment and inflation with a declining public investment ratio and phenomenal current account deficit between 2003 and 2012 implies that budgetary austerity did not redound to curbing inflation and stabilising output and employment, and austerity was not effective in the absence of strong industrial performance that could be operationalised by internationally competitive but not by state-subsidised and rent-seeking entrepreneurs.

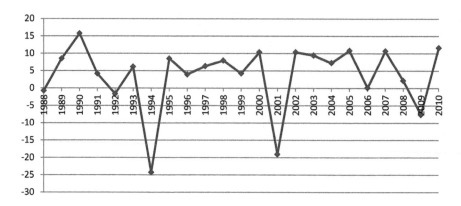

Figure 6.3   Exchange rate volatility in the Turkish economy, 1988–2010
Source: TKB (2013a, Table 3.12).

The budgetary austerity could be suggested to mitigate the adverse impacts of internal/external shocks by provisionally reducing public sector financial fragility, as was partly observed during the 2008–09 crisis. Yet, in the long-run, without increasing the marginal efficiency of investment capital, it has become obvious that Turkey's structural imbalances, such as the phenomenal current account deficit, would not be smoothed by macro-economic games played by an independent Central Bank. The Bank currently *hoards* sizeable foreign exchange reserves in excess of 100 billion dollars, 13 per cent of GDP in 2012, primarily to be able to halt the sharp fluctuations in foreign exchange and short-term (speculative) portfolio investments (see Figures 6.2 and 6.3) under the direct threat of a considerably high current account deficit. The same proportion was only 2 per cent in 1989 when the financial account was fully liberalised and inward foreign portfolio investment was only 0.9 per cent (2.8 per cent of GDP in 2011). Compelling the Bank to be so *generously prudent* is the fact that foreign direct and short-term portfolio investments declined remarkably (Figures 6.1 and 6.2) during the periods of crisis in the Turkish economy (1994, 1999, 2001, 2008–09), driving up real interest rates, debt ratios in Turkish Lira (TL) and the cost of borrowing, thereby depressing output and employment.

Changing Formational Path-Dependencies of the Republic: the Rise and Fall of Conservative Secularism and Outward Etatist Liberalism

In Turkey, the 1950s represents an interim period of structural dissolution of orthodox Kemalism and the inception of a state-led outward liberalism. The sharp-edged termination of this period by a harsh coup d'état in May 1960 predisposed the DP's successor, the AP, towards a more secular and less conservative line

(Levi, 1991). But this could not hinder the former's scaring effect upon the latter's entity and the country's political economy, evolving until the present, particularly as a discursive power for countercyclical actors such as the AKP for substantiating the conservative struggle against the CHP's authoritarian inclinations. It is within this context that Erdoğan, the AKP's former leader and the current President of Turkey, frequently declares that our road is the road of Adnan Menderes, the DP leader hanged by the military junta of May 1960, Necmettin Erbakan, the leader of the NOM, and Turgut Özal, the founder and leader of *Anavatan Partisi* – ANAP, the Motherland Party, the governing party of Turkey between December 1983 and November 1991.

As a reaction to the unchanging path-dependencies of the CHP's authoritarian pragmatism, the DP, governing party of Turkey between May 1950 and May 1960, cunningly developed a politico-economic strategy that lies partway between laicism, capitalism and Islam to cultivate a popular, catch-all identity. The DP can thus be suggested to have crafted a practical ideology to conciliate the then popular demands with vested political institutions and economic developmentalism. In structural terms, this policy choice entailed the perpetuation of liberal etatism by theoretically articulating a progressive strategy of economics as the main catalyst for change in tandem with the expectations of the businessmen, the liberal intelligentsia and international conjuncture. However, it practically perpetuated the etatist pathway, as there was neither an accumulated stock of a path-making entrepreneurial class nor the necessary factors of production in qualitative or quantitative terms.

With this mindset, the Party embarked on revisioning but not reforming the vested political institutions and interests by directing conservatively sensitive discourses towards the peripheral segments of society and emphasising individual rights or freedoms but not creating the practical means for upward social mobilisation: this cosmopolitan strategy was carried out by 'a small group of capital owners along with a larger group of aggressive entrepreneurs with a rather superficial liberal view of economics ... often as the chairman or members of its (the party's) local executive boards' (Karpat, 2004: 41–2). Consolidating the Party's abovementioned strategy was its electoral composition, consisting of underprivileged peasants, artisans, labourers and so on, voting for the Party essentially with a reactionary approach towards the CHP's poor performance during its single-party administration (Ahmad, 2003: 111).

The DP's political initiatives were a formalised and hence more reified reflection of its electorate's reaction to the CHP. The closure of the people houses, as one of the adjunct institutions of orthodox Kemalism, was perceived by its proponents as an assault on Kemalist reforms; resuming the reading of *Ezân*, call to prayer, in Arabic and the reopening of Qur'ân courses; and the general resurrection of an Islamic social image with its conservatively motivating but not formally institutionalised version at the level of discourse (the Party's landslide victory in 1954 spurred the escalation of its reactionary initiatives). In addition to these undeviatingly countercyclical initiatives, the Party stiffened penalties for

Table 6.1 Democrat Party's Economic Performance, 1950–1960

Results of General Elections	May 1950		May 1954		October 1957				
	CHP	39.9	CHP	34.8	CHP	40.6			
	DP	53.3	DP	56.6	DP	47.3			
Governmental Status	DP								Inter.
Duration of Incumbency	May 1950 - May 1960								Oct.
Parameters	1950-53		1954-56		1957	1958	1959		1960
GDP	11,3		2,7		7,8	4,5	4,1		3,4
Agriculture	12,2		0,3		6,5	9,2	0,3		2,3
Industry	10,5		10,0		10,7	5,6	3,6		0,4
Services	11,0		2,9		7,9	0,4	7,6		5,4
Balance of Accounts/GDP	0,1		0,3		0,3	0,2	0,1		-0,1
Current Account Balance/GDP	-1,4		-1,1		-0,3	-0,3	-0,5		-0,7
Foreign trade/Harmonized/GDP	8,7		5,9		3,5	2,2	2,6		4,0
Consolidated Budget Balance/GDP	0,0		-0,3		-0,1	0,0	0,1		0,0
Direct Taxes/GDP[1]	1,7		2,3		2,0	2,0	2,1		2,4
Indirect Taxes/GDP[2]	2,9		2,9		2,4	2,3	2,9		2,5
Public Investment/GDP[3]	1,8		2,3		2,4	2,2	2,4		2,6
Inflation	1,1		10,8		12,5	15,7	22,6		7,4
Unemployment[4]	1,9		3,1		2,7	2,8	2,8		3,1
Wages and Salaries in Public Sector[5]	2,7		2,7		-7,7	-6,2	15,5		-8,8
Worker (Public Sector)[5]	9,4		4,8		-1,3	-2,1	-19,8		4,1
Worker (Private Sector)[5]	12,2		17,3		23,7	20,4	22,9		11,9
Change in Public Sector Employment[5]	5,9		2,7		6,4	4,1	3,7		6,1

Notes: The harmonized GDP data has been used, provided by the TMD (2013) and the OECD (2013).
Source: TMD (2013a): 1, 2, 3 - TMD (1963: 18-19); TUIK, 2012; 4,5 - Bulutay (1995: 239, 294-8).

several basic items in the criminal code, constrained on press freedom, confiscated the CHP's assets and so on. Along with the upper class and landed families, who cultivated prestige, power and money thanks to the CHP's etatist policies, the media, the intelligentsia (while initially reservedly supporting the DP) and, most important, the military began accusing the DP of generating a repressive, commodificatory and religiously sensitive political strategy and being the agent of capitalist countries (on the basis of foreign loans).

Representing a broad alliance, including private industrialists, commercial groups, landed aristocrats and peasants, the DP opted for trade liberalisation and an agriculture-oriented and infrastructure-building development path with an integral emphasis on attracting foreign direct investment. These policy choices did not bring about a decline in the magnitude of the state's investment expenditures, as can be seen in the increasing trend in this figure throughout the decade. Rather, new SOEs were founded in the areas of machinery and chemistry, cement, petrol, paper, iron and steel, banking and transportation and so on. Furthermore, the DP governments pioneered the import-substitutionist production of basic consumption goods (Kepenek, 2007: 113, 142). Yet what changed was the division of labour between the private and public sectors. The latter *specialised in* the provision of key inputs for intermediate and capital goods for the former, while the former utilised these subsidised (inexpensive) inputs to manufacture high-surplus-yielding final consumer goods (Öniş, 1998: 459). Even the SOEs began to be founded in partnership with the private sector, requiring the latter to have at least a 51 per cent share.

The DP's primary target was to liberalise foreign economic relations and attract foreign investment to promote rapid economic development, the main tools of which were the devaluation of the Turkish lira, reducing import quotas, mechanisation and supporting product prices in the agricultural sector, making infrastructural investments, such as railroads, communication and energy, for the extensive development of industrial activities, state guarantees to the private sector for external borrowing and granting permission to foreign companies to explore for and refine oil in the Turkish territory (Aydın, 2005: 31). To finance this state-led outward liberalisation, short- or long-term credit lending by the Party with a high interest burden, especially between 1951–52 and 1954–56, resulted in a financial crisis in 1958 that would be managed by an IMF rescue programme.

In 1956, in view of increasing current account deficits, the government re-enacted the National Protection Law, intensified price controls, restrained credits for commercial banks and so on. In addition, the Party chose to expand public fixed-capital and consumption expenditures, especially between 1954 and 1956, to stimulate import-substitutionist industrial growth (Boratav, 2008: 108). As a result, despite slightly receding deficits, inflation and subsequent black-marketing gathered remarkable pace between 1957 and 1959. The programme primarily aimed to subdue rampant inflation, increase export revenues through devaluation, budget austerity and lifting the constraints on foreign trade (Aydın, 2005: 31).

The targets were not substantially achieved, as observed in the ultimate realisation of the current account and budget balances, rising inflation and receding growth compared to the pre-programme years. Instead, the programme conclusively reduced wages and salaries in the public sector in open conflict with the real increases in private sector workers' wages. The DP advanced this governmental strategy by adopting temporary and palliative measures such as engaging the IMF to enforce a new orthodox economic programme to save its electoral image, a policy choice that became embedded as rather a sticky path-dependence for the governments in coming decades, stretching forward to May 2008.

Along with its political and economic impact, the 1950s marked a turning point in the socio-economic structure of the country. The main signals of transition in this period were accelerating industrial growth, rapid urbanisation and the opening up of rural areas to the market economy, changing consumption patterns and unplanned settlements in the cities, *gecekondus* (Karpat, 1973: 57). This *economisation* of traditions called for the emergence of new demands concerning urban life, namely the roads, water, electricity, hospitals and so on. Under the competitive pressure of a multi-party democracy, the CHP had to reckon with these social demands, beginning in the first half of the decade with a path-dependent change towards 'social democratic Kemalism'. Let us examine the internal/external circumstances of the period 1960–2013, which will provide us with a retrospective/prospective insight into the variants of CHP's politico-economic strategies beginning with this change in the macro-institutional environment.

The Resurrection of Inward-Looking Import-Substitutionism

By the early 1960s, a planning period with five-year sequences was introduced under the guiding role of *Devlet Planlama Teşkilatı* – DPT, the State Planning Organisation of Turkey, a reaction to the unplanned and uncontrolled expansion of the DP era, to diminish the scope of opportunity enjoyed by the landed aristocracy and trade bourgeoisie that gained enormous power during the DP's incumbency. The unique approach to this was to authorise the bureaucracy to control and determine the distributional income of the factors of production in structural terms (Eralp, 1999). The relatively slow growth of industry relative to agriculture was to be inverted; otherwise the former classes would earn easy money by manipulating high inflation and black-marketeering. The aim was also to increase national production and therefore reduce the current account deficit: Kepenek (2008: 145–6) critically emphasised that neither the bureaucracy nor industrial entrepreneurs were equipped for such a sharp change in the economic structure. In a reactionary fashion, the military reformers perceived planning as a magical endeavour that would smooth economic and social imbalances in a short period of time (as Boratav [2008: 117–8] put it, the upshot was that, despite harmonised planning, the money, credit, exchange rate and, at times, the fiscal policies could not be optimised in conjunction with the pre-planned targets throughout this period).

The main economic policy strategy employed between 1960 and 1979, in broad strokes, was inward-looking import-substitution that aimed to produce import goods, chiefly consumer goods and consumer durables, in the country by national enterprises or national-foreign capital partnerships. Yet, as in the DP governments, these enterprises were, in terms of main inputs, especially technology and energy, dependent on foreign markets and utilised the subsidised (inexpensive) inputs that the SOEs produced. The underlying motive behind the steady, albeit slowing, growth during this period, 1960–80, was external borrowing and worker remittances.

Ultimately, in addition to the stagnation in export performance, import-substitutionist industrialisation entailed its own demise by making the country's industrial establishment subservient to foreign capital, especially in intermediate goods, despite the relative progress in investment goods (Hale, 1981). Agricultural goods and raw materials were, as in the 1950s, the main export items, although a notable increase was posted in industrial products with a share of 20–39 per cent in the 1970s compared to 13–18 per cent in the 1960s. The rising share of agricultural products was marketed through the SOEs that quoted a base price for these products as a sort of subsidising strategy, the prices of which were lower than they would have been under free market conditions.

Despite the widespread exchange controls, quotas and fixed exchange rate regime, current account deficits were the result of low value added public investment gathering pace between 1960 and 1965 and populist increases in public sector employment. In this period, however, deposit interest rates that were lower than real inflation and interest rates on credit near the real inflation level imposed by the private banks and the accommodating monetary policy of the government hampered the contraction of private industrial and commercial investments. In the 1960s, *Türkiye Cumhuriyeti Merkez Bankası* – TCMB, the Central Bank of Turkey, by holding interest and exchange rates constant, canalised saved funds to prioritised investment areas through selective credits determined in the five-year development plans. In addition, operationalising monetary policy through rediscount policies and required credits, the Bank provided medium-term rediscount credits to pour the accumulated funds into long-term investments and obliged the banks to maintain a certain amount of middle- and long-term investment credits (Akçay, 1997: 96–8). In the 1970s, however, beginning with the devaluation of the TL at a rate of 66.7 to restrict import demand, an uncontrolled monetary policy was implemented to be enforced in response to the suboptimal increase in the Bank's credits to the public sector to finance the budget deficits of the central government and SOEs, with the consequences of rampant inflation and drastically high interest rates.

Regarding power relations, this era symbolises a delicate conflictual compromise among the bureaucratic elites, industrial capitalists, industrial workers and the peasantry. The protectionist and state-subsidised structure of business formation enabled industrialists to harvest vast oligopolistic profits and rents through readily available domestic market demand. Complementing the conflictual compromises in this period was expansionary fiscal policy in both public sector fixed capital formation and current expenditures (primarily personnel expenditures arising from a high average annual rate of public employment growth of approximately 8 per cent), low and moderate growth in private sector workers' wages, albeit negative growth (1.2 per cent on an average) in governmental wages and salaries, and a moderate level of unemployment (5.8). The Gini coefficient, despite rising to 0.56 in 1968 from 0.55 in 1963, retreated to 0.51 in 1973 and then to 0.49 as of 1980.

Despite a high level of industrial growth, at approximately 10 per cent, the model of inward-looking import-substitution did not realise a self-financing and average higher growth than in the previous period, the establishment of an internationally competitive and self-grounding sectoral endowment, a full employment strategy and well-functioning economic governance. In brief, it failed in stimulating the establishment of a working insider or stakeholder model of capitalism. In the late 1970s, this state-subsidised and debt-financed model fell into a vicious circle with its all trappings: rising balance of account and current account deficits, receding and negative growth rates, soaring PSBR, unemployment, inflation and interest rates, negative growth in public sector fixed capital formation, high real declines in wages and salaries in both the public and private sectors and so on (see Table 6.1, p. 126). Coupled with the social tension arising from the March 1971 military memorandum, the erratic policy choices of the subsequent instable coalition governments, escalating ideologic clashes between left and right groups, heightening with the murders of 1977, political killings, assassinations and massacres that cost the lives of thousands, mounting strikes and lock-outs, this period concluded with the harsh coup d'état of September 1980, ushering in another reactionary structural change.

The military junta, on the political front, suspended political democracy and closed all political parties and labour organisations (Devrimci İşçi Sendikaları Konfederasyonu – DISK [reopened in 1992], the *Revolutionist Trade Union Confederation*, the religiously sensitive Hak-İş [reopened in 1981], the *Hak-Is Trade Union Confederation*, and the radical-leaning trade unions in Türkiye İşçi Sendikaları Konfederasyonu – Türk-İş, the *Turkish Trade Union Confederation*). It then prepared a constitution and submitted it to a referendum. 'Confirmed' by a submissive 93.7 per cent of the electorate, the Turkish Constitution of 1982 subjugated political parties to the systemic control of the Constitutional Court and forbade them from forming national or international complementary bodies, such as youth or women's branches, and engaging with civil society organisations, such as trade unions or business associations.

Intended to depoliticise society, the Constitution prohibited a wide array of individuals from becoming members of political parties, from university teachers to civil servants and so on. A complement to this was the election law that stipulated obtaining at least 10 per cent of nationwide votes to be eligible for seats in the parliament. The Law was apparently intended to support a totalitarian political regime envisaged to cast off political cosmopolitanism and therefore centripetal offshoots. In terms of the separation of powers, as Kalaycıoğlu (2005: 128) put it, the Constitution was designed to devise a 'legislature subservient to the executive, that is only nominally controlled by the legislature, a judiciary strictly monitored and even harnessed by the Ministry of Justice (executive), an omnipotent, yet legally and politically irresponsible, and hence arbitrary Presidency, and a concomitant docile civil society, largely apathetic toward politics … Turkish Presidents seem to "have a cake and eat it too" and resemble Greek Gods'.

In May 1983, the junta allowed the foundation of political parties but stipulated that only the political parties confirmed by the junta could enter the elections of November 1983. One of the CHP's successors, *Sosyal Demokrat Halkçı Parti –* SODEP, the Social Democratic Party of Turkey, founded by Erdal İnönü, the son of İsmet İnönü, was not approved by the National Security Council to compete in the elections. The other, Halkçı Parti – HP, the Populist Party, founded in May 1983, took 30 per cent of the vote, becoming the main opposition party. Then, the 10 per cent threshold enabled that ANAP to consolidate its electoral base, primarily consisting of the conservatively or nationalistically sensitive segments of society including the lower urban classes. The founder and the leader of the ANAP, Turgut Özal, crafted a political ideology combining liberal, conservative and Islamic ideals with a discursive egalitarianism at the level of theory.

In theory-praxis interaction, the Party stood on the centre right with an economically neoliberal, politically conservative-pragmatist and culturally Muslim-pragmatist strategy. This meant that the Party well internalised the institutionalised economic order following the 24 January 1980 decisions and prioritised the embedded peculiarities of the Turkish state from laicism to national-unity-conditioned individual and political rights, from Atatürk's principles to planned economic development. The Party programme highlights that, on the one hand, 'we regard *planning* significant in employing available resources in the most effective manner and realising a consistent, rapid and productive social and economic development', whereas '… a competitive free market economy is our preference', on the other (ANAP, 1983: item 8).

The Party declared that it intended to encourage aggregate savings to stimulate investment and price stability with a passive emphasis on social justice by providing equality of opportunity and the promotion of welfare by 'reducing income differentials'. Complementary institutions for the Party in terms of social policies were the provision of a constrained social security regime and the extension of social aid opportunities and voluntary social self-help (Ergüder, 1991). The Party's strategy, in its operational roots, aimed to dispose its central and provincial organisation under the leadership of conservatively oriented, liberal-minded and secularly adaptive cadres. The religiously sensitive individuals participated in a fragmented manner at the various levels of Party administration, but religion itself was an electorally inclusive rather than politically integral constituent of the Party's mainstream organisation.

Institutional Political Economics of Economic Transformation Costs in the Turkish Context

In economic policy, the accumulated dynamics of the politico-economic crisis of the late 1970s elapsed into changing path-dependencies overnight, as executed first by the junta and then the successive ANAP governments until November 1991. In the Turkish case, in this sense, while the crisis-ridden structures generated the change-laden dynamics from a reactionist standpoint, the coup d'état condensed the pace of these changes into a very limited period of time, not more than a few months. Following the military intervention, in this respect, a technocratic government was installed, and the 24 January 1980 economic decisions, taken by the AP's overthrown government under close monitoring by the IMF and World Bank, were then implemented authoritatively under the technical guidance of Turgut Özal, then deputy prime minister responsible for economic affairs. The programme contained classical neoliberal recipies: the realisation of the budget and balance of payments off-set on the basis of public sector downsizing and the liberalisation of trade and commercial exchange, flexibilisation of prices, exchange and interest rates and so on.

In parallel, in praxis, along with the lifting of import quotas and substantial reductions in tariff rates, the direct state subsidies in the form of inexpensive inputs to the private sector from the SOEs were discontinued (Celasun and Arslan, 2001). Instead of complete elimination, however, the face of state intervention changed, in this case through export-subsidies until the end of 1988, under the shadow of a widespread rent-seeking action and a mechanism that betrayed this intervention, *fictitious exports*. The post-1980 export incentive schemes were: (i) a policy to stimulate exports through exchange rate depreciation until 1988; (ii) direct payments to exporters through tax rebates and cash premia; (iii) preferential and subsidised export credits with a rediscount rate below commercial interest rates; (iv) tax exemptions on imported inputs used in the production of export goods; and (v) corporate tax allowances.

Additionally, public investment expenditures, throughout the 1980s, did not decelerate, but instead were poured into infrastructural areas such as energy, transport and so on. A fragile and vulnerable economic order accumulated during the 1980s in the form of chronic inflation and skyrocketing interest rates, the structuralisation of high unemployment rates with limited growth in public employment and flexibilisation of employment patterns, increasing tax burdens, especially regarding indirect taxes, real declines in the wages and salaries of public and private sector employees until 1988, persistent consolidated budget and current account deficits and a debt-financed, especially foreign debt, growth model incrementally accumulating with the liberalisation of financial accounts in 1989.

At the end of the 1980s, to gain in the forthcoming elections, ANAP began to develop palliative populist policies such as increasing social expenditures and high real increases in public sector workers' wages in tandem with those in the private sector (Bedirhanoğlu and Yalman, 2010). This initiative did not mitigate but rather worsened the distribution of income and resource allocation, as it paved the way for the accumulation of crisis dynamics, such as hyperinflation and higher interest rates, and a fragile financial structure open to supply shocks from short-term portfolio investments. This populism was also quite dichotomous, as the cost of the reductions in direct taxes was compensated by a nearly an equal increase in indirect taxes, remarkably increasing the total tax burden.

From May 1981 onwards, in this new environment, TCMB began to adjust the exchange rate on a daily basis. In July 1984, domestic and external Turkish and foreign exchange transactions were substantially liberalised and interest rates were deregulated as a structural enhancement for the development of the financial sector. In 1981, the Capital Markets Law was enacted to pave the way for the development of securities markets while protecting the rights and benefits of financial investors, and an independent regulatory institution, the Capital Markets Board, was formed to regulate these markets. Government treasury bills and bonds began to be issued in 1985 to finance governmental debts, which had previously been serviced by direct monetisation by the Central Bank (Yeldan, 2001: 127–58).

Figure 6.4 The anatomy of the April 1994 financial crisis in Turkey
Source: TCMB (2002: 32). The boxes comprise direct quotations.

After a sustained rise in the PSBR during 1991-1992, the government modified its domestic borrowing strategy in the last quarter of 1993 with the aim of reducing interest rates on Tbills and curtailing the interest expenditures in the budget. This policy in turn enhanced the uncertainty perceived in the markets, leading to a decrease in the demand for T-Bills and a monetization of debt. As this strategy prevailed in the first quarter of 1994, the Treasury was left with the Central Bank short-term advances as its only domestic source to finance the budget deficit.

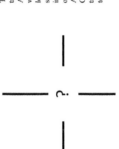

Both factors contributed to the sharp decline in industrial production in the last three quarters of 1994. In the spring of 1994, the government signed a stand-by agreement with the IMF in order to regain credibility. Two further measures were also introduced. First, deposits within the banking system were put under "full insurance" coverage. Second, the government passed a bill aiming at the gradual elimination of public sector borrowing from the Central Bank. With the implementation of the stabilization program, the ratio of the PSBR to GNP decreased from 11 percent in 1993 to 8 percent at the end of 1994

The excess liquidity in the market immediately transformed into a speculative attack on foreign currency. As noted in Ersel and Sak (1995), the Central Bank, while trying to keep the interest rates at their artificially low levels, attempted to defend the exchange rate by selling foreign currency. As a result, both the international reserves and the foreign exchange reserves of the Central Bank declined to their historical low levels. Although the authorities hoped that an increase in the Central Bank's exchange rate might stop this process, the turmoil in the markets continued as exchange rates started to rise at an unprecedented rate (Ersel and Sak, 1995).

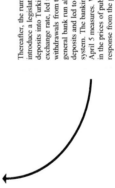

Thereafter, the rumors that the Government was to introduce a legislation to convert foreign exchange (FX) deposits into Turkish lira (TL) deposits at a specified exchange rate, led to a bank run in the form of FX deposit withdrawals from the banking system. This turned into a general bank run also inducing the withdrawal of TL deposits and led to an overall liquidity crisis in the system. The banking crisis led to the introduction of the April 5 measures. With a jump in the exchange rate and in the prices of public goods and services, followed by a response from the private sector, the working capital available for non-financial firms decreased dramatically in real terms. Further, the decline in real income reduced the domestic demand.

The government securities auctions gave rise to the Central Bank's open market operations and the establishment of a secondary bill and bonds market at the Istanbul Stock Exchange, the Interbank Money Market, in April 1986, and the foreign exchange and banknote markets in August 1988. In 1989, capital account was fully liberalised and the convertibility of the TL was recognised, allowing the sale and purchase of national or foreign currencies or securities in the country or abroad. In 1986, monetary policy underwent a structural change from direct to indirect controlling measures.

The pre-1986 period symbolised direct interventions of the Central Bank to control the expenditure and portfolio structures of both the private and public sectors, and the PSBR was financed by Central Bank resources. After 1986, a new policy centred on control over the Turkish lira reserves of the banking system to maintain optimal interest rates and thereby realise indirect control over the money supply. As a complementary initiative, in 1989, the bank limited the exercise of the short-term advance facility by the Treasury. The consequences and effectiveness of these design-centred forms of financial institutionalisation were highlighted by its prime actor, TCMB (2002: 31–6), as follows:

> The capital account liberalization in late 1989 has changed the monetary policy making environment substantially, exposing the economy to strong and mainly short-term capital flows. Thus, the main development on the monetary front has been the gradual but steady decline of the effectiveness of monetary policy and the loss of control of the Central Bank over the monetary aggregates. The aim of the Central Bank through the 1990s was mainly to provide financial stability in the financial markets rather than control inflation. This was due to the high level of dollarization that was indicated by the increase of the share of foreign currency denominated bank deposits in total deposits from 24 per cent in 1989 to 46 per cent in 1999, the acceleration of public sector deficits during the 1990s and increased political instability especially after 1995. Thus, while between the 1989 and the 1994 currency crisis the Central Bank was committed to a certain ceiling on exchange rate depreciation, between late 1995 and early 1998 the Central Bank's main focus was the stability of the real exchange rate … Theoretically, financial liberalization is expected to result in higher savings. When the Turkish case is examined, it is observed that total savings have not shown striking increases in the aftermath of the financial liberalization … The Turkish experience after full liberalization can be well summarized by a very familiar transmission mechanism; large public deficits, putting pressure on shallow financial sector, raise the real interest rates ending up with an increasing dependency on more short-term capital inflows. Eventually, less and less resources were available to production and investment.

TCMB's statement is well reflected during the first and crisis-path-making 1994 economic depression under the incumbency of the DYP-SHP coalition government (Doğru Yol Partisi – DYP, The True Path Party, the AP's successor). The key question in Figure 6.4 refers to whether the ebbing and flowing reactionary policy adaptations were sufficient to smooth the source of the crisis-ridden dynamics in the Turkish economy. The government's ultimate policy set consisted of providing full insurance to bank deposits and gradual termination of the public sector's borrowing from the TCMB. What about the underlying structural imbalances that precipitated the crisis?

In what follows, to determine an inter-temporal response to this question, these structural imbalances are discussed along with their cumulative impact on the making of the 2001 financial crisis. As the SHP/CHP and the DSP were in power between December 1991 and March 1996 and June 1997 and November 2002, a moderately detailed analysis of these particular periods will elicit the practical policy choices and performances of these parties. In addition, such an analysis is of crucial importance in understanding the AKP's economic policy choices and political success, despite enduring structural flaws, between Islamic egalitarianism and neoliberal austerity. In a general sense, the neoliberal transformation and its crisis-generating outcomes have been the major impulse of Islamic, social democratic and liberal interpenetrations from the early 1980s onwards. A set of descriptive data concerning the period 1980–2002 can be found in Table 6.2. The data are presented on an annual basis between 1990 and 2002, as this period will be utilised in due course to examine the economic policy performance of the DYP-SHP and the DSP-led coalition governments in a relatively detailed manner. As Figure 6.5 shows, a systemic analysis of these data between 1989 and 2002 is offered as follows in terms of the basic intersections among the major institutional axes of the Turkish economy.

In the period 1989–2002, the path-dependent imbalances in the Turkish economy are, as described in Figure 6.5, as follows:

a. The inability of the state to collect direct taxes (2) and compensating for this by imposing additional indirect taxes such as the Value Added Taxes (the transfers from the government budget to social security institutions due to an excessive rate of unregistered unemployment at 50 per cent during the 2000s).
b. In addition to inefficient taxation, the low level of public and private savings (1) and delayed pricing strategy of the SOEs (3) with a deficit-increasing impact (6) caused an embedded dependency on domestic and foreign debt (7). The erratic management of this dependency by weak and politically inconsistent coalition governments resulted in persistent financial fragility and consecutive economic crises with soaring interest rates (9), higher interest payments on domestic borrowing (5), and increased credit costs for the real sector (15). The consequence of this cycle is the diminishing marginal efficiency of industrial investment in oligopolistic sectors (4).
c. The unsteady inflow of short-term portfolio capital attracted by the high interest return (13) on, particularly, government securities and its sudden outflow (11) before and during crisis periods triggers real appreciation in

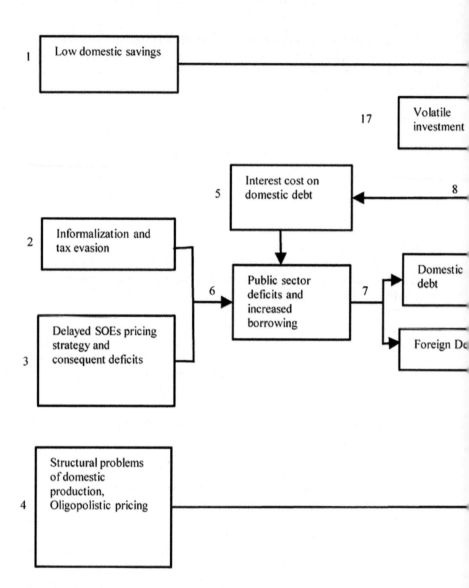

Figure 6.5   Institutional intersections of the Turkish economy under full liberalisation, 1989–2002

Source: Boratav et al. (2000: 7).

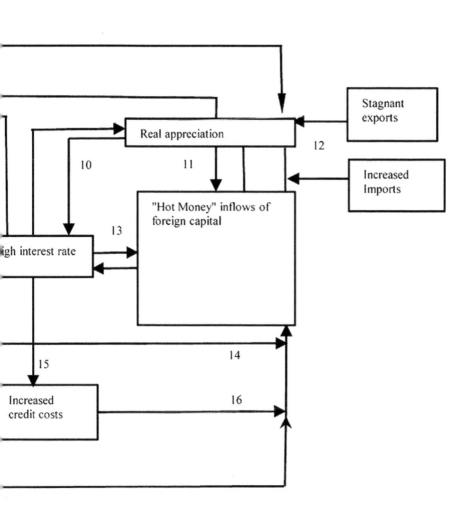

Results of General Elections		Interregnum	Nov.1983		Nov. 1987		October	
			HP	30.5	SHP	24.9	SHP	2
					DYP	19.1	DYP	2
					RP	7.2	RP	1
					MÇP	2.9		
			ANAP	45.2	ANAP	36.3	ANAP	2
					DSP	8.5	DSP	1
Governmental Status					ANAP			
Duration of incumbency*		Dec					Nov.	

Parameters	1980	1981-1983	1984-1987	1988-1990	1991
GDP[1]	-2,4	4,5	6,9	3,9	0,9
Agriculture	1,3	0,2	1,1	2,4	-0,6
Industry	-3,6	7,2	9,8	5,4	2,9
Services	-4,1	4,5	7,9	4,2	-0,5
Balance of Accounts/GDP	-1,4	-0,6	-0,2	1,1	-0,5
Current Account Balance/GDP	-3,7	-1,8	-1,3	0,2	0,1
Foreign trade/GDP	11,9	16,6	20,9	19,3	17,2
Consolidated Budget Balance/GDP[2]	6,6	3,1	3,5	4,4	7,5
Tax Burden/GDP	13,0	12,8	12,4	14,0	15,7
Indirect Taxes/GDP	4,1	4,1	5,5	6,4	6,9
Direct Taxes/GDP	6,6	6,0	4,1	4,5	5,2
Public Fixed Cap. Form./GDP	-8,1	0,4	1,8	-11,1	4,8
Government Final Cons. Exp./GDP[3]	...	-5,5	-1,2	12,5	12,8
Total Domestic Demand/GDP	...	3,5	6,8	4,4	-0,1
Credit of Central Bank to Public Sector/GDP	5,9	4,2	2,3	1,6	2,2
Inflation	101,4	31,3	41,7	65,8	65,9
Unemployment	8,6	7,8	8,2	8,7	8,7
Interest Rates[4]	33,0	43,3	50,0	65,8	80,5
Privatization/GDP[5]	...	...	...	0,2	0,1
Social Expenditures/GDP	3,1	2,8	3,3	5,2	6,1
Gini coefficient	0,49	0,52	0,47	...	...
Public Sector Wages and Salaries	...	...	...	...	...
Wages and Salaries in Public Sector	-1,0	6,7	-6,4	5,4	3,9
Worker (Public Sector)	-27,6	-3,0	3,0	34,2	46,4
Minimum Wage	...	...	...	...	14,2
Worker Private	-22,6	1,5	-1,6	5,3	45,6
Change in Public Sector Employment	2,8	1,6	2,3	2,0	1,5
Civil Servant (Fixed-term contracts)	3,5	1,5	3,7	1,7	1,6
Worker (Temporary)	-25,3	-1,4	-16,2	-2,4	-0,1
Worker (Permanent)	1,6	2,2	-10,4	3,1	0,0
Contracted	9,8	4,9	8,1	42,3	3,9
Employment Strictness	...	...	...	3,76	3,76

mber 1995		April 1999		November 2022	
10.7		CHP	8.7	CHP	19.3
19.2		DYP	12.0	DYP	9.5
21.4		FP	15.4	SP	15.4
8.0		MHP	17.4	MHP	8.3
P 19.7		ANAP	13.2	ANAP	5.1
14.6		DSP	22.1	DSP	1.2

	DYP-CHP	ANAP DYP	RP DYP	ANAP-DSP DTP-Ind.		DSP	DSP-MHP-ANAP	AKP
t.	Mar.	Jun.	Jun.	Jan.		May		Nov.
95	1996	1997	1998	1999		2000	2001	2002
7,2	7,0	7,5	3,1			-3,4	6,8	-5,7	6,2
1,3	4,6	-2,2	9,6			-5,7	7,1	-7,9	8,8
12,5	6,8	10,2	1,8			-4,9	6,6	-7,3	2,7
7,6	7,9	9,9	3,6			-1,5	6,4	-2,5	5,5
2,1	1,8	1,3	0,1			2,1	-1,1	-6,5	-0,1
-1,0	-1,0	-1,0	0,7			-0,3	-3,7	1,9	-0,2
25,3	27,4	29,4	26,9			27,1	31,0	36,9	38,0
3,7	6,5	5,8	7,1			11,6	8,9	12,1	10,0
15,5	16,7	18,6	20,0			21,5	23,8	25,1	23,9
7,4	8,5	9,3	8,7			9,4	10,8	11,1	11,0
5,1	4,9	5,4	6,8			6,9	6,9	7,4	5,9
31,1	18,2	21,8	.8.3			-3,9	5,6	-9,0	2,6
-7,4	7,3	6,0	3,6			19,3	-4,1	5,7	2,7
10,1	6,8	8,1	1,2			-1,9	8,0	-12,0	8,8
1,9	1,9	0,9	0,0			0,0	0,0	0,0	0,0
88,0	80,4	85,7	84,7			64,9	54,9	54,4	45,0
8,1	7,1	7,3	7,4			8,2	7,0	8,9	10,8
21,9	135,2	127,2	122,5			109,5	38,0	96,2	63,8
0,2	0,1	0,1	0,1			0,1	0,8	0,1	0,0
5,6	7,2	8,0	8,3			9,8	...	...	...
...	...	...	...			...	...	...	0,44
...	...	...	...			...	...	...	...
-2,6	11,2	13,4	-3,8			2,8	-13,7	-5,5	6,4
22,5	-23,4	26,8	-6,4			26,4	18,0	-6,9	-11,0
-3,8	19,0	11,3	-7,2			25,2	-14,9	-10,7	5,0
14,2	2,6	0,8	8,0			7,0	10,9	-13,8	-2,8
2,4	-0,5	0,4	6,0			3,4	6,3	-0,4	0,8
2,6	0,8	0,5	6,5			3,5	6,5	-0,1	0,1
0,4	-4,7	-0,6	-0,2			23,9	18,4	-82,7	4,7
0,2	-8,5	-0,3	-2,1			-1,2	-0,7	8,9	0,3
-2,7	-11,2	-5,6	1,3			0,8	7,0	3,4	6,7
3,76	3,76	3,76	3,76			3,72	3,72	3,72	3,72

Table 6.2 Major indicators of the Turkish Political Economy, 1980–2002

Notes: * The months indicate the termination of incumbency in the year. [1]The harmonized GDP data has been used, provided by the TKB (2013a) and the OECD (2014). [2]For 1950–1974, Consolidated Budget Balance/GDP; 1975–2012, PSBR/GDP; - indicates surplus. [3]1970–1988 Deposit interest rates, 1989–2012 average compound interest on domestic borrowing. [4]1989 value represents average of 1985–1989.
Source: TKB (2013a), TUIK (2013), OECD (2013a).

the TL against foreign exchange and drives up interest rates (10), thereby destabilising output and employment and decreasing exports (12).

d. The banking sector's persistent 'investment' in governmental securities using funds borrowed from abroad at relatively lower costs and the quite low marginal propensity of this sector to grant investment credit, declining ratios of total credit to total deposits and total credits to total assets (especially throughout the 1990s when political and economic volatility reached their greatest extents).

e. The social expenditure-reducing impact of high public debt and its constraints on market demand, widening wage differentials and the growing gap between labour productivity and real wages.

What should have been done? Interestingly, with reference to McKinnon (1991), the TCMB (2002: 61–2) offers an evolutionary response to this question in terms of how the institutional design should be phased out throughout the process of financial and commercial liberalisation. According to McKinnon, initially, financial liberalisation should be preceded by fiscal discipline. As the second step, the establishment of overall macro-economic stability should be the main yardstick for the *pace* of liberalising domestic capital markets and the deregulation of banks and other financial institutions, because the shallow financial structures operating under the yet to be institutionalised structures of developing countries cannot cope with the unpredictable volatility in real interest and exchange rates prior to the establishment of price stability. The ultimate step is to liberalise international capital mobility, which should be preceded by the development of a well-functioning domestic capital market at the equilibrium interest rate. In addition, inflation should be at controllable levels to avoid incurring the volatilising impact of exchange rate depreciation or appreciation (see, McKinnon, 1991: Chapter XI).

In terms of the structural imbalances in the Turkish economy, it becomes apparent that these policy prescriptions are in fact also inadequate for establishing a macro-micro equilibrium to achieve sustained and stable growth. This is because the abovementioned prescriptions bear on macro financial variables to a substantial extent but do not comprise their interplay with productive variables in the long run. As can be observed in the outbreaks and evolution of the 1994 and 2001 crises in Turkey, any attempt to manage economic crises through short-run-focused financial games will not stabilise economic conduct but expose it to the former's destabilising cycles (Cizre-Sakallıoğlu and Yeldan, 2000). Another structural result of these crises is that Central Bank independence in no way ensures the optimality of monetary policy adaptations. Rather, as instantiated by TCMB's own acknowledgment cited above, they might manage these crises quite inconsistently while paying no heed to the impact of their policy adaptations on productive variables.

A note from the PhD dissertation of the prime minister of the DYP-SHP coalition government, Tansu Çiller, during the 1994 economic crisis, published in 1972, on the strategy for economic development is that 'It is possible to attain a higher growth rate in both consumption and income in the long run by giving more emphasis to the portion of investment which increases the capacity of the investment goods industries'. She attends to the prospective balance of payment instabilities in the event that such a strategy cannot be operationalised within 12 to 22 years. In October 2013, the deputy prime minister of Turkey responsible for economic affairs, while announcing Turkey's medium-term programme for 2014–16 (TKB, 2013c), placed particular emphasis on the risks of current account deficits for Turkey with respect to the extremely low level of domestic savings, 12.6 per cent. It is a well-established fact that the main reason is the structural dependence of Turkey's industrial establishment on intermediate goods imports. In addition, he argues that a rollback in savings is highly correlated with the current account deficit due to a rising demand for import goods consisting of automobiles, mobile phones, computers and other electronic products.

The meaning of these inter-temporal investigations for this book is that, despite untimely and overnight changes in financial institutions, the productive variables of the Turkish economy remained relatively unchanged over the last four decades. At issue is that the change in financial institutions primarily depends on the enactment of related acts, but the change in productive institutions requires the development of a mode of social order on the basis of institutional complementarities among the state, market, capital, labour, industrial relations, social policy and so on. In this sense, Turkey failed to develop stakeholder or shareholder capitalism between 1950 and 2002 and thereafter (Altuğ and Filiztekin, 2006). The underlying reason is the formation and deformation of the institutional stock on a path of institutional-engineering and re-engineering, irrespective of the evolutionary bases of capital, technology and socio-cultural accumulation. The combinational manifestation of these variables in Turkey ebbed and flowed between institutional time-lags and rushes enforced by conjuncturally adapted *reactionary* strategies in the form of U-turns.

For example, the transition towards an etatist neoliberalism was predicated upon the fact that the import-substitutionist strategy of the previous era failed to achieve its declared aims and proposed an inside-out recipe for an escape from the deep crisis of the late 1970s. An institutionalist analyst should ask the question why an import-substitutionist model had been adopted and on what grounds. The answer is, to a great extent, a reaction to the failure of the outward liberal etatism of the preceding period. As noted earlier with reference to Kepenek, neither were there industrialists nor bureaucrats prepared for such a change. In the sequel, the result of reactionary import-substitionism and etatist neoliberalism can be observed in the longstanding structural imbalances discussed above, the accumulated bill of which manifested itself at the turn of the century, in the 2001 economic crisis.

Beyond its fluctuational specifications, the crisis reveals the highly buoyant financial imbalances of the country and the limited space for political discretion to take structural steps. What the then DSP-led coalition government did was, as can be followed in Figure 6.6, to only make immediate reactions to market signals rather than to take a well-organised set of systemic steps to curb the

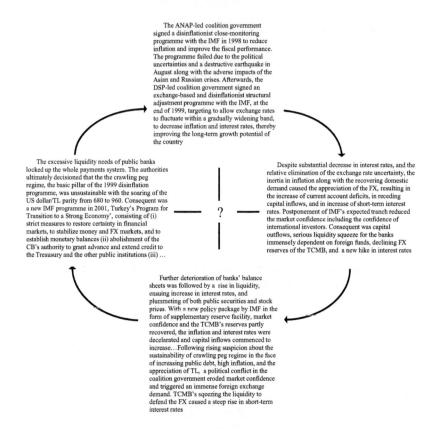

The ANAP-led coalition government signed a disinflationist close-monitoring programme with the IMF in 1998 to reduce inflation and improve the fiscal performance. The programme failed due to the political uncertainties and a destructive earthquake in August along with the adverse impacts of the Asian and Russian crises. Afterwards, the DSP-led coalition government signed an exchange-based and disinflationist structural adjustment programme with the IMF, at the end of 1999, targeting to allow exchange rates to fluctuate within a gradually widening band, to decrease inflation and interest rates, thereby improving the long-term growth potential of the country

The excessive liquidity needs of public banks locked up the whole payments system. The authorities ultimately decisioned that the the crawling peg regime, the basic pillar of the 1999 disinflation programme, was unsustainable with the soaring of the US dollar/TL parity from 680 to 960. Consequent was a new IMF programme in 2001, Turkey's Program for Transition to a Strong Economy', consisting of (i) strict measures to restore certainty in financial markets, to stabilize money and FX markets, and to establish monetary balances (ii) abolishment of the CB's authority to grant advance and extend credit to the Treausury and the other public institutions (iii) …

?

Despite substantial decrease in interest rates, and the relative elimination of the exchange rate uncertainty, the inertia in inflation along with the recovering domestic demand caused the appreciation of the FX, resulting in the increase of current account deficits, in receding capital inflows, and in increase of short-term interest rates. Postponement of IMF's expected tranch reduced the market confidence including the confidence of international investors. Consequent was capital outflows, serious liquidity squeeze for the banks immensely dependent on foreign funds, declining FX reserves of the TCMB, and a new hike in interest rates

Further deterioration of banks' balance sheets was followed by a rise in liquidity, ensuing increase in interest rates, and plummeting of both public securities and stock prices. With a new policy package by IMF in the form of supplementary reserve facility, market confidence and the TCMB's reserves partly recovered, the inflation and interest rates were decelarated and capital inflows commenced to increase…Following rising suspicion about the sustainability of crawling peg regime in the face of increasing public debt, high inflation, and the appreciation of TL, a political conflict in the coalition government eroded market confidence and triggered an immense foreign exchange demand. TCMB's sqeezing the liquidity to defend the FX caused a steep rise in short-term interest rates

Figure 6.6   The evolution of the 2001 economic crisis under IMF surveillance
Source: TCMB (2002: 50–54).

inflation-interest-debt Bermuda triangle. Specifically regarding this case, a highly exceptional event occurred that illustrates the desperateness of the then prime minister, Bülent Ecevit, the ideologue of social democratic Kemalism. He called on the then vice president, Kemal Derviş, of the World Bank for *urgent help* (Derviş et al., 2006: 50–51). I will elaborate on this issue further in due course in terms of the DSP's transformation between 1999 and 2002.

In the long run, it can thus be suggested that Turkey's social actors could not forge a peculiar social model in the form of an organised or market capitalism around economic and political exchanges. The state-subsidised strategy of production from the early twentieth century onwards has always been accommodated by the suppression or control of organised labour and civic organisations through authoritative measures. The generous incentives of the single-party, the exchange-rate and quota-based protection and subsidised-inputs during the import-substitutionist and the wide-ranging export incentives of etatist neoliberal eras have always evolved in patronage-based exchange between governments and business, including the direct engagement of the former's members in business activities.

Turkey's big businesses approached the TKB, Turkish Ministry of Development, with caution in fear that it would render Turkey an overruled economy. Yet, in praxis, they came to buttress its *modus vivendi* regarding its role in the distribution of public resources through its programmes for business incentives, subsidies, protective measures and so on. In the post-1980 period, too, big business maintained its support for the State Planning Organisation, the former title of the TKB, as they utilised the export subsidies and foreign capital permissions given by it (Akçay, 2007: 187). Among them, the most salient is Koc Holding, the largest business group in Turkey.

The company's founder, Vehbi Koc, cultivated his capital by capturing the food expenditures of bureaucratic families and gaining business opportunities through governmental projects. During World War II, as a dedicated member of the CHP, he sold tracks that he had imported to the government at a 90 per cent profit, a watershed in the accumulation of his capital (a similar scenario is the case for the second largest holding in Turkey, the Sabancı Group, offering top-level positions to high-ranking military officials as a strategic attempt to perpetuate its business, especially during military coups [see Buğra, 1994]). At present, Koc Holding is of the opinion that constructing a new national brand of automobile is simply commercial suicide. Rather, Mustafa Koc, Vehbi's son, intends to perpetuate the firm's role as an *assembly representative* of the Italian firm Fiat at the Holding's automotive establishment in Bursa, a city in the Northern Marmara Region, as has been the case since the late 1960s. The explicit meaning of this is the continuing dependence of the Turkish export sector on intermediate goods imports, from the 1950s onwards.

Three intertwined outcomes can be proposed to reveal the suboptimality of the institutional stock in Turkey, as a result of its long-run drift. The first is that Turkey ranked 59th and 44th in global competitiveness in 2006 and 2013, and has the 13th largest GDP of the OECD countries as of 2012. This is not a notable status for a country that has engaged in industrial activities for more than one and a half centuries, which place it far behind nations that were previously under the rule of the Ottoman Empire such as Qatar, Bahrain, Oman, Kuwait, the United Arab Emirates and so on. A study by the Turkish Statistics Institution in 1998 concluded that of Turkish enterprises, 16 per cent are competitive, 35 semi-competitive, 25 highly concentrated and 35 per cent highly monopolised (TCMB, 2002: 43–4). Complicating this panorama is the second observation that, despite extensive neoliberal reforms, Turkey had the second highest status with a score of 3.25 on the OECD's index of product market regulation as of 1998 and fell to fourth with a score of 2.17 in 2013 (OECD, 2013b).

The index indicates the promotion or inhibition of competition in areas of the product market where competition is viable and covers formal regulations in the areas of state control of business enterprises, legal and administrative barriers to entrepreneurship and barriers to international trade and investment. In the employment rigidity index, indicating the strictness of regulations on dismissals under regular contracts, the country only fell to 2.30 in 2013 from 2.39 in 1990. Another nexus, the third, is the drifting structure of the SOEs. Asutay (2010: 94) describes Turkish SOEs as *vote factories* and *out of budget* spending opportunities, stating: 'Despite recent privatisation attempts, SOEs or the state owned industrial companies, remain important producers, distributors, banks and sometimes as the largest buyer or the monopsonist. It is, therefore, still normal to hear increases in the prices of steel or iron or even sugar announced by the government'. These three parameters well demonstrate that, during a period of transition, the country could not enforce a targeted but instead pursued a drifting institutional transformation, ultimately having an *uncompetitive deregulation* that dragged the country's economic structure into deep financial crises.

National and Transnational Actors in the Turkish Political Economy between 1950 and 2013

As stated at the beginning of this chapter, the end of this chapter illustrates the institutional environment of and actors in the Turkish political economy with their strategic policy choices during the periods 1960–79 and 1980–2013 (see Figure I.2, p.). As it is well beyond the scope of this research to elaborate on the foundation and evolution of each actor, I will incorporate them into the analysis in terms of their roles and impacts on the formation, evolution and path-dependent change of Islamic, social democratic and neoliberal institutionalisms in the Turkish context, particularly in the context of their interactions with the NOM-affiliated parties, the AKP, the CHP and the other representatives of Kemalist variants of social democracy and the Third Way.

Table 6.3   Institutional environment and major actors of the Turkish political economy between 1960 and 1979

Institutional Environment

Internal	–A planned, semi-stakeholder capitalism, expansionary fiscal policy, development-oriented monetary strategy, a fixed-exchange rate regime, widespread exchange controls and quotas –Systemic industrialisation, urbanisation, and halfway marketisation of social interaction –An ideologically segregated political structure and an import-substitutionist economic regime –Institutionalisation of organised labour relations under a model of semi-corporatist authoritarianism functionalised by a compromise around oligopolistic profits and moderate wage restraints

External	–Continuing and falling tides of international Keynesianism and European social democracy, the Bretton Woods system, ideologically segregated world politics –Dissipation of the Soviet threat and normalisation of Turkey's relations with the SSCB –Interference of the IMF, the World Bank and, partially, the TNCs in the Turkish political economy

Major Actors and Strategies

Civil-military bureaucracy	–Discontinuing the changes that the DP made to power, prestige and patronage channels –Changing the continuity of crude authoritarianism by adding ideologic content to it

Political Parties

CHP (1923)*	–Changing continuities by crafting revisionist theoretical ideology, left of centre, as a new strategy for resurrecting Kemalism with an egalitarian social face –Reconstructing the basic constitutional, judicial and socio-economic institutions in compliance with planned economic order
AP (1961–81)*	–Perpetuating the DP's practical ideology in politics by striking a pragmatic/flexible balance among secularism, Kemalism and liberal etatism –Discarding anti-systemic tensions in the Party by dissociating from normative gestures to avoid agitating the central forces (the military, bureaucracy and intelligentsia)
MSP-MNP (1969/1971–81)*	Adapting Islamic political economy to the Turkish context and organising religiously sensitive individuals through strong organisational bonds from the early 1970s
MHP (1969–81)*	Developing nationalistically motivated, bottom-up social action with a political vision of 'Muslim-Turk' synthesis

Business and Employer Organisations

TISK (1961)*	Turkish Confederation of Employer Associations –Pursuing a radical employer strategy against the working class by strongly defending lock-outs –Appealing for active state involvement in constructing tri-lateral concession bargaining, leading the development of industrial sectors and adopting protective measures in the face of international competition –Demonstrating strict allegiance to Atatürkism
TUSIAD (1971)*	Turkish Industrialists' and Businessmen's Association –Having an organisational mission to serve Turkey's democratic and planned development with a Kemalist orientation –Adopting a 'progressive conservatism' with a tolerant perspective on organised labour and autonomous collective bargaining and urging the state to address social justice, unemployment, education and health services

Trade Unions

Turk-Is [1952]*	Adapting unconflictual wage unionism and organising primarily in the SOEs with a secularly oriented conservative or social democratic inclination
DISK [1967]*	Adopting a radical trade union strategy with a compromising niche, organising largely in the private sector
Hak-Is [1976]*	Pursuing a conciliative strategy with a religiously sensitive concentration, founded in the MSP-affiliated ministries in 1976

Regional and International Organisations

The EU	The institutional role model for Turkey's civilisational transformation and specifically the CHP's social democracy (in terms of its status for the Turkish political economy). Turkey's never-ending journey towards membership began in 1963
IMF [1946]** World Bank [1947]**	Destructuring import-substitutionist regime by coercing the CHP government of 1978–79 to devaluate the TL, raise the prices of the SOEs' products and reduce public expenditures, converting ($2.8 billion) private sector debt into public debt, accelerating inflation, reducing the rate of capacity utilisation and so on The World Bank's provision of development finance without a systemic impact on economic conduct
ILO [1932]**	Exerting diplomatic pressure on Turkish governments to sign the ILO conventions and execute their requirements and the regulation of labour and collective bargaining laws in parallel with these conventions
ITUC [ICFTU]	International Trade Union Confederation Providing financial, educational and logistical support to enhance the operational effectiveness of the Turk-Is, becoming a member of ICFTU in 1960

Table 6.4   Institutional environment and major actors in the Turkish political economy between 1980 and 2013

Institutional Environment

Internal	–Etatist neoliberalism, venturous commodification and consolidative austerity –Volatile, untimely, reactionary and systemically dichotomous restructurations resulting in structural crises –De-ideologisation (early 1980s), political fragmentation (early 1990s) and re-ideologisation (mid-1990s) –Assimilative and reifying invasion of purposive rationality into social networks –Dissolution of micro-corporatism and shallow structuration of macro-corporatism

External	–Disintegrative conditionalities of centripetal organisations of the transnational neoliberal establishment –Political democratisation and economic consolidation under the aegis of the EU's conditionality –A burred cobweb of overseas networked rationalisation over the dialectics of norms and rationality –Consolidating the social security regime, subjecting rights to means-tested responsibilities and discursive decommodification under unsystemic re-Keynesianisation

Major Actors and Strategies

Civil-military bureaucracy	–Leading the settlement of state neoliberalism by establishing an authoritarian and controlling institutional system in the aftermath of a coup d'état –Perpetuating secular capitalism in the face of the Just Order, the AKP and Kurdish politics by closing political parties affiliated with these currents, enforcing a coup d'état to force the RP to dissolve the government or pressing AKP governments not to attempt the initiatives regarding emancipating religious education or extending the scope of Islamic action

Political Parties

AKP [2002]*	*Conservative Democracy**** Crafting a path-dependently structured change initiative to strike a balance between the unsystemic *implementation* of norm-contingentness among Turkish Muslims and the level of rationality-contingentness that the secular politico-economic institutional environment requires
RP-FP-SP [1983–97–2001]*	*The Just Order**** Continuing path-dependence through a straightforward adaptation of Islamic economics while internalising the punitive reflexes of the Kemalist regime in politics
SHP [1983–95]*	*Third Way Kemalism* (1985–1995)*** First to continue the strategic vision of social democratic Kemalism in response to the electoral demands of both the Party's members and prospective voters but, second, to discontinue its path-dependencies in conciliation with then rising neoliberal market capitalism to leave room for executing the first
CHP [reopened in 1992]	*Kemalist social democracy* (1995–2010)*** To capitalise on the regime-based political tensions by placing Kemalism over social democracy but also to sustain social democratic premises as a means of alternative discourse to the RP's social justice-first politico-economic programme and the AKP's responsible pragmatist social welfare paradigm and a recipe for the commodifactory power of neoliberal hegemony *Social democratic Kemalism* (2010–13)*** To turn the Party's route towards a social policy-centred opposition strategy and use Kemalism as a background motive to be featured in the event of a regime-based threat, essentially from Islamic circles

DSP [1985]*	*Social democratic Kemalism* (Democratic Left)*** Further paradigmatic sidelining of the Kemalist implications in the social democratic Kemalism of 1970s, imposition of adaptive but unsystemic constraints on its social justice-conditioned morphology but essentially continuing the path-dependency of the building blocks of the CHP of 1970–80
ANAP [1983–2009]*	Combining liberal, conservative and Islamic ideals along with a discursive egalitarianism to cultivate a catch-all vision
DYP [1983–2007]*	Perpetuating the AP's practical ideology in politics by striking a pragmatic/flexible balance among secularism, Kemalism and liberal capitalism
MHP [1983]*	Perpetuating a nationalist vision with a regression of engagement in ideologic clashes and in strong counteractions against leftist currents
Business and Employer Organisations	
TISK	–Urging the state to undertake an active role in managing the institutional axes among education, labour markets, research and development, taxes, sectoral subsidies and so on, and flexibly implementing Turkey's international commitments in financial and commercial liberalisation to protect domestic producers –Undertaking aggressive lobbying in the formation of basic individual and organised labour relations arrangements
TUSIAD	–Arguing for active state involvement in developing the educational and technological infrastructure for industrial investment under five-year plans for the industrial sector while avoiding venturing into competitive industries –Proposing the alleviation of poverty and inequality of income as a subsidiary target
MUSIAD [1990]*	Independent Industrialists' and Businessmen's Association –Supporting public-private partnerships from the perspective of Islamic economics, particularly in the sense of business ethics and finance –Urging state involvement in providing export subsidies, increasing research and development support and instituting an import-substitutionist strategy for import goods such as electrical machines, motor vehicles and so on
Islamic Banks [mid-1980s]*	Collecting interest-free funds primarily to provide consumer credits and production financing in the form of murabaha and leasing, respectively, and trivially for business credits in the form of mudaraba
Trade and Civil Service Unions	
Turk-Is	–Adapting a conflictual compromise strategy with a secularly oriented, conservative, nationalist or social democratic inclination –Pursuing an above-party politics, albeit conjunctural engagement with the parties in power
DISK	Adapting a radical trade union strategy with a compromising niche
Hak-Is	Pursuing a conciliative strategy with a religiously sensitive concentration

Memur-Sen [1992]*	Confederation of Civil Servants Union Adapting a prudent conciliative strategy to a religiously sensitive concentration
Kamu-Sen [1992]*	Confederation of Public Servants Union Adopting wage-unionism with a strictly secular nationalist-political and nationalist-Keynesian economic policy vision
KESK [1995]*	Confederation of Public Workers Union –Radical and uncompromising unionism in cooperation with transnational labour movements –Cooperating with other leftist civic organisations in advocating for radical leftist and Kurdish politics

Regional and International Organisations

EU	–Urging Turkey to optimise and consolidate its liberalised institutional stock in strategic cooperation with the IMF-World Bank-WTO-TNCs-OECD –Requiring Turkey to democratise and secularise its political establishment and endorse basic individual and collective rights including the right to strike and collective bargaining for civil servants
Business Europe [TISK's membership in 1987]	TISK's mentor in forming and defending its strategies of flexibilised and deregulated industrial relations and preventing the ESC from becoming a binding forum on the basis of equal power-sharing among the 'partners' (in parallel with the open-ended conduct of the bilateral or trilateral negotiations among the Commission, ETUC and Business Europe)
IMF & World Bank	Conditioning the country to destructure its semi-stakeholder model towards a shareholder one, downsize the public sector, deepen the supply-side austerity and so on
WTO [1995] – TNCs	Conditioning Turkey to liberalise its trade regime, decrease tariffs and quotas, implement the most favoured nation and national treatment principles, eliminate double taxation problems, provide the free expropriation of profits and so on
ILO	Exerting diplomatic pressure on Turkish governments to sign the ILO conventions, execute their requirements and regulate labour and collective bargaining laws in tandem with these conventions
ITUC-GUFs-ETUC	GUFs (Global Union Federations), ETUC (European Trade Union Confederation) Cooperation on information sharing, actions and propaganda, financial assistance, educational training with Turkish labour organisations and voicing their rights and struggles at regional and international bodies (DISK and Hak-Is' joined the ITUC in 1992 and in 1997, respectively; the ETUC in 1985 and in 1997, respectively; Turk-Is joined the ETUC in 1988)

Notes: *Indicates the year of foundation and, if any, closure; **Indicates Turkey's membership; ***Indicates the identity or ideology of the relevant political party.
Source: Eğilmez (1997); World Bank (2005); WTO (1998, 2012); Balasubramanyam and Corless (2001); ABGS, (2007); Togan and Ersel (2005); Usul (2011); Ateşoğulları (1997); Nichols and Sugur (2010); Memur-Sen (2009a, 2009b); Kamu-Sen (2005, 2013); KESK (2013); Önder (1999); Bianchi (1984); TISK (2011, 2012); TUSIAD, (2011); Jang (2005, Chapter 6); MUSIAD (2002, 2012).

PART III
Systemic Versus Reconciliative Changes Between Major Paradigms in Modern Turkey, 1960–2013

Chapter 7

The Floating Evolution of Turkish Social Democracy and Kemalism Between Orthodoxy and Third Way

Turkish social democracy is an area of research that requires adopting a prudent methodology to examine its theory and praxis as it was nurtured in a developing context. A straightforward outcome of this prudency is the subconscious reference in the minds of the Turkish people to the question: 'Is there social democracy in Turkey?' because the main determinant of the response to this question is whether 'Turkish social democracy has the same practical content and value as European social democracy'. From this perspective, naturally, the answer is 'no' (for example, see Kahraman, 1993). Instead, in this particular sub-section, I will concentrate on the formation, evolution and current stage of Turkish social democracy in terms of the institutional stock of social democratic theory enumerated in the first part and examine the theoretical formulations and practical initiatives of Turkish social democrats within the systemic coexistence of this institutional stock rather than the practical manifestations of European social democracy.

In doing so, the main inquiry becomes whether Turkish social democrats, if any, adapted the pure theory of social democracy to the context-specific circumstances of Turkish territory and then initiated systemically meaningful social democratisations in timespace. Ostensibly, the former would not seem to be a prerequisite for the latter. Yet, without the former, the latter would be unfeasible due to the lack of a roadmap presenting the systemic framework by which the latter would be justified, implemented and changed in tandem with the idiosyncratic structure of political, economic and societal culture. In other words, social democratisations should be gauged in terms of the *social democratizabilities* while accounting for the challenges and opportunities that a politico-economic system poses or offers. The reason is that ideologies, especially context-specific ones, do not have to have theoretical consistency but inter-complementary meanings. In our case, these meanings, needless to say, are expected to arise out of the idiosyncratic social action in the Turkish political economy.

In the Turkish case, as the challenges facing the genesis of social democratically inter-complementary meanings are overwhelming, the above-noted prudence becomes indispensable. The major challenges can be suggested to be the volatile and developing politico-economic structure of the Turkish political economy, the unorganised tradition of social exchange between market and political forces, military-dominated power relations (till the early 2010s), the Islamically structured socio-political stock of Turkish people's lifeworld as the key impediment to social democrats obtaining a political majority and the deep-seated path-dependencies of orthodox Kemalism, as the CHP's official and foundational ideology, which has a systemically constraining impact on the practical adoption of citizen-centred and demand-constrained economic and industrial democracy and so on. These challenges can immediately be claimed to exclude the possibility of forging of theory-praxis consistency for Turkish social democracy.

However, there are also remarkable opportunities. In the absence of a systemic implementation of a purely Islamic model with its social-justice-first theory, Turkey's developing structure is the most prolific dynamic for social democrats to legitimate their social welfare-conditioned policy prescriptions in response to the demand for improved welfare among the country's electorate. Another is that orthodox Kemalists have been unable to respond to these demands in both theory and praxis. First and foremost, Turkey's social structure is not alien to *solidaristic* constellations to institutionalise and allocate social welfare under the auspices of an interventionist and regulatory state.

Under the constraining and enabling impact of these challenges and opportunities, the theory and praxis of Turkish social democracy evolved through the social democratic Kemalism of the CHP in the period 1960–79; the Third Way Kemalism of the SHP in the period 1983–95; the Democratic left of the DSP in the period 1985–2002; the Kemalist social democracy of the CHP in the period 1995–2010; and ultimately the resurrected social democratic Kemalism of the CHP in the period 2010–13 in terms of varying combinations of these political parties' policy choices in constructing or reconstructing the intersections of the state, market, class and society. Additional (f)actors determining the conduct of this drift include the transnational environment, the country's institutional stock, these party's power relations with other economic and political actors, the changing morphology of Turkish society among Islam, modernism, capitalism and so on. In what follows, using the main postulates of institutional system analysis, I will examine the path-dependent change in Turkish social democracy in line of its evolution through five various patterns between 1960 and 2013.

Changing Continuities by Continuing Path-Dependencies: the Rise and Fall of the CHP's 'Democratic' Power between 1961–65

Between 1960 and 1979, there were solid dynamics for the development of a social democratic nexus in the CHP's mission, then representative of Turkish social democracy. The most conspicuous of these was the accumulated theoretical, discursive, knowledge, structural and justificatory powers provided by international Keynesianism of the period and established European social democracy, primarily after World War II. The transnational existence of a socially conditioned politico-economic regime, particularly the latter as the unique role model, thus came to feed back into the institutionalisation and change of Turkish social democracy. In a broader context, as Western Europe is an *achieved civilisational project* in the eyes of a vast number of people in Turkey, these feedbacks directly became justificatory niches thereafter.

The basic domestic and structural dynamics that consolidated this turn in the CHP's party mission were the DP's inconsistency in optimally providing and distributing economic and social welfare during the 1950s, when the foundations of Turkish social democracy emerged, the unfolding of a planned and import-substitutionist production regime, the lack of an alternative vision among orthodox Kemalists in counter-manoeuvring the pragmatically crafted new vision of the AP with a catch-all rigour and the lack of a mainstream opposition party to respond to the growing welfare demands of the have-nots in a politically sustainable manner (without clashing with the vested interests of the civil-military bureaucracy and the intelligentsia).

Under these internal and external environmental circumstances, *ortanın solu*, the left of the centre, as the idiosyncratic variety of Turkish social democracy, came into existence as the paradigmatic manifestation of the changing continuity of orthodox Kemalism. Yet, as was the case for the other turning points between 1960 and 2013, it was the structural power resources generated by a military coup d'état, as the main nexus of continuing path-dependence in the CHP's organisational morphology, that both contributed to the development of this paradigm by initiating a planned economic structure and tarnished its traditional pillars by establishing the institutional environment necessary for its embodiment. The latter is the case because a bona fide social democratic regime arose from the civic dynamics of a social system, the precondition for the 'evolutionary embedding' of its institutional pillars as the unique source of its stability and sustainability.

In Ottoman-Turkish society, the military upheavals or coups d'état, from the Janissaries to the Turkish military, were based on the structural tensions among the various institutional power resources. Among them, the coup d'état of May 1960, in terms of its social gamut, was one of the most extensive as it arose from the receding economic power and political prestige of its members in the face of the newly rising landowning aristocrats and business elites and the changing mode of modernisation that wiped out and canalised the Turkish military staff's structural power resources into more civic channels (Karpat, 1970). Extending power and patronage channels into broad-based interest and occupational groups, from peasants to state officials, the social restructuration under the DP governments led to a halt in the strategic convergence in interest cultivation among radical Kemalist civic and military bureaucrats, etatist bourgeoisie, the mainstream media and the positivist intellectuals.

This strategic convergence had been inculcated by engendering a norm-free cultural modernity, cultivating secular knowledge production, embedding secular control over the religiously sensitive masses, making access to generous public subsidies – as the prime source of profitable production – a prerogative for the party's coalitional forces, capturing top governmental cadres and positions and

Table 7.1 Theoretical varieties of Kemalism, social democracy and the Third Way in Turkey, 1960–2013

Parameter	CHP of 1923–60	CHP of 1960–1979	SHP of 1985–1995	DSP of 1985–2002	CHP of 1995–2010
Institutional system	Orthodox Kemalism	Social Democratic Kemalism	Third Way Kemalism	Social Democratic Kemalism (Democratic Left)	Kemalist Social Democracy
Strategy and policy-choices	Continuing changes	Systematisation of changing continuities	Changing path-dependent continuities	Continuing path-dependency	Repositioning continuing path-dependencies
Political democracy	Institutional design by single-party authority	Multi-party democracy	Multi-party democracy	Multi-party democracy conditioned by economic and social democracy	Multi-party democracy conditioned by Kemalist ideals and the politicisation of labour organisations
Economic and social democracy	Authoritarian paternalism	-State-led, unorganised and unconflictual compromise -State-backed industrial democracy	Unconflictual (state-dominated) neocorporatism	Unconflictual (state-dominated) neocorporatism	Unconflictual (state-dominated) neocorporatism
Taxation	Semi-regressive	Progressive	Semi-regressive	Progressive	Progressive
Fiscal policy	Budget discipline	…	Sustainable debt-servicing	Growth-conditioned and investment-based fiscal expansion	Budgetary discipline for sustainable debt-servicing
Monetary policy	Tight	…	…	Development-conditioned	Monetary- targets-conditioned fiscal policy
Public–private choice	Liberal etatism and etatist liberalism	State capitalism through long-term planning	Regulated market economy	Social market economy through long-term planning	Regulated market economy

Market	A means of national modernisation and progress	Dependent variable of economic development	A well-functioning mechanism, if regulated	An independent variable of economic development conditioned by social utility	A well-functioning mechanism, if regulated
Growth and development	Creating national bourgeoisie through state subsidies and guidance	Import-substitutionist industrialisation	Productive solidarity (special emphasis on labour productivity)	Demand-constrained, productive, and planned full employment	Using the catalyst of high-value added production by encouraging research and development
International trade and finance	…	Nationalistically motivated, anti-imperialist conditioning of foreign direct or portfolio investment	Nationalistically sensitive and internationally competitive free trade strategy	Enhancing exports by productivity-based and inertia-preventing subsidies	Selective protectionism and subsidy regime and maximum utilisation of foreign direct investment
Inflation	…	Non-accelerating inflation strategy for full employment	Non-accelerating inflation strategy for productive employment	A disinflationist strategy without causing underemployment	Low inflation with full employment
Interest	…	…	Determined to realise plan targets	To be kept at a rate that stimulates savings but does not cause cost inflation	Price-stability and plan-conditioned to decrease real interest
Unemployment	…	…	Reduced through productive investment and labour productivity, industrialisation and ALMPs	Increasing the marginal propensity to invest by lowering interest rates	…

Parameter	CHP of 1923–60	CHP of 1960–1979	SHP of 1985–1995	DSP of 1985–2002	CHP of 1995–2010
Business cycles	...	A result of underemployment	A result of speculative investments	Eliminating the structural, psychological and social means of pursuing speculative earnings by directing resources to productive areas	Elimination of speculative short-term capital flows by using reserve requirements to sideline borrowing using foreign exchange rates
Social policy strategy	Paternalism	Active decommodification	Universal and productivity-constrained decommodifica-tion	Universal with a balanced regulation of rights and responsibilities	...
Inequality		Equality of outcomes	Semi-equality of outcomes	Systemic elimination	...
Poverty	Alleviation through paternalist social services	Systemic elimination through social citizenship rights	Positive welfare	Systemic elimination	...
ALMPs/ PLMPs	...	...	...	Training for adaptation to new technologies	...
Labour relations strategy	Authoritarian suppression	Authoritarian micro-corporatism	Flexible conduct of organised exchanges	Neocorporatism	–Downsizing restructuration —Commitment to the ILO Conventions

Employment pattern	...	...	Flexible	Permanent	Enhancing productivity by adopting modern management techniques and personnel strategies
Wages	...	Decent wages	Decent wages	Wage restraint and decent wages	Decent wages
The right to organise	Banned	Guaranteed for both private and public sector employees	Enactment of the right to organise and strike with the potential for politicisation	Unconditional for private sector workers and, under certain conditions, for civil servants	Guaranteed for both trade and civil service unions
Collective bargaining and strikes	Banned	Guaranteed for both private and public sector employees	Unconditional guarantee for private sector workers	Unconditional guarantee for private sector workers and, under certain conditions, for civil servants	Guaranteed for both private and public sector employees
Strikes	Banned	Entitlement provided for both private and public sector employees	Unconditional entitlement for private sector workers	Unconditional entitlement for private sector workers	Entitlement for both private and public sector employees

Source: Party programmes. CHP (1935, 1976, 1994, 2013), SHP (1985), DSP (1991).

so on. Despite emanating from the institutional entity of the CHP in terms of the political career of its leader cadre, the DP then established its own patronage linkages and clientelist pillars through all of its outgrowths, a truly new alignment of social status and a *social restratification*, the distinguishing feature of which was that a relative majority of these groups were in touch with the societal norms and values of the electorate and capitalised on the (accumulated) reactionary sentiments of the latter towards the CHP's single-party era. The coup d'état of May 1960 can be suggested to be a systemic manoeuvre by the major proponents of the Kemalist establishment to regain their structural and institutional power resources in an attempt to change its economic premises towards a pattern of planning conditioned by a social-justice-first authoritarianism.

Immediately after the military coup, the junta closed the DP, arrested the ministers from the DP government, detained the landlords affiliated with the Democrats, established committees for investing the wealth of the newly enriched families and dissolved the executive committees of the Chambers of Trade and Industry (Karpat, 2004: 48). After a 'lawful' trial, the prime minister and two ministers were hanged by a special committee founded for this purpose before the general elections of October 1961. The military junta, under the title *Milli Birlik Komitesi* – MBK, 'The National Unity Committee', began drafting a new constitution in close cooperation with their intellectual coalitions. A commission was formed under the leadership of the rector of Istanbul University. This intellectual-military cooperation effectively enforced the new institutional design of the country in systemic terms.

The leader cadre of the military junta came from the well-educated, pro-*status quo* and positivist segments of society and was sympathetic to socialism. General Gürsel as the head of the MBK and the President of Turkey, declared: 'Turkey needed social reforms and "socialism" could be regarded as a possible avenue for development' (Karpat, 2004: 48). The pre-coup plight of military personnel, in both pecuniary and social status terms, and the institution of an outward liberal order, albeit implemented with etatist discretion, must have exerted a decisive impact on this declaration and the ensuing institutional reconstructions. The high real increases in public sector wages and salaries in 1961, as shown in Table 7.2 (p. 164), are the most concrete evidence of this thesis. Instituting a two-house legislature, a constitutional court and judicial immunity, the Turkish Constitution of 1961 established the basic pillars of a new socio-economic order. The foremost of these in political economy terms was the foundation of *Devlet Planlama Teşkilatı* – DPT, the State Planning Organisation (*Türkiye Kalkınma Bakanlığı* – TKB, Turkish Ministry of Development, after 2011) to prepare five-year plans of macro-economic aggregates with their sectoral specifications and develop alternative policy strategies for governments to pursue, primarily, in the long run.

The Constitution defined the Turkish Republic as a secular democracy and social state respectful of human rights and formed a Constitutional Court to judge the constitutionality of all statues. The judiciary, especially *Danıştay*, the Higher Court of Justice, was made a constitutionally omnipotent institution with the power to judge executive authorities. Beyond granting the freedoms and safeguard for individual rights and private property, the Constitution made the state responsible, explicitly and precisely, for directing and implementing social justice. However, to remind succeeding governments that the Constitution had been enforced by a military junta, Milli Güvenlik Konseyi – MGK, *National Security Council*, was established with the role of *assisting* governments with national security and social coordination.

It becomes apparent that the Pashas were the *de facto* supervisors of political governments' major macro-political economy decisions, because the extant Council comprised the president, prime minister, (a few) ministers from the incumbent government, the Chief of the General Staff and the top cadre of the military forces. In the wake of redesigning the institutional stock in a manner compatible with military dominance, the junta had to declare free elections under its supervision (Karaosmanoğlu, 2000). At issue was that plummeting growth and soaring current account balance and unemployment rates lead to greater reactions, from the private sector to workers, the peasantry and the lower-middle classes (Karpat, 2004: 50).

The CHP's position during the construction, execution and development of the military junta's reforms, in addition to the intelligentsia, was *constructive* in the positive sense of the word. The CHP's strategy of *power cultivation* thus came, from the ITF period onwards, to rely on transforming the structural weaknesses of pro-cyclical forces into a countercyclical movement and then embarking on a top-down redesign of social institutions. This strategy, again, was implemented in cooperation with the Party's prime source of structural power, the military. The equation of 'CHP + military = government' became systemically unmistakeable in this regard. İnönü circulated a declaration to the Party's branches, stating, 'the governmental turnover was managed through a few hour-initiative of the Grand Turkish Armed Forces ... and it is a justified revolutionary movement' (Ulus, 17 April 1960, cited in Kili, 1975: 138). In return, the junta 'assigned' 49 members of the CHP to the founding assembly of the Constitution of 1961, which included various private and civic organisations but excluded former DP members. This empowered the Party to exert a substantial impact on the drafting of the Constitution and the Election Law of 1961. Thereafter, the Constitution was approved in a referendum in July 1961 by a majority of '66' per cent.

At this juncture, after grasping political power with the aid of their military partners, the CHP faced two policy choices: (i) consolidate the top-down regulation of the social system such that it could be 'steered' by the Party's hardliners, who had a firm predilection for re-establishing the *old trade-offs* of etatist secularism, or (ii) extend its coalitional composition, at least, to the electoral segments that would be converted to the Party when offered socio-economic opportunities. The Party's choice was to be the latter, social democratic Kemalism, despite severe debates between path-dependent hardliners and path-changing modernisers. The newly founded internal structure, along with the international environmental circumstances discussed in the previous chapter, exerted a consolidative impact on this strategic choice. Amongst them, the inevitability of responding to the accumulated demands for change, particularly in response to the DP's countercyclical reconstructions, can be suggested to be the most crucial, the products of which began in the first part of the 1950s when the CHP was the main opposition party.

For the CHP, the period 1950–60 was, in systemic terms, a process of changing continuity for its ideology. Yet, in this period, a critical path-dependence also accumulated. This era symbolises the embedding of the *regime-based opposition* strategy of the Party while, endemic to this period, denouncing the DP for manipulating religion, violating the requirements of language reforms, exerting pressure on the press, universities and so on. However, as another major source of critique regarding the DP's policy choices that would be regarded as the beginning of the systemic change in the CHP's vision, the welfare-reducing impact of economic downturns came to be an additional opposition discourse. In June 1953, at the CHP's 10th General Assembly, it was declared that etatism should be understood as a regime in which the state takes on the role of an organiser in cooperation with the private sector, intended to increase the citizens' welfare and social equity. Moreover, the first time in the Party's history, the right to strike was granted on the condition of not disrupting national security, public order or public health in addition to the state of law, the division of powers between state organs and the necessity of constitutional regulations to protect individual and political liberties (Bila, 1987: 205–8).

Revealing the then inchoate and undigested nature of this change dynamic was the continuance of the Party's old practices and irreconcilable discourses. In 1954, for example, the candidates in the deputy elections continued to be co-opted by the Party's central administration and selected from retired generals, former general directors and university professors, whereas a proposal to make this selection task over the local branches was repudiated. In the Party's 1954 and 1957 general elections and the declarations of the 14th General Assembly of January 1959, it was distinctly stated, *inter alia*, that 'we will encourage the private initiative ... we will determine a national minimum wage ... we will keep the trade unions out of politics'. In the 1957 general election declaration, moreover, substantial emphasis was placed on the freedom of the press, university and speech, the right to organise trade and civil service unions, the right to collective 'contracts', decent work, the right to paid holidays and so on (Bila, 1987: 233–9).

More consistent with the Party's change towards a social democratic revision in a path-dependent manner, the Party's 15th General Assembly in August 1961 and the election declaration of 1961 proclaimed that an equal distribution of income and education, health and social security institutions should be established to achieve a social alignment on the basis of meritocracy, Turkish workers should receive wages on the basis of equal pay for equal work, heavy industry should be established rapidly and planned economic development should be conducted in parallel with social justice principles, a secure environment for private investment would be provided and the challenges facing the private sector will be eliminated, the most suitable environment will be provided for foreign aid and investment, and the state will not make investments or intervene through unnecessary measures in the sectors in which private initiative is competent, but it will take all measures necessary to carefully stimulate the private sector (Kili, 1975: 168–9).

The results of the October 1961 elections necessitated a coalition government between the CHP and the AP, the successor to the DP. Among the newly established parties in this period, *Yeni Türkiye Partisi* – YTP, The New Turkey Party, was founded by a former member of the DP and the finance minister from the military government of 1960–61. *Cumhuriyetçi Köylü ve Millet Partisi* – CKMP, The Republican Peasants' Nation Party, was a nationalist front that would become the Nationalist Movement Party in 1969 under the leadership of Alparslan Türkeş, a member of the MBK, which planned and executed the coup d'état. The AP was founded under the leadership of a former Chief of the General Staff. The military staff supported him as a bulwark against DP revanchisme, while former Democrats did so to avoid prospective military pressure. In 1964, Süleymen Demirel – a civil engineer, an Eisenhower Fellow in the USA for one year and an employee of a US multinational corporation's Turkish branch – became the chairman of the Party.

Three coalition governments were founded: between October 1961 and February 1965; during October 1961–June 1962 and June 1962–December 1963; and December 1963–February 1965. As both the AP and the YTP recognised, *inter alia*, that their popularity was eroding, they left the first and second coalition governments, respectively, founded under the CHP's leadership. The last term of the CHP's coalition with the Independents ended in the forced resignation of Prime Minister İnönü, as his government's budget proposal was not endorsed by the parliament. Expectedly, such a varied career of incumbency weakened the CHP's organisational vision, reducing its votes in the 1965 general elections by approximately one quarter.

Between 1961 and 1965, the major achievement of the CHP was to found constitutional institutions such as the Constitutional Court and The Higher Court of Justice and to make the press, university and radio acts compatible with constitutional principles. The first five-year development plan was prepared and its first two years were implemented during the third İnönü government. Regarding economic policy, the general performance of the three consecutive CHP governments was nebulous. The period was characterised by moderately high average growth, primarily in the industrial sector, with a notable increase in the current account deficit and a relatively strict budgetary balance; steadily increasing Central Bank credits to the public sector; a remarkable decline in public sector fixed capital formation in 1964; decreasing inflation rates with steady but increased rates of unemployment compared to the previous period; a slight average increase in public sector wages and salaries along with an increasing trend in public sector employment.

In the socio-economic realm, the Party's performance was more promising from a social democratic standpoint. The Party revised the social security act to extend coverage to the employees of small enterprises, to enable the husband/wife

Table 7.2 Major indicators of the Turkish political economy between 1960 and 1980

Results of General Elections		October 1961				Octobe[r]
		CHP	36.7			CHP
		AP	34.8			AP
		YP	13.7			TİP
		CKMP	4.0			MHP
		Indep.	0.8			

Governmental Status	Inter.	CHP AP	CHP-CKMP YP-Indep.		CHP	Indep.
Duration of Incumbency	May	Dec.	Jun.	Dec.	Feb.	Oct.
Parameters	1960	1961	1962	1963	1964	1965
GDP[1]	3,4	2,0	6,2	9,7	4,1	3,1
Agriculture	2,3	-4,9	5,0	9,6	-0,4	-3,9
Industry	0,4	11,7	3,5	12,0	11,2	9,5
Services	5,4	4,2	8,0	8,9	4,8	5,6
Balance of Accounts/GDP	-0,1	0,1	-0,3	-0,3	0,1	0,4
Current Account Balance/GDP	-0,7	-1,6	-1,9	-2,7	-0,7	-0,5
Foreign trade/GDP	4,0	7,9	7,9	7,2	6,1	6,2
Consolidated Budget Balance, PSBR/GDP[2]	0,0	-0,2	0,1	0,1	-0,4	-0,4
Tax Burden/GDP	...	...	...	...	...	..
Indirect Taxes/GDP	...	...	...	...	...	..
Direct Taxes/GDP	...	...	...	...	...	..
Public Growth Fixed Cap. Formation/GDP	...	...	...	...	-6,3	11,5
Credit of Central Bank to Public Sector/GDP	...	...	0,8	1,4	1,8	1,9
Inflation	7,4	1,3	3,8	6,5	0,8	6,7
Unemployment	3,1	3,4	3,3	3,3	3,5	3,6
Interest Rates[3]	...	...	...	...	...	..
Gini coefficient	...	...	...	0,55	...	..
Wages and Salaries in Public Sector	-8,8	16,9	-1,6	3,5	6,7	-4,5
Worker (Public Sector)	4,1	13,0	2,5	-7,5	13,2	0,0
Worker Private	4,3	2,1	-0,9	5,7	7,8	7,2
Change in Public Sector Employment	6,1	7,0	3,0	6,4	5,6	7,4
Civil Servant (Fixed-term contracts)	...	...	...	...	...	..
Worker (Temporary)	...	...	...	...	...	..
Worker (Permanent)	...	...	...	...	...	..
Contracted	...	...	...	...	...	..

October 1969		October 1973		June 1977	
CHP	27.4	CHP	33.3	CHP	41.4
JP	46.5	AP	36.9	AP	36.9
TİP	2.7	MSP	11.8	MSP	8.6
MHP	3.0	MHP	3.4	MHP	6.4

					CHP		AP-MSP			CHP	AP-MSP	CHP	
		Interr.	Indepdendent		MSP	Indep	MP-CGP				MHP	Indep.	AP
		Mar.	May		Jan.	Nov.	Mar.		Jun.	July	Jan.	Nov.	Sep.
1969	**1970**	**1971**	**1972**	**1973**	**1974**	**1975**	**1976**	**1977**	**1978**	**1979**	**1980**
4,1	3,2	5,6	7,4	3,3	5,6	7,2	10,5	3,4	1,5	-0,6	-2,4
-1,4	2,8	5,1	1,0	-8,1	6,2	3,0	6,9	-2,1	2,7	-0,2	1,3
12,0	-0,5	8,9	10,6	12,0	7,1	9,1	8,9	6,6	3,1	-5,0	-3,6
5,4	7,3	7,6	13,4	9,2	0,7	6,4	10,0	3,9	-0,1	1,1	-4,1
0,1	0,9	1,0	0,5	2,5	-0,8	-2,6	-2,4	-2,6	-1,4	-1,1	-1,4
-0,8	-0,6	-0,4	0,0	1,3	-1,4	-2,6	-2,8	-3,8	-1,4	-1,2	-3,7
4,9	6,0	8,1	8,5	9,4	0,0	9,8	9,9	9,2	7,7	6,7	11,9
-0,7	0,1	-1,8	-0,1	-0,4	-0,6	3,6	5,1	6,1	2,4	5,4	6,6
...	...	...	...	...	...	13,7	14,2	14,6	14,1	13,1	13,0
...	...	...	...	...	...	5,8	6,0	5,5	4,9	4,5	4,1
...	...	...	...	...	...	4,9	5,2	6,0	6,5	6,2	6,6
5,6	-4,9	-9,0	3,8	-1,6	3,9	22,2	11,4	12,9	-16,2	-5,4	-8,1
2,0	3,0	3,5	3,4	2,8	3,4	3,6	5,4	8,2	7,5	6,8	5,9
5,7	11,8	21,8	15,3	15,8	15,4	19,0	16,4	22,5	53,3	62,0	101,4
5,8	6,3	6,6	6,2	6,6	7,1	7,4	8,7	9,8	9,8	8,6	8,6
...	9,0	9,0	9,0	7,0	9,0	9,0	9,0	9,0	12,0	20,0	33,0
...	...	...	...	0,51	...	...	...	...	0,51	...	...
-1,5	11,8	6,4	-0,9	0,2	-9,3	-5,0	2,6	3,9	-16,2	-31,8	-1,0
5,8	24,2	-4,5	-10,5	-6,8	10,0	19,0	3,4	3,6	-3,6	-7,3	-27,6
0,6	5,5	8,3	-7,7	4,9	8,9	12,5	21,7	11,9	-1,8	-3,8	-22,6
5,6	4,7	7,9	10,4	12,2	12,1	17,7	10,5	8,8	19,9	12,8	2,8
...	...	...	...	...	...	...	...	8,9	6,5	13,1	3,5
...	...	...	...	...	...	...	...	...	...	46,8	-25,3
...	...	...	...	...	...	...	...	...	...	6,4	1,6
...	...	...	...	...	...	...	...	...	...	-5,4	9,8

Notes: *The months indicate the termination of incumbency in the year. 1The harmonized GDP data has been used, provided by the TKB (2013a) and the OECD (2014). 2 For 1950–1974, Consolidated Budget Balance/GDP; 1975–1980, PSBR/GDP; - indicates surplus. 3 Deposit interest rates.
Source: TKB (2013a), TUIK (2013), OECD (2013a).

or children of active or retired workers to benefit from illness insurance, and the age of retirement for female workers was reduced to 50 from 55. In addition, health centres were founded to spread health services to the rural areas, albeit inefficiently due to a lack of sufficient personnel and equipment. And the employees of the SEEs were allowed to obtain a 10 per cent share in the profits of these enterprises.

From the summer of 1962 onwards, the trade unionists entered into routine discussions with various ministers concerning national issues and their possible solutions. (Kili [1975: 198] argues that the *Ecevit* factor made these developments possible.) Land reform, in the sense of allocating the land to the peasantry, was not enacted by any of the three coalition governments despite some initiatives in this regard. Ultimately, the foremost social democratic step taken by the CHP was to issue the Trade Union Act of 1963, prepared following an analysis of the labour laws of European countries, particularly those of France. In conformity with the ILO Conventions of 1987 and 1998, the right to organise and strike (for both interests and rights) was granted and incorporated into the Turkish Constitution of 1961, for the first time during the Republican Period. The Act prohibited trade unions from engaging with political parties financially or organisationally, while allowing them to endorse or support any party. Despite granting the right to strike, for the first time in the Republican period, the Collective Bargaining Act of 1963 banned strikes in a broad variety of public and private industries along with political strikes (Sönmez, 1968). Furthermore, the ultimate settlement of the disputes in industries in which strikes were forbidden was left to the Higher Arbitration Board. By the same token, on the grounds of national health and security, the Board of Ministers was authorised to postpone a strike that was underway or about to begin.

Systemisation of Changing Continuities: Social Democratic Kemalism in the Making

The period between early 1965 and 1973 witnessed the transformation of the accumulated dynamics of change in the CHP into a systemic framework of reorganisation, the left of the centre. Compelling as this was, the CHP's abovementioned socio-economic policy adaptations between 1950 and 1965 could not cope with the political rigidities that the Party's top-down organisational structure in both intra-party and party-society linkages accumulated over time. No less influential in this respect was the AP's pragmatically infusive, catch-all strategy that defunctionalised the transformation of patchy discourses on *granting* social rights into electoral gains. The most influential, however, was the long-held expectation of the Turkish people from the CUP periods onwards for the genesis of an egalitarian politics that would initiate an equal distribution of socio-economic welfare, such as the implementation of land and tax reforms. Making this politics more compelling in the 1960s was the nurturing industrialisation and consequent urbanisation that required the masses to have regular and decent work and income.

At the 18th general assembly of the CHP, Bülent Ecevit, the minister of labour in three consecutive İnönü governments, first placed the 'left of the centre' on the Party's agenda. Before the convention, he effectively organised a segment of the Party's local branches and began to exert a popular impact on the Party's top cadres. İsmet İnönü supported such a reorganisational initiative and the Convention ultimately accepted this new mission. Significantly, the Party's local branches supported this new vision, while a group of conservative Kemalists vehemently rejected it and broke off from the party. Another group, entitled the 'sixty-threes', began working to obscure these change initiatives while remaining in the Party and voicing a conservative sentiment, claiming that the CHP was on the path towards becoming a socialist party. March 1971 military memorandum had a positive impact on the acceleration of this reorganisation, especially by causing İnönü's resignation.

Ecevit and his supporters rejected participation in the post-coup d'état political design, in contrast to İnönü and his supporters who had accepted the assignment of three CHP members as ministers in the military-supported government under the premiership of a former CHP member who broke off from the party in the face of the reorganisational initiatives. As a turning point in the CHP's political career, at the fifth extraordinary convention of the Party, Ecevit received 826 votes out of 1,416. The remainder went İnönü, who resigned from the Party with a number of his supporters because the Party took a decision to withdraw its members from the government (Ahmad, 1977: 288–340).

The political mobilisation catalysed by the left of the centre in the Party's intra-organisational dynamics manifested itself efficiently, for the first time, in the 1973 general elections. These elections symbolised relatively integrated efforts between the centre and the local branches around the Party's reorganisational impulse. The managerial cadre was transformed into a structure that embraced, albeit to a moderate extent, the direct representatives of the underprivileged such as peasants or workers and a diminishing number of bureaucrats and members of the intelligentsia. Concurrently, two-thirds of the deputies from the previous period were supplanted for the same reason. Another changing continuity in the Party was the tolerant discourses on freedom of religion and thought with an intriguing statement that 'the clerics will be consulted on local (economic) development efforts'.

Ecevit's contribution was to *systemise* and *popularise* these dynamics. His book, *The Left of the Centre*, the major policy strategies of which became the main principles of the CHP's 1976 programme, which can be seen in Table 7.1, is a well-conceptualised restatement of a social democratic regime of the political economy, served as Ecevit's main yardstick on issues ranging from humanism, productive solidarity and an egalitarian income policy to individual rights, fair economic growth and so on, albeit with two main differences. As regards the economic aspect of social democratic institutionalism, the first is that the productive component of *productive solidarity* is not an instrumental component of the systemic interactions in the left of the centre. In other words, the left of the centre was structured on the consequences rather than the constitutive dynamics of social democratic institutionalism. As regards the political aspect, the second is that the left of the centre is a Kemalism-constrained conceptualisation of social democratic policy-making (Ağtaş, 2009). This brought about the incorporation of a nationalist-sensitivity to the protective and anti-imperialist approach of the social democratic perspective on international financial and commercial exchanges and the adoption of an *authoritarian* pattern of etatist corporatism to circumvent order-breaking initiatives.

The left of the centre is a Kemalism-constrained form of social democracy, as Ecevit argued (1968: 69): 'There is no doubt that the mainstay of being a member of the CHP is to join together around the revolutions that Atatürk found enough time to execute. However, it is not the unique precondition. To do by only adopting pure Atatürk revolutions or uniting in Atatürk revolutions would be to break off with Ataturk's revolutionism'. This signifies that sustenance of Kemalism, path-dependence, feeds on making institutional changes to adapt Kemalism to the political economy of contemporary circumstances (p. 88). In this respect, social democratic Kemalism arises out of the adaptation of Kemalism to social democratic postulates. Despite his structural allegiance to Kemalist sensitivities, Ecevit prioritises social democratic institutions in shaping the left of the centre and utilises Kemalism as an unchangeable pillar that amalgamates the state, society and market components of the Turkish political economy. Thus, I designate the left of the centre as the ideologic conceptualisation of 'social democratic Kemalism'. For the period 1995–2010, I will define the CHP's strategy as a Kemalist social democracy because, at the time, the Party's leaders distilled social democratic variables into the uniting framework of Kemalism, but not vice versa.

In the October 1973 general elections, the CHP increased its vote share to approximately 20 per cent and formed a coalition government with Milli Selamet Partisi – MSP, *The National Salvation Party*, lasting between January and November 1974. This was the first and the last partnership between the CHP and a NOM-affiliated party. The underlying reason was Ecevit's conjecture that both parties would likely come to open agreement on nearly all policy choices, as their economic and social strategies converged to a substantial extent. MSP members were assigned to internal affairs, justice, agriculture, industry and technology, while the remaining cabinet positions remained with the CHP. The CHP-MSP coalition shattered as a result of a coalitional power skirmish led by two influential figures in their electorate. The explanation was the structural divergences on a number of social issues such as the banning of pornography in the press, changing the day off from a Sunday to a Friday, the MSP's rejection of the general amnesty and so on.

Yet, Ecevit's resignation was in fact an opportunist initiative to capitalise on the peak of his popularity after Turkey's July 1974 intervention in Cyprus to take the country to an early election (Ciddi, 2009: 59–60). A factor exerting a notable impact on his decision must have been the poor economic performance of the government, moderate growth and increasing budget and current account deficits, resulting in a continued high rate of inflation. Moderately rising public sector investment and substantial increases in public sector employment (12 per cent) did not prevent unemployment from rising to 7.1 per cent in 1974 from 6.6 per cent in 1973. The large real decline (9.3) in public sector wages and salaries despite a higher increase (10.0) in the wages of public sector workers were incompatible with the coalition government's programme.

The second half of the 1970s witnessed politico-economic chaos following the fall of the CHP-MSP coalition. Between March 1975 and January 1978, with the exception of a one-month interval of CHP incumbency, AP-MSP-MHP-CGP national front governments governed the country (these governments' performance are important for our research in terms of the MSP's practice of its theoretical arguments and the social impression that this practice made). Under the political instabilities of such a cosmopolitan governmental structure, the economic performance of these governments resulted in the accumulation of crisis dynamics. Despite relatively high average growth, in addition to the current account deficit, inflation also rose considerably when coupled with the soaring rates of Central Bank credits to the public sector in the same year.

The most salient distinction of these governments was the record annual growth in public fixed capital formation at an average rate of 15.5 per cent between 1975 and 1977, reaching 10 per cent of GNP in 1977. This record was made possible by the nearly two-fold increase in the PSBR in 1977 compared to that in 1975. Another record was achieved in the increase in public sector employment at an average rate of 12.3 per cent between 1975 and 1977. However, the unemployment rate also reached its highest level between 1960 and 1980 in 1977 (9.8 per cent). While public sector wages and salaries remained constant in real terms, the wages of public sector workers increased to a record level (19 per cent) in 1975, the highest between 1960 and 1980, despite marginal increases in 1976 and 1977 of approximately 3 per cent. As another socio-economic indicator, indirect taxes remained constant, while direct taxes rose by 20 per cent between 1975 and 1977.

The ambiguous and poor performance of the compositionally fragile national front governments with limited response to rising demands for decent work and life and the regular provision of public goods such as electricity, water, roads and so on redounded to a substantial improvement in the CHP's electoral performance (from 33.3 per cent in 1973 to 41.4 in 1977) in the 1977 general elections, during which the CHP based its electoral programme on social rights. Paradoxically, the AP's votes also rose considerably during the same period (from 29.8 to 36.9 per cent). The unique loser in the 1977 general elections was the MSP (from 11.8 to 8.6 per cent). It can be suggested that the CHP's stable electoral success in the 1970s was based on the Party's changing continuity under the left of the centre and the bottom-up mobilisation of the Party's local branches, recruiting a new group of supporters from lower classes, shantytown dwellers in Istanbul, in addition to its ordinary electoral base consisting of the urban middle classes, civil-military bureaucrats and the intelligentsia (Özbudun and Tachau, 1975).

In its nearly two-year incumbency between January 1978 and November 1979, despite its 'political achievement', the CHP could not embark on a structural shift but deteriorated the already flawed economic structure beginning in 1977 with high current account and budgetary deficits, hyperinflation and high unemployment. The late 1970s (1977–80) was a crisis-ridden epoch due to the foreign-debt-financed import-substitutionist strategy of the period 1960–80. Following the OPEC crisis of 1973, during an era of internal political chaos and short-lived governments, Turkish governments chose to use short-term foreign debt with high interest rates and thus began to accumulate an unsustainable stock of debt amounting to 15 per cent of GDP in 1980. Under acute financial imbalances, the Party came to pursue a dichotomous economic policy of suppressing the chaotic environment in the markets through price controls and policing. The limited or negative growth, at record levels in 1978 and 1979, was due to negative growth (16.2 and 5.4, respectively) in public sector fixed capital formation (PSFCF). The relatively limited PSBR in 1978 became possible due to this expenditure-reducing impact of the latter's negative growth along with the phenomenal decline (16.2) in public sector wages and salaries and a smaller decline (3.6) in the wages of public sector workers.

Yet, the PSBR soared in 1979, despite continuing negative growth in PSFCS and public sector wages and salaries. The phenomenal increase in public sector employment in 1978 and in 1979 (19.9 and 12.8 per cent, respectively) was the decisive factor in this increase, in addition to the declining trend in tax revenues. A small but substantial detail for the CHP's socio-economic strategies was that a substantial portion of this phenomenal increase comprised the workers employed under temporary contracts. The temporary and fixed-term contracts registered 46.8 and 13.1, respectively, in 1979, whereas fixed-term contracts only registered a 13.1 per cent annual increase. The tax burden declined from 14.6 per cent in 1977 to first 14.1 of GDP and then to 13.1, primarily due to the decrease in indirect taxes from 5.5 in 1977 to 4.5 per cent in 1979, whereas direct taxes rose slightly (from 6.0 per cent in 1977 to first 6.5 in 1978 and then 6.2 in 1979). With the plummeting of domestic savings to 2.5 per cent of GDP and increased public indebtedness (foreign debts increased from 5.1 per cent of GDP in 1977 to 9.1 per cent in 1979), the continuing trend of high Central Bank funding of the public sector resulted in skyrocketing inflation and interest rates, despite the declining rate of industrial capacity utilisation due to the restricting impact of devaluations on intermediate goods imports.

This systemically negative panorama in macro-economics asserted itself in the scarcity of basic consumption goods and black marketeering in socio-economics. The image of this two-year period in the mind of Turkish society was individuals with ration cards in their hands waiting in queues to buy or hoping to buy these goods. The result was that Deniz Baykal, the finance minister of the first and energy minister of the third Ecevit government, and the future leader of the CHP between 1995 and 2010 except for an interval of approximately one and a half years, declared: 'We intended to change our electoral base at the cost of alienating the people who worked with us in the past for the same ideals ... The people who we wished to win (as voters) now watch our situation laughingly' (Bila, 1987: 471). These words were to be the main basis of the establishment of a Kemalist social democracy under his leadership.

The most catastrophic for the CHP's centre of the left ideology during this period was the Party's intimate, albeit conflictual, relationship with the IMF. Oscillating between requesting aid from the IMF or avoiding the political requirements of this initiative, Ecevit applied to the European social democratic governments. However, they also preconditioned a structural agreement with the IMF to open new credit channels! Two stand-by agreements with the IMF in April 1978 and in June 1979 were not, however, successful because the PSBR continued to rise and foreign exchange policy was not effective in increasing exports and curbing inflation. Instead, 23 per cent and 43.7 per cent devaluations in March 1978 and January 1979 further accelerated inflation and increased the volume of imports.

Changing Constraints Versus Constraining Path-Dependencies: the Encounters of Turkish Social Democracy and Kemalism with Islam and Neoliberalism

The post-1980 period, as discussed earlier, was a quite volatile and constraining era regarding both economic interlinkages of decommodificatory discretions and political restructurations for electoral performance. The reason is the exponentially shrinking space for fiscal and monetary policies in structural terms in addition to phenomenal domestic/foreign borrowing. The ratio of foreign debt/GDP mounted to 26.1 per cent in 1990 and then 57.7 in 2001, from 6.3 in 1965 and 12.3 in 1979. Moreover, the ratio of domestic debt/GDP rose exponentially to 50.9 in 2001 from 10.2 in 1980. Furthermore, this era features the lowest rates of growth and public sector fixed-capital formation and the highest average rates of unemployment, PSBR and unemployment compared to the previous periods of 1950–59 and 1960–79. Another constraint on decommodificatory governmental discretion was the ratio of foreign trade/GDP, which rose to 18.5 and 26.6 between 1980–90 and 1991–2002, respectively, from 7.4 between 1960 and 1979 on average.

These structural constraints under the auspices of neoliberal, theoretico-practical reinstitutionalisation became *de facto* challenges in the face of the path-dependency of social democratic Kemalism. The relatively smooth and transitory theoretical blend from orthodox Kemalism to social democratic Kemalism between 1960 and 1980 became increasingly complicated and heterogeneous during this period. Along with abovementioned *de facto* challenges, endemic to Turkish case and as an integral part of the Turkish praxis of social democracy, Kemalist policy-making encountered grave challenges due to the downsizing of etatist discretion and rising conservative and Islamic politico-economic space, as can be traced through the declines in the SHP and CHP's electoral performances (see Table 6.2, p. 138–9). Yet the changing and hardening constraints did not eliminate the requirement of continuing path-dependency in social democratic policies to perform in general elections. To comprehend this pull-push trend that constitutes the main basis of the abovementioned rising complexity and heterogeneity requires examining the changes and continuities in Turkish social democracy and Kemalism, as illustrated in Table 7.1, in terms of the evolution of each institution and the overall complications of inter-institutional intersections throughout this era.

Continuing, Discontinuing and Changing Path-Dependencies in Reconciliation: Third Way Kemalism

Founded in 1985, the SHP became the *de facto* representative of Turkish social democracy until 1995, when it was merged into the CHP (reopened in 1992). The SHP's main strategy was first to continue the strategic vision of social democratic Kemalism in response to the electoral demands of both the Party's members and prospective voters and, second, to discontinue its path-dependencies in conciliation with the then rising neoliberal market capitalism to leave room to implement the first. This two-edged strategy required adopting a theoretical pragmatism while indoctrinating subsequent theoretical ideology as a mixed-blessing of orthodox and social democratic Kemalisms, Third Way Kemalism. (This definition belongs to the author. The party did not use a particular motto to define itself.) The essential nexus of this triologic blend of social democracy, Kemalism and neoliberalism was its indoctrination in a country where the recent social democratic past was most associated with the drastic crisis of the late 1970s and where the balkanised social structure around inter-repulsive ideologic factions resulted in social chaos and substantially unequal distributions of income, prestige and power, the macro-economic structure of which witnessed the systemic failure of protective, inward-looking, foreign-financed and import-substitutionist industrialisation.

The Party predicated its politico-economic indoctrinations on an unconflictual type of neocorporatism and a regulated and planned market economy. In this structure, the role of state is to organise infrastructural public goods and only engage in direct production in the areas that would redound to social utility. The socially contingent status of markets in the CHP's programme of 1960–80 changed to 'a well-functioning-mechanism', if regulated. In the SHP's party programme, the market economy is defined as a multi-dimensional entity consisting of structured production patterns, the division of labour and consumption patterns. In this perception, the private sector was reputed to make a positive contribution to social development through its entrepreneurial (constructive) power. The protective rigour of social democratic Kemalism thus transformed into selective liberalisation in the internationally competitive export sectors, while it was presumed that a special importance should be accorded to national production of intermediate and investment goods from a nationalistically sensitive and protective perspective.

By placing private initiative over public discretion, Third Way Kemalism made *productivity* rather than social solidarity the cement of its tripartite structure. In the Party's programme, the regression of the *social* vis-à-vis *markets* manifested itself in the emphasis on *sustainable debt-servicing*, supply-side taxation and non-inflationist and productivity-constrained employment creation as the main basis, for the Party, for preventing and reducing unemployment. The *social* manifestation of marketisation in this programme is the lack of a clear emphasis on the enactment of the right to collective bargaining and especially striking for civil servants and the very existence of clear emphases on the structuration of *flexible* employment in both the private and public sectors (in the SEEs), and on a positive-welfare strategy along with ALMPs (SHP, 1985).

As can be gleaned from this power-free programme, there is no cross-institutional consistence in a social democratic sense. Despite the explicit declaration of the necessity of politicising civil society organisations, for example, there is no power-balancing factor, the right to strike, for civil service unions. It is assumed that interest will be adjusted to achieve plan targets. However, the question of 'how' remains unaddressed. Beyond theory, this triologic identity was, however, quite challenging in praxis, as it required matching the inter-repulsive factions in the Party, Kemalist social democrats or social democratic Kemalists. The former advocated sidelining social democracy as a complementary and justificatory tool for orthodox Kemalism, whereas the latter advocated the reverse. Ultimately, the structural power skirmish between factions and personalities eliminated the possibility of constructing an intra-party *productivist solidarity* that the Party promised to establish in the macro-political economy.

Receiving 20.8 per cent of the votes cast in the October 1991 elections, the SHP participated in a coalition government under the DYP's leadership. Before coming to power, Erdal İnönü had declared:

> You may not think it credible ... but we are the only one who can cope with inflation when coming to power. We shall pursue a policy of balanced budget. Ours will be a credible, a resolute government. We shall decisively pursue an anti-inflationary policy. We shall consolidate the internal debt. There will be no question such as failing to repay the foreign debt (Mango, 1991: 177).

The praxis of this government, however, was not so progressive. In its first period, between October 1991 and December 1993, the government achieved relatively rapid growth, moderately decreased public investment and moderately increased public final consumption expenditures. Stagnant direct and a notable increase in indirect taxes along with a soaring tax burden was accommodated by a remarkable rise in budget and current account deficits and rising unemployment, astronomical hyperinflation and higher interest rates. The socio-economic policy during this period featured steadily rising privatisations, initially rising but then faltering social expenditures and initially rising and then stagnating public sector wages and salaries in 1992 and 1993, respectively, and moderate increases in public sector employment, primarily of temporary workers. In the 1994 crisis and ensuing 24 April decisions (see Figure 6.4, p. 133), in tandem with classical IMF standby prescriptions, to increase incomes and decrease expenditures, the Central Bank was granted autonomy, and an upper limit was imposed on government borrowing; public fixed-capital formation and final consumption were reduced considerably.

Consequently, total domestic demand declined by approximately 10 per cent along with substantial declines in public sector wages and salaries, and a limited decline and labour shedding in public sector social expenditures and employment, respectively. Despite substantial declines in GDP, monetary emission was extended markedly and the Central Bank's credits to the government remained nearly constant (2.9 per cent of GDP), causing rampant inflation (106 per cent) and much higher interest rates (164 per cent). Although the PSBR receded further from 7.7 in 1993 to 4.6 in 1994, the domestic debt/GDP ratio increased to 15.3 in 1994 from 13.4 in 1993. Beyond conjuncturally adapted policy choices, it was the poor performance of the coalition government during the 1994 economic crisis, as summarised in Figure 6.4, that became the essential source of poor public image of Turkish social democracy.

As an opposition party between 1985 and 1991, the SHP's strategy relied on systemically criticising the incumbent ANAP's socially irresponsible economic performance. The Party managed to take 28.7 per cent in the 1989 local elections and the mayoralties of three metropolitan cities, including Istanbul. Yet its rule is now remembered for corruption scandals. In his research on patronage and clientelism in Turkish social democracy, Schüler (1999: 289) concludes that 'it is unrealistic to state that managers of the SHP were the people dealing with systemic social interests. Rather they were intermediaries for the job demands of the sympathisers of the party in the public sector'. He adds that the Party's members were related neither to the Party's activities nor its political agenda. Their membership in the Party occurred either by means of their friends or other members rather than by ideologic commitments (Schüler, 1999: 270). More pessimistically, Ciddi (2009: 80) argues that 'SHP is remembered for two things, corruption scandals and internal bickering. Throughout the 1980s and into the post-cold war era, the centre left continued to fall short of being an alternative for Turkey's centre right block'.

In July 1995, a number of constitutional amendments were made, including the right for trade unions to engage in politics and for civil servants to establish civil service unions. However, civil servants were not entitled to engage in *collective bargaining*, let alone strike. The Party's Third Way approach, thus, assumes the institutionalisation of the right to found conciliative class organisations but not to *bestow* on them the authority to challenge governmental power. It is within this context that *Ekonomik ve Sosyal Konsey*, the Economic and Social Council of Turkey, was inaugurated in 1995 with 'the aim of composing a common view among the societal partners whose actions exert direct impact on the economy through democratic consultation'. The primary means for this was to found an institution to organise Turkey's information and knowledge interchange with the European Economic and Social Council (27th article of the Ankara Agreement) and enforce the requirements of ILO Convention number 144 on tripartite consultation. The Council comprised 13 governmental representatives, including the prime minister, two members from each the TOBB, TISK and Turk-Is and one member from Union of Turkish Chambers of Agriculture and the Confederation of Turkish Tradesmen and Craftsmen (TKB, 2013b). Apart from its convention in October 1995, the Council was far from having a definitive impact on governmental policies; it was rather a forum in which government *shared* its policy choices with the abovementioned social *partners*. As will be examined in due course, the Council's passive mission has been in place since then.

Overall, the Party's theory and praxis were not complementary to a great extent. In a study conducted by the Turkish Foundation for Social, Economic and Political Research – TÜSES, the founders of which include prominent social democrats, in 1994 (1995: 62), 59 per cent of the electorate who voted for the SHP in the 1991 general elections declared that Turkish political economy was worse than three years previous, while only a quarter stated the reverse. In the same research, the SHP was found to be trusted by a set of selected electoral segments with various political opinions at a rate of 5.9 per cent to improve the quality of democracy and human rights, 3.6 per cent to alleviate the people's daily expenses and 3.8 per cent to eliminate the terror problem. Instead of managing the delicate balances among social democratic egalitarianism, neoliberal progressiveness and Kemalist etatism, the Party's leading cadres dealt with in-party skirmishes and organisational interests rather than striving to develop feasible, long-term focused and egalitarian-conditioned policy programmes (Ergül, 2000: 315–37).

Continuing Path-Dependencies in Theory versus Exhaustion in Praxis

In view of his long struggle in the CHP during 1960–73 to develop the centre of the left as the mainstay of the Party's policy strategies, Ecevit chose to break off from the CHP and establish a new political party in 1985, *Demokratik Sol Parti* – DSP, the Democratic Left Party, formally by his wife, as he was banned from active politics by the junta government. The structural result was: (i) a further sidelining of Kemalist implications in social democratic Kemalism; (ii) imposing adaptive but unsystemic constraints on the latter's social justice-conditioned morphology; and fundamentally (iii) continuing the path-dependency of the latter's building blocks.

The first does not indicate that Ecevit dissociated himself and his party from Atatürk's principles. Instead, these principles were converted into the nurturing background of Turkey's secular democracy, whereas social democracy was continued into the mainstay of the Party's politico-economic vision (Ergül, 1995: 189–90). The second was intended to make certain revisions necessary to perpetuate the feasibility of social democratic Kemalism through its unsystemic adaptation to the neoliberal internal/external institutional environment. Succinctly, in systemic terms, the DSP was founded to keep democratic Kemalism alive, in the form of the left of the centre, with some systemically unchanging adaptive revisions but without seeking a theoretical pragmatism by reconciling its premises to the dominant institutional environment, as the Third Way Kemalists had.

The main philosophy of the DSP for executing systemically unchanging revisions was that, as declared in its programme, the Party adopted a realist but not *realistically conditioned* perspective. Among these revisions, the DSP's prudential approach to the market is the most salient. The programme emphasised making artisans and craftsman, along with workers and apprentices, adaptable to the contemporary *marketing* mechanisms and advanced technologies. Moreover, the Party declared that it would subsidise and provide a wide area of *freedom* for private sector enterprises that would operationalise a policy of social justice-constrained economic development and would not attempt to transform their economic power into political leverage. Other complementary policy choices were a growth strategy on the basis of a *demand-constrained* productive and planned full employment, an anti-inflationist strategy that would not precipitate underemployment, a fiscal and monetary expansion conditioned by budget discipline and the rate of growth, respectively, and an ALMP-based permanent employment strategy.

The party also intended to depoliticise the SEEs by replacing the state representatives in their administrative cadres with their workers' representatives and the intermediation of the public sector in transforming public savings into real investment by establishing large corporations. Yet the Party theoretically committed itself to the perpetuation of its framing strategy of a social market economy using long-term planning, a universal social policy strategy, granting workers the right to organise and strike and permitting civil servants to organise, the adaptation of an equality of outcomes strategy, progressive taxation, an interest rate policy to increase the marginal propensity to make real investments and the elimination of structural-psychological and sociological means of speculative financial investments (DSP, 1991).

Between 1985 and 2013, the DSP came to power twice: in the ANAP-DSP-DTP-Independents coalition government between June 1997 and January 1999, and in the DSP-ANAP-MHP coalition government between May 1999 and November 2002. The former came to power following the overthrow of the RP-DYP coalition by the military on 28 February 1997. Despite Ecevit's valiant stance against military interventions during the 1970s, in this case, the DSP surreptitiously supported the coup d'état of 28 February 1997. When the ANAP-led coalition was in power, Ecevit announced, 'we are conducting our studies rapidly in accordance with the decisions taken at the MGK convention dated 28 February 1997'. The reason that Ecevit changed the party's strategic posture was the strategic convergence between the DSP's policy and the then high-ranking military staff's institutional design project to prevent religious symbols from becoming a discursive power niche in Turkish political economy. This was motivated by the third NOM-affiliated party, *Refah Partisi* – RP, the Welfare Party, having garnered 21.4 per cent of the vote in the 1995 general elections, becoming the largest party in parliament. The convention is known as the platform that *de facto* implemented the coup d'état. Among those studies are three regulations: the amendment on the dismissal of civil servants, eight-year compulsory education and banning students wearing headscarves from university education. The amendment regulated the dismissal of civil servants by the decision of two inspectors, a secret personnel report by their two chiefs and confirmation by the Board of Ministers without any investigation.

Ecevit defended this amendment on the grounds that these dismissal decisions would be suited against. The implementation of eight years of compulsory education in effect aimed to deactivate the *İmam Hatip* schools, religious vocational schools, by both closing their middle sections and imposing a formula that reduced the university entrance examination scores of the graduates of all vocational schools when the graduates of Imam Hatip schools – which teach all of the courses at other middle or secondary schools along with a number of religious courses such as the Qur'ân, Arabic and so on – wished to take courses outside the faculty of theology. This practice, however, also caused the marginalisation of other technical vocational schools and exerted a destructive impact on the supply-demand balance among technical personnel in Turkish industry. Ultimately, in September 1997, a circular from the Turkish Higher Education Council prohibited women wearing headscarves from receiving an education at universities and terminated their educational rights, including those who were about to graduate.

The social emphasis in the ANAP-DSP government's programme was eclipsed by its poor performance in terms of economic policies. The structural challenges of the Turkish economy, summarised in earlier sections, deteriorated under the rule of this government. In 1998, growth remained limited, accompanied by a soaring PSBR rate (Table 7.1). The current account balance recovered as a result of declining foreign trade during the Asian and Russian crises. Public sector capital formation and final consumption expenditures, nevertheless, fell markedly in real terms, as did total domestic demand. These *prudential* measures did not prevent the continuation of extremely high inflation and interest rates. Despite the remarkable decrease in growth, unemployment rose only slightly due to the high increase in public employment. Yet public sector wages and salaries declined in real terms. Even the minimum wage declined at a rate of 7.2 per cent. The tax burden continued to rise, with a noticeable increase in direct taxes, while indirect taxes receded slightly.

The economic performance of the DSP-led coalition government between May 1999 and December 2002 was worse. Taking 22.1 per cent of the vote in the 1999 general elections, the DSP founded a coalition government with the ANAP and MHP. Dichotomous for the DSP was that Ecevit, as in the late 1970s, had signed an IMF standby agreement to curb inflation and interest rates to improve the long-term growth potential of the country using an exchange-based strategy (see Figure 6.6, p. 142). The evolution of the economic cycles until the outbreak of the 2001 crisis and the abandonment of the crawling peg regime, as summarised earlier, indicate the highly *volatile* administrative performance of this coalition government, as manifested in the ebb and flow of the interface between inflation-interest-foreign exchange-capital inflows and outflows in the absence of coordination between the government and the TCMB.

Another indicator in this respect was the steadily volatile (negative-positive-negative-positive) growth rates in addition to record PSBR, a high balance of account and relatively high current account deficits, substantial rises in the indirect tax burden and high real declines in public sector wages and salaries on average between May 1999 and November 2002 (see Table 6.2, p. 139). Public sector employment, following relatively high increases in 1999 and 2000, remained stagnant in 2001 and 2002. Despite rising government final consumption expenditures, public sector fixed capital formation plummeted and total demand only increased at a rate of 2.9 per cent over three and a half years, whereas inflation and interest rates were not reduced successfully.

The volatile and inconsistent administrational strategy of the DSP-led coalition prompted a telephone call from then Prime Minister Ecevit to then vice-president of the World Bank, Kemal Derviş, saying: 'Mr. Kemal, we are in a hard situation. We are passing through a crisis, would you come to help us?' with an urgent request to come to Turkey the next day (Derviş et al., 2006: 50–51). In this process, Derviş' perspective when preparing a new IMF programme following the failure of the previous one was: 'We predicted that a strong financial policy will stimulate the economy as a result of increasing trust' with an understanding that politics should allow free functioning markets (Derviş et al., 2006: 91, 93). He added that 'We learned from history that, without the allocation of resources according to the rules of the market, efficiency and growth would not be ensured in an economy'. Complementary was his emphasis that the main function of the state is to implement a social policy within the context of a market economy (Derviş et al., 2006: 146). Thus, Turkey's Programme for Transition to a Strong Economy was ratified as an IMF programme consisting of strict measures to restore confidence in financial markets, stabilise money and foreign exchange markets, establish monetary balances, abolish the Central Bank's authority to grant advances and extend credit to the treasury and so on at the cost of high real declines in public sector wages and salaries, a 10 per cent fall in total demand, substantial shedding of temporary workers in the public sector and a soaring unemployment rate of 10.8 per cent in 2002 from 8.9 per cent in 2001 (see Table 6.2).

In practice, however, this ambiguous programme turned into an unambiguous austerity. In the Derviş-led economic programme of 2001, the government declared that 'We recognise the need to move to a system of wage and salary determination that focuses increasingly on productivity and profitability rather than inflation. To this end, we will seek a significant reduction of the ex-post indexation element contained in current contracts during the next public worker collective bargaining round and civil service salary adjustment, and will use the Economic and Social Council as a forum for income policy discussions with the private sector' (IMF, 2010). Within this authoritative approach, the coalition government enacted the Public Officials' Unions Law (POUL) in July 2001, which did not grant the civil servant unions the right to collective bargaining, let alone to strike. The unique function of civil servant unions was confined to 'collective meeting' with the government. It is ironic that in the event of a disagreement between these *partners*, it was the Board of Ministers that would make the final decision.

The basic social policy regulation of the DSP-lead coalition government was to implement major revisions in the social security regime. The revisions increased the active/passive ratio by gradually increasing the retirement age to 60 for men and 58 for women, and the minimum premium days required for retirement was increased to 7,000 from 5,000. As the levels of pensions depended on the number of days worked, a later retirement age was encouraged. In 2001, an individual retirement system was introduced and would come into force in October 2003. In addition, the unemployment insurance system was created by Act number 4447. The system was financed by the payment of premiums (2 per cent by workers and the state and 3 per cent by employers on the basis of the workers' monthly earnings subject to the premium) and stipulated making payments and providing services to the unemployed in the form of unemployment benefits, illness and maternity insurance and professional training, provided that the unemployed were dismissed by their employers through the termination of a fixed-term contract and so on (OECD, 2006). The eligibility criteria also consisted of having paid at least a 600-day premium over the last three years and having worked permanently over the past 120 days. The unemployment benefit was set to be no more than the net amount of the minimum wage and less than the half of its net amount.

Overall, it can be suggested that the DSP failed to achieve its basic policy targets, despite some crude socio-economic institutionalisations. Beyond the abovementioned macro-economic and political data, the Party's electoral performance supports this thesis, declining from 22.1 per cent in 1999 to 1.2 in the 2002 general elections. Of the DSP electorate, blue-collar workers, the unemployed and the retired constituted the vast majority. In the 1995 general elections, the DSP electorate comprised the retired (1.72), blue-collar workers (1.55), the unemployed (1.43), employers (0.94), civil servants (0.90) and white-collar employees (0.90) (TÜSES, 1995). Thus, such a phenomenal decline in the Party's performance can be assumed to be the result of the practical *exhaustion* of the left of the centre at the level of praxis in the face of its continuing path-dependence at the level of theory.

Displaced and Redisplaced Continuity of Path-Dependencies: Kemalist Social Democracy and Social Democratic Kemalism in Succession

Streeck and Thelen (2005: 31) define 'displacement' as a pattern of change that emerges when subordinate institutions replace dominant ones in a gradual process on the basis of the 'rediscovery and activation of dormant or latent institutional resources'. The pattern of change in the CHP during the period 1995–2010 was the resurrection of the Kemalist core as the variable determining the Party's programmatic action. Kemalism and social democracy have been the basic path-dependences of the CHP from the 1930s and the 1970s onwards, respectively.

In this sense, the resurrection of Kemalism as a path-dependent change between 1995 and 2010 materialised through the replacement of one path-dependence by another. At issue were the dialectics between Turkey's secular capitalism and Islamic politico-economic survival, a process that gathered *systemic* pace in the early and particularly the mid-1990s and resulted in the rejuvenation of a regime-protective cell in the CHP, as in the 1950s, as the foremost means of vote cultivation. Two main grounds were influential in this rejuvenation.

The first was the narrowed latitude for unsystemic Third Way politics in the face of the RP's social-justice-first theoretico-practical action, earning this party the most votes in the 1995 general elections held following the 1994 economic crisis, because the RP's and the DSP's systemic emphasis on social justice with an anti-imperialist rigour did not allow the CHP to capitalise on the pursuit of a market-pioneering regulatory politics *per se*. The second was the dissipation of the structural, institutional and knowledge power that the external environment provided the Party with in the 1970s. In conjunction with the falling tide of European social democracy, this ineluctably made it a substantial challenge to justify the discourse and praxis of the old social democracy *par excellence*. The most promising option was to cling to a regime-based opposition strategy without actively participating in power from March 1996 onwards, a factor that contributed to the perpetuation of the Party's theoretical rigidity in terms of radical Kemalism.

The Party programme and its praxis explicitly declared, 'we are the guardians of Atatürk's principles and revolutions. Our power is rooted in our historical roots', making a direct reference to the Association for the Defence of the National Rights of Anatolia and Rumelia. The sequence of priorities in the Party's ideologic status was stated as follows: 'The three basic sources of our ideology are Atatürk's modernisation revolution and six arrow principles, universal rules of social democracy and the philosophical accumulation of Anatolia and Thrace' (CHP, 2013: 23–4). In the Party's programme of 1995–2000, the market economy was defined, akin to the SHP's party programme, as a well-functioning mechanism, if regulated, and the state regulation and protection, in contrast, are presumed to be selective.

With this motivation, the Party commits itself to the provision of a secure, stable and feasible investment environment and the minimisation of bureaucratic transactions for domestic and foreign investors. (In the meanwhile, additional emphasis was placed on developing commercial linkages with Islamic countries on the basis of secular exchanges.) For this purpose, the programme emphasises that fiscal discipline should be conditioned by the Central Bank's monetary targets and sustainable debt servicing. Full employment is to be pursued through the catalyst of high-value-added production by encouraging research and development and reducing inflation and interest rates as a nominal complementary tool of this catalyst from a planned perspective. The Party assumed that a declining rate of interest automatically reduces the risk premium, and hence structural improvements in debt servicing results from the fact that decreasing interest payments increases savings. As a corollary, speculative short-term investments would be reduced using reserve requirements to discourage borrowing in foreign currencies.

Despite its open commitment to market mechanisms, albeit prudential, the Party committed itself to establishing a neocorporatist regime, granting the right to collective bargaining and strikes for both workers and civil servants, including both interest-based and political strikes, as in the Collective Bargaining Act number 275 from 1963, provided that they took place 'without suspending compulsory public services' and conditioning strike postponements on certain grounds by authorised judicial authorities (CHP, 2013: 63). In addition to the pursuit of progressive taxation, the Party intends to reduce the tax burden on the have-nots; eliminate certain taxes such as the corporation tax on small and medium-sized businesses; eliminate all taxes on residences used for housing purposes; reduce the income taxes imposed on the artisans, craftsmen and wage-labourers and the social security premiums of workers by 5 per cent and from 10 to 50 per cent within four years, respectively; exempt the minimum wage from taxes; and ultimately reduce value added taxes to 1 per cent on a wide range of goods and services, from basic agricultural inputs to basic food products. On the income side, the Party seeks to finance the consequent losses by reducing unregistered employment to the bare minimum (CHP, 2013: 170–172).

The overgenerous strategy of taxation and social rights provision, especially the right to strike for civil servants, was entwined with the crisis-ridden circumstances of the Turkish economy between 1994 and 2002 and particularly the depressive impact of this structure on the real income losses among workers, civil servants and the retired, the persistence of high unemployment at 10 per cent, a rising tax burden, especially the high successive increases in indirect taxes, and the constrained channels for seeking economic rights through strikes and the inconclusive participation of trade unions in the Economic and Social Council. Between 2003 and 2013, these trends continued in terms of the tax burden, indirect taxes and unemployment, even increasing in some instances (see Table 9.1, p. 208). Under the permanent austerity strategy employed by successive AKP governments, civil servant salaries rose slightly but not in keeping with a model of backward-indexation, and public sector workers' wages slightly declined in real terms.

However, between 1995 and 2010, the CHP's international vision ebbed and flowed between closedness and openness. The Party highlights the preservation of Turkey's unitary structure in the face of the economic hegemony of multinational firms and imperialist incursions. However, it also commits itself to encourage foreign direct investment, regards the G-20 as the major actor in the global architecture and surreptitiously declares its positive stance towards international financial institutions, stating that in the decision-making processes of these institutions, the increasing role of developing countries will be promoted and their crisis-preventing role will be supported. This close/open perspective impelled the Party to minimise its relationship with the Socialist International and the Party of European Socialists between utilising their institutional and discursive support for political popularity and taking the risk of missing catch-all opportunities in an Islamically structured social landscape.

As discussed earlier, as of mid-2010, before the 2011 general elections, there appeared a process of renewal in the CHP (Ete and Eşkinat, 2013). Seemingly, this process unfolded due to Baykal's resignation following allegations regarding his private relationships. Yet, in praxis, it was the outcome of an accumulated process of change that can be observed in the stagnant political performance of the CHP in the 2002 (19.3 per cent) and 2007 (20.8 per cent) general elections in the absence of any prominent rival competing for the votes of the same electoral masses. Underlying this, the key issue was the CHP's refusal to change its regime-based opposition strategy prioritising Kemalism over social democracy. Baykal was well aware that placing social democracy over Kemalism would carry substantial risk, as the history of Turkish social democracy was fraught with theory-praxis mismatches resulting in endemic crises, as in the late 1970s and 1994. Thus, he chose to prioritise the structural and institutional powers of Kemalism over Islamic politics as an *immediate* source of vote cultivation (Keyman and Öniş, 2007) and utilise the abovementioned social democratic promises as a background motive to be rekindled conjuncturally.

The 2008–09 recession rekindled the accumulated change dynamics in the Party given the rising structural and institutional power of Keynesian ideas and interventionist policy worldwide. That the AKP's intervention during the Great Recession came on the supply side substantially contributed to the genesis of the replacement of Kemalism and social democracy with social democratic Kemalism, a process executed by the Kemal Kılıçdaroğlu-led intra-party subversives between May 2010 and July 2011. The primary argument of the subversives was simple, to direct the Party's route towards a social-policy-centred opposition strategy and use Kemalism as a background motive to be employed in the event of a regime-based threat, essentially from Islamic circles (Kiriş, 2012).

The quintessence of this strategy was the enactment of 'family insurance' along with a passive emphasis on labour rights. As a non-reciprocal benefit, as proposed by the CHP, family insurance comprises minimum income security, a payment in the amount of the minimum wage, to be provided to poor families across the country. Priority will be given to families with woman and children in need of care, retired and elderly persons living alone and the unprotected and disabled segments of society. The social security premiums of the families utilising family insurance will be paid out of the central budget. Over a 10-year period, family insurance will cover the entire population. In addition, for workers, the premium days will be reduced to 7,000 days, the unemployed will be provided with health insurance as long as they benefit from unemployment compensation and the retired will receive benefits in proportion to their share of economic growth (CHP, 2011). After the July 2011 elections, social-economics were eliminated from the Party's agenda in tandem with the changing conjuncture of the Turkish political economy due to the peace process and the drafting of a new constitution. (This peace process refers to the democratisation reforms to resolve the Kurdish issue.)

Thus far, we have discussed the development of Turkish social democracy in its dialectics with Kemalism, Islam and neoliberalism. I will present an overall systemic discussion of its evolution and future prospects in Chapter 10 in a comparative perspective with the Turkish Islamic parties and the neoliberal institutional environment. Apparently, this requires first elaborating on the politico-economic evolution of the Turkish Islamic parties, its structural rivals, to which I now turn.

Chapter 8

The Just Order: Re-accumulation of Discontinuing Path-Dependencies Versus the Persistence of Path-Dependent Discontinuities

As discussed in the first chapter of this book, in institutional system analysis, the evolution of political economies is not explicated through *critical junctures* but through turning points or relational transitions on the basis of varying interpenetrations of path-dependence and change dynamics, the main patterns of which are depicted in Figure 1.4 (p. 41). In other words, continuities and discontinuities are dialectic and interconstitutive units of social action. A diachronic examination of the transformation from Ottoman Islam to the AKP's conservative democracy is a case in point. The fact that Ottoman Islam relied upon a normatively contingent social system intensified the inter-repulsive tension between the changes that the secularly motivated civil military bureaucracy attempted to enforce, as previously discussed, and the path-dependencies that conservatively or religiously minded politico-economic actors attempted to resurrect or perpetuate.

In the Republican period, the latter has been represented by the NOM-affiliated parties and, recently, the AKP, the leadership cadre of which was among the top figures of the former, particularly during the 1990s. The path-dependence-sustaining initiatives of these two actors embrace, *inter alia*, adaptive changes to the contemporary internal and external institutional environment, which were dominated by secularly motivated actors until recently. Thus we have to discuss the foundational pillars of these parties and the policy strategies these actors adopted to reconcile these pillars with the prevailing institutional environment between 1970 and 2013.

Foundational pillars point to the structural dynamics that constitute the building blocks of these parties. The Just Order is rooted in the time-specific reinterpretation of the Islamic system of political economy and its Ottoman practice in the early 1970s, initiating the *re-accumulation* of formally exhausted but informally discontinuing path-dependencies in the minds and the spirits of the Turkish people. The AKP's foundational pillars originated in the changing continuity of this process of re-accumulation by prioritising adaptive changes to the internal/external institutional environment. For both the Just Order and Conservative Democracy, this re-accumulation or its changing continuity occurred under the persistence of the path-dependent discontinuity of the unifying bond between formal and informal means of re-Islamicisation.

In other words, and particularly during the reign of the AKP between 2002 and 2013, the process of re-accumulating Islamic political and economic consciousness in formal/public spaces has evolved symbiotically with the process of de-accumulating Islamically or normatively contingent social action in informal or private spaces. As the current mainstream representative of Turkish Islam, the AKP thus stands for the organisational manifestation of the changing continuity of the re-accumulation of discontinuing path-dependencies accruing from Ottoman Islam and Just Order politics in terms of their adaptive responses to the secular capitalist national and international institutional environment. As Ottoman Islam was discussed earlier, in this section I begin with the genesis and evolution of the Just Order as a politico-economic project in the late 1960s.

As previously examined, the formal variables of Ottoman Islam as a social system at the level of theory and praxis were interrupted by changing continuities and continuing changes during the ITF and single-party periods, respectively. Its informal pillars perpetuated its existence as a dynamic of inter-individual and inter-group action to various extents. The formal ramifications of this dynamic were, however, suppressed in an authoritarian manner (particularly during the single-party era, the repressive rigour of the CHP over the masses calmed religiously motivated incidents in rural or urban areas). For example, the Nakşibendi rebellions of 1925 and 1930 were subdued by harsh state intervention. These movements' lack of access to both major and minor resources of power in formal spaces confined their position to a posture of *defence*.

In this context, Yavuz (2003: 133–50) argues that the two main branches of Islamic civic movements in Turkey, the Nakşibendi and Nurcu movements, grudgingly acquiesced to an inward-looking self-enforcement strategy as educational and cultural associations. A tradition-centred Islamic consciousness supported the perpetuation of these movements at grassroots socio-cultural spaces. During the War of Liberation, Nakşibendi leaders played an active role in mobilising mass support against imperial forces and providing shelter for high-ranking Turkish officials, including Mustafa Kemal and İsmet İnönü, from the occupying forces. The National Outlook Movement and Nurcu movement, two basic pioneering social movements that are influential in the Turkish political economy, derived from the Nakşibendi tradition. As a founder of the former, Erbakan was a dedicated member of one of the major branches of Nakşibendis, the *İskenderpaşa* sect. The leader, or *sheik*, of this sect, Mehmet Zait Kotku, adopted a normatively conditioned rationality in construing material and spiritual variables. He encouraged the adoption of technical innovations, industrialisation and economic independence and inorganically played an active part in politics with this way of thinking (Yaşar, 2005).

With the introduction of multi-party democracy, these movements came to engage with the DP and, partially, with the AP during the periods of 1950–60 and 1960–70, respectively, and then with NOM-affiliated parties to a considerable extent. In essence, the proponents of these movements utilise politico-economic power resources to meet their justificational, financial, patronage and clientelistic purposes, the key pillars for them to manifest themselves in everyday life, social linkages, especially the print media, and therefore to aggrandise religious consciousness. The emergence of NOM was retrospectively based on the rejuvenation of the accumulated path-dependant change demands of the religiously sensitive groups of various classes (Gülalp, 2001). Unifying these groups under the roof of a reactionary sentiment towards the civil-military bureaucracy, the DP partly responded to the demands of these individuals by developing at least a motivationally free space of life or providing them with partial access to clientelistic opportunities. These religiously sensitive groups might have preferred to do with this palliative environment provided by the DP as democratic politics was then in an embryonic stage and the political system left an indelicate image in the minds of these groups in terms of the state's prospective reaction to a religiously inclusive organisation.

The AP's dissociation from its Islamically integrative vision and therefore from these groups with a bias towards a more pragmatist and stately orientation, however, left these masses isolated. Kept away from the power, patronage and prestige channels in both the economic and political domains, these religiously sensitive groups that expected change ineluctably searched for a new, genuine alternative. It was the NOM-affiliated parties in which they could not only engage but also partake in the managerial cadres to a greater extent. As far as the theory-praxis trade-off is concerned, the average mindset of the religiously sensitive public in Turkey can be suggested to be the restructuration of Republican institutions by an Islamically contingent initiative that would enable them to have access to the resources of power and prestige, including market opportunities. The pattern of power that the overwhelming majority of Turkish Muslims wish to grasp is not the systemic power to transform the state and market, but the structural power to establish the resources for affecting decision-making processes in the public sector.

Turkish state capitalism, from the ITF onwards, had been based on the patronage and power relationship between the positive-minded businessmen, particularly those operating large-scale modern capitalist enterprises, and their coalitional subsidisers, the CHP and then the AP. Moreover, the small independent tradesmen, merchants and artisans who were unable to utilise these patronage channels, from import quotas to commercial credits, during the reign of the AP, in contrast to that of the DP, denounced the AP for acceding to the demands of the vested interests. The formal emergence of the MNP, the first NOM-affiliated party, was, *inter alia*, related to this type of skirmish in the TOBB, The Union of Chambers and Commodity Exchanges of Turkey (Eligür, 2010). The structural basis of this emergence was urbanisation, social stratification, broader political participation and the ideologic presuppositions towards the foundations and refoundations of the institutional stock in the country and consequent intensification of the subdivisions between major political currents.

Necmettin Erbakan, the founder of the NOM, was elected president of the TOBB in 1966 as the representative of the businessmen running small and middle-sized enterprises confronting large commercial and industrial circles.

However, as the Istanbul and Izmir branches of this union vehemently denounced his views, the AP's ministry of commerce did not recognise these elections. Entering the 1969 elections as an independent candidate from a province known for the widespread presence of religiously sensitive communities, he became a deputy and then founded the MNP in January 1970. Presumably, he conceived of politics as the unique means of taking countercyclical action. Following the closure of the MNP by the Constitutional court in 1971, in the aftermath of the military memorandum of 1971, on the grounds of the Party's involvement in anti-secularist activities, *Milli Selamet Partisi* – MSP, the National Salvation Party, was founded in October 1972 and captured 11.8 per cent of the vote in the 1973 elections from relatively less developed and rural areas or countryside, primarily from the Central and Eastern Anatolian regions. Its electorate primarily comprised housewives, industrial workers and tradesmen and craftsmen, who primarily supported the party for its programme. The Party's deputies in 1973 primarily comprised civil servants, free occupations, farmers, tradesman, builders and clerics (Sarıbay, 1985: 178–9).

A professor of machine engineering and a dedicated Muslim, Erbakan founded the NOM and the MNP with the support of a part of the *Nurcu* sect (Çakır, 2005: 545). I can define NOM as a socio-political front that works to establish the Just Order with its affiliated political parties and civil society organisations. The NOM is a socially integrated, bottom-up organisation, under a strict intra-organisational hierarchy, loyalty and political ambition with a reactive consciousness due to having been sidelined by the Republican order regarding the members' social status and worldview. TÜSES (2002: 54–8) finds that the proponents of the RP, the third NOM-affiliated party, were the segment of the Turkish electorate most committed to their leaders and their party in coping with the expensiveness of life and establishing genuine democracy and human rights.

The Just Order was conceptualised in the late 1980s and early 1990s. Yet, as it relies on the basic postulates of Islamic political economy, it can be suggested to be the manifesto of the NOM's movemental action from its origins until the present. In this sense, in the following, I will first engage with the theory of the Just Order and then examine its praxis by the NOM-affiliated parties during their involvement in one coalition as a minor partner between January and November 1974, two national front governments between March 1975 and June 1977 and July 1977 and January 1978 and ultimately as the senior partner in a collation government between June 1996 and June 1997. It can be argued that because these governments were short-lived and the NOM-affiliated parties were minor partners in the first three governments, this reduces the feasibility of comparing the theory and praxis of the Just Order and its praxis during these governments. Nevertheless, I will make this comparison because these *de facto* experiences with their path-dependent connotations in the minds of Turkish people are the unique material for us to make this comparison and provide insights into the upper limits of the applicability of an Islamically formulated politico-economic project under micro-macro boundaries and challenges of the Turkish context.

Table 8.1 Varieties of Turkish Islam from a political economy perspective

Parameter	MNP-MSP-RP-FP-SP	AKP	HASPAR
Institutional system	Just Order	Conservative Democracy	...
Strategy and policy-choices	Changing discontinuities	Changing continuities	Path-dependent continuity
Political democracy	Normatively contingent, multi-party democracy	Catch-all politics	Beyond group and humanitarian politics
Economic and social democracy	–Unconflictual compromise –Workers should be shareholders in private or publicly owned workplaces	Functionalisation of social dialogue for a healthy and stable political economy	Social-justice-conditioned neocorporatism
Taxation	Progressive production tax	Semi-progressive	Progressive
Fiscal policy	Balanced budgets	Budget discipline for the sake of economic stability	Social-justice-first economic stability
Monetary policy	A valuable TL – inhibition of non-reciprocal money printing and devaluation	Tight monetary policy	...
Public-private choice	–Planned development led by the state's 'organising intervention' –Privatisation under the condition that the shares of the SEEs not be sold to non-Muslims	Privatisation is a precondition for economic effectiveness	Intermediary role of state
Market	A means for realising a just economic order and national independence against international imperialism and Zionism	A foundation of modern life that should be managed effectively to sustain a normatively structured, rational life	A secondary social institution to be regulated according to the establishment of an equal regime of social welfare

Parameter	MNP-MSP-RP-FP-SP	AKP	HASPAR
Growth and development	−Social-development-conditioned economic restructuring −Productive and high-tech-based heavy industrial investment −Mobilising social dynamism through 'religiously motivated (ethnically integrative) national sentiments	−Productive investment is the mainstay of sustainable growth −Economic-stability-first, robust growth	Growth is a secondary institution conditioned by social equity
International trade and finance	−Export-oriented open trade policy with Islamic countries and the elimination of imperial pressure on the country −Protective measures for strategic sectors	−Adopting a liberal trade and flexible exchange rate regime on the basis of export-based economic development −Enhancing international financial transactions by opening the Istanbul Stock-Exchange to global transactions	A tool of capitalist incursion that should be defunctionalised through decommodificatory protective measures
Inflation	A result of money printing	A result of deficit financing and can be curbed through tight monetary and fiscal policy	…
Interest	Main cause of economic imbalances – unfair gain of speculative capital	…	…
Unemployment	−To be erased through a production-based full employment strategy −Means-tested unemployment insurance	A micro-economic issue arising from a cost-productivity mismatch	A systemic but not demand-supply problem

Parameter	MNP-MSP-RP-FP-SP	AKP	HASPAR
Business cycles	A result of interest and speculative investment	A result of uncontrolled fiscal and monetary expansion	...
Social policy strategy	Universal	Austere universalism	Universal
Inequality	Equality of outcomes promoting equality of opportunity and meritocracy-based income differentials	Means-tested equality of outcome	Equality of outcome and the provision of a salary contingent only on citizenship
Poverty	Should be prevented by adopting a universal social policy strategy in addition to Islamic social self help	−Should be alleviated primarily by social self-help organised by civic initiatives −The state should develop social aid services	A systemic challenge to be erased by the provision of equal economic and political power-sharing
ALMPs/PLMPs	Active society, active employment	...	Unemployment is not an individual but a systemic problem
Labour relations strategy	Positive-sum conciliation	Unconflictual compromise	Conflictual conciliation
Employment pattern	Permanent	Human resources perspective	Permanent
Wages	Decent and activating wages	Performance-based	Decent wages
Trade and civil service unions	Civil society organisations to contribute to the effective enforcement of public economics	Should be tolerated	Politico-economic organisations for providing equal power sharing at both the micro- and macro-levels
Collective bargaining	...	For both workers and civil servants	For both workers and civil servants
Strikes	...	For both workers and civil servants	For both workers and civil servants

Sources: Erbakan (1991a, b), AKP (2002), HASPAR (2013).

Table 8.2   Erbakan's comparison of the Just Order with socialism and capitalism

Right-based system	Power-based systems	
The Just Order	*Socialism* (The power of politics)	*Capitalism* (The power of capital)
Balance between private and public property	Public property	Private property
Interest-free profit	Interest free, no profit	Interest and profit
Monopoly-erasing	Public monopoly	Capital monopoly
Credits to production and labour	Credits to public enterprises	Credits to capital
Macro-planning	Macro- and micro-planning	No planning
Full subsidy-full support for productively producing and ethically behaving entrepreneurs	Public suppression in both production and consumption	Enhancement of consumption
Universal welfare	Suppressive welfare	Unequal distribution of welfare
No tax. The state enjoys partnership rights in return for its contribution to production	The poor are made to pay unfair taxes by means of a price mechanism	The poor are made to pay unfair taxes on goods and profits

Source: Erbakan (1991a: 79).

Erbakan's strategy to conceptualise the Just Order was not based on an attempt to reconcile pure Islamic premises with secular Turkish or global capitalism. Instead, he chose to make a straightforward adaptation, particularly in economics, while addressing the harsh political reflexes of the Kemalist regime. He breaks down the Just Order into two major sections, *Adil Ekonomik Düzen* – AED, Just Economic Order – JEO and *Adil Siyasi Düzen* – ASD, Just Political Order (1991b). While delineating the latter, Erbakan sternly denounces the design and imitation-centred institutional stock of the Turkish Republic, transposed from Western Europe, claiming that it caused the inculcation of a flawed and guided democracy. According to Erbakan, the consequence is that the state came to be the master of its citizens rather than vice versa. The ASD is based on the re-establishment of a political order on the basis of the moral and cultural values of Turkish society with an awareness that the state is the servant of its citizens. As the unique way of establishing a substantive democracy, the co-integration of the social motivations of political and civic actors, according to Ersoy (1995), the co-theoretician of the Just Order, should comprise the key constitutive element of a new Turkey. The essential manifestation of the ASD is the freedom for Muslims to practice their religion in the public sphere.

The AED prescribes a mixed-economic system on the basis of productive investment, non-interest financing, optimal pricing through a free market structure regulated by public authorities and a social-justice-first development strategy. Rather than directly referring to Islamic economics, Erbakan (1991a) defines the AED in reference to socialism and capitalism, arguing that it comprises the beneficial aspects of these two regimes. As shown in Table 8.2 in the AED, property is not allocated to either the public or private sectors, as in capitalism and socialism, respectively, but is distributed equilibratingly between them in an inter-reinforcing manner. Ersoy (1994: 64–73) argues that, on the basis of public property, socialism, in its initial stages, substantially increased production capacity. However, socialism was unable to then mobilise social capacity because its heavily bureaucratic content structuralised the imbalances between wealth and responsibility. In contrast, while imposing an unbearable burden on wage labour, capitalism decreases the income of this group and deteriorates the distribution of income. Although capitalism made significant achievements possible, as its progressive mindset paved the way for the exploration of new production techniques, its effectiveness is only sustainable at the firm level because this type of exploitation results in the monopolisation or oligopolisation of production relationships and begets the waste of public resources and opportunities.

Erbakan (1991a) argues that public authorities would effectively invest in, particularly, strategic sectors, as its main function is to provide the foundations for a universal welfare regime in the country. However, in principle, it should leave productive investment to private entrepreneurs to avoid encumbering competitive price formation and market progressiveness, stimulatingly subsidise the entrepreneurs making ethical and high-value-added investments, eliminate the market failures of a capitalist system such as oligopoly, monopoly and business cycles and provide general services such as government, legislation, energy provision, water, road, infrastructure, health, education and so on. The state's primary role in the AED is to proactively prevent interest-based capital accumulation, the main failing of a capitalist system, that Erbakan notes embeds an unequal distribution of income.

Ersoy (2005: 356–7) adds that interest is not the price of capital but a way of making money from money, thereby destroying the production-consumption balance, causing inflation and structuralising income differentials. Interest, thus, would not provide equilibrium levels of savings and investment because money is a nominal, not a real variable. Providing this equilibrium, hence, is the quantitative balance in money and goods markets (the value of money should be measured by the value of the goods that money represents). In the AED, from another perspective, money is the bond given to a person (labourer or entrepreneur) who produces to demonstrate that he/she has a right to consume in proportion to the value of his/her production. (The surplus accruing from the exchange of goods and services is profit, which is the return on undertaking market risks that increase social welfare by creating a progressive pathway.) Unreciprocal money printing, hence, increases the prices of current goods and services, incrementally deteriorates the income distribution and transfers the right of a producer to another individual who does not deserve it. As such, inflation arises from the misuse of government intervention without increasing production. As it makes economic variables such as prices, wages and costs unclear, it imposes a recessionary constraint on the volume of investment credit, output and employment.

In this sense, in the AED, the state is not staffed to establish SOEs for redistributional purposes. Rather, the dissociation of the state from productive activities is not disapproved of, if not urged. It is, however, stipulated that the SOEs should not be sold to foreigners – the imperialists, multinational corporations with non-Muslim shareholders. By the same token, the AED systemically rejects any cooperative linkage with the UN, EU, IMF, WB, WTO and so on, as these organisations are the agents of the worldwide capitalist exploitation of Muslim and the other nations' human, capital and territorial resources (Erbakan, 1991c). Erbakan frequently emphasises financing production through alternative methodologies such as *mudaraba, murabaha, selem* and so on. In his theorisation, the primary means for Muslim countries to finance their economic development is the establishment of an Islamic common market, which is presumed to be politically invigorated by the foundation of the United Nations, the Defence Cooperative Organisation and the Organisation of Cultural Cooperation of the Muslim countries.

His main emphasis is on the development of economic bonds on the basis of technical and human resources and financial complementarity among Islamic countries – a concrete step towards this ideal was the foundation of the Developing Eight (D-8) under his leadership and during his premiership in June 1997 and including Turkey, Iran, Pakistan, Indonesia, Malaysia, Nigeria, Egypt and Bangladesh. In addition to its overt aims, the Just Order is intended to make Turkey a powerful and wealthy nation-state that numbers among the world powers, thereby restoring the spirit of Ottomanism. Despite his harsh discourse on the abovementioned West-originated regional and international organisations, he advocates the development of strong friendships and peaceful bonds with individual industrialised Western countries in the commercial, technological and scientific realms.

In socio-economic terms, this systemically anti-capitalist theorisation involves the complete transformation of the institutional stock from a social-justice-first standpoint. Erbakan (1991a: 83) notes:

> Five viruses of the capitalist order (interest, unjust taxes, money printing, devaluation and the banking system) trigger every kind of economic and social devastation and thus exacerbate the disparity in income distribution by making the rich richer and the poor poorer. *Window-dressing measures* taken to ameliorate the adverse impacts of these viruses arising out of the very origins of (capitalist) order are nothing else except a new unjust oppression and, in essence, cannot change the result.

A study of the societal bases of the MNP demonstrated that its electoral base was primarily located among the poorer and less educated segments of the population. Consistent with this finding, in the 1994 general elections, the RP's electoral support thrived among shantytown dwellers on the outskirts of large cities. The majority of this support came from blue-collar workers (TÜSES, 1995: 47; Gülalp, 2001). The AED's emphasis on the equal distribution of income and the elimination of exploitation was therefore not surprising. Erbakan (1991a: 66, 84) claimed that there would 'not be poverty and starvation in [the] Just Order since the *first and foremost duty* of the state is to provide everyone with the opportunity to live in decent way […] *no matter the situation* [of the economy]'. Accordingly, the state would distribute the national income by imposing a single tax on production.

The production tax should be optimised because capital owners would otherwise impose taxes on customers or cut employee wages, in which case, the demand side of the economy would fall into decline. The state has the right to impose the tax on producers but not on employees, in contrast to its contribution to production. In the current system, state worsens the income distribution and averts sustainable development. Collected taxes should also be employed to meet the needs of unprotected individuals (namely, children and unemployed, poor, ill and elderly individuals), as well as civil servants, workers, the military and the police. In this regard, the Just Order stipulated that the state *must* provide every citizen with an income sufficient to meet a basic standard of living. Providing of this income would be the essential task of the state. Erbakan argues that it would not constitute *hush money* as it does in the capitalist system. He remarks (1991a: 67) that 'social justice services are not delivered as a necessity of humanity but hush money provided so that the capitalist order would be maintained'.

As a result of real-production-centred economic investment and the elimination of the overfinancialization of aggregate economic activity, there would not be unemployment but full employment in the AED. (He claims that, in the current system, two-thirds of the cost of goods is composed of accumulated interest [one-third] and unfair taxes [one-third]. When these are removed, prices will decline by one-third. Therefore, a given enterprise will be able to increase production threefold relative to the present and employ three times more workers. This will also create a comparative advantage and boost exports, especially when the Islamic common market is established.) To maintain full employment in the labour market, the level of wages should be determined according to age, education, service and professional quality within a meritocratic system. Even if they are provided to each citizen on a non-reciprocal basis, social security benefits should also be in line with these parameters and be optimally arranged to ensure that individuals remain active in the labour market. This is because social security in an inactive society would be unsustainable due to ageing and a declining birth rate, as in the European countries.

In the area of the IRs, the Just Order envisions a social contract between the state, employers and workers that will keep employers from abusing workers' rights, workers from abusing their jobs and the state from showing a bias towards either employers or workers. In this peace-based articulation of the IRs, Erbakan does not elaborate on *class* organisations, taking for granted the absence of class-based conflict among the actors of labour relations. Instead, he argues that in the Just Order, everyone will become a member of solidarity organisations like trade unions or guilds (1991a). Their main function would be an intermediary role between the state and their members for apportioning social security and unemployment benefits. In this respect, the term 'trade union' does not refer to contemporary trade unionism but rather refers to those labour organisations that would function as self-help organisations for their members and would participate in the regulation of supply and demand in the labour market under the leadership of the state authorities, in the same way as the Ottoman craft associations. Given the state-dominated structure of Turkish labour relations, the Just Order explicitly tailors a more interventionist function for the state than does pure Islam. However, the mobilisation of workers against political authority by radical means such as mass strikes is not condoned, since it is believed that such methods cannot exert a systemic influence over secular capitalism and serve no other purpose aside from triggering political chaos.

Theory and Praxis of NOM-Affiliated Parties

The Just Order accurately depicts the general framework of the NOM-affiliated parties' programmes, in broad strokes. A point of divergence is that the latter were forged under official responsibility and hence were subject to some corporeal modifications. The MSP's programme (d.a: 8), for example, declared: 'Laicism is the guarantee of the freedom of thought and conscience and acts as a buffer in the face of pressure from one group on the others in an ideologic sense'. This definition was more straightforward in the MNP programme, in which the Party grudgingly presents it as the functional demarcation of religion and state affairs and emphasises that this should not be made a means of suppression over the former.

The MNP's programme featured moral and spiritual values more prominently as a unifying bond between normative and rational constituencies, whereas the MSP placed the primary emphasis on economic development and industrialisation. In the latter, democracy is defined as 'free opportunity spaces that are the most respectful of the law, that presents the freedom to seek for individual rights in the fairest way, and that paves the way for the realisation of the right and the truth' (p. 5). The RP's programme (1986) furthers the adaptive tendency of the NOM-affiliated parties in its opening sentence: 'This programme has been prepared in keeping with Atatürk principles, the constitution and the law of political parties ... [and] with the view that the Turkish Republic is a nation loyal to, above all, to Atatürk nationalism'. In addition, the secular substance of the Republic is underlined more *intimately*: 'Laicism is not the principle of hostility to religion but a principle that protects the freedom of religion and conscience from all kinds of violations' (p. 8). Akdemir, one of the three theoreticians of the Just Order, argues (1991: 222) that laicism is the 'balance in the principle of the separation of powers and religion is the "supervisor" of this balance'.

In the area of economics, in tandem with the AED, the heavy industry strategy is the most widely discussed, along with a production strategy of establishing industrial plants wielding innovative and advanced technologies in the areas of nuclear energy, aviation, shipping, computers and so on, with an internationally competitive and export-oriented capacity. To establish an innovative economic structure, exchange controls should be minimised and customs duties such as licences, quotas and so on should be lifted, with the exception that the state stimulates strategic and young sectors to ensure a sustainable development process. The state's role in this process is both to ensure the feasibility of and construct these industrial plants in cooperation with universities, transfer them to the private sector after ensuring that they function productively and prioritise the policy that the shares of these firms should be held by their employees, who should be provided with the necessary occupational training opportunities to make an efficient contribution to a social-justice-centred development process (see the MNP and MSP party programmes [d.a.]: the RP [1986]).

In terms of the praxis of the Just Order and the performance of the NOM-affiliated parties, the picture is mixed but not positive in a systemic sense. During all three governments in which the MSP and the RP participated, GDP increased at moderately high rates, public sector fixed capital investment rose remarkably compared to the previous period and indirect taxes declined and increased notably during the national front governments and the RP-DYP coalition, respectively. Direct taxes and the total tax burden registered real increases in all three periods. Current account and budget deficits were relatively high during the first two periods, whereas PSBR declined slightly in the last period. The Central Bank's credits to the public sector were either moderately or remarkably high, except the last period. Inflation receded during the first period and the first year of the second period, while it rose at a remarkably higher rate in 1977. Interest rates remained constant during the first two periods. Under the RP-DYP coalition government, inflation recorded slight increases and decreases, whereas interest rates first rose considerably and then declined slightly. Unemployment increased in all periods, whereas public employment increased substantially, except during the last period. Public sector wages decreased rapidly during the first period and increased slightly and remained at a high level during the second and third periods, respectively. During the RP-DYP coalition, there was labour shedding among temporary, contracted and permanent workers, while civil service employment increased marginally. Social expenditures during this period also increased slightly.

Overall, the most concrete trends during all three periods are the increases in GDP and public sector fixed capital formation. The MSP controlled the Ministry of Industry and Technology in the first and second periods. In the second period, Erbakan's opening ceremonies at industrial plants were the most conspicuous demonstration of the Party's policy. The aim was to found 200 enterprises with billion valuations and 70 of them were completed in various sectors such as iron-steel, aviation, tanks, the defence industry and so on. These ceremonies were subsequently presented as the implementation of heavy-industry policy. During this period, the World Bank declined to finance certain projects and, during the second national front government, the MSP rejected the IMF's relief proposal to overcome a foreign-currency shortage (Sarıbay, 1985: 196–203).

Another concrete result of the NOM-affiliated parties' participation in coalition governments was the partial access to governmental opportunities, particularly to the personnel cadre, as reflected in the high public employment rates throughout these governments' tenures, except in the last period. Regarding the RP-DYP coalition, the mostly cited variable is the high real increases in public sector wages and salaries and the minimum wage despite stagnant wages in the private sector. Again, in this period, relative declines in unemployment, social expenditures and inflation would be suggested to be positive signals. During the previous two periods, the MSP was a junior partner, and there was a highly volatile politico-economic environment under the shadow of domestic social chaos, particularly during the second period.

Some positive inferences in terms of the praxis of the Just Order could be proposed, such as a relative decline in indirect taxes and an unchanged interest rate. Yet the negative outcomes are more numerous, such as the persistent current account and budgetary deficits, ambiguous trends of inflation, increases in the tax burden and unemployment, high real decline in wages and salaries in the public sector during the first period and so on. The fragmented ministerial composition allocated among ideologically diverse political parties and the fragile nature of the politico-economic structure in the face of social chaos, particularly during the second period, preclude making clear-cut inferences. The same also holds for the CHP.

It was not the macro-economic performance of the MSP but the performance of the RP local governments that laid the foundations of the rising tide of the RP during the early 1990s. Taking 8.7 per cent of the total votes cast in the 1989 local elections, the RP increased its vote share to 19.0 per cent, the second highest after the ANAP (22.9), in 1994. Despite the closure of the RP in 1998, *Fazilet Partisi* – FP, The Virtue Party, won the 1999 local elections, taking 18.4 per cent of the votes. A major contributing factor to the RP local governments of the period was the conscious that they had, for the first time, such a *massive* opportunity to assert themselves and demonstrate their distinctiveness arising from their Islamic worldview. As the mayor of Istanbul, Erdoğan was the most conspicuous figure to manifest himself with his vivid 'corporatisation' of various municipal such as the Istanbul Natural Gas Distribution Co. – IGDAS, Istanbul Energy Co. and so on. Their activities were predicated upon simple commercial principles enmeshed with the RP's clientelistic and patronage linkages.

It is now a well-established fact that the RP local governments were not operationally unsuccessful. Developing a concept, the social municipality, they directly engaged with civic public, especially with the needy and the underprivileged, who constituted the majority of their electorate, *Beyaz Masa*, white table, became the major means of providing this linkage with the ordinary public; in this system, all inquiries were collected and then addressed with relatively close supervision by the mayoral staff. Through the *Halk Meclisleri*, public councils, the RP municipalities attempted to create a means of consensus building between the public and local politicians in addition to organising wide-ranging national and international conferences, workshops, panels and conventions concerning various social and economic issues (Yavuz, 2009: 63). The fact that the performance of the RP mayoralties was contrasted with the unsuccessful performance of the SHP mayoralties, particularly in Istanbul, where the latter lost to former in 1994 (the RP and SHP's shares of the vote were 10.9 and 36.6 per cent in 1989 and 17.4 and 25.2 per cent in 1994), likely contributed to the latter's image of being 'not unsuccessful'.

The third period, the RP-DYP coalition, featured a clash between the RP and the *defenders* of secular capitalism. Among the latter were the military and civil bureaucracy including 'activist' judges from the judicial cadres, the CHP, mainstream Turkish media, TOBB, TISK, Turk-Is, DISK, Turkish Confederation of Small Business and so on (Kalaycıoğlu, 2005: 58). The defenders employed various methods to force the government to resign, from turning on and off the lights in houses, a direct military memorandum at the MGK of February 1997, to agitating the public's secular sentiments through television programmes and false newspaper articles directed by high-ranking military staff members, rigid implementation of a headscarf ban and so on. The fundamental argument was that the RP had a hidden agenda to transform the Turkish Republic into a religious state. Ultimately, Erbakan was forced to resign as of June 1997 after a one-year incumbency. The RP and its successor, the FP, were closed by the Constitutional Court in 1998 and 2001, two events that led up to the emergence of the AKP, the governing party in Turkey from December 2002 onwards.

Chapter 9

Conservative Democracy as the Second Great Divide [?] in Anatolia at the Crossroads of Continuing Changes and Changing Discontinuities

Extrapolating from the entirety of world history, Roberts and Westad (2003) have argued that the pathway and evolutionary dialectic of civilisational transformation are determined by the *preferences* of a society. This viewpoint would be considered *irrational* by utilitarians because they hold that there is only one impulse that propels all nations onto a monolithic civilisational pathway, utility. As Roberts and Westad put it, the Chinese or Ottoman Empires, however, in their social organisation, did not prefer to engage with capitalist rationalisations before or after Europe experienced the Renaissance. This was neither a weakness nor a strength, but the spatio-temporal outcome of the original consistencies of these empires. As discussed earlier, for example, the Ottoman Empire's social organisation was at odds with capitalist progress. The Empire featured pragmatist discretions in commercial life and established patronage linkages between capitalists and bureaucrats and so on. Yet the foundational pillars and evolutionary dynamics of its social system were not predicated upon corporeal ideals and appeals, but a politically contingent rationality (Aydın, 2009) to eliminate the widening income differentials both between capitalists themselves and among various classes, as can be seen in the relatively positive trend of real wages throughout the Empire's long *durée*.

At this juncture, I believe the question is not why the Ottomans *had* not structuralised a capitalist organisation but why they were unable to *restructuralise* their civilisational pillars to sustain a competitive position across continents. A prospective answer is that the Empire's massive social organisation, established on delicate balances, did not have the dynamics to become the pillars of a liberal market economy. Creating such an economy, from nothing, was inconceivable due to the embedded path-dependencies of abovementioned institutional interlinkages. It was in this context that the first industrialisation initiatives in the long nineteenth century were intended to rejuvenate the Empire's former grandeur through the state itself. Normatively contingent path-dependencies of the Empire, in other words, could not be poured into a rationally conditioned change, as a result of which the ITF emerged at the end of the nineteenth century. From then onwards, the panorama has not changed in systemic terms. Neither have the major politico-economic actors in the Turkish political economy achieved the construction of a truly capitalist mode of production, nor have they laid the foundations of a social market economy. Instead, the Turkish political economy drifted between etatist and (neo)liberal regimes, leading to a systemically catastrophic (2001) crisis at the turn of the century.

For religiously sensitive persons, the outcome of the faltering flow of the Empire's social structure emerged at the turn of the twenty-first century. They have to both develop a rationally motivated, modern restructuration of the country and condition the dosage of this rationality in keeping with their normative constraints. As someone who demonstrated his competency in rational sciences, Erbakan was well aware of these *systemic* facts and blended the normative content of the Just Order with an integral emphasis on technology-centred economic and financial reinstitutionalisation. However, there was a structural obstacle to his project: the systemic mismatch between the institutional mix that he advocated in the Just Order and Turkish society's level of commitment to the theory and praxis of Islamic norms and values. This resulted in the waning of the NOM-affiliated parties, as Turkish society did not provide the required electoral support to these parties, which was indispensable for counteracting the vested, systemic power of Kemalist civil-bureaucratic elites and their coalitional power shareholders, major business and employer organisations and so on (Özbudun, 2006).

That the RP captured 21 per cent of the total vote was, in a systemic sense, entirely insufficient. This is because, given the strong coalitional, institutional and structural veto power of pro-cyclical actors, a change in the *systemic* power resources could not be *initiated*, let alone *achieved*, with such a slight majority. The inconspicuous governing performance of the NOM-affiliated parties played a part in creating the lukewarm support of Turkish society. But it can suggested that the main issue is related to the mismatch between the reformational expectations of religiously or conservatively sensitive persons and theoretico-practical steadiness of the Just Order in strict allegiance to Islamic political economy in the face of these expectations and path-dependent continuity of vested interests of pro-regime political, market or civic forces.

The reformational expectations of religiously or conservatively sensitive Turkish people centre not on the systemic implementation of basic Islamic institutions but on having the freedom to practice Islamic culture freely and reflect these cultural images at the level of politics and economics. This systemic-unsystemic trade-off, as Kalaycıoğlu argues (2007), lies in the commodification of normative values in the face of: the need to pursue a secularly dominated education to qualify for a high-paying job; speaking fluent English and contacting secular images to learn it; engaging with secular social images in movies, social activities and educational facilities; perpetuating a permanent and ever-rising career path in notable professions such as medicine, engineering and business management; adapting familial connections to the power and prestige-imposing business environment; establishing an extensive business or social linkages for advancing corporeal interests irrespective of ideologic credentials; creating a sympathetic image open to communication including to foreigners; engaging with interest-bearing credit agreements or doing business with banks that engage in interest-bearing transactions; living in a salient location, having high-tech and prestigious cars, computers and mobile phones; being open to or beginning to forge intimate clientelistic and patronage opportunities through local or central political channels and so on.

As these *practical constraints* overwhelmed the theoretical normativities in the minds of Turkish Muslims, they chose to vote for the *reconciliative* AKP rather than the *reformist* NOM-affiliated political parties. This is because the margin for a systemic transformation, at least in the area of economics, requires a high level of fidelity and in-group solidarity. Pecuniary evidence of the lack of such a sentiment among Turkish Muslims is their abstention from investing their money in interest-free banks or making their business transactions through the intermediation of these banks. Although the AKP took 50 per cent of the total votes cast, in this sense, these banks only hold 6 per cent of the total deposits in the Turkish banking system. The extent to which Turkish Muslims adopt a systemic or unsystemic approach to Islamic political economy can be well inferred from this fact.

At the turn of the twentieth century, approximately three centuries after the initiation of the Empire's first inquiry (in 1720, see p. 94) into the reformational pillars of European civilisation, (Turkish) Conservative Democracy was conceptualised as a path-dependently structured change initiative to strike a balance between the abovementioned unsystemic *expectation* of norm-contingentness among Turkish Muslims and the level of rationality-contingentness that a secular politico-economic institutional environment required. Akdoğan (2006: 51, 58), the theoretician of conservative democracy and the chief political consultant to Erdoğan, declares:

> The AKP is able to establish a synthesis of classical conservative culture with Islamic values, and to remain a viable party in a functioning democracy, this will be its most lasting legacy ... Conservative democracy supports a gradual and progressive transformation of its functions in order to bring about significant, even revolutionary change for the betterment of society. Such gradual improvements, by genuinely reflecting what has been acquired historically by a society and what gains can naturally evolve in the future, can produce societal transformations that are both fundamental and permanent. Changes that have not materialized gradually are not considered viable or permanent.

In other words, conservative democracy has become a theoretical ideology to create a pragmatist complementarity in the Turkish political economy between normatively contingent rationality and rationality-conditioned normativity in time and to varying extents in the cultural, political and economic realms. I can define the strategic endowment of conservative democracy as the *'timely and justified reification' of the Just Order's norm-contingent rationality* or *the transformation of path-dependently contingent rationality of Islamic political economy into the change-contingent normativity of reconciliation among Islam, neoliberalism and even social democracy under the confines of the internal/external institutional environment*. For adherents of the Just Order, such a reconciliative initiative is the uncreative destruction of the Just Order. For the conservative democrats themselves, it is an entirely new 'identity', not an ideology, crafted to unite the Turkish people under a single roof for the creation of a 'Great Turkey'. Akdoğan (2006: 50) argues that 'According to the conservative democrats, the field of politics should be firmly grounded in the culture of reconciliation. It is possible to solve social differences and disagreements in the political arena on the basis of reconciliation'.

An indicator of this reconciliation is the cosmopolitan nature of the Party's electoral basis and administrational cadres. A survey of the AKP's electoral base indicated that 27 per cent of votes came from the ex-electorate of the FP; 21.9 from the ultra-nationalist MHP; 9.2 from the centre-right ANAP; 7.3 from the centre DYP; and even 6.9 from the centre-left DSP (TESEV, 2002: pp. 70–71). The AKP's supporters were, by and large, members of the rural population, artisans and small traders in the cities, urban slum-dwellers and rising religious entrepreneurs running small or middle-sized businesses. The educational level of these people is in turn primary school (20.6), secondary school (27.6), high school (18.6) and the university (17.2).

The AKP's deputies generally came from families with average or below-average incomes. The deputies had completed primary school (1.4 per cent), secondary school (2.8 per cent), high school (9.9 per cent), university (61.3 per cent) and post-graduate degrees (24.5 per cent). Their mothers and fathers generally only completed primary school, while a limited number had completed secondary school. Among their fathers, 6.3 per cent were university graduates, while 1.0 per cent of their mothers were. In other words, the deputies were prominent figures, but they were not elites by family ties. Instead, they exhibited high personal social mobility and became the representatives of the Party and its friends and supporters in their provinces. Of the Party's supporters, attendants and deputies, 26.8, 55.9 and 73.5 per cent had FP (the fourth NOM-affiliated party) origins, respectively. The percentage of the members of provincial organisations who had worked for the RP and FP was 54.8, 15.5 for the ANAP, 8.7 for the DYP and 6.4 for the MHP (Aydın and Dalmış, 2008). These proportions would well be argued to vary in time.

It can *prima facie* be suggested, as we did above, that the main catalyst for the formation of the AKP was the successive closure of the previous four NOM-affiliated political parties. (Akdoğan [2006: 60] notes that 'The parties *emanating from the National Outlook Movement*, including the AKP, are generally deemed to be …' The leading features of the AKP's founders were the members of the NOM, as well, including the current and previous presidents of Turkey, *Recep Tayyip Erdoğan* and *Abdullah Gül*, respectively, and AKP's second man, *Bülent Arınç*). This hypothesis is rooted in the restructuration of political identities under the constraints of the formal institutional structure, the Kemalist establishment in the Turkish case.

Nonetheless, I believe that it is the *synthesising pressure of timespace and income-lifestyle compression* that initiated the development of conservative democracy as the organisational manifestation of accumulated change demands in the politico-economic ideals of conservatively or religiously sensitive persons in the Turkish political economy. In other words, the disidentifying and integrative power of income-yielding or money-making impulses under a capitalist mode of social exchange has *dragged* Turkish Muslims into a search for a conciliative strategy of politics and economics and matching their lifestyles with the *flow* of this conciliation, cutting through the theory of Islamic political economy and its praxis, as in other contemporary Muslim countries. This *great* reconciliation executed by the leaders of religiously sensitive segments in Ottoman-Turkish society, three centuries after the beginning of reform initiatives in the Empire, symbolises the emasculation of 'group' or 'me' feeling in the Haldunian or Habermasian senses, respectively, among Turkish Muslims with the ideal of rejuvenating the systemic or unsystemic mode of Islamic political economy. The AKP stands for the formal centripetal organisation of informally centrifugal (fragmented) mind-sets (Yılmaz, 2005).

In one respect, the AKP relies upon rationally crafted, delicate balances that would fail during any period of socio-economic or political crisis. However, in another respect, the Party has consolidated Islamic normativity, irrespective of its level of *Islamicness* or *taqwa*, in social and public space and further augmented its support among the Turkish people, garnering a total vote share of 49.9 per cent. As social interaction is a dynamic process, the current prospects for the Turkish political economy will either be in the form of a renormativisation of rationally contingent cycles, namely changing discontinuity or a further denormativisation/ deepening of ongoing *social exchange*, namely continuing changes. A systemic examination of the politico-economic *recipes* of conservative democracy would enable us to have a more crystallised comprehension of it in light of the internal and external institutional environment, inter-actor relationships and power competition.

The AKP's party programme begins with the statement that 'the structure of our country is not irredeemable. The resort is the public itself. *As the Great Atatürk* accentuated, the power to save the public is its own decisiveness and perseverance'. The programme also declared: 'Our party regards Atatürk principles and revolutions as the most significant means of carrying Turkish society to a point above the contemporary level of civilisation and regards this as a tenet of societal peace' (AKP, 2002: 13). In the programme, the key referent for basic rights and freedoms is the Universal Declaration of Human Rights and The European Convention on Human Rights. The Copenhagen Criteria are regarded as the supreme principles of democratisation. According to the programme, laicism is an indispensable precondition for democracy and the guarantee of religious freedoms. Religion is claimed to be one of the most significant institutions of humanity and its political manipulation for political purposes has been explicitly condemned. In international politics, basic vision presented in the programme is the continuation of Turkey's current position in NATO, the strategic cooperation with the USA and the advancement of its candidacy for EU membership. Furthermore, particular emphasis was placed on developing ties with other Islamic countries and enhancing the international role of the Islamic Conference Organisation.

In brief, it can be suggested that, in political terms, the Party has determined a strongly reconciliative strategy with respect to both internal and external *constraints* (Çınar, 2006). The Party's economic strategy gives the same impression. The AKP's framing logic is that economic management should focus on long-term balances, engender trust and be committed to moral principles. As can be observed in Table 8.1 (p. 189), under this mindset, the Party predicates its fiscal and monetary policies on providing and sustaining austerity-contingent economic growth with the aim of laying the foundation for a productive and internationally competitive market economy. In the area of international economics, the Party advocates the adoption of a liberal trade regime and a flexible exchange rate policy to functionalise an export-based economic development strategy. Adopting the perspective that the financial sector is the determinant force in the emergence of high investment capacity, the Party declares its strong support for international capital inflows, the TNCs for their (alleged) contribution in the transfer of knowledge accumulation and industrial experience and international financial institutions and the EU for the consolidation of economic progressiveness.

According to the Party programme (AKP, 2002), public borrowing 'above an acceptable level' results in overall economic imbalances, reduces the borrowable funds available for the private sector and increases the cost of credit. (Thus, to sustain cash balances in public budget, short- or long-run borrowing should only be contracted for projects that would recover their costs.) Inflation, which is a direct result of deficit financing, can only be curbed through tight, rather than discretionary, fiscal and monetary policies. Moreover, inflation is the main cause of business cycles in Turkey. On the income side, the Party promises both to reduce the tax burden as a tool for increasing the marginal propensity to invest and consume and to remove the inequality-creating burden of taxation facing the workers, civil servants, the retired and low-income households.

In socio-economic terms, in the programme, the Party regards unemployment as a micro-economic issue stemming from rigidities between labour productivity and labour costs, namely as a voluntary phenomenon. In this sense, the state should, in principle, not be involved in any type of economic activity, including achieving full employment or redistributing national income, except for regulatory and supervisory functions. As a corollary, privatisation is a must for the establishment of a rational economic structure with a passive emphasis that the shares of SOEs to be privatised should first be offered to their employees, the neighbouring public and sectorally organised professional (trade or employer) organisations. In addition, national targets and strategic priorities will be factored into the privatisation of critical sectors (such as telecommunication and postal services).

Despite their liberally oriented economic and pragmatically crafted catch-all political vision, Turkish conservative democrats, in social policy terms, first and foremost accepted responsibility for social justice. In the Party's programme having a separate section on social policy, it is straightforwardly declared that 'it is *unavoidable* that we should introduce a concept of a social state that cares for the unemployed, poor, needy, ill and handicapped and which allows them to live in a way that is commensurate with human dignity' (AKP, 2002). The social justice ethos of the Party lies in the ideal that 'service to people is service to God' as the previous Prime Minister Tayyip Erdoğan put it while presenting the programme of the second AKP government.

According to the conservative democrats, social expenditures should not, however, interrupt economic stability as a result of inflationist and populist policies. In this regard, the Party believes that the steady increase in social welfare is possible only through an increase in productivity by means of improved competitiveness. It is within this context that special emphasis is laid on the necessity of decentralising the management of social aid and services in coordination with the local administrations (governorship and municipalities) and non-governmental organisations (Akdoğan, 2006). Underlying is the Party's unsystemic approach that poverty is an issue that would be overcome primarily by social self-help to be organised by non-governmental organisations, and by state's social aid services. In a similar vein, privatisation is proposed to be an alternative way of extending social services in the area of health, education and so on.

In Turkish conservative democratic discourse, the state/government has retained a relatively powerful position. In theory, the government is assigned the role of organising the power relations between the employers and the workers by proactively setting down necessary legal regulations to settle and prevent conflicts among them. The unique means for ensuring peaceful IRs is to establish social dialogue as a platform for mutual agreement. From this perspective, trade unions and employer organisations are expected to take a conciliatory stance to attain and sustain peace in a positive-sum relationship. The following declaration in the Party programme describes this approach:

> Our biggest target is to place the social dialogue at the highest level and solve problems through *mutual agreements*, within a triple structure consisting of worker, employer and the government, for the purpose of attaining *peace* for workers and for the maintenance of labour activities in a healthy and balanced manner (AKP, 2002).

The AKP explicitly backs the right to organise and to collective bargaining and to strike for both workers and civil servants. In fact, Erdoğan's discourse rose above a soft support: 'it is our primary responsibility to invigorate trade unionism'. *Daily Radikal* dubbed Erdoğan as the 'Che Guevera of Turkey' and 'Socialist Tayyip' considering this discourse. However, this discourse comes to clash with the fact that the party, in its programme, declares to restructuralise public personnel management in terms of modern management techniques, namely human resources management and the principle that citizens are 'consumers'. A special emphasis

Table 9.1 Major indicators of the Turkish political economy, 2002–12

Results of General Elections		Nov. 2002		July 2007		June 2011	
	CHP	19.3	CHP	20.8	CHP	25.9
	DYP	9.5	DP	5.4	DP	0.8
	SP	15.4	SP	2.3	SP	1.2
	MHP	8.3	MHP	14.2	MHP	12.9
	ANAP	5.1				
	DSP	1.2			DSP	0.2

Governmental Status: DSP-ANAP-MHP | AKP
Duration of Incumbency: Nov.

Parameters	2000	2001	2002	2003	2004	2005	2006	2007	2008	2009	2010	2011	2012
GDP	6,8	-5,7	6,2	5,3	9,4	8,4	6,9	4,7	0,7	-4,8	9,0	8,8	2,2
Agriculture	7,1	-7,9	8,8	-2,0	2,8	7,2	1,4	-6,7	4,3	3,6	2,4	6,1	3,5
Industry	6,6	-7,3	2,7	7,8	11,3	8,6	8,3	5,8	0,3	-6,9	12,6	9,7	2,0
Services	6,4	-2,5	5,5	4,3	10,1	8,7	8,2	6,3	1,2	-3,2	8,5	9,0	2,4
Balance of Accounts/GDP	-1,1	-6,5	-0,1	1,3	1,1	4,8	2,0	1,8	-0,3	0,1	2,0	0,1	2,9
Current Account Balance/GDP	-3,7	1,9	-0,2	-2,4	-3,6	-4,6	-6,1	-5,9	-5,6	-2,2	-6,5	-9,7	-6,0
Foreign trade/GDP	31,0	36,9	38,0	38,2	41,1	39,5	42,7	42,7	45,0	39,4	40,7	48,5	...
Consolidated Budget Balance/GDP	8,9	12,1	10,0	7,3	3,6	-0,1	-1,9	0,1	1,6	5,1	2,3	0,1	1,7
Tax Burden/GDP	23,8	25,1	23,9	25,6	25,7	26,0	26,2	26,5	26,6	27,2	28,4	29,7	27,6
Indirect Taxes/GDP	10,8	11,1	11,0	11,9	12,0	12,4	12,8	12,2	11,6	11,8	13,4	13,5	13,5
Direct Taxes/GDP	6,9	7,4	5,9	5,8	5,4	5,5	5,2	5,7	5,7	6,0	5,6	5,9	6,0
Public Fixed Capital Formation/GDP	5,6	-9,0	2,6	-22,2	-13,5	12,9	2,9	0,2	13,6	-4,0	3,9	...	...
Government Final Consumer Expenditures/GDP	-4,1	5,7	2,7	-4,2	-2,1	-1,3	4,6	3,7	0,1	14,8	-3,0	...	...
Total Domestic Demand/GDP	8,0	-12,0	8,8	8,8	11,7	9,5	7,0	5,7	-1,2	-7,4	13,4	...	...
Credit of Central Bank to Public Sector/GDP	0,0	0,0	0,0	0,0	0,0	0,0	0,0	0,0	0,0	0,0	0	...	...
Inflation	54,9	54,4	45,0	25,3	8,6	8,2	9,6	8,8	10,4	6,3	8,4	6,5	8,9
Unemployment	7,0	8,9	10,8	11,0	10,8	10,6	10,2	10,3	11,0	14,0	11,9	9,8	9,2
Interest Rates	38,0	96,2	63,8	45,0	25,7	16,9	18,2	18,8	19,3	12,7	8,5	8,7	8,8
Privatization/GDP	0,79	0,08	0,04	0,08	0,09	0,24	1,34	0,68	0,49	0,25	0,30	...	...
Social Expenditures/GDP	...	...	...	...	...	9,7	9,8	10,7	11,1	13,3	12,6	12,2	12,3
Gini coefficient	...	...	0,44	0,42	0,40	0,38	0,42	0,40	0,40	0,41	0,40	0,40	0,40
Public Sector Wages and Salaries	6,9	-11,5	-9,2	-2,7	1,7	2,7	-2,7	3,1	-1,9	-0,5	-3,6	...	...
Wages and Salaries in Public Sector	-13,7	-5,5	6,4	2,2	6,7	3,0	4,0	3,4	1,1	6,7	...	...	...
Worker (Public Sector)	18,0	-6,9	-11,0	3,0	5,5	-0,3	-3,0	4,7	-4,0	1,3	-1,4	...	...
Minimum Wage	-14,9	-10,7	5,0	14,4	13,5	4,2	-0,9	-0,7	-1,6	2,5	0,9	...	...
Worker Private	10,9	-13,8	-2,8	-2,1	6,9	1,2	-1,1	1,4	-2,4	1,7	...	...	...
Change in Public Sector Employment	6,3	-0,4	0,8	0,8	0,6	5,9	7,7	3,8	-0,9	1,3	6,7	...	...
Civil Servant (Fixed-term contracts)	6,5	-0,1	0,1	0,9	0,6	4,5	3,6	-0,9	0,9	0,3	5,2	...	...
Worker (Temporary)	18,4	-82,7	4,7	1,2	9,7	4,8	450,6	-74,8	-85,8	-22,6	-17,1	...	...
Worker (Permanent)	-0,7	8,9	0,3	-0,7	-1,2	5,4	58,2	-3,0	1,6	-2,6	0,0	...	...
Contracted	7,0	3,4	6,7	-1,2	18,2	166,2	17,7	109,5	36,3	23,1	28,2	...	...
Employment Strictness	3,72	3,72	3,72	3,72	3,72	3,72	3,72	3,72	3,72	...	...	...	...

Source: TKB (2013a); TUIK (2012).

was made in the programme to the removal of wage and social right distinction between workers and civil servants in the public sector.

  Specifically, during its third term in office, in addition to these programmatic postulates, the Party announced 'The Vision for 2023' (AKP, 2013) including the following targets:

- Be among the top 10 countries in terms of GDP by increasing GDP to two trillion dollars, at a minimum;

- Increase export volumes and per capita income to 500 billion and 25 thousand dollars, respectively;
- Structurally reduce the inflation and interest rates into the single digits;
- Reduce the unemployment rate to five per cent and increase the employment rate to 50 per cent, at a minimum.

While evaluating the practical performance of successive AKP governments, it is a widespread practice among students of the Turkish political economy to *forget* the structural imbalances in the Turkish economy that precipitated the 2001 crisis and claim that they did nothing except implement the IMF programme outlined by Kemal Derviş in 2001. For the AKP's leaders or proponents, the Turkish economy has left behind highly volatile and crisis-ridden periods through the removal of macro-imbalances in structural terms. Despite having some basis in fact, both perspectives lose sight of the evolutionary dynamics and ongoing structural imbalances in the Turkish economy, particularly its socio-economic implications.

During its incumbency from December 2002 onwards, the AKP has maintained its economic policy programme. As can be observed in Table 9.1, the Party's economic performance can be divided into two periods, 2003–07 and 2008–13, as the global downturn began to affect the Turkish economy in the last quarter of 2008. When the AKP came to power, Turkey's Program for a Transition to a Strong Economy was underway, and the Party chose to implement this programme and a successive one signed in 2005, and essentially based on the same structural pillars, until May 2008 under the IMF's supervision. From then onwards, despite substantial negative growth in the period 2008–09, the Party did not change its primarily supply-sided strategy towards a demand-sided one, in contrast to worldwide policy decisions.

In the first period, particularly between 2002 and 2006, the boom period in the global economy and liquidity contributed to the consolidation of a virtuous cycle when Turkey managed to attract a substantial amount of long-term foreign capital (Öniş and Şenses, 2010a: 5–6). A relatively high growth rate (6.9 per cent) was realised with a remarkably higher ratio of current account deficit/GDP (4.5 per cent) on average, stemming from an overvalued TL and the resulting import boom, the primary cause of external fragility. During this period, current account deficits were financed by increased FDI and portfolio investment (see Figure 6.2, p. 123), predominantly short term, as a result of increased uncovered interest arbitrage in Turkey relative to emerging market economies, indicating the net return on domestic short-term financial assets. For Turkey, this arbitrage was 10, 19 and 40 per cent during 1989–94, 1995–2001 and 2002–07, respectively (Demir, 2010: 14–5).

A positive development in this period is the decreasing standard deviation or volatility of GDP and real short-term capital inflows from 5.5 during the period 1995–2001 to 1.2 between 2002 and 2007, and from 4.8 to 1.9 during the same periods, respectively. Real foreign exchange rates were also relatively stable throughout this period (see Figure 6.3, p. 123). The party was able to pursue strict austerity that resulted in a balanced budget, first in 2005 and then 2007, thanks to declining ratios of public sector fixed-capital formation (investment) and final consumption expenditures, which were accompanied by steady rises in indirect taxes and very limited real increases in civil servant salaries, limited increases in average public sector employment and, ultimately, relatively high privatisation revenues, especially in 2006. This austerity coincided with remarkable declines in the rate of domestic and foreign debt/GDP from 42.8 and 56.2 in 2002 to 30.3 and 38.5 in 2007, respectively. The decline in the latter was primarily the result of the primary surplus strategy and the rising parity of TL/dollar. However, private sector foreign debt soared, especially in 2006 and 2007, and created a critical risk factor of exchange rate volatility, although its average duration became relatively longer. Furthermore, inflation and interest rates (average compound interest rates on domestic borrowing) declined from 45.0 and 63.8 in 2002 to 8.8 and 18.8 in 2007. There was one politically small but socially massive problem, the persistence of unemployment above 10 per cent and plummeting total demand from 11.7 in 2004 to 5.7 in 2007 during this first period.

At the beginning of the second period, the main debate centred on the prospective impact of the global downturn on the Turkish economy. Erdoğan claimed that the ongoing crisis would not affect Turkey, even tangentially. The reality was different, at least to an overwhelming extent, as shown by the stagnant and large negative growth rates in 2008 and 2009, respectively. As was the case with Erdoğan's reaction, Turkey's delayed response to the Great Recession was exceptional and socially exclusive relative to worldwide praxis, which revolved around operationalising Keynesian demand-stimulus, lowering interest rates, implementing tax breaks, welfare and employment schemes and infrastructure investment in addition to applying for external funding from international financial institutions to alleviate short-term fiscal constraints and balance of payments problems.

The AKP opted to reduce tax rates on consumer durables instead of basic goods and implemented corporate tax cuts and a range of entrepreneurial supports with a relatively high increase in public sector fixed investment in 2008 and final consumption expenditures in 2009, resulting increased PSBR and domestic debt stock from 1.6 and 28.9 in 2008 to 5.1 and 34.6 in 2009, respectively (Uygur, 2010; Öniş and Güven, 2011: 587). The resumed growth in 2010 and 2011 sharply decelerated in 2012 in conjunction with the phenomenal increase in the current account deficit, which reached 9.7 per cent of GDP in 2011, despite swiftly rising FDI and portfolio inflows in 2010 and 2011. The AKP government resumed its pre-crisis strategy by swiftly reducing PSBR to 1.6 and increasing indirect taxes to 13.5 per cent of GDP in 2012, keeping inflation under control between 6 and 8 per cent and suppressing interest rates (8 per cent as of 2012).

An important factor in the *prudent management* of the crisis would be to avoid falling into the traps encountered in the past due to the fragile nature of macro-economic variables, as in the 1994 and 2001 crises. Babacan, the deputy prime minister responsible for economic affairs (2013), claimed that Turkey overcame the negative impacts of the global crisis through political stability, robust public finance and a strong banking sector, financial discipline, effective monetary policy and the effective utilisation of macro-discretionary measures in 2009. In spite of Babacan's self-confident emphasis on the macro-economic balances, as he himself announced in the declaration of Turkey's medium-term programme for the period 2014–16, the current account deficit and drastically low level of savings continue to be the highest risk factors for Turkey. The government imposed additional regulatory measures, especially on credit cards, to restrict the level of consumption above the real incomes of consumers in addition to the enhancement of private savings by the implementation of a law of leveraging private pension scheme participants' savings using public subsidies at a rate of 25 per cent (OECD, 2012: 5).

During the post-2002 period, it can be argued that Turkish industry transformed into an open economy, with a transition from a specialisation in primary and low technology production to more technology-intensive manufacturing (the medium-low and medium-high technology sectors comprise the chemical manufacturing industry, machinery and equipment, motor vehicles, office, accounting and computing machinery, manufacturing of radios, televisions and communication apparatuses) (Taymaz and Voyvoda, 2010: 167). Structural challenges remain in place, however. Turkey is primarily dependent on imports with medium and high technology content, and the low technology and labour-intensive exports constitute a major portion of total Turkish exports and are subject to fierce competition from large-scale economies such as India and China with lower real wages (Öniş and Şenses, 2010: 308). This structural challenge is rendered more difficult by the lack of investable funds and credits and the unpromising panorama of receding capital accumulation, even during the promising 2002–07 period, and the pragmatist stance of Turkish banks to restrain long-term investment capital to channel additional funds to consumer credit (Öniş and Şenses, 2010b: 313).

Ultimately, the AKP's continued incumbency for more than a decade has, in Turkish case, illustrated that static austerity severely limits the development of a dynamically complementary market structure. From a strategic political standpoint, the Party's economists would claim that an austerity-contingent strategy has been necessary due to the path-dependent fragilities of the Turkish economy. However, for our research, it emerges that tight fiscal and monetary policy might tame inflationary pressures and interest rates somewhat, but such an approach also undermines export performance, severely constrains total demand and fails to curb high levels of structural unemployment. Moreover, the impact of Central Banks' *innovative monetary strategy* of defining a wide interest rate corridor to flexibly change market interest rates in tandem with shifting policy priorities remains ambiguous, as it has failed to deliver low and stable inflation, albeit providing relatively stable exchange rates. A key point, in this respect, is the low marginal propensity of Turkish industrialists to make high value-added investments, as reflected in the declaration by Turkey's largest industrial group regarding the development of a productive automotive industry (p. 143).

In this context, due to the lack of industrial entrepreneurs to make progressive investments in high value-added sectors, the AKP governments chose to pursue their stability-first economic strategy irrespective of its urgent socio-economic consequences. The political quintessence of this strategy is that, thanks to its bilateral political mission, the Party has not been in a position to utilise populist policies to cultivate votes. The first is to make a path-dependent change in the current regime. Path-dependence lies in the inevitability of maintaining the secular, laicist and capitalist roots of the ongoing institutional stock, whereas change requires restructuring the *pliable* components of this stock from an anti-systemic perspective insofar as the Party's social power is capable. The second is to make this path-dependent change in the name of the politically and economically marginalised masses, ranging from the poor and low-income households to small and medium-sized enterprises or educated social groups in need of political patronage for a governmental career, credit, subsidy and so on. The tension between these two major axes provided the Party with a substantial margin: to perpetuate austerity-centred economic stability without adopting expansionary monetary or fiscal policies, even during the Housing Bubble, in contrast to the worldwide tendency.

Before the 2007 general elections, the second variable became a strong tool for the Party to increase its vote share to 46.5 per cent from 34.2 per cent in 2002. The strategy of regime-based protection of Kemalist social democrats, a path-dependency that the CHP has maintained from its opposition to the DP onwards, paradoxically fed back into strong civil support for the AKP. Another feedback into this swift *structural* increase in the Party's votes (to continue and even increase in the 2011 general elections) was the military memorandum of April 2007, just ahead of the July 2007 general elections, implemented by posting a text on the website of Turkey's General Staff openly warning the government to remain in line with Kemalist principles and secular capitalism. The AKP took a firm stance against this memorandum through a counter-declaration simultaneously broadcast on nearly all major television channels.

These dialectic attempts continued with the opening of a closure case by the Chief Public Prosecutor of the Supreme Court of Appeals, in July 2008. The Turkish Constitutional Court decided that the AKP had become the focal point of the activities against the secular political regime while rejecting demands for the Party to be closed by a six to five majority decision. However, political tension persisted thereafter with the opening of an historic case, *Ergenekon*, in July 2008 by a number of public prosecutors under the indictment that a highly cosmopolitan and organised group began developing plans for a coup d'état between 2003 and 2004, entitled *Sarıkız, Ayışığı, Yakamoz and Elviden*, to overthrow the AKP government by escalating social tension through organising assassination groups, executing armed attacks on various targets and persons and so on. The alleged group is composed of the members of Turkish General Staff, journalists, former politicians and political party leaders, the state's special forces, lawyers, trade unionists, a former MGK general secretary, academics, members of police departments, former mayors, former secretary general of the Turkish Orthodox Patriarchate and so on. The local court imposed, generally heavy, penalties and life sentences on 252 out of 275 defendants.

In another case, *Balyoz, de facto* beginning in January 2010, concerning the preparation of a military coup d'état in March 2003, the Supreme Court of Turkey upheld the local court's convictions of 237 defendants and reversed those of 88, the great majority of whom were members of the military staff. The explanation was that the staff had planned initiatives to organise attacks, assassinations and bombings at mosques to create a chaotic social environment, prepare the necessary ground for the proclamation of martial law and ultimately to initiate a coup d'état. It should be noted that the Constitutional Court of Turkey has reversed the judgment of the High Court of Justice and the local courts on the grounds that the right of the defendants to be judged fairly has been violated. In addition, in spite of his party's initial coalitional support to the judicial circles that conducted these cases, Yalçın Akdoğan, the deputy Prime Minister, declared in December 2013 that 'a plot was laid against the national army of Turkey'.

The Ergenekon and Balyoz cases have been the main political tension among the CHP, the AKP and the military staff. Yet, in this instance, the Turkish media, intelligentsia, academia, major business organisations, civil bureaucracy and so on chose not to side with the defendants straightforwardly and structurally. The fact that the history of Turkey is replete with coups d'état that had economically catastrophic consequences for both business and labour, as recently experienced in 2001, might have been a factor in this prudency. The foreground was, nevertheless, the AKP's reconciliative political identity and, most important, the Party's liberally oriented economic strategy with the catalyst of its institutionally notable political reforms on the road to EU membership. The party's internationally cooperative and open policy strategy with Western countries, international financial organisations and so on has consolidated its reconciliative status, as an indicator that it remains aloof from politically anti-systemic radical reforms. Akdoğan (2006: 52–3) writes that 'The AKP has been actively working to reform the system by solving some of these problems without upsetting the status quo entirely. This reform has been accomplished, in part, by developing a modernity that accepts the traditional, a globalism that accepts the local and a stress on smooth, rather than radical, change ... [the strategy] to hinder uncontrolled reaction in favor of controlled alteration'.

This *gradual change* initiative by the AKP, however, could not be implemented smoothly, but occasioned strict opposition from the CHP and central bureaucracy. The process of selecting the President of Turkey was a case in point. According to Article 102 of the Turkish Constitution of 1982, the requirement is that a candidate must obtain a majority of 376 votes in the National Assembly in the first two rounds to win an election. In the third round, this requirement is half of the total, 276, and in the fourth it is a qualified majority. The CHP claimed that 376 votes are necessary to open the Assembly for all rounds of a presidential election and boycotted the elections of Abdullah Gül, who received 357 votes in the first round. The CHP brought this election to the Constitutional Court, which held that a two-thirds majority is necessary to open the Assembly for all rounds. Özbudun (2012: 45), a secular liberal professor of constitutional law, evaluates this decision as *extremely controversial* because there is no arrangement of this type in the Constitution of 1982. As a result, the Parliament, as a constitutional requirement, called new elections and the AKP increased its votes from 34.4 to 46.6 per cent in July 2007. Ultimately, in August 2007, Gül was elected, obtaining 339 votes in the third round of the elections, despite the CHP's continuing abstention. In the referendum of October 2007, *inter alia*, a constitutional amendment on establishing a qualified majority as the unique precondition for the Turkish Parliament to take all of its decisions was also endorsed by 68.7 per cent of voters.

In September 2010, another set of constitutional amendments was put to a referendum and endorsed by a majority of 58 per cent, including the introduction of a new institution, the Ombudsman, a new right for citizens to raise their individual complaints to the Constitutional Court, making the Supreme Military Council's decisions subject to judicial inspection, increasing the number of members on the Constitutional Court, the High Council of Judges and Public Prosecutors to 17 from 11 and to 22 from 5, respectively, to be elected predominantly by the High Courts from their own members rather than by the president as in the pre-amended Constitution. In addition, following the June 2011 general elections, the AKP established a commission to draft a new constitution in October 2011, agreeing to include an equal number of members from the four parties represented in parliament rather than on the basis of their parliamentary seats. At the time of this writing, despite arriving at consensus on 60 articles, this commission was dissolved in the face of the unbridgeable divide between the parties' viewpoints on structural issues such as the coverage and content of the right to education, the official language, citizenship, the unchangeable articles in the Constitution of 1982, the peculiarities of the Republic and so on

The abovementioned constitutional amendments and judicial cases concerning coup d'état initiatives feature discursive, structural and coercive power struggles between the AKP, the CHP and the central bureaucratic establishment, as well as major business and employer organisations. It can be claimed that, to a certain extent, the AKP has succeeded in changing 'malleable' niches in the resources of structural and institutional power in its own favour. The current situation is that the *average demand* of religiously or conservatively sensitive individuals seems to have been met to a structural extent, namely the restructuration of Republican institutions through an Islamically contingent initiative in a manner that would enable them to have access to the resources of power and prestige, including market opportunities. This could be regarded as a threshold in terms of the *structural* power competition between the AKP and the other major actors in the Turkish political economy. I will discuss this perspective in the following sub-sections. Suffice it to say here that, throughout the evolution of the abovementioned political restructurations, the AKP's rule was not free from certain soft-authoritarian implications.

The first, to be elaborated below, is the Party's functionalising an austerity corporatism that leaves little room for organised civil society to participate in socio-economic policy-making. The second, most importantly, is its initiative to raise a hard discourse regarding the oppositional parties, media groups, business organisations, intellectuals and so on. Generally appearing in the words of Prime Minister Erdoğan, these discourses aim to cultivate a consolidative power for the Party to ensure that its ties with its electorate remain dynamic. The underlying motivation is the reactionary sentiments of the AKP's electorate regarding the proponents of the Kemalist establishment. Two main catalysts for this discourse were the CHP's non-political tactics to lock the political system and therefore cultivate additional votes for the sake of regime protection and the 27 April 2007 military memorandum as the pinnacle of military shadow over the AKP government.

An intriguing peculiarity of Turkish political economy under the AKP's reign is *the tensional gap* between the outermost limits of domestic and external policy-making. While Erdoğan, the previous prime minister of Turkey between March 2003 and August 2014, voiced his discourses with persistent harshness, Davutoğlu, previous Minister of Foreign Affairs, did so with persistent softness (Davutoğlu became Prime Minister in August 2014). This, I believe, well reflects the professional policy-making in the AKP on the basis of *tensional dialectics*, a phenomenon directly related, no doubt, to the policy-making style of the AKP's domestic or external rivals. What makes the AKP a persistent image is in this sense the Party's professionalism in ebbing and flowing between soft-harshness and harsh-softness at the crossroads of national and international politics. Erdoğan's storming out of a debate with Israel's President but *procedural* embrace with Obama are consequences of this dialectic. Their longstanding encounters with the Kemalist establishment, from their youth to old age, inculcate this delicate dialectic into AKP members' policy-making initiatives.

In the area of international economics, for example, the AKP does not regard being Muslim or non-Muslim as a determining factor in the development of commercial or financial linkages. The Party's engagement with the IMF, World Bank and FDI and portfolio inflows well reflects this phenomenon. As can be observed in Figure 6.2, between 2003 and 2013, the Party has essentially maintained the country's relationship with the World Bank at the same annual volume of increased credit. Moreover, FDI and portfolio inflows exhibited remarkable increases in the periods 2005–08 and 2004–05/2010–11, respectively. The most important development in this respect was that, as previously discussed, the Party continued the IMF stand-by agreements between December 2002 and May 2008. At this point, the *soft-harshness* of this engagement emanates from the fact that the Party does not hesitate to terminate its relationships with international financial organisations when it feels no need for them. In May 2008, the Party terminated its *de facto* stand-by relationship with the IMF, despite substantial pressure from the TUSIAD to renew the then concluded agreement. The underlying explanation is the Party's path-dependence in self-confidently conducting, and thus keeping occidental organisations away from intervening in, the country's internal affairs.

In cognisance of the inevitability of the abovementioned dialectic in political economy, as the theoretician of the Party's international relations strategy, the previous minister of foreign affairs between May 2009 and August 2014, and the current prime minister of Turkey, Davutoğlu argues that a foreign policy based on sheer resistance irrespective of the strategic opportunities would not halt but only slow the collapse. According to him, it is the accumulated culture of a nation, its *strategic deepness*, which forges the dynamic opportunities to enforce and perpetuate an effective strategy of international relations. He (2007: 68) claims that 'the most significant aspect of the foreign policy experience of the ITF period for today is the risk of seeking for an international power not in proportion with the country's real power ... The powers that tend to gather the necessary momentum during wars must precisely be in a position to have made the necessary preparations for such an attempt in the psychological, strategic, technologic, political, economic and cultural realms'. The main strategy of the pre-AKP era was, according to Davutoğlu, to protect the national frontiers under the auspices of the Western powers against Soviet threat. Even the extremely significant decision to participate in the European Economic Community was a product of the desire to not lag behind in its struggle with Greece. With this reactive mindset, Turkey's international political economy in the twentieth century was trapped between resistance and change, circumventing the eruption of structure-changing initiatives.

At issue is that Turkey began to become a partner of the Western world: the European countries and the USA that regarded the country as an intermediary ally, at best, to execute their strategies regarding the Middle East, the Balkans and the Caucasus. Moreover, the country could not create effective regional coalitions with the nations of these three regions or the other Muslim countries in Southeast Asia and Africa in the economic, political or cultural realms. Turkey's internal conflict-ridden restructuration process created an immense burden on the country that impeded the inception of such transnational discretion. Davutoğlu argues that throughout the AKP era, in essence, this discretion has been realised, as well as the formation of strategic, rather than peripheral, ties with the non-Muslim leading countries, primarily through the catalyst of an *inside-out power* emanating from a stable domestic politico-economic environment (Davutoğlu, 1994: 96–113).

The Party's major policy choices included the decisive steps taken to gain full membership status in the EU, the development of pragmatically crafted diplomatic reconciliations with the USA (such as discourses on the political irreconcilability but not the civilisationally assimilative nature of the USA's invasion of Iraq and so on), and calming political tensions in Cyprus by, for example, complying with the Annan Plan prepared by the United Nations and so on. *Zero problems* constitutes the key principle that the AKP has internalised in structuring Turkey's long-term international relations. For the debate in this book, it is important because it indicates the Party's reconciliative policy choices in international relations beyond religious references. The most conspicuous attempt of the Party, in this regard, was to establish the Alliance of Civilisations in cooperation with Spain and under the auspices of the UN (http://www.unaoc.org/about/). Under this initiative, while not being internationally influential, the UN is researching the roots of civilisational polarisations and developing practical policy recommendations to cope with these challenges.

The thoroughgoing image of the AKP's foreign policy strategy, particularly under the conspicuous leadership of Mr Davutoğlu, passed through a process of stagnation in the wake of the outbreak of the Arab Spring in late 2010, the ensuing civil war in Syria with its bloody massacres by the state's army and the bloody military coup d'état in Egypt in 2013, consigning Turkey's cordial relations with Egypt, Syria and its coalitional allies, Russia and Iran, to a conflictual diplomatic tension. At the crossroads of the Ottoman and subsequent imperialist past, the Middle East has become a diverse political arena in which cosmopolitan social interactions among the Islamic left and right, Islamic modernity-traditionalism-orthodoxy, radical or moderate political associations groupings drifted through formally established authoritarian regimes. The complete overturning of or partial revisions to the formal rule of these regimes – such as in Tunisia, Yemen, Egypt, Libya and so on and in Jordan or Kuwait, respectively, unleashed a process of chaotic transition at the intersection of developing a new institutional stock, revising the old establishment or protecting the vested interests of civic and political actors.

The meaning of this panorama for Turkey is the reorganisational crisis in its previously cordial political relationships with these countries under the constraint of the volume of economic exchange. Turkey's exports to Near and Middle Eastern countries increased from 5.4 to 25.4 billion dollars during the period 2002–08. With the emergence of Arab Spring, this rate declined to 19.2 and 23.2 in 2009 and 2010, respectively (EB, 2013). On the one hand, Turkey has pursued and managed to establish strategic opportunities by utilising its discursive power over the entire Middle East, emanating from its imperial tradition during the pre-Arab Spring period. The fragmentation of socio-political spaces in the Arab world defunctionalised this holistic strategy of the AKP and confronted it with a subtle challenge to enforce the same strategy. A direct consequence is that Turkey is currently unable to use its region-wide prestige as leverage in its relations with Europe, the USA or international organisations. Coupled with the decelerated reform process on the road to EU membership, this loss of power has raised doubts regarding the effectiveness of the Party's international relations strategy.

At this point, one can come to the conclusion that the AKP is an acrobat swinging on the stable axes of Islamic political economy and flexible horizons of a *de facto* political economy, a peculiarity that prevents it from using clear-cut definitions in its policy strategies (Atasoy, 2009: 107–36). Furthering these mixed blessings is the Party's socio-economics. This is because this area constitutes the core component of the institutional intersections between political and economic power and the competition for prestige.

In terms of socio-economics, the AKP's theoretical presuppositions can in this sense be claimed to be implemented under a practical strategy of *austere universalism* signifying that the Party, on the one hand, has initiated developing the means of a universal social policy strategy but has implemented this political choice under the constraints of the economic stability-first social justice strategy, on the other. Elsewhere, I designated this strategy as *responsible pragmatism*. As can be seen in Table 9.1, social expenditures rose steadily, particularly in 2009, and the Gini coefficient first retreated to 0.38 in 2005 from 0.44 in 2002, but then rose 0.42 and finally levelled off around 0.40 till 2011. Constituting the big portion of social expenditures is the increase in social protection expenditures such as pension payments and expenditures of unemployment insurance fund, social aids and unfunded payments. Under the AKP's reign, the salaries of civil servants registered steady but limited increases that were funded partly by real reductions in the wages of public sector workers. The minimum wages have been nearly stagnant, despite high real increases between 2003 and 2004. Having a notable part in high unemployment, the limited increases in public employment on average have been predominantly made up of temporary and contracted workers, and the proportion of permanent employment in the public sector remained limited, especially for workers.

Another cause of the limited decline or stagnancy in the Gini coefficient was the flourishing sentiment of social self-help, particularly between 2002 and 2007 when the number of beneficiaries rose remarkably. This help came from relatives and neighbourhood solidarity as well as from food, fuel and rent aids given by the governorships and municipalities. As appeared in the remarkable rises in social aid expenditures rather than in regular incomes of civil servants, workers or the retired, the AKP's strategy in this context was to enhance this sentiment with a central initiative, the affiliation of *Sosyal Yardımlaşma ve Dayanışma Genel Müdürlüğü*, The General Directorate of Social Assistance and Solidarity, directly with organisation of Prime Ministry. Besides, the AKP government spurred the operations of civil society organisations making in-kind and cash aid to the needy by passing the Law of Association of 2004, restricting governmental control over commercial activities and encouraging private firms and companies to finance social projects in poverty alleviation through the incentive of tax cuts (Grütjen, 2007: 59). The Party issued a draft proposal for civil society organisations to establish their own social service institutions.

In terms of austere universalism, the AKP's most outstanding initiative was the restructuration of the social security regime, primarily for reducing transfer expenditures allocated to meeting the deficits of social security institutions that amounted to 7.4 per cent of the GDP in 2009. The basic target was to attain an equilibrium rate in which four working people would finance one retired and therefore lower the dependency ratio. An integral part of this target, the retirement period was shortened by raising the retirement age for all three groups (workers, civil servants and the self-employed), and the number of qualifying premium days for workers to 9,000 days, albeit during a slow phase-in period (ÇSGB, 2009). Stabilising the pension allowance rate at 2 per cent, with this reform, the pension rate was reduced between 0.4 and 0.6 per cent. These rates have become much higher with the decreasing revaluation rate of the pension base that excludes 70 per cent of the GDP growth rate. In the face of the criticisms, in this regard, the Party declares to have compensated for these declines by extending the coverage of the pensionable earnings. Another structural constituent of this reform was to equalise the qualifying conditions and rights of civil servants, workers and the self-employed and to unite the three separate insurance institutions serving each of these three categories under the roof of a single authority, the Social Security Institution. Overall, the AKP's reform of the social security system engendered an austerity-contingent and state-dominated universalist regime by removing the status discrimination and privilege among the insured and pensioners.

In one of the two basic areas of socio-economics, labour relations, the AKP's choice was to craft a flexi-cure strategy consisting of institutionalising flexible employment patterns and perpetuating the allegedly rigid regulatory framework under the shadow of the former. In OECD employment rigidity index, indicating the strictness of regulation on dismissals for individual and collective regular contracts, the country retreated only to 2.31 in 2004 from 2.39 in 2002. The Act continued the severance payment at the rate of one-month gross wage for each year, legalised the major flexible work patterns (part-time, temporary, on call and so on) and increased the threshold for job security in firms employing 10 to 30 workers, thereby excluding 40 per cent of the workforce from coverage. It further confined job security only for those working for at least six months in the same workplace, but brought in a precondition, a valid reason, for the termination of job contracts of these workers. In order to increase the rate of employment, with the Employment Packet of 2008, the social security premiums for women and unemployed youth between the ages of 18 and 29 were initialled to be met by an unemployment insurance fund for five years following their employment and the employers' portion of social security premiums for all others was reduced by 5 per cent (ÇSGB, 2008). Under the auspices of the European Employment Strategy, the National Employment Agency of Turkey pushed for the ALMPs such as 'employment-guaranteed training programmes', 'get skilled-your job is ready', 'the young businessman' and 'woman entrepreneurship' programmes. However, the labour force participation rate increased quite slightly from 46.3 in 2004 to 50.0 per cent in 2012.

The AKP governments, on the other hand, maintained the authoritarian nature of Turkish industrial relations. The Party's strategy was to create an austerity corporatism with a tactical choice of controlling governance. In doing so, the Party chose to perpetuate the suppressive institutional stock such as the extensive bans on strike postponement, the very existence of a Higher Arbitration Board, the lopsided nature of the Economic and Social Council's power composition and the inconclusive negotiational entity of the EU Joint Consultative Committee – JCC. In this sense, the Party's strategy of *hard pragmatism* in IRs aimed to manage the power flow between governmental discretion, trade union reaction and employer demands through a binary strategy of suppression and support. However, the Party also enacted noteworthy emancipatory regulations. The most conspicuous is the lifting of the ban on general and political strikes for private sector workers, which could well be regarded a structural turn in Turkish IRs. The other is the enactment of the Trade Union and Collective Contract Act number 6356 in October 2012.

The Act reduced the membership age from 16 to 15, replaced the requirement of notary notification for membership with an e-application by workers, realisation of the intra-organisational inspections by the respective trade union councils and audits by independent financial advisors and confining the security of trade union membership to workplaces employing over 30 workers. In terms of collective bargaining, the Act replaced sectoral collective bargaining with framework contracts, legalised group collective labour contracts in which the parties are one trade union and multiple employers who operate enterprises at the same sector, reduced the sectoral barrage for the right to organise from 10 to 3 per cent gradually over the next five years while preserving the 50 per cent majority precondition for the right to organise in workplaces. The Act only lifted the bans on strikes for educational workplaces and notaries, leaving the others intact.

Given this ambiguous socio-economic performance in the areas of social policy and IRs, it becomes an intriguing question to determine how the AKP perpetuates its ever-increasing electoral performance, not only among the ordinary public but also among the working-class, as can be explicitly observed in Figure 9.1. The answer lies in the Party's structurally powerful position in the sense of politicising the normative demands of these individuals at the level of the central government, albeit not eliminating the bottlenecks obstructing the upward mobilisation of the unprivileged members into the Party's managerial cadres. Another possible answer is the poor performance of the main opposition party, the CHP, throughout its incumbency in previous periods. The ideologic allegiance of the working class to the AKP also cannot be taken for granted: those members do not vote

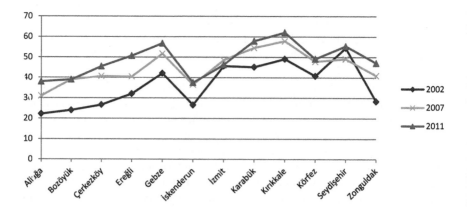

Figure 9.1   The AKP's votes in major working-class towns
Source: Higher Election Council (2013); The towns listed by Yıldırım (2006: 238).

AKP because they are satisfied with the Party's socio-economic performance but instead to support its political mission in forging institutional changes towards a normatively contingent social order. Succinctly, *timely alternativelessness is AKP's greatest resource.*

Overall, the AKP is at the crossroads of continuing changes and changing discontinuities. At this juncture, the Party will either continue to accumulate the former and de-accumulate the latter or vice versa. The former signifies the further assimilation of the Party's Islamic core in the face of capitalist pressure, whereas the latter requires the re-accumulation of the discontinuities, the Just Order's and the Ottoman Empire's strategic depth, by the AKP's leader cadre. This dialectic naturally would not be supposed to unfold on a linear basis. In this respect, in 2010, a new dynamic emerged from the NOM, the HASPAR movement, which could be envisaged, albeit not with a strong possibility, to influence the AKP's pathway on this dialectic. This option, under the current circumstances, is not sufficiently substantial to permit a detailed analysis. However, its delineation is significant in understanding the future evolution of the AKP's party strategies and the prospective institutional mix that the Just Order-based politico-economic currents would adopt under changing circumstances, which I will elaborate on in the next parts. Herein is presented a compact summary of HASPAR's policy adaptations.

A professor of social policy and industrial relations, Numan Kurtulmuş, founded a political party in November 2010, Has Parti – HASPAR, The Party of People's Voice, with a group of intellectuals, academics, lawyers, businessmen and so on. The Party then merged with the AKP in September 2012. What makes HASPAR a matter of debate is its similar emergence and programmatic declarations. Kurtulmuş was the head of *Saadet Partisi* – SP, the Felicity Party, the current NOM-affiliated party. As he did not confirm the entry of certain figures, proposed by Erbakan and the previous leading figures of the NOM, into the SP's managerial cadre, he had to resign from the Party along with 53 provincial chairmen and 65 majors affiliated with the SP to found HASPAR. In addition to embracing a number of socialist intellectuals, the Party's programme offers a moderately radical political economy to cope with the neoliberal challenge on the basis of a bottom-up democratic regime, citizenship rights and humanitarian values. Broadly, the programme can be suggested to be an anti-imperialist and beyond-group manifestation of the Islamic political economy. Its primary difference from the Just Order is that the programme develops a more universal rhetoric in structuring the political economy on egalitarian pillars. The Just Order also makes an appeal to extend economic, political and social justice to all humanity. Yet it predicates this appeal on Islamic ideals. HASPAR bases its social-justice-first manifesto on humanitarian values and norms with soft references to Islamic postulates. This is significant because Erbakan's manner of discourse was somewhat sharp, presumably stemming from his profession, machine engineering. Kurtulmuş is a social scientist and a social policy expert. This left an opening for Kurtulmuş to extend the Just Order vision to the wider masses with a more tolerant and inclusive approach. As far as the profile of Turkey's *average Muslim* is concerned, this is quite an important faculty for political success.

Under the sub-title 'political economy' in HASPAR's programme, it is suggested that social welfare should be the *sine qua non* of political strategies as the independent variable of economic exchange. Moreover, the value of basic public goods such as education, health and security should not be determined by market supply and demand conditions but by public discretion free from competitive concerns. Poverty, according to the Party's programme, is not an entirely economic but essentially a political phenomenon that should not be left to market dynamics, and a *salary of citizenship* must be determined to eradicate it systemically and be a basic right for all citizens. The Party declares: 'For us, rather than growth, an economic or public policy matters based on its impact on social welfare. On the one hand, growth does not spontaneously and automatically support social welfare, and a vast number of growth experiences materialised at the expense of social welfare, on the other'. Namely, the state should take on the role of mediating the production and distribution of social welfare that is not a means of capital accumulation. When economic efficiency or capital conflicts with justice or labour, public discretion must prioritise the latter: this is because the essential factor or value of production is not capital but labour. Underlying this generous welfare perception is the Islamic premise that the resources required to meet the basic needs of humankind are not scarce and should be distributed equally among the various classes (HASPAR, 2012).

PART IV
The Future Prospects

Chapter 10
Is There a Next Way for Turkish Social Democracy?

The contours of the theory and praxis of Kemalism, the Kemalist variants of social democracy and the Third Way evolved under the challenges and opportunities of the external and internal institutional environment. In theoretical terms, Table 7.1 (p. 156) illustrates the main policy strategies of the CHP, the SHP and the DSP, the political parties that conceptualised and implemented these paradigms. Figure 10.1 illustrates the varying combinations of state-market-society and class interaction in terms of the extent to which they were adopted by the CHP and its successors (but not in terms of universally accepted standards of social democracy). In practical terms, Tables 6.3 and 6.4 illustrate the institutional environment under which these political parties have acted and the major actors with which they engaged in power relations. In this section, I will examine these theoretical and practical evolutions within the extent of the theoretico-practical interaction of the Ottoman-Turkish political economy with European and global capitalism, as depicted in Figure II.1 (p. 71). Thus, the theory-praxis-ideology and pragmatism of these parties and their path-dependent changes require a multipronged institutional system analysis. As I have discussed in nearly all analytic material in the tables and figures above, in this section, I will concentrate on the transtemporal, evolutionary and dialectic specifications with a visual reference to the inquiry of *what is next* for these parties.

The main patterns of path-dependent changes in the theories of the Kemalist parties are as follows: continuing changes by the orthodox Kemalists of 1923–60 → the systematisation of changing continuities by the social democratic Kemalists of 1960–79 → changing path-dependent continuities by the Third Way Kemalists of 1985–95 → continuing path-dependency by the social democratic Kemalists or democratic leftists of 1985–2002 → repositioning continuing path-dependencies by the Kemalist social democrats of 1995–2010, and again repositioning path-dependencies by the social democratic Kemalists of 2010–11. The main proposals of each paradigm regarding major social institutions, from taxation to political democracy to international trade and finance, can be found in Table 7.1. Here, I will present the flow of the path-dependent changes in these paradigms from an evolutionarily systemic and cross-institutionalist perspective.

Under the aegis of European trends in social democracy, the Third Way or new left, the conceptualisation of social democratic Kemalism of 1960–79, Third Way Kemalism or new left Kemalism, seems timely. Thereafter, Kemalist social democracy gained a truly reactive ground and symbolised the detachment of Turkish social democracy from its transnational threads. The recent resurrection of social democratic Kemalism has also been a timely initiative to utilise the positive feedbacks of theoretical, knowledge and justificatory power provided by worldwide re-Keynesianisation, albeit unsystemic and palliative. An ideology denotes theoretically established and structurally embedded utterances to attach inter-complementary meaning to social phenomena to conceive, explicate, streamline, vindicate, contextualise and socially organise lived relations. All of the above-noted variants of Kemalism are ideologic theories in terms of these purposeful constituents of an ideology. They could also be suggested to have inter-complementary meanings, the institutional precondition for a paradigm to be termed an ideology. However, as will be detailed below, there are some *systemic gaps* between their theories and praxes.

Under the programmatic implications of orthodox Kemalism and its social democratic and Third Way versions, reported in Table 7.1, Figure 10.1 illustrates the varying scales of state-market-society and class in terms of the extent to which they have been adopted by the CHP and its successors. Thus, for example, 'society', the furthest scale from the origin, refers to a variant or blend of Turkish social democracy and Kemalism, the social democrat Kemalism, that adopts a more socially inclusive theoretico-practical perspective than orthodox Kemalism and Kemalist social democracy. The social democratic Kemalism of 1960–79 supports granting the right to organise and strike for workers from any ideologic front and social rights in a more decommodifactory manner by a redistributionally interventionist state.

Principally, political democracy is systemically conditioned in the left of the centre by the provision of economic democracy and state-backed micro corporatism. Moreover, it is also the most market-constraining of the five major

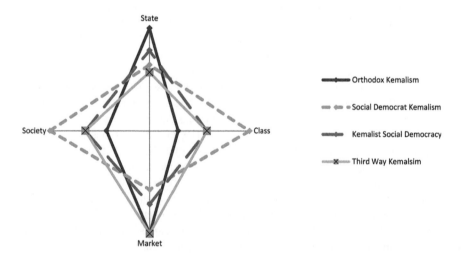

Figure 10.1   Path-dependent change of Kemalism and Kemalist variants of social democracy and the Third Way

variants of Kemalist politics, as it assigns the state an active redistributive and productivist role unconditioned by budgetary balances or inflation in conjunction with a progressive taxation strategy and the systemic regulation of exchange relationships, such as reducing the intermediary stages of supply-demand interaction to minimise prices. (The programme of the third Ecevit government of 1978–79 highlighted: 'In order that the basic consumption goods reach the masses cheaply and their prices are effectively controlled, the necessary measures will be taken to reduce the intermediary stages, the provision of the right to organise to the civil servants' [TBMM, 2013].) The fact that the Party then established a nationalistically sensitive anti-imperialist vision as a normative constraint on foreign direct investment or capital inflows under the systemic priorities of an import-substitutionist industrialisation geared towards full employment further consolidated its market-constraining niche at the level of theory.

Despite being the most socially inclusive of the variants of Turkish social democracy or Kemalism, in terms of the universal principles of social democracy, the left of the centre regards society as a semi-independent but not a *partner* variable in a centrally planned egalitarianism in congruence with its perception of a classless society. According to Habermasian communicative action, politico-economic institutions are and should be the subject of informal institutionalisation. Both orthodox Kemalism and its reformed version, the left of the centre, are theoretical ideologies, and their proponents paid central efforts to put them into praxis. In this respect, there is not a socially contingent perspective that arises on the basis of the norms and values of Turkish society.

If we regard class as the manifestation of income and power differentiation between the haves and have-nots, a social democratic model would include three parameters. The first is its role in a society's division of labour by performing its *productive duty* in compensation for the benefits it obtains in the form of wages and salaries. The second is its right, partly to be bestowed by state and partly to be seized by its organised mobilisation, to have a decent opportunity for work and equal income. The third is to initiate conflictual strategies for realising its rights and interests in the face of the exploitative assaults of both public and private employers. The left of the centre, in its essence, envisions a solidaristic and passive class structure in which the latter right is guaranteed by the former but under the state's controlling power. In his book, Ecevit remarks that class differences are bound to dissolve in the process of the state providing an equality of outcomes, but does not respond to the question of 'if not'.

Kemalism enters the scene at this point. The authoritarian solidarism of the principle of *publicism* requires remaining within the limits of *unconflictual compromise*, namely compromise with compromise. The consequence was the establishment of an authoritarian micro corporatism led and manipulated by a controlling state. The most concrete evidence of the CHP's theoretico-practical pragmatism in its corporatist inclinations was its initiative to sign a 'Social Agreement' with Turk-Is in 1978 to authorise workers to participate in macro-socio-economic decision-making. The background motive for the CHP was to neutralise the escalating rate of strikes in a socially tense environment and establish a wage-control system. However, a brief (one-year) period after its confirmation by both sides, the agreement was abolished (Talas, 1982). As can be observed from the phenomenal declines in public sector wages and salaries in 1978 and 1979, it can safely be argued that the Agreement did not achieve its most basic aim.

Social democracy is a collective initiative of a holistic, theoretico-practical conciliation of inter-repulsive institutional interactions to forge a positive-sum regulative and redistributive order. Its mainstay is therefore the equal distribution of rights and duties by ensuring the necessary power channels for organised labour and civic society to participate in this distribution to provide the right to decent work, just and propitious working conditions, fair wages, equal remuneration for work of equal value and so on. Succinctly, it strives for the elimination of uncertainty over human life and securing self-esteem. From the standpoint of social democratic institutionalism, the ordeal for the left of the centre was how to establish the social optimum in a developing context by keeping society under etatist control, albeit being socially inclusive.

As previously discussed in the introduction of this book, economic development is not a trilateral process comprising only the material endowment of capital, labour and technology, but a long-run evolutionary dialectics of all social institutions, from economic governance to the social psychology of the workers. The genesis of a robust process of fair politico-economic development requires, first and foremost, a dynamic social integrity that, in the long run, would direct the optimal combination of the existing institutional stock by striking a balance between productivity and equality. In social democratic terms, this manifests itself in the embodiment of a solidaristically complementary institutional order on the basis of positive-sum constellations to distribute social rights and responsibilities impartially by creating an equal opportunity for power and therefore to save the human lifeworld from market pressure under the constraining coexistence of conflict, dependence and order. As shown by the practical performance of the CHP in the 1970s, Turkish social democrats were unable to provide such a workable mutuality.

The underlying reason was that, while incorporating social equity and individual liberty as the two of the three preconditionalities for an original social democratic regime into its theoretical construction to varying degrees, the left of the centre lost sight of the other, productivity, to a systemic extent. This is because the then internal and, until the first half of the 1970s, external institutional circumstances provided the CHP of the 1960s and 1970s with systemic power as both a source of theoretical power to systemise the changing continuities in orthodox Kemalism during the 1950s and a source of lethargy to prioritise the benefits rather than costs of or preconditions for a social democratic regime.

The constituents of the CHP's power resources at the time comprised: the institutional power provided by planned, semi-stakeholder capitalism, development-oriented monetary policy, a fixed exchange rate regime and so on; the structural power created by the presence of an import-substitutionist regime, the path-dependent continuity of the Kemalist establishment and the coalitional power provided by the civil-military bureaucracy, the TUSIAD, the TISK and so on; the strategic power created by the wide margin for implementing a social democratic model unconditioned by productivity under these internal and external institutional and structural circumstances; the theoretical, knowledge, discursive and justificatory powers created by the strong presence of European social democracy and international Keynesianism and the internal dynamics, such as growing demands for increased welfare and the commodifying impact of rapid industrialisation on the masses, along with the DP's and AP's poor socio-economic performance, particularly in the second half of the 1950s and 1960s, respectively.

In this sense, the left of the centre, or social democratic Kemalism, as an ideologic theory crafted through the transposition of the rudiments of European social democracy into the Turkish context was, to a certain extent, based on a theoretical pragmatism of exploiting structural opportunities to cultivate votes. In another sense, it was a theoretical ideology developed on the basis of programmatic designs rather than grassroots inspiration. As the CHP of the 1970s did not manage the workable mutualities between its ideologic practices and the social democratizabilities in the then institutional stock of the Turkish political economy, the result was therefore catastrophic in systemic terms for both the vision and mission of Turkish social democracy. The impact on its vision was the *profanisation of its sacrosanct myths*, resulting in the SHP's adoption of Third Way Kemalism as a more *rationalist* conception of the combination of social democratizabilities and Kemalist appeals.

In systemic terms, in its inchoate attempt to reconcile Kemalism with social democracy, the CHP of 1960–79 could not lay the basis for a long-run social democratization by intertemporarily managing the delicate balance between theory and practice to generate *timely* inter-complementary meanings. The *ideologic stability* of the CHP at the time relied on the *ample* power resources and a relatively extensive budget space, as noted above, at the cost of exhausting long-run strategic opportunities. Social democratic and Kemalist sources of knowledge allow one to adopt such a politico-economic strategy of *flexible stability* to establish workable margins between theory and praxis. This is the case because secular theories are constructed and reconstructed on the basis of the structural constituencies of the praxis or the praxis is structured and restructured according to the postulates of theories under the intermeshed evolution of ideology and pragmatism.

For a practitioner organisation, the tension between theory and praxis emerges in the dilemma of striking a balance between the practical adaptation of theoretical postulates under the confines of the inter-complementary coherence of ideologic presuppositions and adopting an effective pragmatism that enables it to steadily ebb and flow across the inter-repulsive relationship of theory, practice and ideology. The CHP of 1960–79 could not functionalise a *dynamic solidarity* with society, as its formally designed and undigested structure did not allow the Party to manage the ebb and flow of its electoral fortunes among theory, ideology, pragmatism and praxis. This occurred despite the fact that the party was reasonably successful in expressing its mission to Turkish society. This was the source of transformation costs in the Turkish political economy attributable to Kemalist politics.

As noted above, the Third Way Kemalism of the SHP between 1995 and 2010 was intended to reconcile social democratic institutions with neoliberal ones in the economic sphere and continue the egalitarian discourses of social democratic Kemalism. The consequence is, as Figure 10.1 illustrates, that the market becomes the primary determinant of social interaction while the interventionist function of the regulatory state recedes to the bare minimum among all variants of Kemalist politics, and society becomes conditioned by the level of competitive productivity rather than productive solidarity. The primary policy tools employed for this purpose were supply-side taxation, budget austerity, a strategy of economic growth that essentially relied on factor productivity, non-accelerating inflation strategy to encourage productive employment and the elimination of unemployment by increasing productivity.

In this rationally structured trade-off among the market, state and society, class was *de jure* granted the right to organise and engage in collective bargaining but *de facto* constrained by an austerity corporatism designed to functionalise a system of positive welfare along with the deregulation and flexibilisation of labour relations. For this purpose, the Third Way Kemalists envisaged and instituted a concession-bargaining mechanism, the Economic and Social Council of Turkey. By all accounts, the general framework of Third Way Kemalism was, in a systemic sense, congruent with Third Way theory, the main policy tools of which are presented in Table 2.1 (p. 56). The primary reference point in this issue is the *systemic dissolution* of social democratic Kemalism and the consequent *double-shuffle* politics caused by a proclivity for a converging divergence with the casino capitalism operating in Turkey at the time. As we discussed earlier, the most conspicuous niche of this convergence is the *flexible compromise* between public and private employers and the workers. The systemic theorisation of Third Way Kemalism, in this respect, subjugated organised labour to unconflictual compromise conditioned by the flexible flow of market praxis.

The SHP was inspired to reconcile the continuing, discontinuing and changing path-dependencies of social democratic and orthodox Kemalism by the changing internal and external institutional environment, ranging from the transition from an inward-looking, etatist liberalism to an outward-looking, etatist neoliberalism and to the decline in the institutional and structural power of European social democracy and Keynesian economics. The demise of social democratic Kemalism provided the SHP with a justificatory power to strike a balance between productivity and equality, even to set the former over the latter, and restrain state discretion and the power of organised labour under the pressure of a liberalised economic structure in the 1980s. Overall, Third Way Kemalism was a search for workable mutualities or rationally designed, secular optimalities among the state, market, society and class. Therefore, it became a mid-range theory between social democratic Kemalism and orthodox Kemalism.

Third way Kemalism grants the most extensive space for market exchange relative to the other two variants and less emancipatory space and more decommodificatory discretion for class organisations and social equality, respectively, compared to social democratic Kemalism and orthodox Kemalism. This is because, in terms of changing path-dependencies of the CHP of the 1970s, the SHP of 1985–95 did not have systemic power resources, in the sense of both electoral support and economic fortunes, to discourse on a generous welfare state unconditioned by productive constraints. The institutional and structural source of power for social democratic politics in the economic sphere ceased to function, and its coalitional power was emasculated by an ideologically impartial but authoritarian influential military organisation. The TISK and TUSIAD's regime-based support for the SHP's open and purely secular posture continued, but the phenomenon of *social democratic businessmen*, and thereby the ideologic thread between the CHP of 1960–79 and these organisations, particularly with TUSIAD, faded away in structural terms, although there was a partial compromise in the structuration of employment relations from a productivity-contingent, flexible perspective.

Further, the Party did not have strategic, theoretical, knowledge or discursive power because, theoretically, it had to adopt a countercyclical position in the face of etatist neoliberalism and authoritarian structured post-1980 political *status quo*, even in the absence of a notable source of coalitional support from the external institutional environment. Turk-Is and the DISK under the aegis of the ILO and the ITUC cannot be considered ardent supporters of the Party's flexi-cure policy strategies in labour relations and social policy. This is because Turkish trade unions of the period yearned for direct, not palliative, support to overcome national and international neoliberal pressure.

Kemalist social democracy, conjuncturally, was structured on the basis of exploiting regime-based political tension by placing Kemalism over social democracy and sustaining social democratic premises as an alternative discourse to the RP's social-justice-first politico-economic programme and then the AKP's responsible pragmatist social welfare paradigm, as well as a response to the commodifying power of neoliberal hegemony. The consequence was a resurgence of an authoritarian state structure, most similar to orthodox Kemalism, that aims to re-establish old trade-offs, namely the dissociation of the public sphere from Islamic images through the apparatuses of the civil-military bureaucracy, ranging from military pressure to ideologically motivated judicial interventions such as the closure of conservatively or Islamically motivated political parties. As a result, social discretion is depressed vis-à-vis state power. Moreover, under the constraints of external institutional dynamics, Kemalist social democrats conditioned their social democratic premises on economic efficiency.

The institutional mix of Kemalist social democracy, therefore, embraced the state authoritarianism of orthodox Kemalism, efficiency-constraintness of Third Way Kemalism and the socially contingentness of social democratic Kemalism. The most conspicuous display of this mix is the theorisation of a multi-party democracy, as discussed in the party programme, conditioned first by Kemalist principles and *then* politically active labour organisations. Complementary examples include budget austerity conditioned by monetary targets, a full employment strategy with a low level of inflation and interest, a selectively protected, liberal international regime of commerce and finance and a productivity-centred development strategy. In terms of power relations, while emphasising granting the right to organise and strike both for civil servants and workers, the Party also presents an unconflictual neocorporatism conditioned by market efficiency and productivity. In the public sector, this efficiency is supposed to be provided through downsizing and the use of modern management techniques and personnel strategies. Overall, Kemalist social democracy differs from Third Way Kemalism in emphasising, albeit tentatively, full employment, decent wages unconditioned by flexible employment, an entitlement to the right to strike for both civil servants and public sector workers, a progressive taxation strategy, conditioning political democracy by the active intervention of organised labour and so on.

The CHP's orientation in the mid-1990s towards Kemalist social democracy rather than the new left was primarily intended to perpetuate the vote-cultivating power of a radical Kemalist posture. After the process of re-ideologisation in Turkish politics, which concluded on 28 February 1997, and normalisation of Turkish politics first in the 2002 and then the embedding of this normalisation in the 2007 general elections when the AKP won a landslide victory, the CHP's power resources for maintaining a regime-based, countercyclical position were systemically attenuated. The TISK, TUSIAD and the major media preferred to provisionally remove their unquestioned coalitional support for the CHP on the basis of regime protection. Underlying was the AKP's *reconciliative* posture towards both the internal and external pillars of a capitalist political economy, particularly the latter's unhesitant efforts to further the process of EU membership, as well as the changed dynamics of politico-economic games under an etatist neoliberal regime, in which the state's *authoritarian* discretion over politico-economic processes, at least after 2002, was reduced to a bare minimum.

Further emasculating the CHP's power was the falling tide of the European social democrats' electoral performance and the dominance of market competition over political competition after a post-crisis structure. At this point, Turkey experienced conservative political stability and austere economic stability following a period of highly volatile coalition governments between 1991 and 2002. Before 2002, the power resources available to the Party were justificatory, consolidative and coalitional. However, in the face of the abovementioned challenges, these power resources also declined substantially, accumulating the dynamics of change towards social democratic Kemalism in mid-2010.

Social democratic Kemalism was an attempt to reverse this trend and redeem the Party's power resources by reprioritising social democratic constituents in the Party's policy strategies. As this process was a pre-election strategy under the discursive and justificatory power provided by international re-Keynesianisation and the AKP's ambiguous welfare performance, it was unable to create a dynamic source of coalitional power, except that provided by the DISK and certain major secular media outlets. Furthermore, under these circumstances, the Party began to voice nationalistically sensitive politics in response to the recent democratization reforms launched in September 2013 to further address the Kurdish question. Under the ambivalent position of the contemporary CHP at the margins of social democratic Kemalism and Kemalist social democracy, a question has lingered in the minds of Turkish people, *what is next* for Turkish social democrats or Kemalists?

To determine a structural response to this question, it is first necessary for an overall exegesis of the theory-praxis match or mismatch in the variants of Kemalist politics between social democracy and Third Way and then assess the suitability of this match or mismatch using social democratic theory. These two analyses will allow us to provide at least a theoretically delineated structural response to the question of what comes next. Throughout the first part of this book, I attempted to argue that the future cannot be precisely foreordained due to the over-complexity of institutional intersections on the evolutionary pathway. My inquiry into what is next is limited to an appraisal of the changes or path-dependence dynamics under the feedback of the legacy of first Kemalist and then Islamic politics. Moreover, *what is next* is not far away, but in the immediate or near future.

Social democracy is principally a normatively contingent regime of political economy, and its mainstay is socially contingent economic efficiency to create and sustain durable institutionalisations. In its European version, social democracy arose from a living and processual culture of dialectics over time among society, economy and polity at the level of theory and praxis that emerged from a radical socialist posture. In terms of institutional system analysis, the foremost imperfection of Turkish social democracy and the Turkish Third Way, in this respect, is their genesis as paradigms formally designed by a group of elitist intellectuals or politicians, and hence they are not bottom-up, accumulated paradigms. Moreover, the consequence, as noted above, has been tremendous structural transformation costs due to the inability of Kemalist politics to determine workable margins or an optimum political economy endowment by undertaking an organising regulatory discretion between the norms and values of Turkish society and its level of political and economic development. This imperfection was entwined with the *secular* pillars of Kemalist politics, which were path-dependently infused into its social democratic and Third Way variants over time. The best structural evidence of this rather pessimistic analysis is how this politics was performed.

One of the two most ubiquitous images of the social democratic and Third Way versions of Kemalist politics is, paradoxically, that of *crisis*. Governments led by social democratic Kemalism, Third Way Kemalism and again social democratic Kemalism resulted in catastrophic crises in the late 1970s, 1994 and 2001. The other is the lack of *systemic initiative* in functionalising a social democratic or a Third Way programme in terms of cross-institutional dynamics. As we discussed regarding macro-political and economic data between 1960–80 and 1980–2002, succinctly, it is inconceivable to suggest a theory-praxis match between the programmes of these parties and their practices.

Our aim is not to seek a valiant expansionary fiscal or monetary policy, a universal social policy and a neocorporatist industrial relations regime on the basis of a balanced distribution of power. Instead, I have attempted to determine the practicability of the programmatic institutions of these parties within the confines of the Turkish political economy for social democratic or Third Way Kemalism. For example, for social democratic Kemalism, there are certain indications in this regard, such as the substantial increases in public sector employment and moderate rises in public sector capital formation (1974) under underemployment conditions, expanded social security coverage (1961–65), notable decreases in indirect taxes and slight increases in direct taxes (1978–79) and so on. However, these *positive clues* were always overshadowed by adverse *structural* dynamics such as a substantial decline in public sector wages and salaries (1974) or volatile business cycles in 1979 and 2001. The same was the case for Third Way Kemalism (1991–95), for which conducting a balanced appraisal of efficiency, equity and voice is not conceivable even with a market-contingent rationality.

Rather, both social democratic Kemalists and Third Way Kemalists, except for undertaking certain noteworthy but crude institutionalisation in the area of social security and industrial relations, made conjunctural policy choices, not strategies, according to short-run oscillations in the existing politico-economic structure. Moreover, in conjunction with the corruption scandals and clientelism-contingent political exchanges, this volatile flexibility generated a dull and even unpromising performance in political economy terms. The crisis-ridden career of social democratic and Third Way Kemalists would have been justifiable to a certain extent, as these parties had adopted systemically decommodificatory strategies, albeit uncontrolled, such as increasing labour's share of GDP through aggressive measures, increasing social expenditures to unreasonable levels and so on. However, this was not the case.

The underlying reason was the inability of social democratic Kemalists to create a solidaristic compromise, let alone a productive one, among the state, market and society under positive-sum regulation. The constraining initiatives of these parties were, to a certain extent, effective such as the relatively emancipatory enactment of the Trade Union Act of 1963. However, these constraints were, in the absence of confirmatory internal and external environmental circumstances, contradictory, such as the enactment of the Public Officials' Union Act of 2001 that denied civil servants the right to collective bargaining, let alone the right to strike. Throughout the 1960s and 1970s and during the period 1999–2001, social democratic Kemalists failed to functionalise a macro-level economic democracy, with the exception of an unsuccessful joint initiative between the Turk-Is and the CHP government in 1978. Furthermore, they failed to adopt an expansionary or contractionary monetary and fiscal strategy for achieving full employment, and they did not fine-tune nominal wages and prices to meet aggregate demand.

The reactionary, rather than strategic, mindset of social democratic Kemalists in managing the ebb and flow between the state and market manifested itself in oversubsidising private industrial establishments, engaging with the IMF for crisis management, making extensive devaluations and failing to institute system-wide decommodificatory policies or an efficient redistributive regime. In a similar vein, Third Way Kemalists could not strike a balance between growth and equality, even in a productivity-contingent manner. Instead, their policy strategies resulted in a catastrophic crisis (1994), coercing the DYP-SHP coalition government to adopt the IMF's neoliberal prescriptions. The pre-crisis period under this government is also quite difficult to categorise into any clear-cut set of policy choices, either neoliberal or Third Way.

In this book, we predicated changes on path-dependencies because social structures change accumulatedly or de-accumulatedly, haltingly and non-routinely. Prospective *systemic change* in Turkish social democracy as a social phenomenon is not free from this basic premise. Systemic change, here, refers to the transformation of its constituents insofar as this change proposes a different combination of politico-economic institutional interactions to cultivate votes from a different or more extensive group of voters, obtain a more diverse status in inter-actor power relations and so on. The genesis of the left of the centre is a case in point. In both internal and external institutional dynamics, there is neither a requirement of nor an alternative to systemic change in Kemalist politics. Rather, its near future should be discussed in terms of its ebb and flow among the four major patterns described in Figure 10.1. The quintessence of such a debate is whether, as the unique major representative of Kemalist politics in the contemporary Turkish political economy, the CHP would reincarnate Kemalist social democracy, refunctionalise a social democratic Kemalism, reorient itself towards a Third Way path or posit its strategies as an intermediate course between the latter two options.

The first option would be operationalised in the event that the AKP opted for a more 'Islamically inclusive' strategic posture in systemic terms. In terms of the Party's discursive power, the leading cadre of the CHP, while strategically prioritising a social democratic discourse, holds a regime-based card that could be employed in such a case. This has been the *sina qua non* of their efforts. A test in this respect were the political cases such as Ergenekon and Balyoz that resulted in the conviction of a remarkable number of high-ranking members of the military. While adapting a relatively prudent posture, the CHP does not hesitate to straightforwardly denounce the judicial authorities for conducting an unfair trial, as they rendered their verdicts under pressure from the AKP government. However, as the AKP effectively managed to transform such a reactive consciousness on the part of the CHP into a means of achieving landslide victories, it is not strategically tenable for the CHP to revive such an orthodox choice, as can be observed in the changing behaviour of the Party in opposition to the entry of deputies wearing headscarves into the Parliament; they did not initiate organised protests as they had during the Kavakçı event when Ecevit raged at a headscarved deputy, *Merve Kavakçı*, into the Turkish Parliament, saying that 'Here is not the place to defy the state. Rup this woman over knuckles' (2 May 1999, Turkish Parliament).

Turkey's ongoing EU membership process is a potential, but not absolute, deterrent for the CHP to place regime-protective politics over social democratic politics in terms of the maintenance of the Copenhagen political criteria, the foremost transnational reference for the CHP's social democratic politics. (It should be borne in mind that the EU does not take a firm stance against any restrictive initiative on the preponderance of religiously sensitive currents in the realm of politics.) The hesitant posture of the TUSIAD, TISK, DISK and the Turk-Is, as well as the major media, towards supporting such a reincarnation is another niche of abstention for the Party. In the present circumstances, the high-ranking military cadre is also not prone to harsh reaction until a *genuine risk* appears. The AKP tailors its political strategy to avoid presenting an image of systemic transformation that would entail the re-embodiment of the spirit of 28 February. Moreover, as such an initiative on the part of the AKP is bound up with a systemic change in the *mould* of an average Turkish Muslim towards an Islamically contingent lifeworld in the economic, political and cultural senses, this initiative is not likely to occur, at least in the near future, as far as the gradual and slow change of social structures is concerned.

In economic terms, the ongoing Great Recession, its impact on the Turkish economy and the AKP's unremitting austerity strategy are justificatory niches for the prioritisation of social democracy over Kemalism under the ongoing, albeit blurred, interventionist waves worldwide and the continuing highly unequal distribution of income in the Turkish political economy (the average Gini coefficient was 0.40 between 2007–11, despite an increase to 0.41 in 2009). Such an initiative would retrieve the active coalitional support of the DISK and the Turk-Is in collaboration with the ETUC, ILO, GUFs and so on, to a certain extent. On the one hand, this support would be solid, as these organisations are in urgent need of the coalitional support of a political party to retrieve the structural power they have lost since the 1980 coup d'état. On the other hand, it would be moderate and lukewarm, as these organisations continued to lose their power at an even greater pace during the DSP-led coalition government between 1999 and 2002 due to the dark shadow of a crisis cycle.

This is an impasse in every sense, originating in an adverse internal and external institutional environment that precludes systemic cooperation between economically countercyclical actors. Furthermore, as labour organisations are unable to convince even their own members to vote for a certain political party (Yıldırım, 2006), the leveraging power of such a coalition would be very limited for the CHP compared to its prospective loss of coalitional support from the politically much more influential TISK and TUSIAD. While urging the state to take discretion in managing the institutional axes between labour markets, the educational system, research and development, and sectoral subsidies under a long-term plan, the latter organisations, however, are not prone to espouse either a regime-based politics or a systemic decommodificatory strategy in a social democratic direction. This is because the restructured institutional environment in the post-1980 period prompted them, particularly the TUSIAD, to change the social liberal posture they had adopted in the 1970s.

As the CHP is prone to refunctionalise the *systemic leisure* of the late 1970s, the EU, given its coalitional posture regarding the IMF-WB-WTO and the TNCs, would also not back the CHP's orientation towards a social democratic pathway.

When asked from whence the necessary funds for financing the family insurance would be obtained, the CHP's main policy proposal during the 2011 election campaign, Kılıçdaroğlu gave a highly bizarre answer: 'My name is Kemal. I would find it'. This means that the European social democrats 'intentionally' lost the opportunity to cultivate additional votes by developing a *generous discourse*, regardless of its feasibility! Moreover, as Ecevit did during the 1970s, Kılıçdaroğlu did not emphasise one of the contemporarily non-negligible requirements for the sustainability of a social democratic optimum, efficiency.

Considering the substantial degree of politico-economic compression in the current circumstances, it is obvious that this *easy pragmatism* is untenable and unsustainable in the Turkish context, as the late 1970s explicitly demonstrated. For example, how could the CHP replace a prospectively substantial outflow of foreign direct or portfolio investments under a fragile economic structure constrained by a tremendous and structural current account deficit? It is true that, in the long run, Turkey should structurally reduce its dependency on unproductive and speculative finance capital. However, the question is how the CHP could do this without triggering another catastrophic crisis, at least in the short run? The recent past of social democratic Kemalist politics during the 2001 crisis did not give any impression that its proponents would manage this delicate balance between state and market with even moderate success.

This point reveals a substantial risk for social democratic Kemalism. As the CHP's social democratic past is overwhelmingly unpromising in a systemic sense, a prospective recurrence of poor performance resulting in a structural crisis during its incumbency would exhaust not only the possibility for revitalisation, but also the Party's resources of power, even discursive power, not in the near but a relatively long future. It is impossible to state that Kılıçdaroğlu and his team are well aware of this risk. Furthermore, in terms of the theory-praxis trade-off, there is a substantially more challenging internal and external institutional stock regarding the creation of sufficient room to operationalise social democratic politics.

This is because doing so would require them to manage the ebb and flow among: constructing a dynamic balance between the systemic consistency of a demand-constrained Keynesian social democracy and desystematising inconsistency of supply-sided neoliberalism; decommodificatory regulation and commodificatory deregulation; market-friendliness and worker-friendliness; demand-sided economic democracy and supply-sided governance; productivist, authoritarian and competitive solidarity; progressive and regressive taxation; output gaps and price stability; fixed-exchange rate regime and hard currency; social citizenship and market citizenship; rights with responsibilities and no rights without responsibilities; solidarist and positive welfare; stable and flexible working patterns; binding collective bargaining and opt-out options; conflictual and unconflictual compromises and so on. The difficulty of managing these trade-offs would naturally change according to whether the current national and transnational neoliberal stock persists or is restructured towards, at least, a moderately regulatory pathway.

In essence, to realise a path-dependent change in the manner of repositioning continuing path-dependencies, as the current, Kılıçdaroğlu-led CHP administration initiated in mid-2010, the CHP seems far from functionalising an adequate mix of systemic power, given the opportunities and challenges that the national and transnational institutional environment offers or poses for social democratic Kemalists. The power resources available to the CHP are discursive, justificatory, theoretical and structural and reside in the ongoing crisis of neoliberalism, unsystemic re-Keynesianisation, the AKP's ambiguous social policy performance and so on. On the eve of the 2011 general elections, the CHP effectively utilised these resources of power. The crux of the argument is that these resources did not allow the Party to come to power and initiate social democratic restructurations. On the contrary, its main rival, the AKP, holds nearly all of the resources of systemic power, even in an evolutionarily consolidated manner, although it has reached its natural boundaries.

Third way Kemalism has less clear options under current conditions. The determinant parameter is that, despite the ambiguity of its overall socio-economic performance, the AKP managed to reduce poverty rates from 30.3 per cent to 2.7 and from 3.0 to 0.1 for purchasing power parity below 4.3 $ and 2.15 $, respectively, it did not adopt aggressively neoliberal but moderate concession bargaining to determine civil servant salaries and minimum wages, enacted a relatively emancipatory trade union act and so on. In conjunction with the ongoing, albeit faltering, economic stability in terms of the investment climate, these parameters are adequate, at least for 50 per cent of the Turkish electorate, of which the working class represents a remarkable portion, to vote for this party. Thus, the CHP's orientation in a Third Way direction would diminish the discursive and justificatory power that it cultivated by reprioritising social democratic variables in its electoral campaigns.

However, this programmatic change would enable the Party to obtain the coalitional support of the TISK and TUSIAD, as well as the European Union to a certain extent, with the consolidative power of its purely secular posture depending on the institutional mix of the programme to be adopted. For example, given the delicate structural balances of the Turkish economy at the crossroads of consolidating macro-austerity and undertaking expansionary discretion to spur output and employment, the Party would adopt a prudent strategy of a moderately more egalitarian version of Third Way economics. It would have to avoid increasing macro-financial fragility by initiating uncontrolled expansionary measures while also ensuring that it did not perpetuate jobless growth. A risk emerges at this point, 'AKPisation', in the sense that the AKP has already in essence functionalised such an austere dosage of egalitarianism. In cognisance of this risk, the CHP's current orientation is, as noted above, to prioritise the political critique of market capitalism in crisis and capture popular electoral support in the short term with limited respect for a theory-praxis match. In this sense, a Third Way or new left approach does not seem highly likely under current circumstances, but it is also not possible to foreordain considering the transitory nature of the international system.

Chapter 11

The Political and Economic Future of the Ottoman-Turkish Islam

The evolutionary contours of Ottoman-Islam, the Just Order and Conservative Democracy can be seen in Figure II.1 (p. 71) in dialectic interaction with Kemalism, Turkish social democracy and global capitalism. Under the constraints and opportunities of the internal and external institutional environment and inter-actor power relations, the patterns of change in Ottoman-Turkish Islam, in political economy terms, have been changing continuities in the face of continuing path-dependencies over the first three quarters of the nineteenth century (before the first Constitutional Monarchy), continuing path-dependencies in the face of changing continuities between 1876–1908 (during the reign of Abdülhamit II), the re-accumulation of discontinuing path-dependencies vis-à-vis the persistence of path-dependent discontinuities (the Just Order) between the late 1960s and the early 2000s and, finally, the great reconciliation between continuing changes and changing discontinuities (Conservative Democracy) from 2002 onwards.

The first two patterns of path-dependent change in the Empire, as noted above, were based on contriving a new means of combining the institutional stock to resurrect the Empire's grandeur under the confines of its original and structural consistencies. The ITF and Republican periods transformed this path-dependence-contingent strategy towards a change-contingent one, first in the form of changing continuity by discontinuing path-dependencies and then continuing changes systemically through sharp-edged institutional break-offs. From the late 1960s to the late 1990s, the NOM strived to re-accumulate the path-dependent discontinuities of Ottoman praxis under the aegis of a pure theory of Islamic political economy. As this re-accumulative initiative of the NOM, as a systemically countercyclical actor, could not cultivate adequate support from Turkish society, there emerged a reconciliative change initiative, the Conservative Democracy represented by the AKP, between the path-dependencies of the Just Order, the dominant Kemalist and neoliberal institutional environment, and the continuing changes in the lifeworld of the conservatively or religiously sensitive Turkish people.

The current prospect is that the AKP is at the crossroads of continuing changes and changing discontinuities. The latter refers to the re-accumulation of the re-accumulative spirit of the Just Order, at least as the determinant variable in the Party's policy strategies, whereas the former denotes the further de-accumulation of the path-dependencies of the Just Order in the Party's centre of gravity in favour of neoliberalism and Kemalism. The question of *what is next* for the Party is strictly bound up with and for the Turkish political economy, as well, as the

Party's electoral performance is currently at approximately 50 per cent. To obtain structural insights into this question, let me begin a trans-temporal and cross-paradigmatic journey across the theory-praxis boundaries of pure Islamic theory, Ottoman Islam, the Just Order and Conservative Democracy, given the challenges and opportunities that the internal and external institutional environment of Turkish political economy present.

The Just Order, broadly, is a state-dominated version of the pure theory of the Islamic political economy. In this sense, it has been contextualised into Islam's preconstructed institutional basics. The *ex post*, mundane reinterpretation of these basics by the Just Order theoreticians, primarily Erbakan, resides in engaging with the technical implications of contemporary capitalism and complying with the political constraints that Turkish secular capitalism imposed. As the Just Order perpetuates the *systemic cores* of Islamic economics and politics, this methodology would be suggested to be consistent with the methodology of path-dependently-conditioned change in Islam. The Just Order's methodology is also congruent with the Ottoman praxis of Islam, in strategic terms, crafting a delicate and sensitive balance among Islamic theory, the practical exigencies of the internal and external geocultural and geostrategic idiosyncrasies and conjunctural pragmatic choices. Of these three parameters, the Just Order prioritised Islamic theory, particularly Islamic economics, as its economic manifestation, AED – the Just Economic Order, is a theoretical paradigm conceptualised regardless of the constraints of the national or internal institutional environment on the feasibility of its theoretical axioms. (This methodological posture, in terms of the performance of the NOM-affiliated parties, created a dichotomy between the high expectations of their electorate in theory and inadequate responses by these parties in praxis.)

A taxonomy of the consequent institutional mix of the Just Order, the theoretical framework of the NOM-affiliated parties, and that of Conservative Democracy can be found in Table 8.1 (p. 189). Regarding this taxonomy, the state's role in the Just Order is more dominant than the organising, regulatory role of the state in Islamic political economy. This arose from the practical path-dependence that the Ottoman-Turkish state had created in dominating the institutional organisation and reorganisations and from the developing structure of the Turkish economy that, in the absence of self-guiding entrepreneurs, required efficient state discretion to structure it from a social-utility-contingent perspective. As in its Ottoman practice, state regulation in the Just Order is envisaged in the form of *organising intervention* by making direct investments, particularly in the industrial sector, and supervising the allocation of private investments under a planned path of development, thereby going beyond providing social harmony and full-employment-centred economic stability, in addition to supplying infrastructural public goods, as stipulated in pure Islamic theory.

Another strategic divergence of the Just Order from Islamic theory is that it stipulates a macro-economic and a micro industrial democracy, structured on the principle of unconflictual compromise, whereas Islam leaves an open room for right-seeking conflictual initiatives by organised civic associations. In Ottoman practice, such conflictual exercises occurred, albeit at infrequent intervals. This normatively contingent compromise with the Just Order's compromise strategy results in the denial or omission by the state of the right to collective bargaining and strike for labour organisations, albeit while permitting all workers the right to organise as self-help constellations. In the absence of intermediary organisations playing a decisive role in macro-politico-economic management, in the Just Order, the state's decommodificatory discretion theoretically generates an uncontrolled or patrimonial egalitarianism. Underlying this is the perception that the state is always a reliable institution, the Muslim managers of which would not make fundamental mistakes. This is, in systemic terms, not congruent with either Islamic politics or, particularly, Islamic economics, in which equal power sharing is a necessity for Muslims to form and sustain an interstabilising and interconstitutive order of positive-sum conciliation. The consequence is the risk that, in the absence of effective civic supervision, the state would become an end in itself rather than a means serving the ultimate aim of achieving the social optimum. This risk could be suggested to have been the case in Ottoman praxis to a certain extent.

However, the Just Order's state-first approach is not absolute, as it presumes a social-justice-first economic and political development, the main policy choices of which are the equal redistribution of welfare through a progressive tax regime, full-employment of the factors of production, a universal social policy regime, a decent work and life balance and so on. Moreover, the Just Order is a strictly anti-capitalist paradigm that stipulates the systemic elimination of interest from both individual and organisational credit interlinkages to eliminate the risk of social exploitation by leisure or speculative capital. In terms of its theory-praxis consistence with Islam, in this respect, the Just Order exceeds Ottoman praxis in which interest-bearing transactions were permitted, albeit exceptionally. The other institutional formulations of the Just Order that are consonant with Islamic economics are its demand-constrained and real production-centred economic policy strategy and its prioritisation of balanced budgets and, particularly, strictly avoiding inflationist monetary policy. These policy choices were, by and large, also employed by the Ottomans, despite their exceptional decisions to engage in devaluation to finance budget deficits. The Just Order's emphasis on the necessity of prioritising a decent work and life balance, even at the expense of budgetary balances, is another structural area compatible with the latitude Islamic economics that allows for deficit financing for development or social policy purposes.

Overall, as shown in Figure 11.1, the Just Order is the most state-dominated project among the three variants of the Islamic paradigm in the Turkish context. It prioritises society over markets but does not systemically enable labour organisations to balance against the state's organising interventionist role in terms of its social consequences. It is also the least secular one. In this respect, Erbakan did not attempt to adopt a systemic pragmatism. Rather, he did so by discursively reconciling the NOM-affiliated party programmes with the formal requirements of policy-making in the secular and Kemalist establishment. Otherwise, his discourse was simply straightforward. However, I believe, he could not fine-tune the theory-

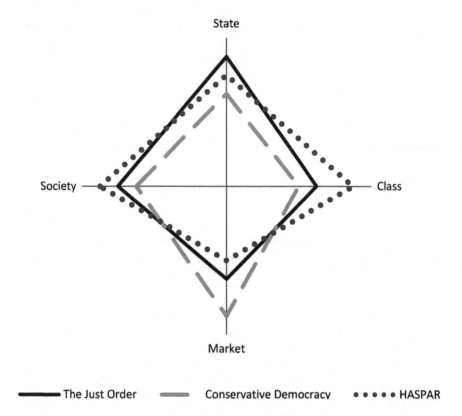

The Just Order   **Conservative Democracy**   •••••**HASPAR**

Figure 11.1   Path-dependent changes of the Just Order, Conservative Democracy and the HASPAR Movement

praxis match utilising *flexible stability* and created difficulty in explaining the coalition government's performance in which the MSP and the RP participated. (A compact and summarising exegesis of these coalition governments can be found on pages 168 and 197) – this is because the picture was nebulous and systemically not in parallel with the theory of the Just Order, such as the notable increase in indirect taxes, labour shedding, the rise and fall of interest and inflation rates and so on. It is this gap between theory and praxis that ensured, at least, a conjunctural de-accumulation of the Just Order project, giving way to a successive project, Conservative Democracy, which aims to reduce this gap by adopting a sustainable pragmatism in the middle term.

In a long-run perspective, it can be suggested that *Conservative Democracy is the contemporary paradigmatic manifestation of Ottoman-Turkish society's nearly three-century search in its incessant encounters with European and global capitalism.* This is why I termed it the 'great reconciliation', which is not necessarily intended to have a positive or negative connotation. The synthesising pressure of timespace and income-lifestyle compression has catalysed the development of conservative democracy as the organisational manifestation of the accumulated change dynamics in the lifeworld of the conservatively or religiously sensitive segment of Turkish society at the turn of the twentieth century. These dynamics are aligned not with the pure and systemic realisation of basic Islamic premises but rather the creation of space for this segment to practice their Islamic culture freely and have access to politico-economic institutional power resources. In this respect, conservative democracy stands for the inter-repulsive and inter-complementary manifestation of the formal and informal institutions in the Turkish context, at least for the half of Turkish society, and it is the outcome of the dialectic evolution of the NOM-affiliated parties with the orthodox Kemalism of civil-military bureaucracy and the regional and international actors in the Turkish political economy.

The AKP's methodology in adopting conservative democracy as its framing identity is to change the continuities of the Just Order and the rudiments of the Islamic political economy. The latter would be suggested to be relevant for the AKP in terms of its adaptation by the Just Order politics as the politico-economic programme to which the Party leader's cadre and mainstream managers were strictly committed before becoming conservative democrats. In doing so, the AKP's political strategy is to craft a catch-all politics by deranging the systemic coherence of Just Order politics and engaging in neoliberal disorder and Kemalist secularism with a socially sensitive but not socially contingent perspective. Such a strategic posture prompted the blurring of timespace in the Turkish context between the de-accumulation of the paradigmatically contingent political stabilities of the Just Order and the accumulation of the pragmatically crafted flexibilities of conservative democracy. In a methodological sense, this way of action is at odds with Islamic theory, the Just Order and Ottoman praxis in that it does not rely on a strategy of change conditioned by the path-dependencies of Islamic theory. This does not, however, signify that conservative democracy is free from normative tenets and is simply a neoliberalised version of the Just Order. Rather, it is an interim identity that ebbs and flows between these two paradigms under a subconscious reference to a purely Islamic theory of political economy and its Ottoman praxis. This is why the question of what is next becomes intriguing and appealing in the Turkish case.

In political economy terms, as observed in Figure 11.1, the Party confined the state's organising intervention role in the Just Order to organising regulation and left directing the conduct of financial and commercial structuration to the private sector. Between the state and market, therefore, society becomes vulnerable to the latter's commodificatory impact in the absence of efficient neocorporatist surveillance. The economic and social dialogues in the Party's programme are negotiational forums to provide for the smooth functioning of economic conduct. In the Just Order, the same is the case to a great extent. In Islamic theory, economic governance should be structured on the basis of equal power sharing among major political economy actors to allocate the factors of production and the distribution of income. In one respect, the path-dependence in the state-led social order becomes the determinant factor in the AKP's approach to economic governance. In another respect, however, the Party perceives the market as a building block of modern life that should be managed effectively to make a normatively contingent lifeworld possible and applicable.

As the Party precludes the state from undertaking direct regulatory intervention in national or international markets, in conservative democratic theory, the state's role is to prevent organised action from becoming a straitjacket for market exchange. Complementary policy instruments of this role include tight monetary policy, budget austerity, the privatisation of the SEEs and semi-progressive taxation. In systemic terms, such a supply-sided approach to economic policy diverges from the social market model envisaged by the Just Order and Islamic economics, which call for a demand-constrained structuration of market exchange. The AKP's macro-economic strategy would be suggested to be in partial line with that of the Ottomans in the sense of prioritising the state's financial balances without adopting a systemically progressive tax regime. However, the Ottomans also conditioned market exchange from a demand-constrained perspective via the strategy of organising intervention. The consequence is that, despite undertaking a universal strategy of social policy, the Party conditions this strategy by budget austerity and economic efficiency, in structural contrast to the Just Order and Islamic theory.

The theoretical construction of the AKP's party programme can be suggested to take a conservatively constructed, Third Way identity between Islamic and neoliberal institutionalism in terms of adopting a form of knowledge management between normatively contingent rationality and rationality-contingent normativity, organising regulation and deregulative regulation, decommodification and commodification, progressive and regressive taxation, equality of outcomes and equality of opportunity and so on. In terms of the interaction between Islam and neoliberalism, however, it would be proposed that the AKP gives precedence to conjunctural constraints in configuring its politico-economic strategies while taking on an open-ended responsibility for adapting structural constraints by constructing a universal social policy strategy and enabling organised workers to have the right to collective bargaining and strike.

What makes the AKP more similar to neoliberalism than its antecedents – the Just Order, pure Islamic theory and Ottoman praxis – is the *open-endedness* of the constraints that, in praxis, make social conduct vulnerable to the decommodificatory impact of market exchange (see the comparative discussion on the systemic impact of neoliberalism on Islamic and social democratic structures, pp. 69–70). While this does not reach the point of systemically subsidising private risks, it contributes to the infusion of the neoliberal sentiment of *cooperation through voluntary exchange* into the Turkish context. The outcome of this infusion, on the one hand, is that the coalitional impact of power, prestige and money becomes the driving force that unifies Turkish society under the cement of the AKP's formal organisation and around the common end of increasing per capita income.

In Khaldunian terms, therefore, the group feeling of the NOM-affiliated parties becomes centrifugal political professionalism under the auspices of the AKP. On the other hand, this is not a sharp-edged but gradual change accommodated by the renormativisation of the public sphere, both in terms of the conflation of secular formal institutions with the Islamically motivated managerial conduct of the AKP cadres and the spillover from this process onto the Turkish people by way of releasing pent-up Islamic consciousness and adjusting the centre of gravity of their action between value and purposive rationality. As this process unfolds in a society that evolves under the path-dependent continuities of its past with time-lags and time-rushes in various sequences, it becomes impossible to make a clear-cut definition of the current panorama of this binary coexistence of value and purposive rationality in Turkish society.

To be concise, to conceptualise the AKP's party programme using clear-cut definitions is infeasible in a structural sense. The reason is that, from a practitioner's perspective, the tension between theory and praxis arises in the dilemma of (i) striking a balance between the practical adaptation of theoretical postulates under the confines of the inter-complementary coherence of ideologic presuppositions and (ii) adopting an effective pragmatism that enables her/him to steadily ebb and flow along the inter-repulsive relationship among theory, practice and ideology. The AKP's perspective is, in this regard, to develop a theoretical ideology to be practised with a practical pragmatism under the confines of practical exigencies.

What makes the Party a persistent and prevailing image is its dynamic efficiency in playing at the workable margins of theory and praxis with the assistance of conjunctural circumstances. For example, throughout its time in power between 2002 and 2013, the AKP has neither discoursed nor practised a strategy of *unconditional egalitarianism*, namely rights without responsibilities. The Party also did not exploit political business cycles to cultivate additional votes. Instead, it clings to *feasible equalities* and legitimates this vision through its role as *stabiliser*. Albeit paradoxical, *prima facie*, this strategy has enabled the Party to cumulatively increase its votes under the grim legacy of the crisis-ridden past of the Turkish political economy, particularly between 1994 and 2002.

However, I believe the AKP's Third Way strategy, situated between theory, praxis, ideology and pragmatism, has already reached its natural boundaries in cultivating votes by ebbing and flowing at the institutional margins that have thus far been tolerated by the Turkish public by suppressing the people's demands for increased equality in the face of political and economic stability. This tolerance was based on the AKP's mission of reforming the centre-periphery alignment of Turkish political economy in favour of conservatively or religiously sensitive individuals. As noted previously, in this respect, informal institutions such as shared values and norms can be expected to bestow a relatively longer-term structural power to their adherents, whereas formal institutions such as government would provide their holders with a relatively shorter term of power. This is because the latter's resources, such as money and popularity, are much more fluid in nature. The AKP utilised the norm-contingent demands to consolidate its structural power for over a decade. To continue in power, it must begin prioritising the normative demands of its electorate, such as social equity and secure jobs. This inquiry takes us to the question of *what is next*. Before seeking a structural response to this question, a compact analysis of the Party's practical performance will enable us to comprehend why the AKP needs a new dynamism that will constitute its future foundations.

When the internal and external constraints listed in Table 6.4 are taken into account in the context of the structural volatilities of the Turkish political economy between 1980 and 2013 (see pp. 246–247), the relative priority of a secular, neoliberal vision in the AKP's programme can be better understood. Obviously, at the turn of the twenty-first century, the Turkish economy was at a critical juncture between a structural reconstruction or perpetuating the status quo, which was ultimately to take the country to an outright memorandum. In the political realm, political dissolution, in the form of both a catastrophic economic crisis and the inability to circumvent Islamic politics through successive closures, brought about a systemically dark picture far from creating a positive dynamism to overcome both economic and structural challenges. The systemic power of the civil-military bureaucracy and pro-cyclical actors, ranging from the DSP, the CHP and the ANAP to the TUSIAD, the TISK and major media outlets, began to decay, as their coalitional mindset authorising them to overturn the RP-DYP coalition could not yield a means of justifying or providing the sustainability of the then existing politico-economic regime. This could be likened to the Empire's inability during the eighteenth and, particularly, nineteenth centuries to devise a new institutional system to redeem its former grandeur, which served as the main source of systemic power for the ITF and then Republican elites to transform the institutional stock of the Empire towards a secular capitalist pathway.

The AKP's systemic power is apparently much weaker than the ITF's and, particularly, the CHP's during the single-party era because their power also derived their ownership of the overwhelming gravity of institutional power and the strategic convergence of their policy choices with the dominant global actors in initiating denormativising restructurations. Despite pro-cyclically engaging in the neoliberal establishment and cooperating with occidental organisations, ranging from the IMF and WB to the WTO and G-20, the AKP is, in both institutional and structural terms, a countercyclical actor, at least potentially, not only for Turkey's secular capitalism but also for transnational neoliberalism. (The latter is because the Party holds a niche of structural and strategic power, albeit a weak one, to mobilise a vast number of Islamic countries to increase their politico-economic power through various economic organisations. The D-8 is a case in point. Trade among its member countries increased from 14 to 129 billion dollars between 1997 and 2011.) This is why the EU, IMF, WTO, OECD and the TNCs are able to exert a surreptitious constraint on the AKP's structural posture at the margins of Islam and liberalism.

In other words, the AKP lacks the coalitional support of these transnational organisations in terms of strategic, knowledge and theoretical political power resources. In this sense, its practical pragmatism is systemically structured on the basis of the fine-tuning of its political countercyclicality through economically pro-cyclical, unsystemic adaptations to the national and international institutional environment that provide the Party with a justificatory power for its catch-all politics. As in its rejection of a new stand-by agreement with the IMF as of May 2008, the Party does not pursue a straight-line but a conjuncturally flexible approach in blending the constituents of its systemic power resources. (This was a timely initiative in consolidating the Party's discursive power over its electorate, which gave the impression that the Party did not voluntarily pursue global capitalism but engaged with it due to conjunctural inevitabilities.)

Another conspicuous nexus in the AKP's systemic power is its integrating the normative niches in Turkish society around an Islamically contingent, conservative thread. This was and in fact is possible through the existence of a framing identity, conservative democracy, under the leadership of a charismatic figure, Erdoğan, who eloquently manages the varying tides of conservatism, Islamism, neoliberal capitalism, nationalism, clientelism, egalitarianism and so on. (Despite becoming the President of Turkey and formally detached from the AKP in August 2014, Erdoğan acts as the *de facto* leader of the party.) As in the Ottoman context, this balance is quite delicate. What capacitates the AKP to perpetuate this delicate power is that, as previously discussed, its leader cadre, including Erdoğan himself, comes from underprivileged segments of society in terms of their origins. This feature enables them to dynamically consolidate their coalitional ties with their electorate on a bottom-up basis, an organisational versatility that the CHP lacks to a structural extent. The AKP effectively marshals patronage and clientelistic linkages in a manner that does not disrupt its organisational unity under the unifying cement of its overall political mission, which was, paradoxically, further consolidated by the regime-based reactions of the civil-military bureaucracy and the CHP of 1995–2010. However, there is no solid guarantee that the Party will be able to perpetuate this delicate balance permanently, in both a formal and informal sense.

The abovementioned niche is complemented by the coalitional power that the MUSIAD, Hak-Is and Memur-Sen provide the Party in implementing basic political and democratisation reforms, particularly in the enforcement of central countercyclical initiatives such as taking a firm stance against military pressure and the creation of opportunity spaces for conservative patronage and power networks. As the AKP's reformist initiatives, particularly in structural reconstructions such as changing the judicial system or providing employment opportunities to headscarf-wearing women in the public sector, arose during a transitory period, the discursive, coalitional and justificatory powers that these three organisations provide the Party are significant in embedding the sources of its structural power over time. The Hak-Is and Memur-Sen's support for the AKP, albeit prudent, also has a structurally appeasing impact on labour militancy. In the absence of Turk-Is' support, the KESK and DISK's countercyclical attempts to politicise labour disputes have generally remained insufficient to coerce the AKP to change its structural economic or IR strategies.

The AKP's abovementioned swings between countercyclicality and pro-cyclicality outfit the Party with the ability to gain the support of the TUSIAD and TISK on economic issues, and the Party utilises this support as leverage to keep the political tension between secularism and Islam stable over time. Moreover, the AKP utilised the TUSIAD, TISK, MUSIAD and the EU's support for its economic-stability-first social justice strategy to consolidate its coercive power in enforcing the deregulative IRs arrangements such as the implementation of flexible working patterns or justifying austerity-contingent wage and salary management. In terms of the diplomatic resources of enforcive power, the ITUC, ETUC and GUFs' initiative in coercing the AKP government to comply with the ILO conventions by declaring their transnational discursive and operational support for the Turkish labour confederations generated some conclusive but limited results in view of the Party's coalitional power with international financial and commercial organisations, the TNCs and the EU in executing supply-sided policy measures.

In conjunction with the ILO's and the EU's persistent critiques and increasing tensions with the national trade and civil service unions, the AKP legalised general, political and solidarity strikes, authorised the confirmation of trade union membership by e-mail, reduced the sectoral barrage from 10 to 3 per cent and so on, notable steps in terms of the reorganisation of Turkish IRs. In this respect, it could be argued that the Party has taken countercyclical demands seriously to the extent that they do not disrupt its structural economic policy choices. The most conspicuous choice in this regard is the Party's refusal to confirm the 5th and 6th articles of the European Social Charter or extend the right to collective bargaining and strike to civil servants. It pursues the same strategy in the case of social policy. On the one hand, the Party raised the retirement age and increased the number of qualifying premium days; however, it also steadily increased social expenditures, remarkably reduced poverty, repealed tuition fees at public universities and constructed nearly 615,000 middle- and low-income housing units using a public-run construction institution, TOKI, for which the poor, admittedly, paid reasonable costs and enjoyed favourable payment options compared to the market average.

What would be next for the Party? I have hitherto argued that changes should be path-dependent, as social phenomena accumulate or de-accumulate gradually, haltingly and non-linearly. The AKP's path-dependence consists of the Just Order, the Islamic theory of political economy and Ottoman praxis. The last is particularly relevant for its geopolitical and geostrategic discursive and justificatory power over Muslim communities. What is next for the AKP's political strategies is either to de-accumulate or re-accumulate these path-dependencies. As can be inferred from the discussion above, in terms of the overall institutional stock, the Party already de-accumulates them in structural terms, while continuing unsystemic re-accumulations. The key point for what is next is thus whether the party will begin to re-accumulate path-dependencies at the level of theory and praxis. It is beyond theoreticians' ability to make clear-cut predictions of the far future, particularly in highly complex world politics and economics as exists at present. However, in light of the historical data that we have provided thus far, a structural analysis could be made of the Party's prospective institutional preferences.

I believe that we have to look upon the neoliberal centre of gravity of the Party's strategic choices as a pivotal path-dependence dynamics for its ensuing policy adaptations, under the possibility of *Islamisabilities*. As stated in our earlier discussion on *social democratisabilities*, irrespective of the internal and external threats and opportunities, we could not make a theory-praxis match or mismatch in political economy terms. In this respect, and in view of the structural imperfections of Turkish politics and economics at the turn of the century, on the one hand, the AKP's performance can be suggested to have left an opening, at least, for a more effective interventionist role in erasing income inequalities given the Party's abovementioned egalitarian, albeit palliative, socio-economic policy choices. On the other hand, we could not identify a structural transformation in the Party's strategic choices from the increasing proportion of indirect taxes to the refusal to adopt a demand-side strategy, even during the Great Recession.

The unsteady increases in public sector fixed capital formation or government final consumption expenditures cannot be regarded as concrete indicators of the possibility of such a decommodificatory intervention. Other parameters, in this respect, are the Party's poor performance in functionalising the ESC and public sector collective contract processes and the consequent low but steady critical voices arising from even the Party's coalitional partners, the Hak-Is and Memur-Sen. To a certain extent, it would be understandable that, in a post-crisis period, the Party chose to first consolidate macro-economic balances by substantially reducing the debt ratio, PSBR, interest rates, inflation and exchange rate volatility, namely to palliate the overall macro-economic fragility. To claim that the AKP's austerity strategy sought to cultivate the funds necessary for future egalitarian interventions, such a strategy would and should have been conducted through the gradual adaptation of a structurally decommodificatory strategy to alleviate one of the highest levels of income inequality among the OECD countries (Turkey's Gini coefficient has been 0.40 from 2004 onwards), particularly by establishing an effective economic and industrial democracy. (Between 2003 and 2007, average economic growth was steady at 7 per cent.)

In the short-run, as a result, the AKP's turn towards establishing a social market economy, as envisaged by the Just Order and Islamic theory, while not particularly likely, is also not inconceivable. The former option would first be pursued because the impact of liberal economic exchange is more independent and less subject to the AKP's discretion. Previously, we have argued that economic institutions are much more fluent in nature than political ones. Yet, if the former has become gradually structuralised in social praxis, its durability would become consolidated and could thus only be de-accumulated over a certain period of time. Thanks to the overwhelmingly liberalised institutional stock of Turkish capitalism, neoliberal disorder has aggressively infused into the everyday life of the people, Muslim or non-Muslim, intensifying the process of income-lifestyle compression.

At this point, the ambiguous performance of the NOM-affiliated parties serves as concrete proof that the embedded cointegration of normative or rational secularism and individually adopted neoliberal values inspired by network rationalisation could not be harnessed overnight solely by crafting and path-dependently defending a political programme. This is why Akdoğan emphasises gradual change. Furthermore, as the Turkish economy has already been completely liberalised and its foreign trade volume reached 48.5 as a share of GDP as of 2011, such a turn is strictly dependent on the resurgence of international Keynesianism, and its regulatory policy tools, over international financial and commercial exchange regimes. In this respect, for the AKP to turn towards a social market economy, there would need to be a process of discontinuing path-dependence in neoliberal institutionalism and its outgrowths in inter-individual, intergroup and inter-organisational actions at the national and international levels.

Moreover this discontinuing path-dependence should be accommodated by the changing centre of gravity in the systemic power relations among the major actors in the Turkish political economy. The 10-year path-dependence of the Party in managing economic governance does not allow us to have promising expectations in this regard. Although we take it for granted that the AKP would initiate such a turn by re-accumulating its path-dependencies, there is a systemic bottleneck resulting from the path-dependencies of Turkey's major business and labour organisations. Turkish civil or trade unions do have a history of acting reactively, not strategically.

The rather poor performance of these organisations in establishing intra-union democracy and effective recruitment strategies enmeshed with a macro-visionary organisational development strategy does not portend a promising future with respect to creating and sustaining a positive-sum relationship among themselves in terms of cooperation on their common areas of interest against public or private employers, let alone with public or private employers. The sharp ideologic polarisation among the DISK/KESK and Hak-Is/Memur-Sen, the Turk-Is and the Kamu-Sen profoundly damages the possibility of such a conciliation among labour organisations. The TUSIAD, TISK and MUSIAD are prone to suppress rather than cooperate with labour organisations under their structural power engendered by their holding the most precious thing of value in neoliberal times, capital, and have been further consolidated by this incompetence on the part of labour organisations (MUSIAD's emphasis on public-private partnerships could be considered a tolerant approach. However this approach is based on *concession* rather than *collective* bargaining). The strategic convergence among the institutional priorities of these business and employer organisations, the AKP, EU, IMF, WB, WTO, TNCs and the OECD, makes it exceedingly difficult for labour organisations to accumulate any niche of systemic power except for raising inconclusive discourses using the justificatory power resulting from their representation of the exploited, the workers. Furthermore, the coalitional partnership in political pro-cyclicality is not a determining parameter in this context, as seen in MUSIAD's rigid rejection of Hak-Is' organising attempts in the enterprises affiliated with itself.

Another issue is that, instead of venturing into competitive sectors and establishing their progressive strategies regarding the sustainability of productive relations in cooperation with their employees, Turkish employer or businessmen organisations expect the state to create a favourable investment environment, particularly by granting export subsidies, establishing an easily usable technologic and research and development infrastructure, developing protective measures to enhance the competitive strength of certain sectors and so on. Given the embeddedness of monopolistic and oligopolistic structures in the Turkish industrial sector, it is not tenable to expect them to play a conciliatory role in the formation of positive-sum cooperation between major *social partners*. This directly bears on the inconclusive initiatives of the ITUC, ILO and the GUFs to establish a binding transnational governance structure with the IMF, WB and WTO that would function to provide and sustain the inclusion of labour and social rights as binding constraints in the conduct of structural and development programmes and in the dispute settlement system to prevent a race-to-the-bottom. This is because the Turkish state and employer and businessmen's organisations reap structural and institutional power from refusing to take part in the institution of productive solidarity, and this prevents Turkish labour organisations from obtaining justificatory power to contribute to such a positive-sum outcome.

By all accounts, there are solid pro-cyclical factors that make it difficult for the AKP to exercise countercyclical regulatory discretion. However, there are other structural facts that could well require the Party to do so. The first is that the party has already exhausted its credit on the part of its electorate through its strategy of *responsible pragmatism* in social policy and *hard pragmatism* in industrial relations; hence, it should develop a more structurally clear-cut and conclusive decommodificatory strategy. This point is consolidated by the persistent critiques of labour organisations, particularly the Party's coalitional allies, the Hak-Is and Memur-Sen and the Party's electoral coalition, predominantly consisting of the rural population and urban slum-dwellers. The EU's 'soft' pressure on the Party to confirm the 5th and 6th articles of the European Social Charter and effectively implementing labour rights in keeping with the ILO conventions would be suggested to reinforce this option in terms of its coercive power stemming from Turkey's overall democratisation performance.

Second, to maintain its electoral performance, the AKP should extend its vision towards a broader segment of Turkish society, which would require a more inclusive and beyond-group discourse on the basis of humanitarian and citizenship rights. Such an expanded vision is a must for the Party to enforce its 2023 targets by creating a *societal dynamism*. In other words, to ensure sustainable politico-economic development, there should be a 'Turkish social model' such that fleeting and conjunctural political and business cycles would not deviate it from its stable trajectory, at least substantially, and the Turkish political economy has a dynamic ability to contain the internal and external unexpected shocks and adapt to ever-changing transnational dynamics, ranging from production techniques to competitive cycles.

Another parameter in this regard is that the ongoing global recession cast a shadow over the Party's most significant discursive power, economic stability. The Party must compensate for this decline in its core strategy by touching upon the *receptive cells* of the Turkish public to create the space required to justify its organisational mission and vision, at least in the run-up to the 2015 general elections. In this regard, the main opposition Party, the CHP, has turned to a social-policy-centred electoral strategy that, in dialectic terms, would predispose the AKP to retaliate. This issue would become more determinant if the regional or international political economy were to take on a Keynesian trajectory; whether this development will occur is unclear.

Given the above-noted countercyclical dynamics for the AKP to make a strategic turn towards a path-dependent trajectory, as a political movement that emerged from the NOM, HASPAR's annexation by the AKP takes on structural importance. This is because HASPAR adopted the strategy of social-justice-first economic stability under the supervision of a professor of social policy and industrial relations, Numan Kurtulmuş. One, and in fact currently the most likely, prospect is that Kurtulmuş, one of the four deputy prime ministers of the AKP government, and his ideas would not have a notable impact on the Party's major strategies, as the centre of gravity of the AKP's policy strategies cannot be expected to be amended by a person whose political popularity was trivial (HASPAR's electoral support was 0.77 in the 2011 general elections). In another respect, the above-noted, solid countercyclical factors urge us to reckon with such an option seriously, albeit prudentially.

Another parameter favouring the likelihood of such an option is the AKP's recent political reforms. After consolidating its power base both formally and informally, the Party *de facto* succeeded in repealing the ban on headscarf-wearing students from education and, most important, the right of women wearing headscarves to work in the public sector, except in judicial, military and security positions. These were the most structurally challenging issues for Islamic politics. However, as the main basis for exercising the above-noted prudence, it can be argued that, in contrast to economics, politics allows for much more independent governmental discretion for two primary reasons. The first is that the timespace inseparability of politics and culture requires the conditioning of political action by normative values. While both culture and politics experience the disidentifying impact of neoliberal values, they might be more effectively safeguarded and nationally regenerated in politics, at least compared to economics, the constituents of which are highly internationally mobile.

This is why, for example, nationalism is the most widespread common point in all countries, from the USA to France or to Iran, and why Turkey still strives to become a member state of the EU, despite having entered into the Customs Union in 1996. Moreover, the *most structural indicator* of this thesis is the limited market share, 6 per cent, of Islamic Banks, despite the 50 per cent support for an Islamic party and, most important, the trivial amount of funds earmarked for the mudaraba style of productive finance. This apparently demonstrates the stickiness of capitalist networks, even in a country ruled by a political party with leaders who come from a tradition that predicated its economic model on the eradication of interest-bearing transactions from the agenda of the Turkish political economy. A similar nexus is that the EU is Turkey's largest trading partner and the AKP has unhesitatingly advocated becoming a member of this regional organisation, despite the fundamental difference in its civilisational references.

Conclusion
The Turkish Social System at a Critical Turning Point among Islam, Neoliberalism and Social Democracy: What is the Next?

The book consists of two parts. The first aims to present the analytic framework of the institutional system analysis and the cross-paradigmatic examination of Islam, neoliberalism and social democracy. The second is the case study section that in light of the theoretical discussion in the first section, explains the evolutionary dynamics of the Ottoman-Turkish political economy in terms of its formational, evolutionary and current structures along with a systemic insight into its future prospects. In this concluding section, I will not summarise the explanatory framework of the institutional system analysis, as I already did so at the end of the first chapter (pp. 51–54). Instead, I will directly focus on the future prospects of Turkish social system in light of this explanatory framework.

Hitherto, the discussion has demonstrated that the Ottoman-Turkish political economy and its *odyssey* over time, particularly from the early nineteenth century to the present, could not have been examined without adopting a systemic perspective. This is because the spiralling of normative and de-normative rationalisations in the nineteenth and first half of the twentieth century (by the Tanzimat bureaucracy and the ITF and Kemalists, respectively) and then the rational re-normativisations from the third quarter of the twentieth century to the present (by the NOM-affiliated parties and AKP governments) to varying extents and in multiple compositions in the political, economic and social realms, as well as with their national, regional and international outgrowths, could in no way be conceptualised using a theory or analytic paradigm, the components of which are not inter-connective, inter-testifying and inter-reinforcing in explaining the structural intersections of macro-formal institutional axes and their informal underpinnings.

Specific to the Ottoman-Turkish case, the particularisation of this non-autopoietic social system (particularly from the early nineteenth century), not only in terms of individualisation but also its nearly unbridgeable fragmentation of formal and informal meaning structures, poses a formidable challenge in both specifying and clarifying the nexus among the inter-repulsively contingent intersections of Islamic, (neo)liberal and social democratic formal and informal institutions. Institutional system analysis in political economy, in this sense, has provided an explorative cement for us to identify and theoretically contextualise the primordial and reformational path-dependencies of Ottoman and then Republican

Turkey, respectively, along with their in-time entanglements and various patterns of change dynamics.

The transformation of the *patterned* social system or Islamic regime of the Empire, albeit de-accumulated over time, into the *unpatterned* social system of Republican Turkey through a reactively constructed de-normativising process precipitated the patterns of path-dependent changes to inter-repulsively overwhelm one another along an unsteady path of power relations among ideologically balkanised politico-economic actors. This has meant that the inter-actor power relations from the ITF onwards either rush into authoritarianly de-accumulating vested Islamic institutions and establishing secular ones through the orthodox, social democratic, third way strands of Kemalist politics or into reactively re-accumulating the former by the Islamically or conservatively motivated NOM-affiliated parties or the AKP.

The price has been the *political and economic transformation costs* manifesting themselves in the fact that *stable institutionalisations* in the Turkish political economy have yet to be initiated, and the future prospects for such an advance are hardly promising. Rather, the present-day, *patched structures* of the country that have persisted for more than one century are on the path towards reorganisational crisis under the grim legacy of path-dependent deadlocks, from the dependent conduct of the economic system to the Kurdish issue. In the background lies the inability of the Ottoman rulers of the eighteenth and nineteenth centuries and then the overly rational ITF and Republican reformers to reconstruct *original consistencies* peculiar to the natural flow of indigenous societal transformations.

As a permanently destabilising *systemic flaw*, this point circumvented both the orderly re-accumulation of old consistencies and the de-accumulation of formal-informal inconsistencies through democratic dialectics of bottom-up societal discretions. This is why Turkey has been unable to develop a clear-cut version of an Islamic, liberal or social democratic model peculiar to the *modus vivendi* of its social system. The currently floating blend of these paradigms in the Turkish political economy poses an intricate challenge for its actors to take its political and economic development in stride. First and foremost, the Turkish public is unable to attach common meanings, at least, in the areas of common politico-economic interests. Evidence of this is the highly volatile and fluent composition of the Turkish electorate, particularly during the 1990s and early 2000s, when the Turkish political economy passed through a 'Bermuda triangle' of economic crisis, political chaos and societal diffusion.

From a communicative action standpoint, the lack of a *successive unifier* of the transitional bonds from the Empire to the Republic precluded the recombination of the ensuing differences of personality, culture and society around shared utterances, thereby tempting the country's rulers to craft formally adopted institutional constructions. And this, in economic terms, hindered the realisation of the social optimum by means of optimising the regulation of the dynamic accumulation of rational resources of knowledge and technological capabilities, namely evolutionary creativity, of the inequalities in income and power, and of the transformation cost and opportunities to halt systemic leisure and the depletion of social time. While seeming relatively uncomplicated when theoretically delineated, adjusting the combinational sequence and timing of these delicate balances is quite difficult to realise in praxis. This is because the theoretical constructions should be accompanied by practical performances in terms of ideologic doctrinations but not 'patched' by pragmatic adaptations among the state, market, society and class. In the Turkish context, the ideologic clashes among economic actors, major business or employer organisations, trade and civil servant unions are a substantial challenge to the development of an optimising regulation, although political actors intend to do so.

The indecisive nature of the evolution of the Kemalist variants of social democracy and the third way, and the intricate mix of Islamic politics and economics in the AKP's conservative democratic identity are direct results of the abovementioned instable institutionalisations. Particularly relevant in this respect is the displaced and re-displaced continuity of Kemalist social democracy and social democratic Kemalism between 1995 and 2011 in reaction not to bottom-up societal motivations but to Islamic politics. These successive displacements were also not systemically in keeping with international trends of transition between social democracy and the third way. Such a reactive mindset was nothing new but rather a path-dependency dating back to the ITF's strategy of changing continuities through sharp-edged institutional breaks to embed the path-dependent discontinuities of the Empire.

The AKP's stability in remaining in power is due to its aggregative role over a mosaical electorate by reconciling their expectations in various common interest areas, ranging from the resonance of religious ideals in the public sphere to the Europe-centred modernisation initiative at the workable margins. Furthermore, ostensibly, this topical point is one of resistance for Turkish political economy vis-à-vis regional and global capitalism, particularly for Islamically sensitive groups. However, it seems inconceivable to claim that the AKP's austerity empire would continue to retain its buffer role in the absence of a dynamically inter-complementary institutional stock and given the existence of path-dependent deadlocks among Islam, secularism and capitalism.

Revolving around these three major trends, the inter-repulsive dialectics among Islam, social democracy and neoliberalism, primarily by the AKP and the CHP in attempts to capture systemic power resources, engender a highly structural impediment to the establishment of workable mutualities as the unifying cement of a society for developing an optimum political economy endowment. This is because inter-repulsiveness makes it impossible to adjust the levels of normativeness or rationality, either to eradicate social norms and values by overly rational methods (timelessly reified justifications) or by failing to internalise rational methods of development due to extreme normative adaptations. The AKP's strategy of formally reconciling these extreme edges through a theoretico-practical pragmatism would, in one respect, be a transitory solution. However, in the long run, such a palliative functionality should not be assumed to persist, in that the dissolution of the Turkish social system evolves through not the regression of still-resisting workable mutualities, as in countries with organised capitalism, but the deepening of counteractive communications.

In other words, the path-dependent changes in the Turkish context evolved through the drifting reactions between changes and path-dependencies rather than through the dynamically reconciliative dialectics of formal and informal institutions. Turkey's *communicative convergence* with the EU would redound to the rational rationalisation of the country's institutional stock in formal interactions. Yet, as can be retrospectively inferred from the construction of Turkish social democracy by means of ideologic transpositions from European models, the country's formal reflexes are unable to mutate *transposed identities* into *locational originalities*. Thus, formal repositionings under the aegis of the EU conditionalities would not, in structural terms, be claimed to underpin the informal adaptations of a civic initiative consisting of fragmented mindsets that make it quite difficult to structuralise social action on the trilogic trade-offs among conflict, dependence and order.

These *inconveniencies* become increasingly difficult under the ever-rising transnational timespace and income-lifestyle compression of flexible individuals, organisations and markets, requiring nations to have and permanently develop dynamically competitive social discretions with their inter-complementary formal and informal institutional stocks. The continuing transitory nature of the international system as the encompassing environment for various national environments condenses this requirement into immediate conjunctural terms and leaves no room for making *irredeemable institutional mistakes*. In the context of its abovementioned national grievances, Turkey's discretion to *blossom* in the international political economy muddles through, despite some promising signals, particularly during a period in which the latter's pivotal actors are grappling with internal economic crises.

Ultimately, there is no doubt that the near future of the Turkish political economy will unfold under the above-noted challenges and limited opportunities. The ability of Turkish society to cope with the delicate cross-trade-offs between theory-praxis-ideology and pragmatism based on conflict, dependence and order would shift itself to a pattern of path-dependent change that could form the basis for political and economic positive-sum mutualities at, at least, workable margins. The evolutionary dialectics of its major political and economic actors could nonetheless not be claimed to be up-and-coming in this regard to steer these quite vulnerable margins onto manageable pathways. In this sense, the change the AKP has created might give only a *partial hope* for the Party's *believers*. However, providing nations with systemic power in international platforms would only make sense when wielded in a manner that unleashes all human, capital and technologic potentials of a country, particularly in the context of the ongoing global recession. The prerequisite for such a common action is the reconciliation of the intra-system resources of power on the basis of workable mutualities by the pivotal actors and not its unilateral control by one or another faction.

References

Acemoğlu, D. and Robinson, J. (2012), *Why Nations Fail: The Origins of Power, Prosperity, and Poverty* (New York: Crown Publishers).
—— (2009), 'The Crisis of 2008: Lessons for and from Economics', *Critical Review*, 21:2–3, 185–94.
ABGS – Turkish Ministry for EU Affairs (2007), *Political Reforms in Turkey* (Ankara: Ministry of Foreign Affairs Secretariat General for EU Affairs).
Adler, E. and Bernstein, S. (2005), 'Knowledge in Power: The Epistemic Construction of Global Governance', in M. Barnett and R. Duvall (eds), *Power in Global Governance* (Cambridge: Cambridge University Press), 294–318.
Ahmad, F. (2003), *The Making of Modern Turkey* (London: Routledge).
—— (1977), *The Turkish Experiment in Democracy, 1950–1973* (London: C. Hurst & Company).
Ahmad, Z. (1991), *Islam, Poverty, and Income Distribution* (Leicester: The Islamic Foundation).
Ağtaş, Ö. (2009), 'Ortanın Solu: İsmet İnönü'den Bülent Ecevit'e', in T. Bora and M. Gültekingil (eds), *Türkiye'de Siyasi Düşünce: Sol* (İstanbul: İletişim), 197–261.
Akçay, Ü. (2007), *Kapitalizmi Planlamak: Türkiye'de Planlama ve DPT'nin Dönüşümü* (İstanbul: Sosyal Araştırmalar Vakfı).
Akçay, M.A. (1997), *Para Politikası Araçları: Türkiye ve Çeşitli Ülkelerdeki Uygulamalar* (DPT Uzmanlık Tezi, Ankara: DPT).
Akdağ, M. (1963), *Celâli İsyanları, 1550–1603* (Ankara: Ankara Üniversitesi Basımevi).
Akdemir, S. (1991), *Sosyal Denge Modeli II: Devletin Unsurları ve Kuvvetler Dengesi* (İstanbul: İz).
Akdoğan, Y. (2006), 'The Meaning of Conservative Democratic Political Identity', in M.H. Yavuz (ed.), *The Emergence of New Turkey* (Utah: Utah University Press), 45–66.
Akgündüz, A. (1988), *İslam Hukukunda ve Osmanlı Tatbikatında Vakıf Müessesi* (İstanbul: Osmanlı Araştırmaları Vakfı Yayınları).
Akgür, T. (1988) 'Cumhuriyet Dönemi (1924–1986) Mevduat Kredi ve Para Serilerinin Oluşturulması', *ODTÜ Gelişme Dergisi*, 15: 3–4, 181–211.
AKP (2013), *Türkiye Hazır Hedef 2023*, Available at: http://www.akparti.org.tr/site/hedefler, retrieved on 07.08.2013.
—— (2012), *AK Parti 2023 Siyasi Vizyonu: Siyaset, Toplum, Dünya*, Available at: http://www.akparti.org.tr/site/akparti/2023-siyasi-vizyon, retrieved on 07.08.2013.

———— (2002). *Kalkınma ve Demokratileşme Programı* (Ankara: AKP).

Al-Faruqi, I.R. and Al-Banna, G. (1984), *Towards Islamic Labour & Unionism: Three Papers* (Cairo: International Islamic Confederation of Labour).

Alexander, J.C. (1987), 'Action and Its Environments', in J.C. Alexander and B. Giesen (eds), *The Micro-Macro Link* (Berkeley: University of California Press), 289–318.

Altuğ, S. and Filiztekin, A. (2006) 'Productivity and Growth, 1923–1950', in S. Altuğ and A. Filiztekin (eds.), *The Turkish Economy: The Real Economy, Corporate Governance and Reform* (London: Routledge), 15–62.

Akalın, G. (2008), *Atatürk Dönemi Maliye Politikası* (Ankara: Maliye Bakanlığı).

Akural, S.M. (1984), 'Kemalist Views on Social Change', in J.M. Landau (ed.), *Atatürk and the Modernization of Turkey* (Colorado: Westview Press), 125–52.

ANAP – The Motherland Party of Turkey (1983), *Parti Programı* (Ankara).

Andersen, E. (1990), *Three Worlds of Welfare Capitalism* (Cambridge: Polity).

Arnakis, G.G. (1953), 'Futuwwa Traditions in the Ottoman Empire Akhis, Bektashi Dervishes, and Craftsmen', *Journal of Near Eastern Studies*, 12:4, 232–47.

Arrow, K. (1967), 'Public and Private Values', in S. Hook (ed.), *Human Values and Economic Policy* (New York: New York University Press), 3–21.

Arthur, B.W. (1994), *Increasing Returns and Path Dependence in the Economy* (Michigan: Michigan University Press).

Asad, M. (1961), *The Principles of State and Government in Islam* (Berkeley: University of California Press).

Asutay, Mehmet (2010) 'Deconstructing the Functioning of Political Manipulation of the Economy in Turkey', in Tamer Ç. and F. Yılmaz, (eds), *Understanding the Process of Economic Change in Turkey: An Institutional Approach* (New York: Nova Science Publishers), 91–112.

Atasoy, Y. (2009), *Islamic's Marriage with Neoliberalism: State Transformation in Turkey* (Houndsmill: Palgrave McMillan).

Ateşoğulları, K. (1997), *Uluslararası Çalışma Örgütü ve Türkiye* (İstanbul: Petrol-İş).

Aydın, E. and Dalmıs, İ. (2008), 'The Social Bases of the Justice and Development Party', in Ü. Cizre (ed.), *Secular and Islamic Politics in Turkey: the Making of Justice and Development Party* (London: Routledge), 201–22.

Aydın, S. (2009), *Algılar ve Zihniyet Yapıları: Devlet Ekseni* (İstanbul: TESEV).

Aydın, Z. (2005), *The Political Economy of Turkey* (London: Pluto Press).

Ayres, C.E. (1962), *The Theory of Economic Progress: A Study of the Fundamentals of Economic Development and Cultural Change* (New York: Schocken Books).

Babacan, A. (2013), 'Küresel Ekonomideki Gelişmeler ve Türkiye Ekonomisi', Available at: http://www.hazine.gov.tr/File/?path=ROOT/Documents/ Bakan%20Konu%C5%9Fmalar%20ve%20Sunumlar/SN_AB_20121103_ Sunum.pdf, retrieved on 8 August 2014.

Baer, G. (1970), 'The Administrative, Economic and Social Functions of Turkish Guilds', *International Journal of Middle East Studies*, 1: 1, 28–50.

Balasubramanyam, V.N., and Corless, N. (2001), 'Foreign Direct Investment in Turkey and the Transitional Economies of Eastern Europe', in S. Togan and V.N. Balasubramanyan (eds), *Turkey and Central and Eastern Euoropean Countries in Transition: Towards a Membership of the EU* (New York: Palgrave McMillan), 51–64.

Beckert, J. (1999), 'Agency, Entrepreneurs, and Institutional Change: The Role of Strategic Choice and Institutionalized Practices in Organization', *Organization Studies*, 20:5, 777–9.

Bedirhanoğlu, P. and Yalman, G.L. (2010), 'State, Class and the Discourse: Reflections on the Neoliberal Transformation in Turkey', in A. Saad-Filho and G.L. Yalman (eds), *Economic Transitions to Neoliberalism in Middle-Income Countries* (London: Routledge), 107–27.

Beetham, D. (1991), *The Legitimation of Power* (Houndmills: Palgrave).

Berkes, N. (1964), *The Development of Secularism in Turkey* (Montreal: McGill University Press).

Besanko, D, Dravone, D. and Shanley, M. (2000), *The Economics of Strategy* (New York: Wiley).

Bieler, A. Higgott, R. and Underhill, G. (2004), *Non-State Actors and Authority in the Global System* (Routledge: London).

Bianchi, R. (1984), *Interest Groups and Political Development in Turkey* (New Jersey: Princeton University Press).

Bila, F. (1987), *Sosyal Demokrat Süreç İçinde CHP ve Sonrası* (İstanbul: Milliyet Yayınları).

Boisot, M. (2003), 'Is There a Complexity Beyond the Reach of Strategy?', in E. Mitleton-Kelly (ed.), *Complex Systems and Evolutionary Perspectives on Organizations: The Application of Complexity Theory to Organisations* (Amsterdam: Pergamon), 185–202.

Boratav, K. (2007), *Türkiye İktisat Tarihi, 1908–2007* (Ankara: İmge).

———, Yeldan, E. and Köse, A.H (2000), 'Globalization, Distribution and Social Policy, 1980–1998', CEPA, Working Paper Series I: 20, Available at: http://core.kmi.open.ac.uk/download/pdf/6363400.pdf, retrieved on 12.08.2012.

Borch, C. (2005), 'Systemic Power: Luhmann, Foucault, and Analytics of Power', *Acta Sociologica*, 48:2, 155–67.

Bowles, S. and Gintis, H. (2005), 'Power in Competitive Exchange', S. Bowles, M. Franzini and U. Pagano (eds), *The Politics and Economics of Power* (London: Routledge), 10–24.

Bromley, D.W. (2009), *Sufficient Reason: Volitional Pragmatism and the Meaning of Economic Institutions* (Princeton: Princeton University Press).

Brucan, S. (1975), 'The Systemic Power', *Journal of Peace Research*, 12:1, 63–70.

Buchanan, J.M. (2000 [1977]), *Democracy in Deficit: The Political Legacy of Lord Keynes* (Indianapolis: Liberty Fund).

——— (1999 [1962]), *The Calculus of Consent*, The Collected Works of James M. Buchanan, *Vol. 3* (Indianapolis: Liberty Fund).

Buckley, W. (1967), *Sociology and Modern Systems Theory* (New Jersey: Prentice Hall).

Buğra, A. (1994), *State and Business in Turkey* (Albany: State University of New York Press).

Bulutay, T. (1995), *Employment, Unemployment and Wages in Turkey* (Ankara: ILO and State Institute of Statistics).

Bulutay, T., Timur, S. and Ersel, H. (1971), *Türkiye'de Gelir Dağılımı – 1968* (Ankara: Sevinç Matbaası).

———, Tezel, Y.S. and Yıldırım, N. (1974), *Türkiye Milli Geliri, 1923–1948* (Ankara: Sevinç Matbaası).

Celasun, M. and Arslan, İ. (2001), 'State-Owned Enterprises and Privatization in Turkey: Policy, Performance and Reform Experience, 1985–1995', in M. Celasun (ed.), *State-Owned Enterprises in the Middle East and North Africa* (London: Routledge), 224–52.

Chang, H.J. (2007), 'Institutional Change and Economic Development: An Introduction', in H.J. Chang (ed.), *Institutional Change and Economic Development* (Tokyo: United Nations University Press), 1–16.

Chapra, M.U. (2000), *The Future of Economics: An Islamic Perspective* (Leicester: The Islamic Foundation).

CHP (2013), *CHP Parti Programı* (Ankara: CHP).

——— (2011), *Aile Sigortası: Güçlü Sosyal Devlete Doğru* (Ankara: CHP).

——— (1994), *CHP Programı: Yeni Hedefler, Yeni Türkiye* (Ankara: CHP).

——— (1976), *CHP Programı* (Ankara: CHP).

——— (1935), Parti Programı (Ankara: CHP).

Choudry, M.A. (1999), *Comparative Economic Theory: Occidental and Islamic Perspectives* (Boston: Kluwer Academic).

Ciddi, S. (2009), *Kemalism in Turkish Politics* (London: Routledge).

Cizre-Sakallıoğlu, Ü. and Yeldan, E. (2000), 'Politics, Society and Financial Liberalization: Turkey in the 1990s', *Development and Change*, 31, 481–500.

Clegg, S. (1989), *Frameworks of Power* (London: Sage).

Commons, J.R. (1959), *Institutional Economics: Its Place in Political Economy* (Madison: The University of Wisconsin Press).

Crouch, C. (2001), 'A Third Way for Industrial Relations', in S. White (ed.), *New Labour: The Progressive Future?* (Basingstoke: Palgrave), 93–109.

Cypher, J.M. and Dietz, J.L. (2004), *The Process of Economic Development* (London: Routledge).

Çakır, R. (2005), 'Milli Görüş Hareketi', in Y. Aktay (ed.), *Modern Türkiye'de Siyasi Düşünce: İslamcılık* (İstanbul: İletişim), 544–75.

ÇSGB (2009), *Sosyal Güvenlik Reformu* (Ankara: ÇSGB).

——— (2008), 'İstihdam Paketi Yasalaştı', Available at http://www.csgb.gov.tr/ article.php*article_id =501,
retrieved on 10.06.2008.

Çınar, M. (2006), 'Turkey's Transformation under the AKP Rule', *The Muslim World*, 96, 469–86.

Çiller, T. (1972), *The Strategy of Economic Development: The Turkish Case*, PhD Dissertation (Connecticut: University of Connecticut).

Çizakça, M. (1996), *A Comparative Evolution of Business Partnerships: The Islamic World & Europe with Specific Reference to the Ottoman Archives* (Leiden: Brill).

——— (2000), *A History of Philanthropic Foundations: The Islamic World from the Seventh Century to the Present* (İstanbul: Boğaziçi University Press).

Daily Telegraph (26 July 2009), 'Queen Told How Economists Missed Financial Crisis', Available at: http://www.telegraph.co.uk/news/uknews/theroyalfamily/5912697/Queen-told-how-economists-missed-financial-crisis.html, retrieved on 12.03.2014.

Darling, L.T. (2006), 'Public Finances: The Role of the Ottoman Centre', in S. Faroqhi (ed.), *The Cambridge History of Turkey, Vol. 3: Later Ottoman Empire, 1603–1839* (Cambridge: Cambridge University Press), 118–34.

David, F.R. (1993), *Strategic Management* (New York: McGraw Hill).

Davutoğlu, A. (2007), *Stratejik Derinlik: Türkiye'nin Uluslararası Konumu* (İstanbul: Küre).

——— (1994), *Civilizational Transformation and the Muslim World* (Quala Lumpur: Mahir Publications).

Demir, F. (2010), 'Turkish Post-crisis Development Experience from a Comparative Perspective: Structural Break or Business as Usual', in Z. Öniş and F. Şenses (eds), *Turkey and the Global Economy* (London: Routledge), 11–33.

Derviş, K., Asker, S. and Işık, Y. (2006), *Krizden Çıkış ve Çağdaş Sosyal Demokrasi* (İstanbul: Doğan Kitap).

Dopfer, K. (2005), 'Evolutionary Economics. A Theoretical Framework', in K. Dopfer (ed.), *The Evolutionary Foundation of Economics* (Cambridge: Cambridge University Press), 3–60.

Dosi, G., Marengo, L. and Fagiolo, G. (2005), 'Learning in Evolutionary Environments', *The Evolutionary Foundation of ...*, 255–338.

DSP (1991), *DSP Programı* (Ankara: Sistem Ofset).

Dugger, W.M. (1980), 'Power: An Institutional Framework of Analysis', *Journal of Economic Issues*, XIV: 4, 897–907.

Durkheim, E. (1994 [1893]), *The Division of Labour in Society* (Houndsmills: MacMillan).

Dursun, D. (1989), *Yönetim-Din İlişkileri Açısından Osmanlı Devletinde Siyaset ve Din* (İstanbul: İşaret).

Easterlin, R.A. (2006), *Growth Triumphant: The Twenty-First Century in Historical Perspective* (Michigan: University of Michigan Press).

Easton, D. (1965), *A Systems Analysis of Political Life* (New York: Wiley).

Ecevit, B. (1968), *Ortanın Solu* (Ankara: Tekin Yayınevi).

——— (1973), 'Labor in Turkey as a New Social and Political Force', in K. Karpat (ed.), *Social Change and Politics in Turkey: A Structural-Historical Analysis* (Leiden: Brill), 151–81.

Eğilmez, M. (1997), *IMF, Dünya Bankası ve Türkiye* (İstanbul: Creative Yayıncılık).

EB – Turkish Ministry of Economy (2013), 'Ülke Gruplarına Göre İhracat', Available at: http://www.ekonomi.gov.tr/upload/AB0B1F4B-D8D3-8566-45203214B0010CCC/eko04.xls, retrieved on 8.10.2013.

Eldem, E. (2006), 'Capitulations and Western Trade', in S. Faroqhi (ed.), *The Cambridge History of Turkey: The Later Ottoman Empire: 1603–1839* (Cambridge: Cambridge University Press), 283–335.

Elster, J. (1989), *The Cement of Society: A Study of Social Order* (Cambridge: Cambridge University Press).

Eralp, A. (1999), 'The Politics of Turkish Development Strategies', in A. Finkel and N. Sirman (eds), *Turkish State, Turkish Society* (London: Routledge), 219–254.

Erbakan, N. (1991a), *Adil Ekonomik Düzen* (Ankara: Semih Ofset).

——— (1991b), *Türkiye'nin Meseleleri ve Çözümleri* (Ankara: p.a).

——— (1991c), *Körfez Krizi, Emperyalizm ve Petrol* (Ankara: Rehber).

Ergüder, Ü. (1991), 'The Motherland Party, 1983–1989', in M. Heper and J.M. Landau (eds), *Political Parties and Democracy in Turkey* (London: I. B. Tauris), 152–69.

Ergül, T. (2000), *Sosyal Demokraside Bölüşme Yılları, 1986–1991, Vol. 2* (İstanbul: Gündoğan).

——— (1995), *Sosyal Demokraside Ayrışma Yılları, 1980–1995, Vol. 1* (Ankara: Gündoğan).

Ersel, H. (2010), 'Turkish Public Finance in the Post-crisis Era', in Z. Öniş and F. Şenses (eds), *Turkey and the Global Economy* (London: Routledge), 34–49.

Ersoy, A. (1995), *Silm Sosyal Yapılanma Modeli* (İstanbul: Yörünge).

Ete, H. and Eşkinat, D. (2013), 'Siyaset Arayışından Arayış Siyasetine Cumhuriyet Halk Partisi, 2010–2013', Available at: http://setav.org/tr/siyaset-arayisindan-arayis-siyasetine-chp/analiz/3476, retrieved on 16.05.2013.

Faroqhi, S. (1994), 'Crisis and Change, 1590–1699', in H. İnalcık and D. Quataert (eds), *An Economic and Social History of the Ottoman Empire* (Cambridge: Cambridge University Press), 411–36.

——— (1991), 'The Field Glass and The Magnifying Lens: Studies of Ottoman Craft and Craftsmen', *The Journal of European Economic History*, 20:1, 29–57.

——— (2005), 'Guildsmen Complain to the Sultan: Artisans' Disputes and the Ottoman Administration in the 18th Century', in H.T. Karateke and M. Reinkowski (eds), *Legitimizing the Order: The Ottoman Rhetoric of State Power* (Brill, Leiden), 177–93.

——— (2006), *Osmanlı Şehirleri ve Kırsal Hayatı*, Transl. by E.S. Özcan (Ankara: Doğu-Batı Yayınları).

——— (2009), *The Ottoman Empire: A Short History* (Princeton: Markus Wiener Publishers).

FP – Fazilet Partisi (d.a), *Kalkınma Programı* (Ankara: FP).

Foucault, M. (2003), *Society Must be Defended*, Transl. by D. Macey (New York: Picador).

Friedland, R. and Alford, R.R. (1991), 'Bringing Society Back in: Symbols, Practices and Institutional Contradictions', in W.W. Powerll and P.J. DiMaggio, *The New Institutionalism in Organizational Analysis* (Chicago: Chicago University Press), 232–63.

Friedman, M. (2002 [1962]), *Capitalism as Freedom* (Chicago: The University of Chicago Press).

―――― (1980), *Free to Choose: The Classic Inquiry into the Relationship between Freedom and Economics* (New York: Harcourt Brace Javonich).

―――― (1968) 'The Role of Monetary Policy', *American Economic Review*, LVIII: 1, 1–17.

Galbraith, J.K. (1954), *The Great Crash of 1929* (Harmondsworth: Penguin).

Genç, M. (2000), *Osmanlı İmparatorluğunda Devlet ve Ekonomi* (İstanbul: Ötüken).

Gerber, H. (2005), 'Osmanlı Sivil Toplumu ve Modern Türk Demokrasisi', K.H. Karpat (ed.), *Osmanlı Geçmişi ve Bugünün Türkiye'si* (İstanbul: Bilgi Üniversitesi), 243–60.

―――― (1994), *State, Society, and Law in Islam: Ottoman Law in Comparative Perspective* (New York: State University of New York Press).

Giddens, A. (1984), *The Constitution of Society: An Outline of the Theory of Structuration* (Cambridge: Polity).

―――― (1998), *The Third Way: The Renewal of Social Democracy* (Cambridge: Polity).

Gökalp, Z. (1959), *Selected Essays of Ziya Gökalp*, Transl. by N. Berkes (New York: Columbia University Press).

Gözaydın, İ.B. (2004), 'Türk Hukukunun Batılılaşması', in T. Bora (ed.), *Modern Türkiye'de Siyasal Düşünce, Volume 3* (İstanbul: İletişim), 286–97.

Greif, A. (2006), *Institutions and the Path to the Modern Economy: Lessons from Medieval Trade* (Cambridge: Cambridge University Press).

Grütjen, D. (2007), 'Social Security in Turkey: An Example of the Southern Model? The Role of State, Market, and the Family in Welfare Provision', Netzwrk Türkei Working Paper, No. 1, Berlin.

Gülalp, H. (2001), 'Globalization and Political Islam: The Social Bases of Turkey's Welfare Party', *International Journal of Middle East Studies*, 33, 433–48.

Gülmez, M. (1982), *Türkiye'de Çalışma İlişkileri: 1936 Öncesi* (Ankara: TODAİE).

HASPAR – Halkın Sesi Partisi (2012), *Parti Programı*, Available at: http://hasparti.wordpress.com/tuzuk/program/, retrieved on 08.09.2012.

Habermas, J. (1984), *The Theory of Communicative Action: Reason and the Rationalization of Society, Vol. 1*, Transl. by T. McCarthy (Boston: Beacon Press).

―――― (1987), *Lifeworld and System: A Critique of Functionalist Reason, Vol. 2*, Transl. by T. McCarthy (Boston: Beacon Press).

——— (1974), *Theory and Practice*, Transl. by John Viertel (Boston: Beacon Press).

Hale, W. (1981), *The Political and Economic Development of Modern Turkey* (New York: St Martin's Press).

Hall, P.A. (1989), 'Introduction', in P.A. Hall (ed.), *The Political Power of Economic Ideas: Keynesianism across Nations* (Princeton: Princeton University Press), 3–26.

Hanioğlu, M.Ş. (2008), 'The Second Constitutional Period', in R. Kasaba (ed.), *The Cambridge History of Turkey, Volume 4: Turkey in the Modern World* (Cambridge: Cambridge University Press), 62–111.

——— (2001), *Preparation for a Revolution* (Oxford: Oxford University Press).

Hayek, F.A. (1998a [1973]), *Law, Legislation and Liberty, Vol. 1*. Rules and Order (London: Routledge).

——— (1998b [1973]), *Law, Legislation, and Liberty, Vol. 2, The Mirage of Social Justice* (London: Routledge).

——— (1998c [1979]), *Law, Legislation, and Liberty, Vol 3, The Political Order of a Free People* (London: Routledge).

Hechter, M. and Opp, K. (2001), 'What We Have Learned About the Emergence of Social Norms, in M. Hechter and K. Opp (eds), *Social Norms* (New York: Russell Sage Foundation), 394–417.

Helmke, G. and Levitsky, S. (2004) 'Informal Institutions and Comparative Politics: A Research Agenda', *Perspectives on Politics*, 2:4, 725–40.

Horne, C. (2001), 'Sociological Perspectives on the Emergence of Norms', in M. Hechter and K. Opp (eds), *Social Norms* (New York: Russell Sage Foundation), 3–35.

Huo, J. (2009), *Third Way Reforms: Social democracy after the Golden Age* (Cambridge: Cambridge University Press).

Howell, C. (2004), 'Is There a Third Way for Industrial Relations?', *British Journal of Industrial Relations*, 42:1, 1–22.

IMF (2010), 'Turkey Letter of Intent dated 28 January 2002', Available at: www.imf.org/Ext ernal /NP/LOI/2002/tur/01/INDEX.HTM, retrieved on 08.08.2013.

İnalcık, H. (1987), *An Economic and Social History of the Ottoman Empire, Vol. I, 1300–1600* (Cambridge: Cambridge University Press).

——— (1978), *The Ottoman Empire: Conquest, Organization and Economy* (London: Variorum Reprints).

——— (1964), 'The Nature of Traditional Society; Turkey', in R.E. Ward and D.A. Rostow (eds), *Political Modernization in Japan and Turkey* (Princeton: Princeton University Press), 42–63.

Issawi, C. (1980), *The Economic History of Turkey, 1800–1914* (Chicago: The University of Chicago Press).

Jackson, G. (2010), 'Actors and Institutions', in G. Morgan, J.L. Campbell, C, Crouch, O.K. Pedersen and R. Whitley (eds), *Oxford Handbook of Comparative Institutional Analysis* (Oxford: Oxford University Press), 63–86.

Jackson, W.A. (2009), *Economics, Culture and Social Theory* (Cheltenham: Edward Elgar).

Jacoby, T. (2004), *Social Power and the Turkish State* (London: Frank Cass).

Jang, H. (2005), 'Taming Political Islamists by Islamic Capital: The Passions and the Interests in Turkish Islamic Society', PhD Dissertation (Texas: University of Texas).

Jevons, S. (2005 [1888]), *The Theory of Political Economy*, Liberty Fund, Available at: http://oll.libertfund.org/EBooks/Jevons0237.pdf, retrieved on 13.01.2013.

Kahraman, H.B. (1993), *Sosyal Demokrasi, Türkiye ve Partileri* (Ankara: İmge).

Kalaycıoğlu, E. (2005), *Turkish Dynamics: Bridge across Troubled Lands* (New York: Palgrave).

——— (2007), 'Politics of Conservatism in Turkey', *Turkish Studies*, 8:2, 233–52.

Kamu-Sen (2013), 'Türkiye Kamu-Sen'in Krize ve İşsizliğe Çözüm Önerisi', Available at: http://www.kamusen.org.tr/habergo ster.php?Id=4322, retrieved on 15.06.2013.

——— (2005), 'Sosyal Politika ve İstihdam', Ankara.

Kaplan, M. (1965), *System and Process in International Relations* (London: John Wiley & Sons).

Karakışla, Y. (1995), 'The Emergence of the Ottoman Industrial Working Class, 1839–1923', in D. Quataert and E. Zürcher (eds), *Workers and the Working-Class in the Ottoman Empire and the Turkish Republic* (London: I.B. Tauris), 19–34.

Karaosmanoğlu, A.L. (2000), 'The Evolution of the National Security Culture and the Military in Turkey', *Journal of International Affairs*, 54:1, 199–216.

Karpat, K. (2001), *The Politicization of Islam: Reconstructing Identity, State, Faith, and Community in the Late Ottoman State* (Oxford: Oxford University Press).

——— (2004), *Studies on Turkish Politics and Society* (Leiden: Brill).

——— (1970), 'The Military and Politics in Turkey: 1960–64: A Socio-Cultural Analysis of a Revolution', *American Historical Review*, 75:6, 1654–83.

——— (1966), 'The Turkish Left', *Journal of Contemporary History*, 1:2, 169–86.

——— (1959), *Turkey's Politics* (Princeton: Princeton University Press).

Kazancıgil, A. (1995), 'Türkiye'de Modern Devletin Oluşumu ve Kemalizm', in E. Kalaycıoğlu and A. Y. Sarıbay (eds), *Türkiye'de Süreklilik ve Değişim* (İstanbul: Der), 185–204.

Kazgan, G. (2004), *Tanzimat'tan 21. Yüzyıla Türkiye Ekonomisi* (İstanbul: Bilgi Üniversitesi Yayınları).

Kazıcı, Z. (2003), *Osmanlı Vakıf Medeniyeti* (İstanbul: Bilge).

Keane, M. (2005), *Dictionary of Modern Strategy and Tactics* (Annapolis, MD: Naval Institute Press).

Kelly, M.G.E. (2008), *The Political Philosophy of Michael Faucault* (London: Routledge).

Kennedy, P. (1988), *The Rise and Fall of Great Powers: Economic Change and Military Conflict from 1500 to 2000* (London: Unwin Hyman).

Kepenek, Y. (2007), *Türkiye Ekonomisi* (İstanbul: Remzi).

KESK (2013), 'Türkiye'nin Ekonomik Görünüm Raporu – I' (Ankara: KESK).

Keyder, Ç. (2009), *The Definition of a Peripheral Economy: Turkey: 1923–1929* (Cambridge: Cambridge University Press).

Keyman, F. and Öniş, Z. (2007) 'Globalization and Social Democracy in the European Periphery: Paradoxes of the Turkish Experience', *Globalizations*, 4:2, 211–28.

Keynes, J.M. (1964 [1936]), *General Theory of Employment, Interest and Money* (London: H. Hamilton).

Khaldun, İ. [1967 [1375]), *The Muqaddimah: An Introduction to History*, Transl. by F. Rosenthal (Princeton: Princeton University Press).

Kili, S. (1975), *1960–1975 Döneminde CHP'de Gelişmeler: Siyaset Bilimi Açısından Bir İnceleme* (İstanbul: Boğaziçi Üniversitesi).

Kiriş, H.M. (2012), 'The CHP: From the Single Party to the Permanent Main Opposition Party', *Turkish Studies*, 13:2, 397–413.

Köker, L. (2005), *Modernleşme, Kemalizm ve Demokrasi* (İstanbul: İletişim).

Kritzman, L.D. (ed.) (2003), *Politics, Philosophy, Culture: Interviews and Other Writings, 1977–1984* (New York: Routledge).

Leeuwen, T.V. (2008), *Discourse and Practice: New Tools for Critical Discourse Analysis* (Oxford: Oxford University Press).

Levi, A. (1991), 'The Justice Party, 1961–1980', in M. Heper and J.M. Landau (eds), *Political Parties and Democracy in Turkey* (London: I.B. Tauris), 119–33.

Lewis, B. (1937), 'The Islamic Guilds', *The Economic History Review*, 8:9, 20–37.

Luhmann, N. (1995), *Social Systems*, Transl. by J. Bendraz (Stanford: Stanford University Press).

Lukes, S. (2005), *Power: A Radical View* (London: Palgrave McMillan).

Mango, A. (1991), 'The Social Democratic Populist Party, 1983–1989', in M. Heper and J.M. Landau (eds), *Political Parties and Democracy in Turkey* (London: I.B. Tauris), 170–187.

Mannan, M.A. (1983), *Islamic Economics: Theory and Practice* (Lahore: Ashraf Printing Press).

Mardin, Ş. (2000), *The Genesis of Young Ottoman Thought* (Sycrause, NY: Syracuse University Press).

Mantzavinos, C. (2001), *Individuals, Institutions, and Markets* (Cambridge: Cambridge University Press).

McKinnon, R.I. (1991), *The Order of Economic Liberalization: Financial Control in the Transition to a Market Economy* (Baltimore: The Johns Hopkins University Press).

Memur-Sen (2009a), *Ekonomik Kriz ve Kamu Çalışanları Etki-Analiz Araştırması* (Ankara: Memur-Sen).

———— (2009b), 'Yeni Anayasa Raporu' (Ankara: Memur-Sen).

Mentzel, C. (1994), 'Nationalism and the Labor Movement in the Ottoman Empire, 1872–1914', PhD Dissertation (Seattle: University of Washington).

Meyer, T. and Hinchman, L.P. (2007), *The Theory of Social Democracy* (Cambridge: Polity).

MNP – Milli Nizam Partisi (d.a.), *Parti Programı ve Tüzük* (İstanbul: Haktanır Basımevi).

MSP – Milli Selamet Partisi (d.a.), *Parti Programı* (Ankara: Elif Matbaacılık).

Muslehuddin, M. (1999), *Sociology and Islam: A Comparative Study of Islam and Its Social System* (Kuala Lumpur: Islamic Book Trust).

MUSIAD (2002), 'MÜSİAD Ne Dedi? Ne Oldu?' (İstanbul: MÜSİAD).

────── (2012), 'Kalkınma Yolunda Yeni Eşik: 2012 Türkiye Ekonomisi Raporu' (İstanbul: MÜSİAD).

Neumann, C.K. (2006), 'Political and Diplomatic Developments', in S. Faroqhi (ed.), *Cambridge History of Turkey, Volume 3, The Later Ottoman Empire: 1603–1839* (Cambridge: Cambridge University Press), 44–64.

Nichols, T. and Sugur, N. (2010), *Turkey and the EU: A Survey Report on the Views of Turkish Trade Unionists and Those in Seven EU Member States – Belgium, France, Greece, Italy, Sweden Slovakia and the United* (Brussels: European Trade Union Confederation).

North, D. (1990), *Institutions, Institutional Change and Economic Performance* (Cambridge: Cambridge University Press).

Notermans, T. (2007), *Money, Markets, and the State: Social Democratic Economic Policies since 1918* (Cambridge: Cambridge University Press).

NTV (2013), 'Ecevit'in 28 Şubat MGK'sı Hakkındaki Konuşması', Available at: http://arsiv.ntvmsnbc.com/ntv/metinler/neden/20071211.asp, retrieved on 08.03.2014.

OECD (2014), 'Income Distribution and Poverty Statistics', Available at: http://stats.oecd.org/, retrieved on 08.02.2014.

────── (2013a), 'OECD Labor Statistics, Available at: http://stats.oecd.org/, retrieved on 05.09.2013.

────── (2013b), 'OECD Public Sector, Taxation, and Market Regulation Statistics', Available at: http://stats.oecd.org/, retrieved on 05.09.2013.

────── (2006), *Turkey: Public Expenditure Review* (Paris: OECD).

Olson, M. (2002 [1965]), *The Logic of Collective Action: Public Goods and the Theory of Groups* (Cambridge MA: Harvard University Press).

Ortaylı, İ. (2008), *Türkiye Teşkilat ve İdare Tarihi* (Ankara: Cedit).

────── (2006), *İmparatorluğun En Uzun Yüzyılı* (İstanbul: Timaş).

────── (2004), *Osmanlı İmparatorluğu'nda İktisadi ve Sosyal Değişim*, Makaleler I (Ankara: Turhan).

Önder, T. (2005), 'Para Politikası: Araçları, Amaçları ve Türkiye Uygulaması' (Ankara: T.C. Merkez Bankası).

Önder, N. (1999), 'The Political Economy of the State and Social Forces: Changing Forms of State-Labor Relations in Turkey', PhD Dissertation (Toronto: The University of York).

Öniş, Z. (1998), *State and Market: The Political Economy of Turkey in Comparative Perspective* (Istanbul: Boğaziçi University Press).

———— and Şenses, F. (2010a), 'The New Phase of Neo-liberal Restructuring in Turkey: An Overview', in Z. Öniş and F. Şenses (eds), *Turkey and the Global Economy* (London: Routledge), 1–11.

———— and Şenses, F. (2010b), 'Turkish Economy at a New Stage of Integration into the Global Economy: Toward a Synthesis and the Challenges Ahead', *Turkey and the Global Economy ...*, 304–14.

———— and Güven, A.B. (2011), 'Global Crisis, National Responses: The Political Economy of Turkish Exceptionalism', *New Political Economy*, 16:5, 585–607.

Özbek, N. (2006), *Cumhuriyet Türkiyesinde Sosyal Güvenlik ve Sosyal Politikalar* (İstanbul: Tarih Vakfı Yayınları).

———— (2002), *Osmanlı İmparatorluğu'nda Sosyal Devlet: Siyaset, İktidar ve Meşrutiyet: 1876–1914* (İstanbul: İletişim).

Özbudun, E. and Tachau, F. (1975), 'Social Change and Electoral Behaviour in Turkey: Toward a Critical Realignment', *International Journal of Middle East Studies*, 6:4, 60–80.

Özbudun, E. (2006), 'Changes and Continuities in the Turkish Party System', *Representation*, 42:2, 129–37.

———— (2012), 'Turkey's Search for a New Constitution', *Insight Turkey*, 14:1, 39–50.

Pamuk, Ş. (2014), 'Fiscal Centralisation and the Rise of the Modern State in the Ottoman Empire', *The Medieval History Journal*, 17:1, 1–26.

———— (2010), *Osmanlı Ekonomisi ve Kurumları* (İstanbul: İş Bankası Kültür Yayınları).

———— (2003), *Osmanlı-Türkiye İktisadi Tarihi: 1500–1914* (İstanbul: İletişim).

———— (2000), *İstanbul ve Diğer Kentlerde 500 Yıllık Fiyatlar ve Ücretler* (Ankara: Devlet İstatistik Enstitüsü).

———— (1994), *Osmanlı Ekonomisinde Bağımlılık ve Büyüme: 1820–1913* (İstanbul: Türkiye Ekonomik ve Toplumsal Vakfı).

Parla, T. and Davison, A. (2004), *Corporatist Ideology in Kemalist Turkey: Progress or Order* (Syracuse, NY: Syracuse University Press).

Parsons, T. [1991 (1951)], *The Social System* (London: Routledge).

Pierson, P. (2004), *Politics in Time: History, Institutions and Social Analysis* (Princeton: Princeton University Press).

Polanyi, K. (1989 [1944]), *The Great Transformation: The Political and Economic Origins of Our Time* (Boston: Beacon Press).

Przeworski, A. (1993), *Capitalism and Social Democracy* (Cambridge: Cambridge University Press).

Putnam, R.D. (1988), 'Diplomacy and Domestic Politics: the Logic of Two-Level Games', *International Organization*, 42:3, 427–60.

Quataert, D. (1999), *Ottoman Manufacturing in the Age of the Industrial Revolution* (Cambridge: Cambridge University Press).

Rawls, J. (1996), *Political Liberalism* (New York: Columbia University Press).

————— (1999 [1971]), *A Theory of Social Justice* (Cambridge, MA: Belknap Press).

Reader, Z. (2003), *Islam, Postmodernism and Other Futures* (London: Pluto Press).

Resmi Gazette (2014), 'İş Kanunu ... Değişiklik Yapılmasına Dair Kanun', Available at: http://www.resmigazete.gov.tr/eskiler/2014/09/20140911M1–1. htm, retrieved on 13.12.2014.

Richter, R. (2008), 'On the Social Structure of Markets: A Review and Assessment in the Perspective of the New Institutional Economics', in A. Ebnerand and N. Beck (eds), *The Institutions of the Market: Organizations, Social Systems, and Governance* (Oxford: Oxford University Press), 157–79.

Roberts J.M. and Westad, O.A. (2003), *The New History of the World* (Oxford: Oxford University Press).

RP – Refah Partisi (1986), *Parti Programı* (Samsun: Eser Matbaası).

Rutherford, M. (1994), *Institutions in Economics: The Old and New Institutionalism* (Cambridge: Cambridge University Press).

Russell, B. (1997 [1938]), *Power: A New Social Analysis* (London: Routledge).

Sarıbay, A.Y. (1985), *Din ve Parti Politikası: MSP Örnek Olayı* (İstanbul: Alan).

Scharpf, F.W. (1997), *Games Real Actors Play: Actor-Centered Institutionalism in Policy Research* (Colorado: Westview).

Schumpter, J.A. (2008 [1934]), *The Theory of Economic Development: An Inquiry into Profits*, Transl. by R. Opie (New Brunswick: Transaction Publishers).

Schüler, H. (1999), *Türkiye'de Sosyal Demokrasi: Particilik, Hemşericilik, Alevilik* (İstanbul: İletişim).

Scott, W.R. and Meyer, J.W. (1994), *Institutional Environments and Organizations: Structural Complexity and Individualism* (London: Sage).

Shaw, S. (2002 [1976]), *History of the Ottoman Empire and Modern Turkey, Vol 1, Empire of the Gazis: The Rise and Decline of the Ottoman Empire, 1280–1808* (Cambridge: Cambridge University Press).

————— (1979), *History of the Ottoman Empire and Modern Turkey II* (Cambridge: Cambridge University Press).

SHP (1985), *SHP Programı* (Ankara: SHP).

Skidelsky, R. (2009), *Keynes: The Return of the Master* (BBS-Public Affairs, New York).

Smith, A. (1976 [1776]), *An Inquiry into the Nature and Causes of the Wealth of Nations, Vol. 1 and 2* (Oxford: Clarendon Press).

Sönmez, F (1968) *Türkiye'de Sendika Hürriyeti ve Teminatı*, İzmir: Ege Üniversitesi Matbaası.

Steinmo, S. and Thelen, K. (1992) 'Historical Institutionalism in Comparative Politics', in S. Steinmo, K. Thelen and F. Longstreth (eds), *Structuring Politics: Historical Institutionalism in Comparative Analysis* (Cambridge: Cambridge University Press), 1–32.

Stiglitz, J.E. (2010), 'The Financial Crisis of 2007–8 and Its Macroeconomic Consequences', in S. Griffith-Jones,

J.A. Ocampo, and J.E. Stiglitz (eds), *Time for a Visible Hand* (Oxford: Oxford University Press), 19–49.

Streeck, W. (1997), 'Beneficial Constraints: On the Economic Limits of Rational Voluntarism', in J.R Hoolingsworth and R. Boyer (eds), *Contemporary Capitalism: The Embeddedness of Institutions* (Cambridge: Cambridge University Press), 197–219.

——— (2009), 'Institutions in History: Bringing Capitalism Back in', MPifG Discussion Paper 09/8, Available at: http://www.mpifg.de/pu/mpifg_dp/dp09–8.pdf, retrieved on 15.05.2014.

——— (2008), 'Flexible Markets, Stable Societies?', MPifG Discussion Paper 08/06, Available at: www.mpifg.de/pu/workpap/wp08–6.pdf, retrieved on 15.05.2014.

——— and Thelen, K. (2005), 'Introduction: Institutional Change in Advanced Political Economies', in W. Streeck and K. Thelen (eds), *Beyond Continuity: Institutional Change in Advanced Capitalism* (Oxford: Oxford University Press), 1–39.

Talas, C. (1982), *Bir Toplumsal Politika Belgesinin Yorumu: Toplumsal Anlaşma* (Ankara: Ankara Üniversitesi Yayınevi).

Tanör, B. (1992), *Osmanlı-Türkiye Anayasal Gelişmeleri* (İstanbul: Der Yayınları).

Taymaz, E. and Voyvoda, E. (2010), 'Industrial Restructuring and Technological Capabilities in Turkey', in Z. Öniş and F. Şenses (eds), *Turkey and the Global Economy* (London: Routledge), 145–72.

TCMB – Central Bank of Turkish Republic (2002), *The Impact of Globalization on the Turkish Economy* (Ankara: TCMB).

TISK – Türkiye İşveren Sendikaları Konfederasyonu (2012), *Türkiye'nin Büyüme Stratejisi: Yapısal Analiz ve Politikalar* (Ankara: TISK).

——— (2011), *TISK's Basic Views and Proposals* (Ankara: TISK).

Tibi, B. (2001), *Islam between Culture and Politics* (New York: Palgrave).

TKB – Turkish Ministry of Development (2013a) *Ekonomik ve Sosyal Göstergeler: 1950–2010*, Available at: http://www.dpt.gov.tr/Kalkinma.portal, retrieved on 09.01.2012.

——— (2013b) 'Ekonomik ve Sosyal Konsey Mevzuatı', Available at: http://www.dpt.gov.tr/PortalDesign/PortalControls/WebIcerikGosterim.aspx?Enc=83D5A6FF03C7B4FCB7549B778EA1FEDD, retrieved on 12.05.2013.

——— (2013c), 'Orta Vadeli Program, 2014–2016', Available at: http://www.dpt.gov.tr/DocObjects/View/15282/ OVP.pdf, retrieved on 19.11.2013.

——— (1963), *Birinci Beş Yıllık Kalkınma Planı, 1963–1967* (Ankara: DPT).

TKBB – Participation Banks Association of Turkey (2013), 'Türk Finans Sisteminde Katılım Bankaları', Available at: http://www.tk bb.org.tr/genel-sunum.aspx?pageID=52, retrieved on 09.10.2013.

Togan, S. and Ersel, H. (2005), 'Macroeconomic Policies for Turkey's Accession to the EU', in B. Hoekman and S. Togan (eds), *Turkey: Economic Reform and Accession to the European Union* (Washington: The World Bank), 3–37.

Toprak, Z. (1982), *Türkiye'de 'Milli İktisat', 1908–1918* (Ankara: Yurt Yayınları).
Tsebelis, G. (2002), *Veto Players: How Political Institutions Work* (New York: Russell Sage Foundation).
TBMM – Turkish Parliament (2013), III. Ecevit Hükümeti Programı, Available at: http://www.tbmm.gov.tr/hukumetler/HP42.htm, retrieved on 09.10.2012.
TUIK – Turkish Statistical Institution (2012), *İstatistik Göstergeler: 1923–2011* (Ankara: TUIK).
Tuna, O. (1969), 'Türkiye'de Sendikalar ve Sendikacılarımız', *Sosyal Siyaset Konferansları*, 8, 255–68.
Turner, S.P. (2010), *Explaning the Normative* (Cambridge: Polity Press).
TUSIAD (2011), *Türkiye'de Büyümenin Kısıtları: Bir Önceliklendirme Çalışması* (İstanbul: TÜSİAD).
TÜSES (2002), *Türkiye'de Siyasi Partilerin Seçmen Yandaş Profili* (1994–2002), Ankara: TÜSES.
Usul, A.R. (2011), *Democracy in Turkey: The Impact of EU Political Conditionality* (London: Routledge).
Uygur, E. (2010), 'The Global Crisis and the Turkish Economy' (Malaysia: The Third World Network).
VanderLippe, J.M. (2005), *The Politics of Turkish Democracy: İsmet İnönü and the Formation of the Multi-Party System, 1938–1950* (Albany, NY: State University of New York Press).
Veblen, T. (1912), *The Theory of Leisure Class: An Economic Study of Institutions* (New York: The Macmillan Company).
Wallerstein, I. (2004), *World Systems Analysis: An Introduction* (Durham: Duke University Press).
——— (2011a), *The Modern World-System I: Capitalist Agriculture and the Origins of the European World-Economy in the Sixteenth Century* (Berkeley: California University Press).
——— (2011b), *The Modern World-System IV: Centrist Liberalism Triumphant, 1789–1914* (Berkeley: California University Press).
——— (1980), *The Capitalist World-Economy* (Cambridge: Cambridge University Press).
Weber, M. (1978), *Economy and Society: An Outline of Interpretive Sociology*, Transl. by E. Fischoff et al. (Berkeley: University of California Press).
Webster, D.E. (1939), 'State Control of Social Change in Republican Turkey', *American Sociological Review*, 4:2, 247–56.
White, S. (2004), 'Welfare Philosophy and the Third Way', in J. Lewis and R. Surender (eds), *Welfare State Change: Towards a Third Way* (Oxford: Oxford University Press), 25–46.
Whittington, R. (1993), *What is Strategy – and Does It Matter?* (London: Routledge).
Whyman, P.B. (2006), *Third Way Economics: Theory and Evalution* (New York: Palgrave Macmillan).

Williams, M. (2010), 'Governing the Global Regulatory System', in S. Griffith-Jones, J.A. Ocampo and J.E. Stiglitz (eds), *Time for a Visible Hand* (Oxford: Oxford University Press), 200–218.

Woodruff, W. (2002), *A Concise History of the Modern World: 1500 to the Present* (Houndsmill: Palgrave McMillan).

World Bank (2005), 'Türkiye'de Dünya Bankası, 1993–2004: Ülke Yardım Değerlendirmesi', Available at: http://ieg.worldbank.org/Data/reports/turkey_cae_turkish.pdf, retrieved on 12.05.2014.

World Economic Forum (2013), 'Global Competitiveness Report, 2013–2014', Available at: http://www.weforum.org/reports/global-competitiveness-report-2013-2014, retrieved on 5.01.2015.

Wrong, D.H. (1979), *Power: Its Forms, Bases and Uses* (Oxford: Basil Blackwell).

WTO (1998), 'Trade Policy Review of Turkey' (Geneva: WTO).

WTO (2012), 'Trade Policy Review of Turkey' (Geveva: WTO).

Yaşar, M.E. (2005), 'İskenderpaşa Cemaati', in Y. Aktay (ed.), *Modern Türkiye'de Siyasi Düşünce: İslamcılık*, (İstanbul: İletişim), 323–45.

Yavuz, M.H. (2009), *Secularism and Muslim Democracy in Turkey* (Cambridge: Cambridge University Press).

Yeldan, E. (2001), *Türkiye Ekonomisi* (İstanbul: İletişim).

Yıldırım, E. (2006), 'Labor Pains or Archilles' Heel: The Justice and Development Party and Labor in Turkey', in M.H. Yavuz (ed.), *The Emergence of a New Turkey* (Salt Lake City: Utah University Press), 235–57.

Yılmaz, İ. (2005), 'State, Law, Civil Society and Islam in Contemporary Turkey', *The Muslim World*, 95, 385–410.

Zürcher, E. (2010), *The Young Turk Legacy and National Building: From the Ottoman Empire to Atatürk's Turkey* (London: I.B. Tauris).

Index

For Product Safety Concerns and Information please contact our EU representative GPSR@taylorandfrancis.com Taylor & Francis Verlag GmbH, Kaufingerstraße 24, 80331 München, Germany

Batch number: 08151583

Printed by Printforce, the Netherlands